P9-DMB-742

pgs have
been wet
04/08 mk

NAZI
GAMES

FEB - - 2008

Also by David Clay Large

And the World Closed Its Doors:
One Family's Abandonment to the Holocaust

Berlin

Where Ghosts Walked: Munich's Road to the Third Reich

Germans to the Front:
West German Rearmament in the Adenauer Era

Contending with Hitler:
Varieties of the German Resistance in the Third Reich
(editor)

The End of the European Era: 1890 to the Present
(with Felix Gilbert)

Between Two Fires: Europe's Path in the 1930s

Wagnerism in European Culture and Politics
(coeditor)

The Politics of Law and Order:
A History of the Bavarian Einwohnerwehr, 1918–1921

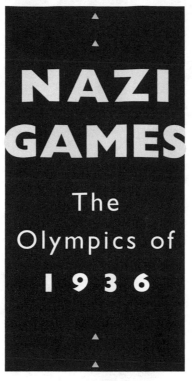

NAZI GAMES

The Olympics of 1936

David Clay Large

W · W · Norton & Company

New York

London

ELTHMMA PUBLIC LIBRARY

Copyright © 2007 by David Clay Large

All rights reserved
Printed in the United States of America
First Edition

For information about permission to reproduce
selections from this book, write to Permissions,
W. W. Norton & Company, Inc.
500 Fifth Avenue, New York, NY 10110

Manufacturing by R. R. Donnelley, Bloomsburg Division
Book design by Margaret Wagner
Production manager: Julia Druskin

Library of Congress Cataloging-in-Publication Data

Large, David Clay.
Nazi games : the Olympics of 1936 / David Clay Large.—1st ed.
p. cm.
Includes bibliographical references and index.
ISBN-13: 978-0-393-05884-0 (hardcover)
ISBN-10: 0-393-05884-0 (hardcover)
1. Olympic Games (11th : 1936 : Berlin, Germany) 2. Sports—Germany.
3. National socialism and sports. 4. Sports and state—Germany.
I. Title.
GV7221936 .L37 2007
796.48—dc22

2006101366

W. W. Norton & Company, Inc.
500 Fifth Avenue, New York, N.Y. 10110
www.wwnorton.com

W. W. Norton & Company Ltd.
Castle House, 75/76 Wells Street, London W1T 3QT

1 2 3 4 5 6 7 8 9 0

For
Joshua John Henry
and
Alma Esmeralda

Contents

Acknowledgments

xi

Introduction

A Bridge to the Ancient Greeks?

3

I

"Faster, Higher, Stronger"

The Modern Olympics from Athens to Amsterdam

17

II

Enter the Nazis

49

III

Boycott Berlin!

69

IV

The Winter Games

110

V

On to Berlin

147

VI

"Holy Flame, Burn"

The Ceremonial Games

190

VII

"Darktown Parade"

Track and Field

227

VIII

Of Pools, Mats, Rings, and Rough Waters

260

IX

Olympia

295

Epilogue

"The Games Must Go On"

316

Notes

345

Index

379

Acknowledgments

D URING the long process of researching and writing this book about the 1936 Olympics, I sometimes imagined, in more grandiose moments, that the task at hand might be nearly as arduous as actually competing in an Olympic event—say the marathon. This project has certainly required as much support and coaching. Without the assistance of family, friends, colleagues, and the staffs of a couple of dozen research institutions, I could not have gotten through the first mile here, much less made it to the finish line.

The idea of revisiting the story of the 1936 Nazi games in light of more recent Olympic controversies, including the contentious award of the 2008 Summer Games to Beijing, came to me via my editor at W. W. Norton, Steve Forman, who then helped to push the project along at strategic moments.

My friend Howard De Nike, who is much better versed in the arcana of sports history than I am, read through the entire manuscript in its first draft, pointing out many errors and making useful suggestions for improvement. Earl Gustkey, a former sportswriter for the *Los Angeles Times*, also vetted most of the manuscript and shared with me his reportage on the boxer Max Schmeling. Professor Barbara Keys, formerly of Sacramento State University and currently at the University of Melbourne, read several chapters in draft and furnished me with an early version of her forthcoming book, *Globalizing Sport: National Rivalry and the International Community in the 1930s* (forthcoming from Harvard University Press). Joshua Large scrutinized the manuscript with the hypercritical eye of a history graduate student, a soccer nut—and a son. I also profited from readings by Professors Jonathan Schneer of Georgia Tech University and Billy G. Smith of Montana State University in Bozeman. David Guss of Tufts University provided me with useful information on some of the Olympic athletes. Sue Llewellyn did an excellent job of copyediting.

While working on this book I was able to share some of my preliminary findings in presentations at Montana State University, Princeton University, Heidelberg University, Georgia Tech University, Sacramento State University, the University of New Mexico, and the World's Fair Symposium in San Francisco in 2005. I'd like to thank Professors Billy G. Smith, Constanza Güthenke, Heiner Must, Jonathan Schneer, Barbara Keys, Christine Sauer, Charles McClelland, and Robert Rydell for arranging these occasions.

Although (thankfully) it doesn't cost as much to write about the Olympic Games as it does to put them on, the far-flung research travels for this project did not come cheaply, and I am grateful to the Research and Creativity Committee of Montana State University for a generous grant in support of my work. My thanks, too, to Professors Noel Cary, Jeffry M. Diefendorf, and Peter Fritzsche for writing in support of my grant application.

My work on this book took me to archives and libraries across the United States and Europe. For their patient assistance and invaluable expertise I would like to thank the staffs of the following institutions: Amateur Athletic Federation, Los Angeles; American Jewish Committee Archive, New York; Bibliothèque Nationale, Paris; Blaustein Library, New York (especially Cyna Horowitz); British Library, London; Bundesarchiv, Berlin; Bundesarchiv, Koblenz; Bayerisches Hauptstaatsarchiv, Munich; Carl und Liselott Diem-Archiv, Cologne (especially Michael Winter and Karl Lennartz); Center for Jewish History, New York; Columbia University Library; Deutsche Sporthochschule, Cologne; Doe Library, University of California at Berkeley; Emory University Library and Archives, Atlanta; Firestone Library, Princeton University; Greene Library, Stanford University; Heidelberg University Library; Heidelberg University, Institut für Sport und Sportwissenschaft; Hoover Institution, Stanford; Institut für Zeitgeschichte, Munich; International Olympic Committee Olympic Studies Center, Lausanne (especially Ruth Beck-Perrenoud); Library of Congress, Washington, D.C. (especially Dave Kelly); Markt-Archiv, Garmisch-Partenkirchen; Montana State University Library; National Archives, College Park (especially John E. Taylor); New York Public Library; Österreichische Nationalbibliothek, Vienna; Osterreichisches Staatsarchiv, Vienna; Politisches Archiv des Auswärtigen Amts,

Berlin; Public Records Office (National Archives), London; Regenstein Library, University of Chicago; Richard Strauss Institut, Garmisch-Partenkirchen (especially Christian Wolf); Seattle Public Library; Staatsarchiv, Munich; Staatsbibliothek zu Berlin; Sterling Library, Yale University; Tulane University Library and Archives; University of Illinois, Urbana-Champaign Library and Archives (especially William Maher and Debbie Pfeiffer); Widener Library, Harvard University; Yale University Manuscripts and Archives.

Writers of books like this one often test the patience not only of archivists and librarians but also of their families. I would like (once again) to thank my wife, Margaret, for putting up with my frequent bouts of bitchiness and my frequent (perhaps not entirely unwelcome) absences. I'd also like to thank, for the first time, my three-year-old daughter, Alma, for slowly coming to accept the sad fact that her father would choose to spend more time writing about games than playing them.

NAZI
GAMES

Introduction

A Bridge to
the Ancient Greeks?

AT precisely noon on July 20, 1936 fifteen Greek maidens outfitted in minismocks of rough serge solemnly entered the ruins of the ancient stadium at Olympia and, with the help of a concave glass reflector crafted by Germany's Zeiss Optics, focused the heat of the noonday sun on a fagot topped with flammable material. They then carried the blazing staff past the Temple of Hera to the fire altar in front of the Altis, the sacred enclosure where an "Olympic flame" had allegedly burned during the ancient games. There the maiden in the lead touched the torch to an oil-filled brazier, another gift from the Germans. During the lighting ceremony an orator chanted Pindar's *Olympic Hymn* to the accompaniment of ancient musical instruments.*

Following this artistic interlude, an official of the International Olympic Committee (IOC) read a message from Baron Pierre de Coubertin, the seventy-three-year-old Frenchman who in 1896 had restarted the tradition of quadrennial "Olympic" festivals after an interregnum of some fifteen hundred years. In his message Coubertin invoked, among other ideals, the spirit of "an eternal Hellenism that has not ceased to light the way of the centuries and whose ancient solutions remain today as applicable as they ever were." Then, as if to suggest which nation in the modern world was most capable of applying those "ancient solutions," the German ambassador to Greece apos-

---

*Sixty-eight years later, one of those Greek maidens, Maria Horss, twelve years old in 1936, would direct the torch-lighting ceremony at Olympia preceding the 2004 Athens Olympics. "We go out to do a very important act for our country, like the soldiers who go out to fight," Horss said of her maidens in 2004. "We are also soldiers for an idea."

trophized the Olympic flame as a greeting across the ages "to my Führer Adolf Hitler and his entire German people."

To underscore the ambassador's point, a German band struck up the German national anthem followed by the "Horst Wessel Lied," the bloodthirsty marching song of the *Sturmabteilung* (SA), the Nazi Party army. No one seems to have questioned the suitability of including this reminder of Nazi Germany's violent ethos in a solemn ceremony celebrating the "peaceful" athletic prowess of the world's youth. On the contrary, according to an on-the-scene reporter for Germany's official Olympic newspaper, the *Olympia-Zeitung*, the flame-lighting ceremony was convincing proof that "in far-away Germany the Olympic idea is celebrating its most glorious reawakening."

Once brought to life in the ruins of Olympia, the Olympic flame was transferred to a torch carried by a slender boy who began slowly jogging out of the compound in the general direction of Athens. This was the beginning of an epic relay run in which more than three thousand torchbearers transported the flame across seven countries to its final destination in the Olympic Stadium in Berlin.

Like all aspects of the 1936 games, the torch relay had been scripted long in advance by the German organizers, who planned it as meticulously as their predecessors had any Prussian military campaign. In 1935 two members of the German Organizing Committee (GOC) reconnoitered the prospective route by car, an arduous undertaking given the lack of paved roads in some sections and the necessity of crossing high mountain passes. On the basis of this advance reconnaissance, the planners decided that each relay runner should cover about one kilometer, taking an average of five minutes but no more than fifteen. The total distance of 3,075 kilometers was to be covered in twelve days. Allowing for breaks for speeches and ceremonies, the flame was scheduled to arrive at the Olympic Stadium in Berlin on August 1 at exactly 4:00 P.M.

The 1936 Olympic torch relay was an "invented tradition" within the invented tradition of the modern Olympic Games. There had been no such torch relays in the ancient games or, for that matter, in any of the ten (official) modern Summer Olympics preceding the Berlin games. The torch relay was but one of many ways in which the Nazi games helped define the modern Olympic experience as we know it today. In contrast to the essentially innocuous Olympic torch relay spectacles that have become familiar to us in recent years, however, the original German relay did more than simply promote interest in the upcoming games: It carried some very heavy ideological baggage.

Initially proposed by the Nazi Propaganda Ministry, and orchestrated primarily by Carl Diem, the indefatigable secretary-general of the GOC, the relay turned into an advertisement for the new Germany across southeastern and central Europe, a region coveted by Nazi proponents of Lebensraum (living space)—and eventually overrun by the Wehrmacht. The seemingly innocuous torch trek from Olympia to Berlin prefigured the naked aggression to come.

At the same time, as if to provide an illustrious pedigree for the new Germanic empire envisaged by Hitler, the relay quite overtly and ostentatiously posited a symbolic bridge between modern Germany and classical Greece. According to Diem the Olympic flame was an ancient "symbol of purity" prefiguring the purity of the modern German nation. He saw the torch relay as a reawakening of the mythic cult surrounding Prometheus, whose theft of fire from the gods for the betterment of mortals had been honored in antiquity by torchlight parades. But Diem got a little confused in his imagery. As a logo for the relay he selected a relief from the Palazzo Colonna in Rome, supposedly depicting "torch runners at the finish line." In fact the "runners" in question were two *putti*, usually associated with erotic love.

The first stages of the 1936 torch relay took the Olympic flame across the rugged terrain of the northern Peloponnesus to Corinth. The Greek authorities had intended to build a new highway from Olympia to the mountain town of Tripolis, but the project was not completed in time for the relay, and automobiles accompanying the runners had great difficulty negotiating the serpentine cart road over the passes. The area up in the mountains was so thinly populated that the runners had to be dropped off in advance, and for security reasons the route was closed to all traffic save for a convoy consisting of an official IOC car provided by the Opel company and two vans carrying German radio reporters and cameramen from Leni Riefenstahl's film company, who were shooting the relay for inclusion in Riefenstahl's now-famous documentary film on the 1936 games, *Olympia*.

Riefenstahl herself showed up to direct the filming of the torch-lighting spectacle and the first stage of the relay. She was distressed that the lighting site, jammed as it was with cars and dignitaries in suits, did not at all fit the image she had in mind of ancient Olympia. Nor, in her view, did the torchbearers look like ancient athletes. With the exception of the first lad, who wore nothing but close-fitting shorts, the Greek runners sweated over the hills in full folkloric costume: white leggings, flared skirts, long-sleeved dark tunics, and elaborate brocaded vests. Riefenstahl would have preferred that they run entirely in the nude, in homage to the athletes at ancient Olympia, who generally competed naked save for a slathering of colored oil. When she and her team finally came upon a runner who, at least in his physique and bearing, resembled what they imagined an ancient torch runner—had such an animal existed—might have looked like, the young fellow turned out to be a Russian émigré named Anatol, who was not anxious to be photographed, even with his clothes on. Eventually the Germans got him to run for their cameras, and he ended up accompanying them all the way back to Berlin, where he helped with the *Olympia* filming.

In Athens, whence the relay progressed after crossing the Gulf of Corinth by boat, the mayor himself insisted on carrying the flame through the heart of the city, pausing so often to catch his breath that he far exceeded his allotted fifteen minutes of torch time. Greece's King George II presided over a torch-welcoming ceremony in Athens' Panathenian Stadium, site of the first modern Olympics in 1896.

At Diem's instigation the relay took a detour west from Athens to Delphi, where another torch-blessing ceremony was conducted in the ancient stadium high above the sacred temple of Apollo on Mount Parnassus. Here Diem added a theatrical prop consisting of a large black rock freshly inscribed with the five-ring symbol of the modern Olympics, which Baron Pierre de Coubertin had devised in 1914. In the late 1950s two British archaeologists stumbled on this artifact and insisted it proved that the ancient Greeks, not Coubertin, had come up with the five-ring device. This "discovery" was picked up by a historian of the ancient games and cited as proof that "the interlocking circles found on the altar at Delphi [were] definitely connected with the ancient Games."

At each village stop along the route in Greece, local orators expressed the gratitude of the "new Hellas" to the "new Germany" for having instituted the Olympic torch relay. According to an account of the relay published in the Reich, some Greek villagers even shouted "Heil Hitler!" as the torch went by.

The German hand lay heavy on every aspect of the relay, including the design of the torches themselves. In the spirit of aping the ancients, Diem initially planned to use stalks of narthex, a fennel-like plant from the Ephesus highlands, which allegedly retained fire for long periods of time. Extensive testing revealed, however, the narthex stalks' staying power to be yet another ancient myth. Eventually the GOC elected to go high-tech, commissioning German chemists to design a magnesium-burning element that would stay lit regardless of weather conditions. The organizers prevailed on Krupp, the famous arms-manufacturing company, to create stainless-steel handles for the torches. Krupp later used one of these devices to ignite its newest blast furnace in Essen.

When the relay left Greece to enter Bulgaria, the chairman of the Greek Torch Relay Committee passed the blazing baton to his Bulgarian counterpart. In Bulgaria elaborate festivities were held at every stop, most prominently in Sofia, where priests of the Greek Orthodox Church blessed the pagan fire in front of the Central Cathedral, which had been bedecked with Nazi swastikas for the occasion.

According to the German *Official Report* on the games of 1936, the ceremonial transfer of the fire at the Bulgarian-Yugoslav border stood as a testament of "Bulgarian-Yugoslav friendship"—an emotional bond of which the two peoples seem not to have been as cognizant as one might have hoped: There were scuffles in the background.

On one stretch in Yugoslavia several of the torches proved faulty and could be kept alight only by temporarily sheltering them inside the accompanying Olympic car. In case one of the torches went out entirely, the car carried a spare "Olympic flame" in the backseat. When the flame passed through two Yugoslav villages inhabited by the descendants of earlier German settlers, the townsfolk took advantage of the occasion to celebrate their Germanic heritage, some even proclaiming their loyalty to the new Nazi Reich.

In Hungary the relay runners made such good time across the flat terrain that the welcoming ceremonies could be gratifyingly drawn out. In the village of Kecskemét, famous for its fruit, an Olympic altar made entirely of apricots adorned the market square. Gypsy musicians serenaded the runners at various stops, and in Budapest the chief of the Hungarian Gypsies, Magyari, performed a special blessing ceremony.

At the Austrian border Dr. Theodor Schmidt, head of the Austrian Olympic Committee, took possession of the torch and carried it the first kilometer, looking distinctly un-Olympic with his bulging gut, bald head, and extralarge track suit. In Vienna the relay's contemporary political symbolism reached its apogee. Two years earlier Austrian Nazis had tried to seize control of the country but had managed only to murder the chancellor, Engelbert Dollfuss. Now, taking advantage of the impending arrival of the Olympic torch at Vienna's Heldenplatz, local Nazis signaled their desire to "come home to the Reich" by singing the "Horst Wessel Lied." When, at nightfall, the torchbearer finally burst into the square, a huge roar of "Heil Hitler!" went up, prefiguring the rapturous welcome that would greet the Führer on his own entrance on this very square some two years later. The Nazi demonstrators shouted down the Austrian president, Wilhelm Miklas, and then turned their attention to Vice-Chancellor Ernst Rüdiger von Starhemberg, who had great difficulty conveying the torch through the boisterous crowd to the next relay station, on the Ringstrasse. "When I reached the Ring," Starhemberg wrote later, "I felt I should never get through. The path had narrowed still further. The light of the streetlamps fell upon faces filled with hatred and distorted by shouting."

Describing the same scene the German *Official Report* delicately stated: "The entrance of the Olympic Fire into Vienna took the form of a triumphal procession of quite unexpected proportions." Realizing that the Vienna demonstration could undercut Germany's deeply disingenuous official stance that the 1936 games stood "entirely above politics," Propaganda Minister Joseph Goebbels ordered the German press not to play up the Austrian demonstration and to comment that "the use of the Olympic flame for political purposes is exceptionally regrettable."

As in Austria, the Czech portion of the relay stoked the fires of German ethnic pride, but also of anti-German feeling. A Propaganda Ministry poster advertising the event showed the Sudetenland, the heavily ethnic German territory in western Czechoslovakia, as already belonging to the German Reich (it would be annexed by Germany per the infamous Munich agreement of 1938). Czech patriots decried the poster as "a singular provocation." Realizing that they may have gone too far, the Germans withdrew the poster, claiming it had been a mistake. This allowed the relay to pass through Czechoslovakia as planned, though hardly without incident. Although Czech president Edvard Beneš gave his personal support to the venture, it occasioned so much animosity among the Czechs that the runners passing through the Slavic portions of the country had to be protected by police escort. In the Sudetenland, by contrast, ethnic German crowds greeted the Olympic flame as if it were a beacon sent directly from Berlin.

The "sacred flame" reached German soil on July 31 at 11:45 A.M., exactly on schedule. The young man who grasped the torch at this point was slim and fit, as were all the runners after him. "Every one of us had to be a Super-Aryan," recalled one of the German torchbearers fifty years later. "Only blue-eyed blonds were acceptable."

The rest of the journey to Berlin resembled a victory lap. Hitler Youth trumpeters greeted the runners as they entered Saxon villages along the way. In Dresden the flame was transferred to a special altar at the Königsufer, on the bank of the Elbe River, allowing a lengthy ceremony replete with gymnastic presentations, musical performances, and a windy oration by the regional leader of the German Association for Physical Training (DRL). In Luckenwalde, in the district of Berlin-Brandenburg, the welcoming ceremony was held at the war memorial, where the mayor drew a parallel between Germany's Olympic athletes and the warriors who had fought and died for the fatherland in World War I. From Luckenwalde it was only a short haul to Greater Berlin and the Olympic Stadium.

THE German organizers' contention that the torch relay symbolized links between Nazi Germany and ancient Greece was not simply a piece of promotional hucksterism. The torch relay was part of an extensive and very serious reworking of the ancient Olympic legacy by the organizers of the 1936 games. In many ways Germany's Olympic officials and their backers in the Nazi government believed themselves to be closer in spirit to the ancient games—with their exclusive cast of freeborn Greek males, cult of pagan religiosity, bloody combat sports, glorification of death in the arena, and unabashed celebration of victory as the only worthwhile outcome—than to the uplifting ideals of peaceful "fair play" and international understanding surrounding the modern Olympic festivals.

The Nazi appropriation of the ancient Olympic heritage in 1936 harmonized well with a larger effort by Hitler's Germany to cast the modern German *Volk* as the true heirs of the ancient Greeks, and even to posit a racial kinship between the two peoples. This claim of blood ties represented a significant departure from the "spiritual kinship" with classical Hellenism asserted by earlier German intellectuals and scholars like Johann Joachim Winckelmann, Ernst Curtius, Johann Wolfgang von Goethe, Friedrich Schiller, and Heinrich Heine. Rather than the well-known cultural "tyranny of Greece over Germany," this supposed racial affinity amounted to a kind of tyranny of Germany over Greece, resting as it did on claims that the ancient Greeks were actually of Germanic stock.

In a book titled *Olympia 1936* the Nazi propagandist Willi Koenitzer asserted that Hercules, the mythical founder of the ancient games, belonged to the "Nordic tribe of the Dorians," whose highest goal had been "the harmony of body, intellect and soul," a goal the Germans under Hitler had supposedly realized by establishing a "moral and physical primacy" over all that was degenerate and debased. Hitler himself, a fervent admirer of classical Greece, insisted that the Dorian tribe, which had migrated into Greece from the north, was of Germanic origin. Thus the Führer claimed that Nazi Germany, in adopting a neo-Dorian architectural style for many of its public buildings, including those of the Olympic Games, was returning to its racial roots. Similarly Goebbels could hail the Acropolis as the cradle of Aryan culture. Alfred Rosenberg, the regime's chief ideologue, sought to document the putative affinity between Germany and Greece by equating the Nordic *Nibelungenlied* saga with Homer's *Iliad*, and the construction methods of Greek temples to those of Gothic cathedrals.

It was not Periclean Athens that most excited the Nazis' admiration, however, but Sparta, the warlike city-state that had not only vanquished Athens in the Peloponnesian War but also dominated the four main ancient Greek athletic festivals, producing more than half the known Olympic victors. German scholars during the Nazi era churned out monograph after monograph on Sparta, "proving," among other things, that the Spartans were just Germans waiting to happen. Although the Nazis admired the Spartans for their sporting prowess, their primary interest in this people concerned their pioneering work in "racial hygiene." Had the Spartans not shown how crucial it was for racial health to kill off weak or deformed newborn babies? The Spartans were also famous, of course, for fighting to the death rather than surrendering. Carl Diem would repeatedly invoke the Spartans' heroic sacrifice at the Battle of Thermopylae in his efforts to draw connections between war and sports—a connection he believed the modern Germans had mastered.

According to Nazi theorists the Greek empire eventually fell from its noble pinnacle because the classical Greeks (especially the Athenians) started allowing racial mixing and began experimenting with democracy—policies that expanded the citizenship base and diluted the power of the aristocratic minority. A Nazi directive on teaching Greek history in German schools took the

Greeks' decline as a cautionary tale for their self-appointed modern heirs: "The history of the Greeks has its origins in Central Europe. It is to be emphasized that they are racially our closest cousins. Class warfare in the south was based on racial hostility; in Sparta as well as Athens, the citizens were only a minority. However, with the removal of class differences through democracy and with the consequent unrestricted mixing of races, the fate of Nordic man in Greece was sealed." The Nazis would not make that same mistake, Hitler vowed.

As part of its campaign to portray Nazi Germany as the modern era's classical Greece—minus that culture's lamentable loss of racial discipline and political toughness—Hitler's government undertook to complete a program of archaeological excavations at ancient Olympia that German researchers had begun in 1875 and abandoned in 1881. After visiting the Olympic ruins in 1935, Hans von Tschammer und Osten, Nazi Germany's Reichssport-führer (Reich sports leader), suggested to Hitler that by uncovering ancient Olympia's architectural glories Nazi Germany would garner "the admiration of all the world's advanced cultural nations and establish a permanent monument to the greatness of the Third Reich." Hitler enthusiastically embraced this proposal, and during the opening ceremony at the Berlin games in 1936 he formally announced the project.

As noted, Hitler's favorite filmmaker, Leni Riefenstahl, was present at Olympia during the torch-lighting ceremony. The bizarre scene there, along with dreamlike images of the surrounding ruins and of the Acropolis in Athens, figured prominently in the prologue to her film *Olympia*, which premiered roughly two years after the Berlin games ended. Like the torch relay and an exhibition during the Berlin games called "Sport in Hellenic Times," the film served further to buttress the claimed ties between Hitler's Germany and classical Greece. In the end, *Olympia* proved to be one long visual ode to the "body beautiful," whose cult is shown to have had its roots in antiquity. Parallels between ancient Greek athletic aesthetics and those of Nazi Germany are often drawn quite overtly. In the film's prologue, for example, a statue of Myron's discus thrower morphs into a modern athlete in the person of Germany's decathlon champion, Erwin Huber. Since its premiere in 1938 *Olympia* has been shown thousands of times around the world. To the extent that people "know" about the 1936 Berlin Olympics these days, they tend to see this historical spectacle primarily through the movie version.

FOR those whose conception of the 1936 Olympics derives largely from the Riefenstahl film, or perhaps from the legend about Jesse Owens being "snubbed" by Hitler after winning the first of his four gold medals in Berlin, this book will offer up a host of new vistas and perspectives. I have framed my story within the larger context of the modern Olympic movement and set it against the backdrop of the political crises that afflicted Europe and the world in the first half of the twentieth century. General accounts of the Third Reich tend to ignore the 1936 games entirely or to mention them only in passing. Yet the Olympic festival constituted the Nazis' first big international show—their coming-out party on the world stage. On the domestic front, the games were a crucial part of the Nazi regime's "spiritual mobilization" to win the hearts and minds of the German people, more than 50 percent of whom had still not voted for the Nazi Party in the last "free" parliamentary elections of March 5, 1933, when the new Hitler government used terrorist methods to swing the outcome in its favor. In this book I try to give the 1936 German games the prominence they deserve within the history of the National Socialist movement and the modern world.

THE Nazi games almost did not come about at all. The IOC awarded the 1936 Summer Games to Berlin in 1931, when that city was still the capital of a parliamentary democracy—albeit a beleaguered one. Before the Nazis came to power in 1933, they had often expressed contempt for the ideals of the modern Olympic movement, whose professed commitment to world peace and international understanding clashed dramatically with their own worldview. When Hitler and his cohorts eventually embraced the idea of hosting the games—and indeed promised to put on the biggest and best Olympic party ever—many on the prospective guest list, above all the Americans, expressed serious reservations about accepting the German invitation. Even though the international boycott effort ultimately failed, it has much to tell us about attitudes around the globe toward Nazi Germany in the early years of the Third Reich, and about the inner workings of the Hitler regime as it struggled to defeat the boycott, consolidate its power at home, and step out impressively on the world stage.

Given all the political infighting and acrimony leading up to what one Olympics scholar has labeled "the most controversial Olympics," the athletic competitions in 1936 have often taken a backseat to the political drama in accounts of the games. But of course it does not make much sense to write a book about the Olympic Games while leaving out the actual games, and so I have devoted considerable space to the various athletic events and to the athletes who (Adolf Hitler notwithstanding) were the real stars of the show.

While the athletes set a host of new world and Olympic records in 1936, and the crowds that came to watch them perform their wonderful feats were the largest to date in modern Olympic history, these games also set new standards in media coverage, with more reporters (print and radio) than ever before, and with the first live telecasts. In addition to inaugurating the Olympic torch relay, the Germans, it turns out, also set the stage for subsequent frantic scrambles to garner rights to televise the games in nations around the world—competitions that in terms of the Olympic movement's financial well-being eventually came to overshadow anything that happened on the field.

THE story of the 1936 Games has been told before, more than once, but in my view what has been lacking so far is a comprehensive study for general readers that takes full account both of the vast specialized secondary literature and the extensive archival record now available. The documentary record is especially revealing on the boycott movement and on the organization of the Winter Games in Garmisch-Partenkirchen, which served as a rehearsal for the larger Berlin festival to follow (and about which much less has been written). In addition to facilitating a wider and deeper exploration of the issues surrounding the 1936 games, the original documents open a fascinating window on the motivations and perspectives of the central players. Believing that God—and in this case also the devil—is in the details, I have decided to let the actors speak in considerable specificity about what was on their minds.

In addition to trolling the archives and sifting through reams of published literature, I managed to speak with a number of people who, in their youth, personally witnessed the 1936 Olympics. I also made it a point to inspect most of the sites connected with the Nazi games. I have walked the grounds of the former Reichssportfeld, toured the Olympic Stadium, run most of the marathon course, sculled on the Müggelsee (venue of the rowing events), hiked the ski hills above Garmisch-Partenkirchen, and prowled around the ruins of the Olympic Village in Döberitz. (To check out what remains of the Olympic Village I had to vault a security fence festooned with signs warning of the presence of unexploded munitions.)

Not surprisingly, after some seventy years—and rather eventful ones at that—the Olympic sites have undergone significant alterations, but not everything has changed. The exterior of the Olympic Stadium in Berlin looks much as it did in 1936, and some of the Nazi-era statues that decorated the old Reichssportfeld surrounding the stadium remain in place. So do the giant reliefs carved in the stone gates at the ski-jump stadium in Garmisch-Partenkirchen. Most of the buildings at the Olympic Village in Berlin are long gone, but the hut in which Jesse Owens lived still stands.

The surviving artifacts from Olympia 1936 may also serve to remind us that these games are among the few undertakings of the Nazi era that many Germans even today believe reflect a more "positive" side of Hitler's Germany (the Autobahnen would be another such example). Anchoring this overly favorable view of the games is a widespread belief that the 1936 Olympics were largely untainted by Nazi ideology and represented a brief moment of tolerance and good feeling—a kind of oasis of decency—in the twelve-year nightmare of National Socialist rule. This was the main theme of the public commemorations in Berlin and Garmisch-Partenkirchen in 1986, marking the fiftieth anniversary of the German games. These festivities were full of nostalgic ruminations about the technical competence and innovative brilliance of the organizers, the orderliness and conviviality of the proceedings, and the "idealism" of the athletes in comparison to "the spoiled professionals of today." On these occasions many of the athletes themselves hotly disputed the notion that the Hitler regime had in any way "misused" the games for political purposes. Their cry was then taken up by some conservative journalists and sports historians, one of whom, Willi Knecht, argued that it was simply "ignorant" for historians to posit extensive ties between the Hitler regime and the '36 games.

But it is not, in my view, only the German keepers of the 1936 Olympic flame who harbor abiding misconceptions about this fascinating chapter in their nation's history. In my many discussions about the 1936 games with colleagues, friends, and captive strangers on long airplane flights, I have discovered that the general stock of information out there is not only insubstantial but also often distorted or downright wrong. Confusions abound about the place of the '36 games in modern Olympic history; the festival's impact on Nazi policies toward the Jews and other "enemies of the Reich"; the organizational qualities of the enterprise; the reception that America's black athletes, not only Jesse Owens, received in Hitler's Germany; the effect that the American blacks' victories had on racial dogma in Germany (and, for that matter, in the United States); the games' echo in the international press; the propaganda value of the games to Hitler's government; and finally, the ideological content of Leni Riefenstahl's film and her relationship to the rulers of the Third Reich. In *Nazi Games* I hope not only to open some new vistas but also to clear the air.

"Faster, Higher, Stronger"

The Modern Olympics
from Athens to Amsterdam

▲

▲

THE modern Olympic movement had a split personality from the beginning. In pointed contrast to the ancient games, which were reserved for citizens of the Greek empire and held exclusively at Olympia, Baron de Coubertin set out to create an international festival that would travel from city to city like a movable athletic feast, transcending borders and uniting the youth of the world in glorious play. Idealizing the ancient Greek tradition of the "Olympic truce," which forbade attacks on pilgrims going to and coming from the games but emphatically did not outlaw or even discourage warfare among the city-states during the festivals, Coubertin insisted that the modern Olympics would reduce the potential for military conflict among nations. Yet at the same time the baron was motivated by strong nationalistic passions, for one of his primary concerns in organizing the games was to strengthen— to "rebronze"—the physical and moral fiber of French youth following France's humiliating defeat by the German states in the Franco-Prussian War of 1870–71. Although he insisted that the modern games were about *individual* athletic prowess, about man's push to be ever stronger and faster, he undercut this principle by requiring that competitors participate as members of national teams. As a result nationalism came to play a powerful role in the games, which were increasingly perceived as measuring rods of national vitality.

Germany, that new nation born in the crucible of military conflict, was understandably quick to embrace the notion of Olympic competition as war by other means. And yet, right from the outset, Germany harbored ambivalent and convoluted views regarding Coubertin's Olympics project. In the nineteenth century Germany's preeminent form of sporting activity was not—as it was in Britain and America—team sports and traditional track and field events, but *Turnen*, elaborate group gymnastics and synchronized calisthenics designed to foster collective discipline and national brotherhood. As pioneered by Ludwig "Turnvater" Jahn (1778–1852), the *Turner* movement took on a *völkisch* and xenophobic quality that put it at odds with Coubertin's cosmopolitan ideal. As soon as the baron announced his Olympics project, the leader of Germany's *Turnerschaft* dismissed it as both un-Greek and un-German: "An *international* Olympic festival makes no sense. . . . However, if we were to celebrate a *national* Olympics, a *German* Olympics, we would be truer to the ideals of the ancient warriors."

Germany's relationship with modern Olympism remained ambivalent and tortured throughout the games' early development. Having decided, after initial misgivings, to demand a place for itself at Coubertin's table, Germany lost its first opportunity to host the games in 1916 because of World War I. Also on account of its role in that conflict, Germany was excluded from the first two postwar Olympiads. Carl Diem, the key figure in German sports at the time, oscillated between claiming that his country had no use for the Olympics and insisting that the modern games were nothing without Germany.

A Rocky Beginning

The modern Olympic movement was fortunate to survive its infancy and childhood. For our purposes, however, what is noteworthy about the fledgling Olympic enterprise has to do less with its precariousness than with its display of many of the troubling features that would cause so much controversy in the midthirties. Although, as we shall see, the Germans in 1936 would come to violate the Olympic principles in an especially egregious fashion, and indeed break new ground in that domain, the five-ringed flag they dragged through the mud was anything but pristine.

GERMANY almost did not take part in the inaugural Athens Olympics of 1896. Baron de Coubertin did not include a German representative in the Sorbonne congress in 1894 at which he first presented his Olympic program. He had been warned that if the Germans were admitted to the congress, the

French Gymnastics Union would not participate. The Germans were incensed over this slight, and they became even more indignant when Coubertin was quoted in the French magazine *Gil Blas* to the effect that no one had missed the Germans at the Sorbonne meeting and no one would be heartbroken if they did not show up in Athens in 1896. Whether or not Coubertin actually said these things remains unclear—the baron was quick to disavow the statements—but many Germans were not to be placated. One newspaper urged that any German athletic official favoring participation in the Athens games should be expelled from the German sports community. The head of the *Turner* movement said it would be "beneath the honor of a German man" to participate in the Athens Olympics.

At heart Coubertin would probably have been happy enough to leave the Germans out of his Olympic dream, but on a practical level he understood that the absence of such an important country would diminish his enterprise. He therefore went out of his way to assure Germany that it would be welcome in Athens. Fortunately for this purpose, he found a strong German ally in Dr. Willibald Gebhardt, a Berlin sports official who had long opposed the *Turnerschaft*'s parochialism. Gebhardt won over Kaiser Wilhelm II, who was eager to see Germany cut an impressive figure in international athletic competitions. With the kaiser's help, a new "Committee for the Participation of Germany in the Olympic Games" managed at the last minute to secure the endorsements and funding necessary to assemble a national team for the Athens games.

As soon as it became clear that the games would indeed go on, various ethnic and national quarrels of the day manifested themselves in disputes over political affiliation. The Hungarians, unwilling to participate alongside the Austrians as members of an Austro-Hungarian imperial team, paid their own way to Athens and competed under their own green-and-white colors. Similarly the Irish refused to compete as part of the British Empire team. The Turks refused to compete at all (in fact, as old enemies of the Greeks, they hadn't been invited), and they denounced the Athens games as a tool of Greek expansionism in Asia Minor.

The United States managed to send a small team to the inaugural games despite a general lack of American interest in the Olympic revival and the impediment of distance. The team consisted largely of Princeton students and members of the Boston Athletic Association (BAA), of whom four were Harvard men. The Princetonians had been given time off from their studies due to the intervention of Professor William Milligan Sloane, a charter member of the IOC. The Harvard boys had it harder. When John Connolly, a triple-jump specialist and freshman at Harvard, asked his coach if he could take time off to represent his country at the Athens games, the coach replied that he had never heard of any "Athens games" and supposed the young man simply wanted to go to Greece "on a junket." The Harvard faculty stipulated that if Connolly and the other students insisted on going to Athens they would have to resign from the university and reapply for admission on their return. Connolly said to hell with Harvard and quit for good.

Although the Americans arrived exhausted from their long and arduous trip, their previous experience in intercollegiate sports gave them an advantage over most of their competitors, many of whom knew precious little about training and high-level competition. The BAA runner who won the four-hundred-meter race was so far ahead of the pack in the home stretch that he slowed his pace to a walk. The Princeton man who won the discus throw, a legacy of the ancient games, had never even seen a discus before the morning of the contest, but his experience in putting the shot and throwing the hammer gave him the edge. America dominated the track-and-field competition in these first games, and many other events as well.

The Greek spectators at first took umbrage at the frequent hoisting of the American colors over the stadium (one of those intrusions of national display that became integral to Olympic pageantry), but eventually they embraced the spirited young Yankees. They even made peace with the incomprehensible cheers of the visiting Boston contingent—"BAA! Rah! Rah! Rah! Sis-Boom-Bah!"—which they imagined to be "the yell of wild Indians." On the other hand Frenchman Charles Maurras, the noted royalist writer and anti-Semite, remained completely unamused by the American antics. Anticipating the disgust with which many Europeans would later greet the hypercharged chanting by American fans at Olympic events, Maurras sniffed that the Yankee rooters were "like overgrown children."

The Germans were considerably less popular in Greece than the Americans—and indeed, less popular than any of the other foreign teams. Although the main German gymnastics association refused to have anything to do with this "un-German" affair, a rump squad of gymnasts did make up part of the German contingent, and they alienated the locals by going through their routines in a robotic and brutally efficient manner. The German gymnasts' victory over the graceful but less disciplined Greek team only made matters worse. The only competitor to be booed by the Athens crowd was an exceptionally ugly German wrestler who triumphed over two Greeks and a comely young Englishman.

By far the most anticipated—and widely watched—event at the 1896 Athens games was the marathon, which in its inaugural edition covered forty kilometers (a little more than twenty-four miles). This race had been included by the Greek organizing committee as a bow to the legend of Philippides, a military messenger who supposedly carried the news of the Greek victory over the Persians at the Battle of Marathon in 490 B.C. On his arrival in Athens he reportedly called out, "Be joyful, we win!" and then dropped dead. Coubertin had his doubts about including this ghastly trial, which had figured neither in the ancient games nor in any of the modern track-and-field contests. Even the Germans advised against a marathon race, fearing it might claim fatalities. "Hopefully in this regard one won't insist upon emulating the legendary inspiration," wrote one German newspaper.

As it turned out, although none of the contestants in the 1896 marathon actually expired, the event certainly took its toll. Not having a clue about how to run a race of this distance, many of the runners blasted out at full throttle, only to drop out after a few kilometers. An American runner, Arthur Blake, his feet bloody and his mind confused, quit the race a little over halfway. Another casualty of this ordeal was the Frenchman Albin Lermusiaux, a colorful figure who wore white gloves in competition. Lermusiaux had already run in the one-hundred-meter and eight-hundred-meter races at Athens before embarking on the marathon. Asked by an American journalist how he trained for races of such disparate lengths, he responded, "One day, I run a leetle way, vairy quick. Ze next day, I run a long way, vairy slow." Although he had spent the previous evening drinking "bottle after bottle" of the local retsina and was accordingly quite shaky on his feet, Lermusiaux set a furious pace and led for much of the race. However, in the last kilometers he began staggering in pain and finally had to be carried from the course. The same fate befell one of the men who passed him, Australia's Edwin Flack. On the outskirts of Athens, Flack dropped in his tracks, unconscious and covered in vomit.

The runner who went on to win, a Greek peasant named Spiridon Louis, had prepared for the race by fasting and praying. Wisely he held himself in the back of the pack in the early going, taking only a little wine as refreshment and gradually reeling in the front runners. Racing through the streets of

Athens on his way to the stadium, Louis occasioned outbursts of patriotic enthusiasm that reached fever pitch as he entered the great arena and made for the finish line, which he crossed in a credible time of 2:58:50. As one commentator reported: "The spectacle that the stadium then presented was really indescribable. . . . The atmosphere resounded on every side with unending cries of victory. Women waved their handkerchiefs, the men their hats; little Greek flags, carefully concealed until now, were unfurled; quite beside themselves, the people demanded that the band play the national hymn." Noting the wild enthusiasm of the Greek crowd, Maurras said insightfully to his countryman, Coubertin: "I see your internationalism does not kill national spirit—it strengthens it."

Despite the failure of the Athens games to attract many foreign guests and to produce more than a few notable athletic performances, the Greek organizers were pleased enough with what transpired to demand that Greece keep the games in perpetuity. Some foreign observers, including the American consul in Athens, agreed this would be a good idea, arguing, "Olympic Games would hardly seem worthy of the name if held in any other country." But Coubertin insisted that "the sole means of assuring the [modern] Games' success and of rendering them as splendid and brilliant as possible consists in giving them a great variety of aspect." With the help of his allies in the IOC, including the German, Gebhardt, Coubertin was able to keep the games ambulatory. The next stop was his native city of Paris.

ON returning to Paris after the Athens games and starting work on organizing the 1900 festival, Coubertin was painfully reminded that his Olympics project had not generated much enthusiasm in fin-de-siècle France. In order to win support for his Parisian games he had to agree to hold them as a mere appendage to the Exposition Universelle Internationale, France's spectacular world's fair. This proved to be a grave mistake, for the exposition organizers had no interest in or knowledge of athletics. The chairman of the exposition, Alfred Picart, thought that sports were for morons. To make matters worse France was still preoccupied with all the bitter controversy surrounding the Dreyfus case. What chance did the fledgling Olympics have when wedged between the fair and L'Affaire?

Showing a complete disregard for the principles of dramatic compactness, the organizers of the exposition spread out the athletic competitions over a five-and-one-half-month period, from May 14 to October 28. To fill up this eternity they padded the program with a host of bizarre (and, thankfully, mostly unrepeated) events, including ballooning, firefighting, tug-of-war, car racing, motorboating, croquet, falconry, cricket, pelota, golf, fishing, boules, and even pigeon shooting (advertised as a "*un sport très aristocratique et très brilliant*").

All the competitors had to contend with eccentric facilities. The swimming events took place in the Seine, where swift currents made for fast times but the heavy pollution brought on nasty skin diseases. The track-and-field events transpired in Paris's great park, the Bois de Boulogne, which the organizers refused to blight with regulation facilities. Thus the sprinters ran on an undulating grassy surface, while the discus and javelin throwers had to be careful not to hit the trees or strolling lovers. The marathon was run under conditions that made this event even more brutal than usual. By starting the race at the absurd time of 2:30 P.M. on one of the warmest days of the year, the organizers treated the contestants to temperatures ranging from 95 to 102 Fahrenheit, the hottest Olympic marathon in history. Because the course wound confusingly through the streets of Paris and was poorly monitored, contestants ended up running all over the place. One of the French competitors wisely concluded his race at a café after having run a considerable distance in the wrong direction. Two Americans who had taken an early lead and thought they had stayed in front the whole way were dumbfounded upon finishing to discover that a pair of Frenchmen had taken first and second place. The frustrated Yanks could not recall ever having seen these guys, let alone being overtaken by them. Later the Americans suggested uncharitably that the local boys might have taken some convenient shortcuts.

To underscore the athletic component's subordination to the exposition's central focus on industrial and technological progress, sporting events often transpired under rubrics that had nothing to do with sports; thus the ice-skaters and fencers were officially registered in the cutlery competition, while the rowers were relegated to commercial shipping. Rather than call their sad excuse for an athletic program *Jeux Olympiques*, the organizers referred pompously to *Concours Internationaux d'Exercices Physiques et du Sport*. No wonder some of the athletes who had appeared in Paris were quite surprised to learn later on that they had competed in an "Olympic Games."

If organizational savvy was not much evident in Paris, politics were present once again, and with a vengeance. The exposition took place against a backdrop of rising tension between the Western colonial powers and Chinese nationalists, which culminated in the Boxer Rebellion of 1900. Japan was on a collision course with Russia that would bring military conflict between the two powers in 1904. With East Asians being decried in Europe as the "yellow peril," it is not surprising that (apart from Australia) the only non–Western Hemisphere nation to compete in Paris was India. The Americans who journeyed to Paris in 1900 were still basking in the glow of their nation's trouncing of Spain in the Spanish-American War. American athletes expected to replicate on the playing field of Paris what U.S. troops had accomplished in Cuba and the Philippines.

Within Europe the ongoing Franco-German animosity was reflected in an effort by French president Felix Fauré to keep the Germans out of the Paris games altogether. When that effort failed—Coubertin himself successfully lobbied for the *Boche*—French organizers went out of their way to make the Germans feel unwelcome. No one met the German team on its arrival in Paris, forcing the Germans to walk across the city in search of their accommodations. On locating them, they discovered graffiti on the walls saying, *Cochons—à bas la Prusse!* ("Pigs—Down with Prussia!") Team captain Fritz Hoffmann found an enormous pile of excrement in his bed. Kept in the dark regarding the competitive schedule, German sprinters arrived at the track just as the starting gun went off for the one-hundred-meter dash. German gymnasts were not allowed to train on the French equipment prior to the Games. Not surprisingly Germany finished low in the national standings, and some German medalists never did get their awards.

The Paris games could have taken place on the moon, for all the Parisians knew or cared. Despite increased tourism for the exposition, attendance at the athletic competitions was extremely low. Coubertin was understandably vexed by this entire fiasco, which he attributed to the mistake of allowing the games to be relegated to the status of "a mediocre sideshow, without prestige."

YET Coubertin and the rest of the IOC made exactly the same mistake with the next Olympics, the St. Louis games of 1904. These were held in conjunction with the Louisiana Purchase Centennial Exposition, America's own world's fair. Coubertin had doubts about holding the games in St. Louis, which had wrested the festival away from Chicago, the site preferred by the IOC. Privately Coubertin said he feared that "the [St. Louis] Olympiad will match the mediocrity of the town." He also worried that the athletic contests there might again get lost in the larger exposition agenda, and that the protracted competition schedule—six months—would be an organizational nightmare. Moreover, as a patriotic Frenchman, Coubertin was aggrieved that "his" games should be held in conjunction with a celebration of France's 1803 "fire sale" of its North American holdings to the U.S. government. He therefore refused to travel to St. Louis to attend the festival.

In electing to miss the St. Louis Games, Coubertin had a lot of European company. With the long travel distance and high costs of a six-month stay in the American hinterland, most of the European nations either stayed away entirely or sent relatively small teams. Even the IOC, which generally held business meetings in the host city during the games, chose in 1904 to meet in London instead. The British capital seemed a safer and altogether more congenial gathering spot than the American alternative, which many Europeans imagined was still threatened by hostile Indians.

The Germans, at least, had heard of Missouri and St. Louis, since many of their kinfolk had settled in the region. However, financial considerations, combined with a continuing Olympic boycott by the *Turnerschaft*, mandated a very small team. (A group of gymnasts not sanctioned by the *Turnerschaft* traveled separately to St. Louis, where they were put up by the local beer baron, Adolphus Busch.) Considering that they had only ten entrants, the Germans did well in St. Louis, capturing eight medals in swimming, including a clean sweep of the one-hundred-yard breaststroke, as well as two medals in track.

German successes notwithstanding, the 1904 games were predictably dominated by the United States, whose team was by far the largest (of the 554 athletes in St. Louis, 432 were Americans). In the twenty-three track-and-field events the host country captured twenty-two gold medals, twenty-two silvers, and twenty bronzes. For the first time America also did well in gymnastics, obviously taking good advantage of the light European competition. George Poage and Joseph Sandler became the first African Americans to medal in the Olympics: Poage took third in the four-hundred-meter race, while Sandler placed second in the standing high jump.

The most revealing competitions in 1904 were not part of the official Olympic program. For two days during the games so-called Anthropology Days contests took place involving Africans, Asians, Filipinos, and American Indians, all dressed in folkloric costumes and competing in "native games" along with conventional European-derived events. This degrading sideshow was fully of a piece with the exposition's larger celebration of white America's expansion from sea to shining sea and Washington's recent establishment of an American empire at the expense of Spain, all of which was portrayed as the "manifest destiny" of a superior Anglo-Saxon race. Summing up the Anthropology Days, a St. Louis newspaper wrote: "The meeting was a grand success from every point of view, and served as a good example of what little brown men are capable of doing with training." The organizers ignored the conventions of Olympic amateurism by awarding the tribal winners small cash prizes. The native athletes' eligibility for genuine Olympic contests was not a concern, said the officials, since on the whole these men were hardly of Olympic caliber, and in any case they "would not have understood the principles of amateurism."

Coubertin, who was kept abreast of the developments in St. Louis by his IOC colleagues in attendance at the games, considered the Anthropology Days a disgrace, but in his anxiousness to keep America in the Olympic fold he tried to be philosophical about this travesty. "In no place but America," he wrote later, "would one have dared to place such events on a program—but to Americans everything is permissible, their youthful exuberance calling for the indulgence of the Greek ancestors, if, by chance, they found themselves at that time among the amused spectators."

At the IOC's 1904 meeting in London, Coubertin initially engineered a vote for Rome to host the 1908 games. Explaining this option, the Frenchman said that after its unhappy sojourn in "utilitarian America," Olympism needed "to don once again the sumptuous toga, woven of art and philosophy, in which I had always wanted to clothe her." However, squabbles among the Italian organizing committee, combined with the natural disaster of a volcanic eruption of Vesuvius in 1906, prompted Rome to pull out. British IOC members, who had harbored doubts about Rome from the outset, now offered London as an alternative, which the IOC promptly accepted. As Coubertin summed up these developments: "The curtain descended on the Tiber's stage and soon rose on that of the Thames."

In terms of the number of participating nations and the size of the audiences, as well as the quality of the athletic facilities, the London games of 1908 were a huge improvement over their French and American predecessors. Yet these games, too, were rife with accusations of home-team favoritism and displays of nationalistic excess. Moreover, the backdrop for the London games was yet another large exposition, in this case the Franco-British Exhibition, a festive commemoration of Britain's recent decision to mend fences with its old rival across the Channel so as not to stand alone against that new bully on the block, Germany.

London, as the world's greatest imperial city, was in a good position not only to impress the French and other exhibition visitors, but also, perhaps, to intimidate the Germans. Accordingly, for the first time in the history of the modern games the host city built an Olympics-specific stadium from scratch. The new White City Stadium at Shepherd's Bush, constructed in less than two years, could hold seventy thousand spectators. Also for the first time, the host nation organizing committee, the British Olympic Council, sought to pull together a program fully in harmony with the plans of Baron de Coubertin. Britain even agreed to adopt the metric system as the standard for all the distance competitions except the marathon. No wonder Coubertin came to look with especial fondness on the London games, seeing them as a wonderful display of the noble ideals he had always hoped the games would embody.

Coubertin's idealistic vision, of course, was fully compatible with national posturing, various forms of which were amply on display at the opening ceremonies presided over by King Edward VII and Queen Alexandra. For the first time athletes marched into the stadium grouped by nation. The Finns, whose land had been annexed by Russia in 1809, insisted on entering the arena separate from the Russian imperial squad and carried no flag so as not to have to bear the Russian colors. The large American team, stacked with athletes of Irish descent, refused to dip its national flag while passing in front of the royal couple. One of the American athletes reportedly claimed of the Stars and Stripes: "This flag dips to no earthly king." Deeply aggrieved by the Americans' rudeness, the British fans let out a chorus of catcalls.

In the athletic competitions the rivalry between the world's two sports superpowers, Britain and America, turned ugly. The American public saw the 1908 games as an integral part of America's larger challenge to Britain's political and economic leadership in the world. Headlines in American papers reflected the Yanks' brash confidence: AMERICAN ATHLETES SURE OF SUCCESS; BRITISHERS FEAR YANKEE ATHLETES; WE WILL KNOCK THE SPOTS OFF THE BRITISHERS. But the Britons turned out to be tough to beat on their own turf: In the end Britain won fifty-seven gold medals to America's twenty-two.

Before the games began American officials had worried about possible bias among the judges in London, virtually all of whom were British. The worry seemed borne out (at least in American eyes) when an American runner, J. C. Carpenter, was disqualified in the finals of the four-hundred-meter race for obstructing the British favorite, Wyndam Halswelle. British officials yelled, "No Race!" and broke the tape when Carpenter ran wide to prevent Halswelle from passing him in the final stretch. The officials then ordered the race to be rerun two days later. The Americans were so livid over Carpenter's disqualification that two other U.S. runners who had qualified for the final refused to participate.

In the tug-of-war, a British specialty, the Americans were "pulled over in a rush" in their heat against the Liverpool police, a humiliation the Yanks attributed to their adversaries' use of heavy iron-reinforced boots. America's protest against Liverpool's "illegal" equipment was immediately brushed aside by the officials governing the event.

The biggest row, however, arose over the marathon, that perennial problem child of the early Olympic Games. For this event the British eschewed the metric system, settling on the odd but now-standard twenty-six-mile, 385-yard distance in order to have the race begin at Windsor Castle and finish exactly in front of Queen Alexandra's box in the White City Stadium. The first runner to reach the stadium was an Italian named Dorando Pietri, but he was so exhausted and disoriented that he turned the wrong way on entering the arena, then collapsed in a heap on the track. Since it looked as if he might die in the presence of the queen, doctors rushed to his side and sufficiently revived him so that he was able to stagger on, but he collapsed again and again as he wobbled toward the tape. Finally, unable to bear this grisly spectacle any longer, the head organizer of the race simply *carried* Pietri across the finish line. The second man to cross the line was American John Joseph Hayes, who, when he learned how Pietri had been assisted, understandably thought that *he* should have the victory. The Americans immediately lodged a protest. In this instance the officials felt obliged to accept the American argument. Hayes was duly awarded the gold medal. Fan sentiment, however, remained very solidly on the side of Pietri, who had hovered near death while the American protest was being considered. In honor of his near-fatal effort Queen Alexandra personally awarded him an enormous cup containing far more gold than Hayes's medal.

At one of the banquets held for Olympic guests, Coubertin uttered the now-famous phrase, "The importance of the Olympics lies not so much in winning as in taking part." No doubt some Olympic competitors—mainly those without any chance at a medal—subscribed to this bromide, but the American team of 1908, which firmly believed it had been cheated out of many victories, was not inclined to accept mere participation as a sufficient reward for their efforts. John Sullivan, the head of the Amateur Athletic Union (AAU) in America, publicly excoriated the British judges as "cruel, irresponsible and absolutely unfair." President Theodore Roosevelt agreed, expressing indignation over "so-called British sportsmanship" in a letter to the American ambassador in London. The president personally endorsed a ticker-tape parade in New York City for America's Olympians at which the revelers dragged a papier-mâché effigy of a British lion.

And what about the Germans in London? Their appearance in the British capital should be seen within the broader context of a growing Anglo-German antagonism fueled by the kaiser's anti-British bluster and an accelerating naval arms race. In effect looking for reasons to be offended by the British during the London games, the Germans found plenty of them. The German press complained about the "cool" reception given the German team when it entered the White City Stadium. German Olympic officials considered it unfair that there were several "British" entries (separate squads from Canada, Australia, and South Africa) rather than a single British Empire team. If the British Empire could field so many teams, why couldn't the Germans have separate entries for Prussia, Bavaria, and Saxony?

When it came to the competitions, the Germans agreed with the Americans that the British judges were hopelessly biased in favor of their own athletes. Having performed considerably less brilliantly than they had hoped (they came in sixth), the Germans blamed, in addition to the judges, the miserable English weather and London's heavily polluted air. The Germans should have done better in gymnastics because for the first time the *Turnerschaft* sent a large contingent. Perhaps fearing failure in direct competition with the powerful Scandinavians, however, the *Turner* elected to participate only in exhibitions. These matches drew virtually no spectators, which the Germans saw as another calculated snub. Embittered, they repaired to a German-run pub in North London for "German beer, German food and German service."

IN hopes of staging the 1912 games in Berlin, German members of the IOC persuaded Coubertin to hold the IOC's tenth annual meeting (1909) in the

German capital. Shortly before the meeting began, however, Berlin withdrew its bid because the GOC had not managed to secure the financing to build a stadium, which was now seen as a precondition for hosting the games. On withdrawing their bid, the Germans promised that for the following games, those of 1916, they would definitely have a suitable stadium in place, and they were more or less assured of getting the 1916 games should that indeed be the case.

At the 1909 IOC meeting in Berlin, Stockholm—the only serious bidder left in the running—garnered the right to host the 1912 games. In light of all the past embarrassments and organizational snafus, Coubertin and his IOC colleagues were counting on the stolid Swedes to run a tight and tidy ship.

That the Swedes did. The Stockholm games, everyone agreed, were the most successful to date. Swedish organizers built a beautiful new stadium that Coubertin considered "a model of its type." For the first time the Olympic festival included ancillary arts competitions in architecture, sculpture, painting, literature and music—programs that Coubertin had long advocated as a means of enhancing the games' civilizing mission. He himself won first prize in the literature competition with a saccharine "Ode to Sport," written under a pseudonym. In the lineup of athletic events the Swedes introduced the modern pentathlon, a grueling five-event military competition in which a then-twenty-six-year-old U.S. Army lieutenant named George S. Patton, Jr., came in fifth. This was a great disappointment to young Patton, who had pulled out all the stops to win, going so far as to train on a diet of raw steak and salad and to inject himself with opium before the cross-country race.

Other firsts at Stockholm included the use of electronic devices for timing the footraces and a public address system. Over the objections of Coubertin, who believed that women's only place in the games should be "to crown the winner with garlands," the Stockholm games included female athletes in the swimming and diving competitions (an innovation that caused an Australian journalist to fret that the appearance of women in swimming suits might incite lust among the spectators, causing them to behave like "primitive blacks"). To the frustration of the IOC the Swedish organizers refused to allow a boxing competition on grounds of humanitarianism. Such scruples did not, however, prevent the Swedes from selecting as honorary president of the games none other than King Leopold II of Belgium, already infamous for his nightmare fiefdom in the Congo. In hopes of avoiding judging scandals, the Swedes brought in an international panel of judges.

As successful as the Stockholm games turned out to be, however, all was not sweetness and light. Once again the opening ceremonies belied the Olympic principle of international harmony. As they had in the 1908 games, the Finns paraded flagless into the stadium to avoid marching as part of the Russian Empire team. Upon entering the arena, they received a huge ovation from the largely Scandinavian audience, much to the irritation of the Russians. Later on, when the Russian flag went up to honor the victory of Finnish runner Hannes Kohlemainen in the ten-thousand-meter race, the Finn protested: "I would almost rather not have won, than to see that flag up there." Czech athletes not only marched separately from the Austrian team but also competed as an independent squad, prefiguring the Czechs' bolt from the Austro-Hungarian Empire following World War I. The Germans, for their part, marched in a tight, disciplined formation that elicited murmurings about "Prussian militarism" from the Swedes.

Racism, like nationalism, was a lamentable part of the Stockholm games. The United States sent a large team to Sweden that, according to American press reports, reflected America's "melting pot" population by including athletes of diverse racial and class backgrounds. America's team did in fact include blacks, a Hawaiian, and the great Sauk and Fox Indian, Jim Thorpe. The Europeans, including the Germans, protested America's inclusion of nonwhites as a violation of the Olympic ethos of "gentlemanly" competition. By contrast many American commentators took public pride in the fact that their nation's success at the games—the United States won the most gold medals and came in a close second to Sweden in the total medal count—had derived from America's "assimilation of many races."

The subsequent experience of Jim Thorpe, however, showed that for all America's professed pride in its "melting pot" team, the U.S. athletic bureaucrats fully shared the racial and class-based prejudices of their European colleagues. As is well known, Thorpe won both the classical pentathlon and the decathlon by wide margins. (Among those he defeated in the classical pentathlon was Avery Brundage, who would go on to become the head of the American Olympic Committee during the great battle over the Nazi games of 1936 and, from 1952 to 1972, president of the IOC.) King Gustav V of Sweden pronounced Thorpe "the most wonderful athlete in the world"—to which Thorpe modestly replied, "Thanks, King." But the athlete's glory was short-lived, for in 1913 American newspapers reported that he had been paid a small sum to play semipro baseball before competing at Stockholm. Sensitive to complaints from Europe about their use of non-Anglo (and working-class) athletes, officials of the AAU, which had presided over the selection of the U.S. team for Stockholm, promptly stripped Thorpe of his victories. Furthermore the AAU returned Thorpe's medals to the IOC and requested that his name be expunged from the official Olympic record books. The Americans insisted on this draconian punishment even though the IOC did not demand it. Defending the action, AAU president Sullivan allowed that while it had probably "come naturally" to a man like Thorpe to violate the gentlemanly code of amateurism, his "strange origin" was no excuse for his failure to inform the AAU of his previous play-for-pay.

IN 1913 Coubertin argued that the Olympic Games, if they did not manage entirely to take the place of military conflicts, would certainly render any future wars more "fair" and less lastingly divisive: "The idea of sporting war— the phrase is carefully considered—seems increasingly taking hold: a contest that is hard but that leaves behind less hatred and bitterness. An army of sportsmen will be humane and fair during wartime and calm and collected thereafter." World War I—a four-year industrial slaughter that made a mockery of Coubertin's idea of "sporting war"—broke out a year later.

1916: The Berlin Games That Weren't

At its meeting in Stockholm in 1912 the IOC voted unanimously to hold the 1916 Olympic Games in Berlin. The German capital had bolstered its cause by finally securing funding for the construction of an Olympic stadium. During the next two years the promised structure went up on the grounds of a race track located on the western outskirts of the city. The Union Racing Club, owners of the track, put up most of the money to build the stadium, which they intended to use for their own purposes after the Olympics.

On June 8, 1913, Kaiser Wilhelm II personally attended the formal dedication of the thirty-thousand-seat facility, christened the Deutsches Stadion. In addition to sporting exhibitions, the ceremony included maneuvers by companies of the Royal Guards, which in full battle kit stormed over two-meter-high-barriers, the military equivalent of the high hurdles. During the maneuvers one trooper broke his arm trying to impress the kaiser. There were also flyovers by a zeppelin and a two-decker Albatross, a new class of military aircraft that would soon see action in World War I. Addressing his majesty and a group of assembled dignitaries, Viktor von Podbielski, president of the Deutscher Reichsausschuss für die Olympische Spiele (German Imperial Committee for the Olympic Games [DRAFOS]), called the new stadium an arena for "steeling the national will and cultivating patriotic spirit."

The stadium dedication was emblematic of Wilhelmine Germany and its brash new capital, Berlin. The kaiser presided over a nation with the most potent land army in Europe and an emergent naval fleet that challenged Britain's claim to supremacy on the high seas. It boasted an extremely sophisticated technological infrastructure and some of the best universities in the world. The city of Berlin, elevated in 1871 from capital of Prussia to capital of the German Empire, was by 1912 the fourth largest metropolis in Europe, having in the past few decades grown faster than any other major European city. In acknowledgment of its late arrival, rapid growth, and rough-edged swagger, Mark Twain famously labeled Berlin "the German Chicago." Most Berliners preferred comparisons with New York, for they were beginning to see their town as a true "world city." Although in truth Wilhelmine Berlin was by no means as "worldly" as New York, London, or Paris when it came to urban sophistication, it was finally getting some first-class hotels and restaurants, and its mass transit system rivaled those of Paris and London for speed and efficiency. On the day the Deutsches Stadion was dedicated, a new subway station opened at the Olympic site, capable of moving four thousand people an hour.

The German athletic officials behind the 1916 Berlin games proclaimed their determination to stage the most impressive Olympic festival to date. Two of the officials involved, Carl Diem and Theodor Lewald, would go on to play key roles in the organization of the German games of 1936.

Carl Diem, though generally staying in the background, did more than anyone else in the Reich during the first half of the twentieth century to advance German sports and German Olympism. A short, barrel-chested man who remained in excellent physical condition even in his later years (he loved nothing better than to take younger men out on long jogs and then run them into the ground), Diem was raised in humble circumstances. He once likened his childhood to "a gray rainy day never enlivened by the sun." Too poor to finish secondary school, much less attend a university, Diem became a lifelong autodidact, reading widely in philosophy, history, and literature, and eventually sitting in on a variety of courses at the University of Berlin. In 1904, after halfheartedly undergoing a training program in business administration, Diem volunteered for the army with the ambition of becoming a professional soldier. His lack of a high school diploma, however, precluded him from consideration for the officer corps, and in 1905 he abruptly left the military.

Throughout this record of failure and frustration there was one bright spot in Diem's life: sports. From childhood on Diem was obsessed with sports—not just with participating in them but also with studying them, writing about them, and organizing them. Because he was never a particularly gifted athlete himself, the organizational side of his obsession quickly came to the fore, and at age fourteen he set up his first sports club. A few years later, in 1908, having cofounded the Berliner Athletikerverband, he helped popularize sports in the capital by organizing Berlin's first "marathon"—a relay race that served as a model for the 1936 Olympic torch relay he helped devise.

Diem's active engagement on behalf of German sport naturally brought him into contact with his country's fledgling Olympic movement. He was a cofounder of the DRAFOS in 1904 and accompanied the German team to an off-year (and unofficial) Athens "Olympiad" in 1906. His experience in Athens so impressed him that he used a new job as a sportswriter for the Berlin paper *Sport im Bild* to proselytize for the Olympic movement. In recognition of his service to the Olympic cause he was chosen to lead the German team into the stadium in Stockholm in 1912. Shortly thereafter he was appointed general secretary of the DRAFOS, with the primary task of preparing for the 1916 Berlin Games.

As Diem set about this task, he advanced the argument that sport, including Olympic sport, was vital to Germany because in strengthening the bodies and moral fiber of its young men it could also strengthen the military potential of the nation. In fact he had been taking this line since his return from the second Athens games, when he wrote: "Perhaps these Olympic Games will bring us the insight that we must do more, much more, for the cultivation of sports if we wish to keep our people fit and militarily strong." As general secretary of the DRAFOS, Diem strove to get the army behind the games by arguing that what was good for the Olympics was also good for the military.

It was clear to Diem from the outset, however, that if the Olympic idea was to capture the hearts and minds of the German military, and indeed of the

Volk as a whole, German Olympic teams must perform significantly better than they had in the games so far. One needed "victory all down the line," as he put it. But how could this be achieved in the short period before the crucial home-field test in 1916? The key to future German success, Diem concluded, was to learn from the nation that theretofore had enjoyed the greatest Olympic success—the United States.

In 1913 Diem set off on a "study trip" to America, determined to plumb the Yanks' training secrets and, if possible, to bring back an American coach or two to help with the training of the German team. Diem's two-month trip was a great success. He visited universities and training facilities and interviewed dozens of American athletes and coaches. Most important, he managed to hire a former American track star, Alvin Kraenzlein, then a coach at Princeton, to take charge of the preparation of the German team for 1916. Conveniently for Diem, Kraenzlein was of solid Germanic stock (his father, who ran a general store in New York City, remained so tied to the old country that he refused to serve customers who spoke English). The thirty-six-year-old German American had won four track championships at the 1900 Paris Olympics and then become a successful coach at the University of Michigan before moving on to Princeton. Even the hypernationalistic *Turner* movement welcomed Kraenzlein's appointment, noting that the Reich was "waiting for the [American] coach as if he were the Messiah. . . . He who teaches sport has to know something about it."

Of course, everyone knew that Germany needed more than a well-trained home team to stage a successful Olympic spectacle. Money was required, and lots of it, to build additional Olympic facilities and to promote the games. The Swedes had set a high organizational standard in 1912, and Diem and his DRAFOS colleagues feared that Berlin would not be able to trump Stockholm without extensive subsidies from the Reich. In Diem's eyes much was at stake here, for the 1916 Olympics afforded Germany the chance to demonstrate superiority all around, not just in sports. His goal was to use the games as a vehicle "to show the visiting world our fatherland in all its economic, industrial and military might."

For all his propagandistic gifts, Diem was not the man to secure the necessary funding for the 1916 games—he lacked the proper social and political connections. Fortunately for Germany's Olympic cause, Theodor Lewald, a high-level government official and later member of the IOC and president of Germany's organizing committee for the 1936 games, was as well connected in politics as he was passionate about sport. Yet it must be noted at the outset that Lewald had his own "disadvantage" to overcome: He was half Jewish. Throughout his long career in German politics and sports administration he had to contend with the argument that it was shameful for Germany to have a person of his ethnic background in a position of prominence. On the other hand, as we shall see more clearly later on, it was precisely Lewald's ethnicity that made him especially useful to the anti-Semitic system he loyally served, for it afforded that system a veneer of fair-mindedness and respectability in its dealings with the outside world.

Lewald was born in 1860 in Berlin. His father, a noted jurist, came from a prominent German Jewish family in Königsberg that had converted to Protestantism in the early nineteenth century. His mother's ancestry boasted noted preachers, artists, and journalists, some of whom were democrats. Lewald's own upbringing was, however, uncompromisingly conservative, and he (like Diem) remained a proponent of nationalistic authoritarian values all his life.

Typically for someone of his background, Lewald followed his father's footsteps into the law, all the while careful to downplay his part-Jewish ancestry. He even decided against marrying a Jewish girl he deeply loved for fear of damaging his career prospects. On completing his legal studies he fulfilled his required one-year-service obligation in the military, which entitled him to become a lieutenant in the reserves, a distinction he bore proudly all his days. A coveted position as a legal assessor in Potsdam gave him entrée into influential governmental circles and social salons. In 1891 he shifted from the Prussian to the imperial bureaucracy by taking a post in the Reich Interior Ministry.

As an ambitious, multilingual, and suave young bureaucrat, Lewald represented his government at both the Paris International Exposition of 1900 and the Louisiana Purchase Exposition in St. Louis in 1904. This duty brought him into contact with Olympic sports, which (as we have seen) transpired within the framework of the expositions. Although not much of an athlete himself, Lewald loved sports passionately and was able in his governmental capacity to steer some modest Reich subsidies to the German Olympic teams in 1900 and 1904.

By 1910 Lewald had climbed to the rank of *Ministerialdirektor* in the Interior Ministry with the primary task of representing his ministry in its relations with the Reichstag. He was no admirer of the German parliament, filled as it

then was with (in his eyes) uncouth Social Democrats, but he was sophisticated and flexible enough to work effectively with all sides. This talent served
him well when, in early 1914, he chose to exploit his considerable influence
to help the DRAFOS acquire substantial Reich funding for the 1916 Berlin
games.

It turned out that Lewald's intervention was absolutely necessary, for on
May 12, 1914, the Reichstag's budget committee unanimously recommended
that the DRAFOS's request for a two-hundred-thousand-mark subsidy be
rejected by the full house. This action provoked outrage among Germany's
pro-Olympic faction, one newspaper speaking of a "dereliction of duty." In
the plenum debate two days later the SPD delegate urged rejecting the subsidy on grounds that the Olympic movement was a bourgeois endeavor with
no appeal to the working masses. Speaking in favor of the subsidy request,
Lewald pointed out that Germany's reputation vis-à-vis the rest of the world
was at stake. It would be unworthy for "a great nation and a great people" to
invite foreign guests to their capital and then lay a meager table. Moreover,
he noted, Germany had to keep in mind its strong ties to the ancient
Olympic heritage: "If thirty years ago the German Reichstag could approve
the resources that made possible the excavation of ancient Olympia, then
surely the Reichstag cannot now deny the resources for the first modern
Olympics on German soil."

Largely because of Lewald's intervention, the Reichstag voted to subsidize
the Berlin games after all. This decision represented a novelty for the young
Olympic movement, since the organizational costs for all the previous festivals had been borne largely by private contributors or lotteries.

Following the Reichstag's historic vote, the entire German nation seemed
to catch Olympic fever. Gustav Krupp von Bohlen und Halbach, head of the
Krupp munitions firm, kicked in 25,000 marks of his own money to help
with the Olympic preparations. Kaiser Wilhelm II endowed a special medal
to be awarded to victors in the trials for the national team. Cast at the Royal
Mint, the medals bore a bust of the kaiser on one side and the victor's name
on the other.

The Olympic trials, which were held at various venues around the Reich
in May 1914, attracted large and enthusiastic crowds. By order of the kaiser
active-duty soldiers were allowed to compete. Of particular interest to them
were the equestrian events and the modern pentathlon, which tested such
military skills as shooting, fencing, and riding. A dress rehearsal for the 1916

games, involving members of the newly selected national team, took place in the Deutsches Stadion on June 26–28, 1914.

As historical irony would have it, just as German marksmen were competing in the shooting championships in Berlin on June 28, down in Sarajevo, Bosnia, a nineteen-year-old Bosnian Serb named Gavrilo Princip was putting holes in Archduke Franz Ferdinand, heir apparent to the throne of Austria-Hungary—a bit of almost accidental marksmanship that ignited the diplomatic crisis culminating in World War I, and the cancellation of the 1916 Olympic Games.

GROWING tensions between Germany and its chief European rivals had been clouding the Olympic picture even before the war broke out. In early 1914, with the prospect of an international conflict looming, the British Foreign Office advised against Britain's participation in an Olympic contest on German soil, as did the British army. French athletic officials, who likewise felt uncomfortable with the idea of their sportsmen competing against the *Boche* on German territory, saw the increased tensions as a good excuse to try to move the games out of Berlin.

Once the hostilities actually began in August 1914, it became highly likely that, unless the conflict ended soon, the 1916 games would indeed be moved or called off altogether. In 1915 the head of the British Olympic Council, Theodore Cook, summed up popular feeling in his country when he wrote that a "British team" was certainly on its way to Berlin, but the team in question wore military kit rather than sporting gear. Cook demanded the ouster of Germany's only remaining representative on the IOC, Count Adalbert von Stierstorpff. When Coubertin rejected this demand, Cook himself left the IOC. Meanwhile, the German *Turner* demanded categorically: "Away with the internationalist Olympic Games!"

With much of Europe caught up in bloody fighting, a bevy of non-European cities offered to host the 1916 games in place of Berlin. Among the aspirants was Cincinnati, Ohio, whose Chamber of Commerce promised a half-million dollars to help defray the costs of building a stadium and bringing European athletes to America. Berlin, however, had not given up its claim to host the games. Carl Diem, who had gone off to fight on the Western Front, argued that the games should be held in the German capital as soon as the fighting stopped. The IOC, which alone had the authority to move or cancel the festival, was also still hoping to stage the competitions in Berlin on the conclusion of peace.

Even Coubertin, who like Diem had answered his country's call to arms (albeit in a noncombatant role because of his advanced age), remained committed to Berlin for several months into the war, hoping that some kind of "Olympic truce" might be arranged, as "in olden times." In April 1915, discouraged by his own nation's indifference toward his Olympic project, and believing that a movement dedicated to transcending national boundaries could function better if based in a neutral country, he transferred the IOC headquarters to Lausanne, Switzerland, its home to this day.

Calls for abandoning Berlin took on added intensity following Germany's deployment of poison gas in the Ypres salient of the Western Front in spring 1915. The use of poison weapons (though in fact hardly unknown to the ancient Greeks) seemed so antithetical to the Olympic spirit that the IOC, Coubertin included, finally washed their hands of the German capital in mid-1915. Rather than try to find a replacement site for 1916, the committee decided to scrap that year's Olympics entirely. At the same time, however, in order to project an illusion of Olympic continuity above politics and strife, the IOC chose to count the nongames of 1916 as the "Fifth Olympiad." As Coubertin argued: "An Olympiad does not have to be celebrated, but it must be counted."

Although the decision to cancel the 1916 games was understandable enough under the circumstances, this move underscored the vulnerability of the modern Olympics to political and military pressures. Despite Coubertin's repeated admonitions that the games must remain above the fray, the contests had never been an athletic ivory tower. Indeed, few international institutions were more caught up in the political passions of the day than the modern Olympic Games.

The Not-So-Roaring Twenties

The nationalist passions and hostilities that were inflamed by the war lived on long after the guns fell silent, affecting virtually everything about the postwar order, including the Olympic movement. Over Courbertin's objections, the first two Olympiads after the war transpired without the participation of the Germans, Austrians, Bulgarians, Turks, and Hungarians, whose wartime "aggression" was said to have made them unfit for a peace-loving enterprise like the Olympic Games.

Another significant nonparticipant was the new Soviet Union, whose representatives professed no interest in a "bourgeois" undertaking like the Olympics. For its part the IOC acted as if the USSR did not exist, retaining a delegate from the defunct Russian monarchy, Prince Lev Urusov, in his seat until his death in 1933. Not until 1952 would the USSR finally participate in the Olympic Games.

Because the exclusion of the defeated powers was hard to reconcile with the professed Olympic ideals of neutrality and internationalism, the IOC did not itself impose the ban on the former Central Powers. Rather it left the matter up to the organizing committees in Antwerp, the host of the 1920 games, and Paris, the host in 1924, both of which simply neglected to send invitations to the countries in question. Meanwhile the Versailles treaty, which established the peace terms for Germany, forbade (in article 177) any contact between German sporting organizations and the national War Ministry.

The selection of Antwerp as host for the 1920 games was itself a legacy of World War I—compensation to "brave little Belgium" for having been invaded and pillaged by the Huns. As one commentator put it, "The decision [to hold the games in Antwerp] was, of course, intended as a tribute of honor to the gallant Belgians, who had been the victims of unprovoked aggression five years before; it was universally popular throughout the world." Belgium's Count Henri de Baillet-Latour, an influential member of the IOC and (as of 1925) president of the committee, had lobbied hard for the selection of his own country.

The choice of Antwerp may have been popular, but it was not necessarily wise considering Belgium's sorry condition after four years of "hosting" World War I. A general lack of resources, combined with an inadequate lead time for preparations, guaranteed some rough moments for the relatively few athletes who managed to make the trip to Antwerp, and for the equally sparse audiences.

Even America, which had emerged more powerful than ever from the war, was hard put to assemble and transport a credible team to Antwerp. With isolationist sentiment already running strong in the United States, the AOC had trouble finding the necessary funding. Employing the patriotic sloganeering familiar from war-bond drives—"Our wonderful war showing has led all European nations to expect that every future American invasion will be concluded upon a winning side"—the AOC managed to raise $163,000, about $40,000 short of its goal.

No sooner had these moneys been secured than the problem of transport arose, since the private shipping lines were all booked up and military vessels were technically off-limits to civilian traffic. In desperation Gustavus Kirby, the new president of the AOC, persuaded Congress to make an exception for the American Olympians, who were permitted to sail for Europe on a U.S. Navy ship, the *Princess Matoika*. This proved to be no great bargain, as one of the passengers, Daniel J. Ferris of the AAU, attested:

> The government gave us this great rusty old transport, the *Princess Matoika*. When we arrived to board, they had just taken off the bodies of 1,800 war dead from Europe. When the team filed up the gangplank, the caskets were sitting there on the docks, lines and lines of coffins. It was a shocking way to start.
>
> The athletes were quartered down in the hold. The smell of formaldehyde was dreadful. What a black hole that was for them. The athletes had to sleep on triple-decker bunks that hung on chains. The place was infested with rats. The athletes used to throw bottles at the rats. It was terrible, but we had to go this way because we had no money. No money at all.

Conditions in Antwerp were not much better than on the ship. American athletes complained about their hard bunks at the local YMCA, the miserable food, and the poor surface of the track. American female swimmers, appearing for the first time in Olympic competition, were horrified by the icy water in the pool. In their frustration the Americans practically staged their own little Bolshevik Revolution in the middle of the competition.

No doubt the Yanks were spoiled. The Europeans, having just endured four years of deprivation, were satisfied enough with the facilities and accommodations in Antwerp. For Coubertin and his friend Baillet-Latour it was triumph enough just to be throwing this peaceful party after an eight-year Olympic interregnum. King Albert I of Belgium, too, was proud to preside over the festival, though he had to admit, "It certainly lacks people." Noting that athletes from twenty-seven nations (actually twenty-nine) had somehow managed to get to Antwerp, the American journalist Arthur S. Draper concluded: "It was the best League of Nations meeting since the war."

The sparse crowds attending the Antwerp games witnessed some significant Olympic innovations. For the first time the now-familiar five-ringed Olympic flag, which Coubertin himself had designed in 1914 as a representation of the five continents participating in the games, flew over an Olympic stadium. New also was an Olympic oath, in which the participants promised to respect and observe "the rules of the Games in the true sporting spirit, in the name of sport and for the honor of our countries."

One country that came away with considerable honor was little Finland, whose total medal haul was second only to that of the vastly larger United States. Paavo Nurmi, the "Flying Finn," won three gold medals, beginning his multiyear domination of the middle-distance races. Despite the icy pool water, American Ethelda Bleibtrey won gold medals in all three women's swimming races. Seventy-two-year-old Swedish shooter Oscar Swahn won a silver medal in the (now discontinued) team double-shot running-deer event, thereby becoming the oldest Olympic medalist in the history of the games.

Germany, having been booted from the Olympic temple, was of course not on hand in Antwerp to witness any of this. The fledgling Weimar Republic, caught up as it was in the travails of establishing new governmental institutions, fighting off putsch attempts from Left and Right, and contending with the worst currency inflation a modern industrial nation had ever seen, was arguably better off not having to worry about fielding an Olympic team.

In any case the German sports community was at this point as disinclined to be part of the Olympic movement as the IOC was to include them. The DRAFOS, which in 1917 had changed its name to the more patriotic sounding Deutscher Reichsausschuss für Leibesübungen (German National Association for Physical Training [DRL]), announced at its inaugural meeting that it intended to cultivate purely German sport, developing national sporting traditions to a degree that would "make the German race unbeatable." Accordingly, after the war the DRL began organizing militarized national competitions (*Deutsche Kampfspiele*) in place of Olympic trials and preparations.

In the view of Carl Diem, now a leading figure in the DRL, these national games were an adequate replacement for the Olympics and closer in spirit to the ideals of the classical Greeks, who had kept the ancient games to themselves. In a 1923 polemic Diem argued, with some justice, that the IOC had violated its own internationalist principles by not postponing the 1920 games until a time when the wounds of war might have healed sufficiently to allow all nations to participate. Noting that the IOC had decided to hold the next Olympic Games in Paris, Diem added that this decision was also a violation of the Olympic spirit, since Germany, even if invited, could hardly send a team to a nation that had imposed a military occupation on German territory (the 1923 French occupation of the Ruhr Valley). Alluding to France's use of Moroccan troops in its occupation, Diem fumed: "What German would be willing to attend an international festival in Paris so long as blacks in French military uniforms stand on the German Rhine! For us Germans, our national competitions are a fully adequate replacement."

Diem undoubtedly meant what he said about the German national competitions being a satisfactory alternative to the Olympics, but his commentary has the ring of protesting too much. The Germans, nationalists like Diem included, were deeply angered by their exclusion from the Olympic movement, to which they believed they had a special claim. Diem was briefly heartened by the fact that, by 1923, Germany was once again being included in many international sporting societies, a trend he thought portended a possible early readmission to the Olympic fold. "Without Germany," he wrote, "the Olympics are a partial creation." Any chance, however, that Diem might have managed to secure Germany's inclusion in the Paris games of 1924 was eliminated when he refused Coubertin's informal invitation to attend the IOC's 1923 meeting in Rome on grounds that he had not been formally invited.

At the moment Diem was professing his allegiance to purely German sports, the political movement with which he would later be closely allied in the organization of the 1936 games, the Nazi Party, was first making its presence felt in the German sporting world. The Nazis staged a violent protest demonstration at the 1923 German Gymnastics Festival being held in Munich, the party's birthplace. The Nazis and their *völkisch* allies from Austria and Bohemia were indignant that this festival allowed Jews and other "non-Germans" to participate. Hitler himself signed a petition protesting the "provocative character" of an event that brought "Jews, Frenchmen and Americans" into "the heartland of the *völkisch* liberation ideal." In this instance the Nazis were unable to achieve their aim—their protest march through Munich was broken up by the police—but within ten years their racist perspective would come to dominate the German sports community.

At its annual meeting in Paris preceding the 1924 games, the IOC welcomed two German members, Theodor Lewald and Oskar Ruperti, into its ranks. France, however, was determined that Germany must not participate in the Paris games, which the French government saw as a vehicle for demonstrating the unique power and glory of France. Fully accepting the oft-asserted linkage between high-level sport and military prowess, France's intelligence agency, the Deuxième Bureau, warned that Germany was already using athletic training and sports competition as a means to circumvent the military restrictions of the Versailles treaty and to rebuild its military might. The bureau further contended that Germany's sporting community was "animated by the most violent hatred" toward France. Caught in the bitter rivalry between Paris and Berlin, the IOC simply threw up its hands and allowed France's politicians to make the vital decisions regarding who would participate in the Paris games of 1924.

Germany and the other former Central Powers missed out not only on the Summer Games of 1924 but also on the inaugural Winter Olympics, held in Chamonix, France, in February of that year. (There had been plans to stage Winter Games on the Feldberg in Germany's Black Forest in 1916, but, like the projected summer festival in Berlin, this event fell victim to the Great War.) Of course there was something rather un-Olympic about Winter Games, the ancient Greeks not having been known for their prowess in skiing and skating. Moreover, most of the competitors would inevitably have to come from countries with mountains or at least suitably cold winters, limitations that were hard to square with Olympic universalism. For these reasons Coubertin was not enthusiastic about the idea of separate Winter Games.

One would think the Scandinavians would have been eager for the introduction of Winter Olympics, but they had their own Nordic Games and worried that Olympic Winter contests would undercut these. The Winter Olympics came about largely because IOC delegates from France, Switzerland, Italy, and Canada effectively argued that this venture would expand the reach of Olympism to the growing world of winter sports. The IOC's lingering doubts about its experiment with the Winter Games were reflected in its initial decision to label the Chamonix affair an "International Sports Week" rather than an Olympic festival. Only after the event proved reasonably successful did the committee officially classify it as the first Winter Olympiad. At the 1925 meeting at which this reclassification was made, the IOC also announced that henceforth the nations hosting the Summer Games would have first call on that year's Winter Games, providing they had the requisite terrain and climate. For the Germans this meant that when they eventually won the right to host the Summer Games of 1936, they would also have first crack at that year's winter festival.

With respect to Germany's (though not just Germany's) Olympic future, the 1924 Paris games were significant in showing that the Americans, while still very strong, were increasingly vulnerable in a number of areas, including track-and-field. A Jewish runner from Britain, Harold Abrahams, won the one-hundred-meter race, while E. H. Liddell, a Scottish Evangelical Christian who refused to race on Sundays, took the four hundred meters (events commemorated in the 1981 film *Chariots of Fire*). America's William DeHart Hubbard, in taking the long jump, became the first black athlete to win an individual Olympic competition. Another notable American participant in 1924 was Benjamin Spock, a member of the Yale University crew that won the coxed eights rowing event. The future pediatrician Spock, of course, went on to write the hugely influential parental guide, *The Common Sense Book of Baby and Child Care*, which made him the bête noire of social conservatives who accused him of corrupting a whole generation of Americans through his counseling of "permissive" child rearing. Spock and the other American competitors in 1924 were cheered on so loudly and aggressively by supporters from the United States that the French spectators took passionate umbrage. One Frenchman went so far as to severely cane an American fan during the Franco-American rugby match. (Rugby Union football was discontinued as an Olympic sport after 1924.)

As they had in Antwerp, the Finns performed magnificently in Paris. Paavo Nurmi won five gold medals to add to the three he had won in 1920. His teammate Ville Ritola earned four gold and two silver medals. In all the Finns bagged thirteen gold, thirteen silver, and five bronze medals. Finland's amazing prowess generated a great deal of speculation on the secret of their success. Some theorists focused on the Finns' nasty but nutritious diet of dried fish, hard bread, and sour milk; others spoke of the "wild Mongol strain" from which the modern Finns supposedly descended; while still others emphasized the virtues of the sauna ritual, reasoning that any people who could roast themselves pink and then roll in the snow had to be tough as nails. Finally there was the notion that the Finns' relative poverty and hard rural lifestyle gave them an advantage over rich, soft, citified nations.

The Germans, having earlier looked to America for guidance in matters athletic, now turned to Finland as a possible model, and one that might be easier to emulate. After all, Germany, too, had strong rural traditions, plenty of simple but fortifying food, and a new poverty that might bring it back to its robust tribal roots—to those rough-hewn ways that in olden days had allowed the Teutons to be the terror of the civilized world. Put in still more ancient terms, might not the Germans play Sparta to America's (and France's and Britain's) Athens?

Germany, it turned out, would once again be given the chance to show the world its athletic mettle in the games of 1928, sixteen years after that nation's last Olympic appearance.On May 26, 1926, Germany was invited to send teams to the 1928 Summer Games in Amsterdam and the Winter Games in St. Moritz, Switzerland. Diem had prepared for this moment by drumming up Olympic enthusiasm among the German people. Once again he took a pronounced nationalistic line, hoping to overcome the reservations of the xenophobic *Turnerschaft* and its nativist backers: "Being German must no longer mean being easily satisfied," he declared. "To be German must mean to claim the world for Germany. Since the war the key goal for us in the realms of culture, science, art and industry has been to reclaim as rapidly as possible our place in the sun; similarly, German sport, an integral part of German life and culture, must not avoid the international arena by cowering in its own little sulking-corner."

Diem's prodding was effective, and Olympic fever once again gripped the nation. An Olympic subscription drive generated more than a million reichsmarks among private and corporate donors to support the German teams bound for St. Moritz and Amsterdam. Those teams were selected by means of special qualifying competitions held in schools all around the country—an innovation borrowed from Finland. Diem did not manage fully to overcome the *Turnerschaft*'s opposition to Germany's participation in the Amsterdam games, but he and Lewald did get the group to join the newly formed German Olympic Association (GOA), which succeeded the DRAFOS and operated as the parent organization for the German Organizing Committee.

The preparation paid off handsomely in the Amsterdam games. The Germans placed second to the Americans in the national medal count, garnering eleven gold, nine silver, and nineteen bronze medals. Just as important, German successes came in a wide range of competitions—equestrian events, wrestling, water polo, swimming—and, yes, even track and field.

As for America its overall victory was tempered by a relatively weak performance in track and field, where the total U.S. medal count was equaled by that of the Scandinavians. Finland's Nurmi once again showed American middle-distance runners his heels, prompting one New York sportswriter to liken him to the fleet-footed hero in the Finnish epic, the *Kalevala*, who "runs as if air were his road." In the track events no American won a gold medal until the last day of competition, when Raymond Barbuti took the four-hundred-meter race—which he managed to do only because James Ball of Canada made the mistake of staying in his lane on the back straight rather than running in a direct line to the tape, as he could legally have done.

The 1928 games were doubly disappointing to the American team because the AOC was then under the stern tutelage of Gen. Douglas MacArthur, who had promised a convincing win. Much like Carl Diem, MacArthur considered the Olympic Games to be a kind of "war without weapons." To ensure victory in this war he personally accompanied the American team on its journey to Amsterdam, all the while reminding his "army" of Olympians of their manifest destiny to demonstrate American superiority across the board. "I told them," he recalled in his memoirs, that "we represented the greatest nation in the world." And he added, "We have not come so far just to lose gracefully, but rather to win, and to win decisively." In Amsterdam, MacArthur allowed his troops to leave their ship, the *President Roosevelt*, only for competitions. This would protect them from unsavory temptations in a notoriously sinful city and prevent competitors from "spying" on them.

Upon returning from America's less-than-stellar performance on the athletic battlefields of Amsterdam, MacArthur remained undaunted despite press criticism that he had mishandled his Olympic command. In typically bombastic fashion he told President Calvin Coolidge that if he, General MacArthur, were "required to indicate today that element of American life which is most characteristic of our nationality, my finger would unerringly point to our athletic escutcheon."

Also characteristically, MacArthur failed to give due credit to the skills of America's competitors, including the second-place Germans. The Germans themselves did not make that mistake. Their surprising success in Amsterdam (which easily compensated for their lackluster performance in the Winter Games at St. Moritz) generated even more Olympic enthusiasm across the nation. President Paul von Hindenburg personally congratulated the team at an official reception in Berlin. Diem ascribed the good showing to a combination of hard work and superior national character. Germany's Olympic victors, he said, were not freaks of nature but "normal, skilled, highly trained, strong-willed fighters—the national fruit of a healthy people."

For Diem and other German Olympic enthusiasts, the success in Amsterdam provided the boost they needed to strive for a bigger prize—the role of host for the games of 1936. Was it not right and just, they reasoned, that an honor that had been lost to war in 1916 should now be regained by virtue of Germany's obvious commitment to Olympic excellence and its respectable standing among the peace-loving nations of the world?

Enter the Nazis

THE 1930s, that "rotten decade" indelibly associated with the Great Depression, the Nazi takeover in Germany, Stalin's ruthless purges, the Spanish civil war, and the buildup to World War II, was also a seminal period in the history of the modern Olympic movement. At the beginning of the decade the IOC tapped Berlin to host the 1936 Summer Games. Then, in 1932, the committee girded its loins for its second experience with American-hosted games—the Winter Games in Lake Placid and the much more ambitious Summer Games in Los Angeles. Within a few months of the conclusion of the LA games, Hitler assumed the chancellorship in Germany. This was a man who as late as 1932 had denounced the Olympic Games as a "plot of Freemasons and Jews." The prospect of a Hitler-led Germany possibly hosting the next Olympic Games presented the young Olympic movement with its greatest crisis to date.

The Decision for Berlin

Germany had begun its campaign for the 1936 Olympics even before the Amsterdam games. On behalf of the German Olympic Association and the city of Berlin, Theodor Lewald tendered Berlin's bid at a meeting of the IOC in Monaco on April 27, 1927. This was the first step in a lengthy process. Baillet-Latour, who had taken over as president of the IOC in 1925, let it be known that the venue decision for 1936 would not be made until 1931. In putting forth Berlin, Lewald conveniently sidestepped the fact that two other

German cities, Nuremberg and Cologne, had also applied to represent Germany in 1936 and were still technically in contention; shortly thereafter Frankfurt also threw its hat in the ring. Lewald's cavalier brush-off of the non-Berlin bids infuriated the partisans of the other cities, who saw this behavior as typical Berlin bullying. Konrad Adenauer, the mayor of Cologne, protested in vain over the pro-Berlin bias in the committee. Years later, as the first chancellor of the post–World War II Federal Republic of Germany, he would get his revenge on Berlin by cold-shouldering the former German capital, then divided into Allied occupation zones and isolated deep within the Soviet-dominated German Democratic Republic.

In pushing for Berlin, Lewald did not initially enjoy solid support from Berlin's municipal administration. The city was flat broke and the municipal council sharply divided over the advisability of hosting the games. Everyone knew the project would be very expensive and that the old Deutsches Stadion, built for the cancelled 1916 games, would have to be expanded and modernized. Lewald countered that the games would undoubtedly be an economic bonanza for Berlin: He estimated a windfall of ten million marks. Ultimately, with crucial help from Foreign Minister Gustav Stresemann, Lewald browbeat the city council and Berlin mayor Gustav Böss into accepting the challenge. Stresemann also promised that the republican government would stand behind Berlin's application.

In 1930 Lewald persuaded the IOC to hold its Ninth Olympic Congress in the German capital. This was a brilliant stroke, for the congress, attended by everybody who was anybody in the Olympic movement, afforded ample opportunity for the Germans to show off Berlin and to glad-hand the IOC delegates. President Hindenburg personally opened the congress at a ceremonial gathering in the main hall of Berlin University, where he emphasized that the Reich government, which was subsidizing the congress to the tune of fifty thousand reichsmarks, stood fully behind Germany's Olympic project. Lewald himself pointedly reminded the delegates of the great contributions to Olympic scholarship made by J. J. Winckelmann and Ernst Curtius (the latter having presided over the German excavations at Olympia in the late nineteenth century). Using some of Hindenburg's money, Berlin laid on an opulent banquet for the delegates at the city hall. To demonstrate their organizational prowess, German Olympic officials amassed a fleet of two thousand rowboats to ferry the delegates and their extensive retinues around the proposed rowing course at Grünau. Guests were also shown plans for the renovation of the Deutsches Stadion. Lewald concluded the congress with the words: "*Auf Wiedersehen* 1936 in Berlin!"

At the time the 1930 Olympic Congress took place, Berlin's primary competitors for the 1936 Summer Games were Rome and Barcelona. Rome, of course, was then under the strongman rule of Benito Mussolini. According to Lewald the IOC was "strongly repelled" by the fascist government's domination of Italian sport, though the committee also believed it could count on "disciplined" and "energetic" support for the games from Mussolini.

In the eyes of most Berlin boosters, Barcelona was the more serious threat, since Spain had strong sporting traditions and a number of IOC delegates were known to favor the Catalan city. Dictator Miguel Primo de Rivera had recently resigned and gone into exile. To undercut the competition from both Barcelona and Rome, Lewald secretly commissioned a study from the Prussian Meteorological Institute showing inhospitable weather patterns in those two cities during the Olympic month of August; Diem then had the results published in a Dutch newspaper. Lewald also took the (then) unusual step of writing personal letters to his IOC colleagues, urging them to commit to Berlin before the committee's April 1931 meeting in Barcelona, where the venue decision was to be made. He pointed out that Coubertin himself favored Berlin, noting that the Frenchman thought the Germans to be excellent stewards of the traditions of modern Olympism. Finally Lewald advised delegates who supported Berlin, but who would not be attending the Barcelona meeting, to express their sentiments to Baillet-Latour in writing.

When the IOC met on April 24–26 in Barcelona to decide on the host city for 1936, the delegates could scarcely focus on the business at hand due to chaos in the streets. The advent of the Second Spanish Republic had just been declared in Madrid, prompting the flight of King Alfonso XIII, while in Barcelona itself Catalan nationalists had proclaimed an independent Republic of Catalonia. Under these conditions only nineteen of the sixty-four IOC members managed to make it to Barcelona for the meeting. The delegate from Italy, apparently aware that Rome had no chance for 1936, retracted that city's bid for the eleventh games while expressing Rome's hopes for 1940. Given the obvious lack of a quorum, the IOC elected not to make its venue decision for 1936 at the Barcelona meeting but to cast ballots by mail, with the result to be announced in Lausanne in May.

Lewald used the days immediately following the Barcelona meeting to put more pressure on his IOC colleagues. He had Germany's ambassador to

Tokyo personally call on the two Japanese IOC members, both of whom eventually voted for Berlin. (In exchange for their backing, Lewald and his German colleagues later supported Tokyo's bid for the 1940 games.) Following an appeal from Lewald, the Chilean IOC delegate, Alfredo Ewing, cabled his pro-Berlin vote to Lausanne, adding the quaint explanation that he considered the "happiest memories of my youth" to have been his two years' service as a visiting officer with the Imperial German Army.

On May 13, 1931, Baillet-Latour announced the results of the vote by mail: forty-three for Berlin, sixteen for Barcelona. Many of the delegates who voted for Berlin said they wanted to show support for Germany's democratic government, which, with the onset of hard economic times following the American stock market crash in 1929, was once again under attack from leftist and rightist extremists. Lewald's personal intervention with his colleagues also seems to have had a positive effect. Carl Diem, who had worried that the time might not yet be ripe for a successful German Olympic bid, generously attributed the result solely to Lewald's efforts. (Diem, we should note, admired Lewald and worked closely with him despite their significant differences in background.)

Nowadays, of course, we are used to all sorts of skulduggery in connection with Olympic bids, but in the games' earlier years this sort of under-the-table politicking was unusual. At the time only insiders like Diem knew the extent to which Lewald had gone to win the games for Berlin. When the award was announced, no one could have known that Lewald would later prove just as instrumental in ensuring that the German capital managed to hold on to what it had won in 1931. But before that crucial showdown could transpire, the Olympic movement had yet another challenge to meet: staging its second Olympiad in the New World at a time of a crippling worldwide depression.

"A Home for Neo-Olympism": The Los Angeles Games

If Los Angeles had had its way, the Olympic Games would have been held in that city as early as 1924, rather than eight years later. During the Antwerp games, Los Angeles officially bid for the '24 festival, arguing, as LA real estate mogul and later IOC member William May Garland put it in a letter to Coubertin, that the United States "was entitled to the international recognition" attendant on hosting the games, and that of all American cities Los

Angeles had the strongest claim "because the Olympics have never been held in the West and because Los Angeles can extend a bid with the greatest number of advantages." Among those advantages were a superb climate and the promise of a new 75,000-seat stadium.

Coubertin advised Garland in 1921 that the IOC was already committed to Paris for 1924 but that LA should nonetheless hold itself ready in case "political and social problems in Europe" forced a last-minute shift to America. The elderly Frenchman, who had become a California fan by virtue of an earlier visit to the Golden State, suggested that Los Angeles might even become "a kind of home for neo-Olympism."

At its Rome meeting in 1923, the IOC, with Coubertin's blessing, voted to award the 1932 Games to LA. Although some of the European Olympic officials still harbored bad memories of the first American Olympics in St. Louis in 1904, the IOC expressed enthusiasm for its choice. The American Olympic Association, dominated as it was by East Coasters, was rather less enthusiastic about the games going to LA. According to Avery Brundage, the Easterners had "considerable doubt that 'these inexperienced provincials' . . . were competent to handle a sport event of this magnitude." Undeterred by the carping, the Los Angeles Organizing Committee promised the grandest games ever. Of course none of the LA boosters could have foreseen that America and the world would plunge into deep depression some three years before the Olympics were set to begin.

The LA Organizing Committee suffered a momentary crisis of confidence even before the onset of the Great Depression. In the immediate aftermath of the Amsterdam games a member of the committee, Zack Farmer, submitted a gloomy report casting doubt on the Europeans' willingness to travel six thousand miles to compete in California and on California's willingness adequately to fund the affair. In Garland's absence the committee passed a resolution to abandon the Olympic project. This attack of cold feet subsided, however, when "Sell 'em Sunshine" Harry Chandler, the ebullient publisher of the *Los Angeles Times*, persuaded the committee to reverse its stance and to go ahead with the games after all. Chandler and other boosters promised the Olympics would bring a huge economic bonanza to the city and "put Los Angeles on the map" in a domain other than mere moviemaking.

The committee stuck to this decision even after the Depression descended, largely because it had already invested a great deal of time, energy, and money in the project, and also because in November 1928 California voters had passed a million-dollar bond appropriation for the games. In March 1931, when California had almost a million people unemployed and soup kitchens were springing up all over Los Angeles, local voters approved another funding measure to pay for expanding and improving the Olympic stadium—and this despite an anti-Olympic protest movement that sent marchers to Sacramento carrying signs demanding "Groceries Not Games." Following its renovation and expansion, the massive Los Angeles Memorial Coliseum, the architectural centerpiece of the games, could hold 105,000 people (not a mere 75,000). It was by far the largest facility of its kind.

The very commodiousness of the Coliseum, however, raised understandable worries about filling the damn thing with paying customers when the Olympics finally rolled around. Even more worrisome was the possibility that some foreign nations might not be able to send athletes at all. To avert this catastrophe the organizers took the innovative step of negotiating with the major steamship lines a 20 percent discount on transatlantic travel for all Olympic participants and officials; to this they added a 40 percent reduction on railroad travel within the United States.

The organizers were even more innovative when it came to housing the athletes, a potential budget buster for the visitors given LA's standard hotel rate of seven dollars a day. To bring down housing costs, the committee came up with the novel idea of a built-to-order "Olympic Village," which could offer decent if not luxurious lodging for two dollars a head per day. When completed just two months before the games, the village, set in the majestic Baldwin Hills overlooking the Pacific Ocean, provided comfortable four-to-a-room accommodations in cream-colored "cottages" surrounded by flowering plants and cooled by the morning fog. This mini–Lotus Land also boasted dining halls serving a variety of ethnic menus. Celebrities like Douglas Fairbanks, Jr., and Will Rogers ambled around the grounds, signing autographs. Tough-looking cowboys on horseback provided security. Unfortunately for the female athletes—and also for the males—the Baldwin Hills facility housed only men. The women had to stay in the Chapman Park Hotel downtown, which had a strictly American menu.

Reassured by these generous arrangements, twenty-seven European nations—and thirty-four nations in all—accepted LA's invitation to attend the Tenth Summer Olympiad. Japan sent a large team despite its preoccupation with the conquest of Manchuria, which had taken place shortly before the games opened. In an effort to win international sanction for its aggression, Tokyo submitted an additional entry application for Manchuria, but the Los Angeles Organizing Committee, backed up by the IOC, refused the entry. The very threat of participation by Manchuria stirred China to become part of the Olympics for the first time. A lone sprinter represented this nation of four hundred million. (The sprinter in question, Liu Changchun, had originally been tapped by the Japanese to enter the LA games under the flag of their new puppet state of Manchuria, but Liu hotly refused, stating that he was "of the Chinese race and a descendant of the Yellow Emperor" and would never betray his own nation to "serve others like a horse or cow.")

Even with all the special provisions, travel to Los Angeles was very difficult for some teams. Brazil, for example, dispatched its team of sixty-nine athletes on a freighter loaded with fifty thousand sacks of coffee, which the Olympians were supposed to sell at ports along the way to defray the costs of their stay in LA. Alas, no one had money to buy the coffee, and in the end only twenty-four members of the Brazilian team could afford to leave the ship when it docked in San Pedro; the rest sailed home.

Although some athletes had to stay away, spectators turned up in abundance, much to the relief of the organizers. Perhaps hoping as much to see screen stars in the stands as athletes on the turf, tens of thousands of people, mostly Americans, bought tickets. More than one hundred thousand folks showed up for the opening ceremony, and the crowds remained respectable for all fourteen days of the competitions. The LA games thus became the first Olympics to turn a profit—some $150,000. This being America, however, a court case immediately ensued over who had legal title to the surplus. In 1935 the California Supreme Court ruled that the Tenth Olympic Committee was the owner of the surplus, with the power to donate it to the state, the county, and the city.

Considerably less successful than the LA games was an "Anti-Capitalist-Olympiad" sponsored by the Communist Party (USA) at the University of Chicago's Stagg Field on July 28–August 1. It attracted little attention at the time but can be seen as a precursor of the "alternative games" of 1936 and of the various protest counterattractions to the Olympics ever since.

THE German team did not have to sell apple strudel or beer to get to Los Angeles, but financial constraints mandated a somewhat smaller team than was originally envisaged. Some Germans had insisted that the country had no business sending a team at all in the midst of a depression, but Lewald effectively argued that if Germany stayed away from LA it would endanger its own games scheduled for 1936. "Let's be honest with ourselves about what we would lose in terms of international reputation, faith in German national willpower, and moral and economic credit if we were to stay away from Los Angeles," he admonished. "[We would] undermine our right to carry out the 1936 Games in Berlin." Promising to be as frugal as possible, Lewald and Diem managed to drum up private contributions to supplement a bare-bones state subsidy of one hundred thousand reichsmarks, enabling Germany to deliver a respectable eighty-two-person team to California.

The team Germany sent to the Summer Olympics in LA was expected to make a much stronger showing than had the country's small contingent at the Third Winter Games in Lake Placid in February. Consisting exclusively of bobsledders, hockey players, and figure skaters, the German squad in Lake Placid had managed to bring home only two medals—bronzes in four-man bobsledding and hockey. With respect, however, to Germany's prospects for the Summer Games, Daniel Ferris of the AAU predicted after viewing training facilities and Olympic preparations in that country that the Germans would dominate the LA games.

But dominate they certainly did not. While U.S. athletes won a total of forty-one gold medals, the Germans came away with just three (in wrestling, weight lifting, and rowing), plus a meager sprinkling of silvers and bronzes. Germany was outclassed not only by America, but also by Italy, Sweden, Finland, Japan, Hungary, and France. The Italians did especially well, "Mussolini's boys" placing a surprising second to the Americans. Japan performed exceptionally well in men's swimming, gaining more medals in that domain than the hitherto dominant Americans.

If the German team came away from Los Angeles with much less than it had hoped for in terms of medals, German officials accompanying the team took home a haul of technical information and observations that would prove invaluable for 1936. Carl Diem, as he had done on his earlier study trip to the United States, made a detailed investigation of American procedures and facilities. He took careful notes on the design of the sports complexes and on the arrangements for transportation, housing, publicity, and broadcasting. He spent a lot of time at the Olympic Village, inspecting the cottages and interviewing cooks about the menus. He visited a downtown department store that claimed to have clerks on hand who spoke every language represented at the games, as well as Esperanto. At the Coliseum he marveled at the giant Olympic flame that burned throughout the duration of the games. First introduced at the Amsterdam games, the Olympic flame became a standard feature of Olympic theatricality. An LA innovation that Diem would later copy in Berlin (and that reappeared in all subsequent Olympiads) was the practice of having the three top finishers in each event receive their medals on a tiered podium—the gold medal winner looking suitably patriotic and humble as his or her national anthem sounded over the loudspeakers.

Like Diem, Theodor Lewald saw much to admire in Los Angeles—but he was convinced that Berlin could do a lot better. After all, Berlin and Germany were the repositories of great intellectual and cultural traditions, and (at least in German eyes) they had profound ties to the ancient originators of the Olympic Games. In a speech at the conclusion of the Los Angeles Games, Lewald promised that Berlin would put on a "true festival of the peoples" characterized by an emphasis on the "spiritual content" of the ancient Olympic heritage. "We can expect," he said, "that Berlin as a city of the arts, and Germany as a citadel of the intellect, will bring out the most important dimensions of the Olympic festival. . . . On to Berlin in 1936!"

Hitler and Nazi Sportsmanship

Although Diem and Lewald left Los Angeles at once impressed by the Americans and determined to outdo them in 1936, a powerful constituency at home was broadcasting its contempt for the Olympic movement in general and for the developments in Los Angeles in particular.

On July 31, 1932, a day after the LA games began, Adolf Hitler's Nazi Party scored a spectacular victory in the national parliamentary elections, garnering 230 (out of 608) seats and thereby becoming the largest faction in the Reichstag. The Nazis' perspective on all manner of topics, including the Olympics, now had to be taken very seriously indeed.

And what was that perspective? Like the nativist German *Turnerschaft*, which in the 1920s called for a "National Olympiad" in place of the multinational festival, the Nazis had always shown disdain for international sporting contests, preferring purely German competitions and fitness programs. In the early twenties they had objected to Germans' competing with athletes from the Allied countries, which had imposed the "yoke" of Versailles on the fatherland. They had also objected to "Aryans" competing with "racial inferiors" like Slavs, blacks, and Jews.

The Nazi objection to competing with blacks was particularly relevant because black athletes, having had a modest presence in the Olympics of 1920 and 1924, performed especially well in the LA games of 1932. U.S. runners Eddie Tolan and Ralph Metcalfe, labeled "the Sable Cyclones" in the American press, excelled in the sprints, with Tolan setting a world record in the one-hundred-meter race and an Olympic record in the two-hundred-meter event. R. M. N. Tisdall, one of Britain's first black Olympians, won the four-hundred-meter race.

Commenting on the blacks' success, American comedian Will Rogers proposed that the slave traders must have operated with the Olympics in mind, "for these 'senegambians' have just about run the white man ragged." A German journalist tacitly acknowledged the black runners' superiority by hailing the German sprinter Arthur Jonath, who finished behind Tolan and Metcalfe in the one-hundred-meter race, as the fastest *white* man in the world. The *Turnerschaft* and the Nazi press, however, took the uncompromising view that "Aryans" like Jonath should not have deigned to compete at all with the likes of Tolan and Metcalfe. A *Turner* newspaper labeled it a "disgrace" that white men had entered the field with "wooly-haired niggers with protruding lips." Looking toward the 1936 Games, the *Völkischer Beobachter* editorialized: "Blacks have no place in the Olympics. . . . Unfortunately, these days one often sees the free white man having to compete with blacks, with [Neger], for the victory palm. This is a disgrace and a degradation of the Olympic idea without parallel, and the ancient Greeks would turn over in their graves if they knew what modern men were doing with their sacred national Games. . . . The next Olympic Games will take place in Berlin. Hopefully, the men in control will do their duty. Blacks must be excluded. We demand it."

Comments like these, especially the ugly slur from the main organ of the party that might soon run the nation scheduled to host the next Olympic Games, understandably alarmed the IOC. Although the IOC did not say as much at the time, it knew that if the Nazis took power in Germany and then tried to instigate a black-free (or Jew-free) Olympiad in 1936, the Olympic authorities would be hard pressed to keep the games in Germany.

Hoping to learn how Hitler himself stood with respect to the games, Baillet-Latour asked a recently appointed German IOC member, Karl Ritter von Halt, to query the Nazi leader on this point. Halt was a logical choice for this assignment. He was a five-time German decathlon champion and influential banking executive who had developed close ties to the Nazi Party, which he would join in 1933. He would also go on to play an instrumental role in the organization of the 1936 Olympics, especially the Winter Games in Garmisch-Partenkirchen. In 1932 Halt duly relayed Baillet-Latour's query to Hitler's office. The Führer's office responded that Hitler regarded the question of hosting the Games "with great interest." For a man who had recently condemned the Olympics as a plot by Freemasons and Jews, this was a welcome change—one that undoubtedly reflected Hitler's dawning appreciation that hosting the games might provide a Nazi-led government with intriguing propaganda opportunities, not to mention an excuse to do some grandiose building. Nevertheless Hitler's rather laconic response to Baillet-Latour's overture obviously left a number of questions open. Indeed, the IOC and the rest of the world would not get a clearer idea about where Hitler stood on the 1936 games until after the Nazi leader had assumed the German chancellorship.

ADOLF HITLER was appointed chancellor by President Hindenburg on January 30, 1933. At that moment the Nazi leader's views on a variety of topics were fairly well known, but this knowledge did not include his perspective on sports because the whole world of athletics had thus far played a peripheral role in his life and political career. The Führer was certainly not much of a sportsman himself. He couldn't swim; the closest he came to water was the bathtub. He claimed to have skied in his youth but this is doubtful. He was a very poor rider and hated horses. In *Mein Kampf* he compares horses to Jews: "[The Jews'] will to self-sacrifice does not go beyond the individual's naked instinct of self-preservation. . . . The same is true of horses, which try to defend themselves against an assailant in a body, but scatter again as soon as the danger is past." Nor did the Führer dance (if that can be considered a form of sport). Dancing, he said, was "an undignified activity for a statesman." Apart from taking regular walks at his mountain home on the Obersalzberg and holding up his right arm for long periods of time—a feat for which he later joked he should be awarded a gold medal—Hitler eschewed all serious exercise, and he stayed resolutely clear of all competitive games even at the risk of looking rather less svelte and physically hardened than what might have been expected of the leader of the "master race." (In his failure to conform to the *Herrenvolk* physical ideal, Hitler of course was hardly unique among top Nazi leaders: Göring became immensely fat, Goebbels had a club-foot, and Himmler wore milk-bottle-bottom glasses.) Following his arrest in connection with the abortive Beer Hall Putsch (1923), when Hitler had begun packing on pounds during his confinement in Landsberg Prison, Ernst "Putzi" Hanfstaengl, one of the Nazi leader's early followers, advised him to join his fellow prisoners in their various pickup games. "No, no!" replied Hitler, "that's out of the question. That would be bad for discipline. A Führer can't take the risk of being beaten by his followers in anything, including gymnastics or games." To Hanfstaengl's rejoinder that it might be better to lose a game or two than to look like a dumpling, Hitler countered that he could easily *talk off* his excess poundage when he got out of prison.

Hitler was indeed an indefatigable talker, and his long hours on the stump gave him an excuse not just to avoid playing physical games but also to escape watching them. His later regular attendance at the Olympic contests in 1936 constituted only a partial departure from this pattern of indifference, for his interest then applied primarily to the German performances and the national medal count, not to the technical aspects of the competitions, about which he remained as clueless as ever. The only sport that seems to have genuinely piqued his interest was boxing.

When it came to the question of sports and physical fitness for his follow-ers and the rest of the German *Volk*, however, Hitler was considerably more enthusiastic. He approved a provision in the 1920 Nazi Party platform for state-sponsored gymnastics and sports programs for German youth, and he insisted that his SA troopers learn to box, so as to enhance their aggressive instincts and physical toughness. In *Mein Kampf* he wrote: "Not a day should go by in which the young man does not receive one hour of physical training in the morning and one hour in the afternoon, covering every type of sport and gymnastics." Here he also proposed that what made the Greek ideal of beauty immortal was "the wonderful combination of the most glorious phys-ical beauty with a brilliant mind and the noblest soul." And he revealingly added: "A decayed body is not made the least more aesthetic by a brilliant mind, indeed, the highest intellectual training could not be justified if its bearers were at the same time physically degenerate and crippled, weak-willed, wavering and cowardly individuals." Yet for all the value Hitler ascribed to sport in the breeding of tough minds and aesthetically pleasing bodies, the Nazi Party, unlike its Socialist and Communist rivals, did not form sports teams of its own. True, the SA was initially registered with the police as a "sports association," but this was primarily for camouflage, and apart from the occasional boxing match the only "sport" the group practiced with any rigor was street brawling.

Like other militant nationalists, Hitler and his Nazi colleagues believed in the value of "*Wehrsport*" (military sport) as a means of promoting martial values and skills, but this kind of activity—hand-to-hand-combat training, rope climbing, and the like—had little in common with most conventional athletic competition. In the early 1920s, as we have seen, the Nazis shared the *Turnerschaft's* contempt for traditional team sports, especially those carried out on the international level. They regarded the modern Olympics as the worst offenders in this domain because of the games' professed dedication to peaceful competition among the peoples of the world, independent of religious, racial, and ethnic considerations. In 1923 the *Völkischer Beobachter* proposed that "an Olympiad of the Nordic peoples" should replace the Olympic Games. Another Nazi organ, the *Nationalsozialistische Monatshefte*, decried the Olympics as "artificial and mechanical . . . without inner necessity and culturally unproductive, [an enterprise] whose chief political consequence is the enhancement of Bolshevism's war against the white race." In 1928 Alfred Rosenberg faulted the Olympics for lacking a racial basis, comparing the Games dismissively to the League of Nations.

Some Nazi sport functionaries also fiercely rejected the notion that sports should stand above politics—an ideal to which the modern Olympic movement subscribed in principle, if not necessarily in practice. Bruno Malitz, the Berlin SA's sports authority, wrote categorically: "For us National Socialists, politics belongs in sport—first, because politics guides everything, and second, because politics is already inherent in sports." Malitz also insisted that the cult of individual achievement promoted by the Olympics was antithetical to Nazi ideals of *Volksgemeinschaft*. "The National Socialist can see sports only from the perspective of the folk community. From this perspective he understands that the liberal-individualistic pursuit of records leads to the degradation of sport and the destruction of community morality in athletics." For Nazi zealots like Malitz, indeed, the cultivation of elite, high-performance athleticism would always remain incompatible with true National Socialist collectivism.

At the end of the 1920s, however, the Nazi movement began to back away from its categorical opposition to German participation in the Olympic Games, while continuing to reject most of the ideals the Olympics stood for (or at least professed to stand for). The main reason for this subtle shift in posture was the Nazis' shared excitement over the German team's showing in the Amsterdam games. It was gratifying to see German athletes running roughshod over their European neighbors, for one could imagine in these victories similar conquests on the battlefield. Thus, in 1929, the *Völkischer Beobachter*, rather than positing a flat *nein* to any further German participation in the games, declared that Germans should not participate until their country "recovered all its rights and the full respect of the rest of the world." In the wake of the LA games the *Völkischer Beobachter* focused not on *whether* Germany should have participated but on *how* it had fared in the competition. The paper blamed Germany's generally poor performance in LA on a failure by the nation's bourgeois sports officials to instill a proper "fighting spirit" in the German athletes. "The people of [meek] 'Poets and Thinkers' belongs to the past," said the paper. "The motto of the twentieth century is *struggle* in everything, especially in the world of sport." Arguing that Germany's Olympic future should not be in the hands of "fine gentlemen" who lacked a taste for blood, another Nazi paper, *Der Angriff*, demanded the resignations of Lewald and Diem. It should be recalled, too, that the *Völkischer Beobachter*'s post-LA editorial regarding proper procedures for 1936 did not argue that Germany should not host the games but that no blacks should be allowed. When word of this demand provoked an uproar in the world press, especially that of the United States, Hitler himself rushed to control the damage, letting it be known that the Nazi Party would "present no difficulties" to a German-hosted Olympic festival and that, "rumors" to the contrary, the Nazis had no objections to blacks coming to Germany for the games. Ritter von Halt also communicated these reassurances to the IOC.

While it had been useful for the IOC to know where Hitler and his party stood on the Olympics *before* the Nazi leader took power, his assumption of the chancellorship in early 1933 elevated his perspective on this issue to a whole new level of importance. Although no one could be sure that Hitler would still be in power in 1936, his government would undoubtedly hold sway during the crucial buildup to the games, allowing his regime to define the political atmosphere in which the preparations took place. Given the Nazi movement's open avowals of racism in all dimensions of life, including sports, anyone with an investment in the Olympic ideals of openness and fair play had to worry about what it would mean to hold the five-ringed festival in Germany.

One figure who was very clearly worried about the fate of the Olympics in the new Nazi state was Theodor Lewald. Hoping to protect Germany's Olympic preparations from the ideologues in the Nazi movement who demanded strict adherence to racist principles, Lewald established, just six days before Hitler took power, a new German Organizing Committee (GOC) for the Eleventh Olympic Games and staffed it with non-Nazi proponents of traditional sporting ideals.

Once Hitler was in power, Lewald made an even bolder move to secure the games' status and to screen their preparations from unwanted influences by appealing directly to the Führer for his personal support. Expressing his "warmest congratulations" to Hitler on his "powerful victory" in the recent Reichstag elections (March 5), Lewald requested a meeting with him to discuss preparations for the 1936 games. On March 16, 1933, he duly met with Hitler, Goebbels, and Interior Minister Wilhelm Frick to discuss the planning and financing of the games. Revealingly he asked Hitler to act as "honorary chairman" of the GOC, clearly hoping to deploy the Führer's prestige as an imprimatur for this undertaking. He also proposed that Hitler personally enlighten German youth regarding the importance of the Olympics and immediately enlist Germany's schools and sports associations in the search for the nation's future Olympic warriors. "The Olympic Games in Los Angeles showed that the enormous energy invested by Mussolini in preparing Italy's youth for the games produced great results," Lewald reminded Hitler.

Pegging the costs of renovating and expanding Berlin's designated Olympic facilities at about five million reichsmarks, Lewald requested a government guarantee of six million reichsmarks. Because the games were certain to bring in between five and six million reichsmarks in revenue, he said, the Reich would run no risk in putting up the financial guarantee. Finally Lewald emphasized "the enormous propaganda effect" for Germany that would come with hosting the games. At least one thousand journalists representing newspapers from all over the world would come to Berlin to cover the games, he said. "No other event can even remotely match [the Olympics] in terms of propaganda value."

In response to this barrage Hitler curtly refused Lewald's invitation to become honorary chairman of the GOC. (President Hindenburg, who was to die in August 1934, had already assumed patronage of the games.) On the other hand, shortly after the meeting, Hitler strengthened his earlier endorsement of the 1936 games, stating for the press: "I will advance the games as well as all sports interests in every manner possible." The Reich Interior Ministry offered financial support for the project, although it insisted on keeping the state outlay "in appropriate limits."

While Lewald did not get all he wanted from this meeting, the games now enjoyed Hitler's formal blessing, which of course was crucial. Immensely grateful for the Führer's support, Lewald wrote Hitler a fawning thank-you letter in which he pledged the loyalty of his planning staff to the new order: "True to its past, [the German Olympic movement] will do all in its power to ensure that the powerful current of national revival is channeled into all the rivers, streams and springs of our great gymnastics and sports community in order to preserve the power of German youth, strengthen national sentiment, and breed a fighting race."

Lewald had also asked Propaganda Minister Goebbels for help with the promotion of the games. Following Hitler's press announcement endorsing the venture, Goebbels invited Lewald and Diem to his office and informed them of his intention personally to direct the Olympic publicity campaign, which he said could begin in the coming summer. He soon established a special committee within the Propaganda Ministry to take charge of Olympic publicity. Clearly Goebbels did not want to be left out of the action.

When Hitler and Goebbels belatedly climbed onto Germany's Olympic bandwagon they certainly did not intend for their decision to have any significant impact on the way they conducted their primary business of consolidating power and ridding Germany of its "internal enemies." On March 23, 1933, following an arson attack on the Reichstag Building attributed by the regime to a demented communist, the national parliament, totally cowed by the Nazis, passed the Enabling Act, which gave Hitler dictatorial powers. On April 1 the Hitler government officially launched its anti-Jewish crusade with a state-sponsored boycott of Jewish businesses and services. To help people identify which shops and offices to boycott, SA men painted anti-Semitic slogans on targeted businesses and stood guard in front of them. A week later, on April 7, the government introduced the Law for the Restoration of the Professional Civil Service, which was designed to rid the state bureaucracy of anyone the Nazis considered politically or racially unacceptable—mainly leftists and Jews. Paragraph 3 of the law—the so-called Aryan paragraph—required that officials deemed "non-Aryan" resign immediately. A supplementary decree to the law defined "non-Aryan" as "anyone descended from non-Aryan, particularly Jewish, parents or grandparents. It suffices if one parent or grandparent is non-Aryan."

The "Coordination" of German Sport

The Hitler government's program of anti-Jewish persecution embraced from the outset the world of sport, which was "coordinated"—forced into conformity—with Nazi dogma along with most other dimensions of public life. Addressing the imperative of a thorough purge of German sports, Bruno Malitz ranted that Jews, pacifists, and pan-Europeans were "worse than cholera, tuberculosis, and syphilis, worse than burning hordes of Kalmucks, worse than fire's heat, hunger's pain, floods, great drought and poison gas." Accordingly, as early as April 1933 the German Swimming Association adopted the Aryan paragraph and banned Jews from its member clubs. Germany's Davis Cup tennis team expelled one of its top stars, Dr. Daniel Prenn, because he was Jewish. The German Boxing Federation forbade Jews to fight in or officiate over German championship contests.

Meanwhile Lewald's and Diem's status as top German sports bureaucrats became precarious in the new state despite their prominence in the international sporting world and their protestations of loyalty to the regime. As we have seen, various voices in the Nazi movement had been calling for their heads even before the Nazi seizure of power, but the press attacks took on added virulence in early April 1933, with the *Völkischer Beobachter* insisting that in Lewald's case a non-Aryan had no business leading Germany's Olympic Committee and its primary national sports organization, the DRL. Moreover, complained the paper, Lewald and Diem had calculatedly avoided bringing representatives of the *völkisch* movement into their Olympic operation. The "sporting youth of Germany needs new leadership!" proclaimed the Nazi organ. *Der Angriff,* Goebbels's mouthpiece, declared that "Lewald plus Diem equals Ullstein [the Jewish publishing house]."

Lewald reacted indignantly to the Nazi press attacks against him. In a letter to Hans Lammers, chief of the Reich Chancellery, he noted that these smears deviated sharply from the warm reception he had recently received from Hitler, Goebbels, and Frick. He reiterated his conviction that "the great task of furthering German sports could prosper only alongside the promotion of nationalistic education, empowerment of the Volk, and military preparedness." Mindful that Germany needed IOC sanction to host the games, Lewald pointedly warned Lammers (and thereby Hitler) that Lausanne would not look kindly on attempts by forces outside the Olympic community to dictate the composition of the German Organizing Committee. "If [the government] wishes to hold the Olympic Games in Berlin it will retain me in my position of leadership despite all the attacks." Yet, in a handwritten addendum scrawled on the back of this letter, Lewald showed how defensive and vulnerable he remained on the delicate subject of his Jewish heritage: "To the charge of Semitic origins I would like to point out that my mother was the daughter of [Friedrich Georg] Althaus, the general superintendent of Lippe-Detmold, and came from a centuries-old family of Lutheran pastors in Westphalia. My father was baptized as a young boy."

At first the Hitler government paid little heed to Lewald's protestations and threats. The press attacks on him stopped, but he was demoted from the presidency of the GOC to the role of mere adviser to the committee. This action indeed brought criticism from the IOC and the international community, just as Lewald had predicted. The IOC sharply reminded Hitler's government that Germany's Olympic officials answered to the international Olympic authorities, not to German politicians. If the Reich chancellor could not accept this reality, "it would be better if Berlin withdrew from its projected role as host of the 1936 Games." Even a domestic paper, the *Deutsche Allgemeine Zeitung*, counseled that Lewald (and Diem) were too well connected, and too knowledgeable about Germany's Olympic planning, to be let go. As a result of all this pressure, Lewald was soon reinstated in his position as head of the GOC. However, in a nod to the Nazi zealots, he was forced to resign his presidency of the DRL. More important, he signed a secret Interior Ministry document stating that while the GOC retained the authority to deal directly with the IOC, Germany's Olympic organizers must defer to Reich officials "in all essential matters of policy." The GOC's "independence," therefore, was purely for show.

Carl Diem might seem to have been in a stronger position than Lewald with the Nazi authorities because he was not Jewish and if anything more rabidly nationalist than his colleague. But he too was "tainted" with Jewish connections because his wife Liselott was one-quarter Jewish and he himself had maintained contact with Jews during his work at the Deutsche Hochschule für Leibesübungen (German University for Physical Exercise), a high-level sports study center he had helped establish in the early twenties. Nazi zealots branded Diem a "white Jew."

In April 1933 Diem passionately defended himself against charges raised in the *Völkischer Beobachter* that he was not enthusiastic enough about the new order to help lead Germany's Olympic planning for 1936. In a feisty letter to one of the Nazi sports functionaries, he declared that if one examined his thirty-year record as a German sports organizer one would not find "a single line that speaks against the national revival of our people." He reminded his rightist critics that he hated the Socialists as much as they did, and noted that said Socialists had always denounced him as a "war-monger and a nationalist." As if to prove his loyalty to the new order, during a meeting of the DRL on April 11 he pushed for that group's immediate and voluntary subordination to the Nazi establishment. And, like Lewald, he agreed to accept the regime's behind-the-scenes control over the organization of the 1936 games. But even Diem could not completely purge himself of the "stain" of Jewish associations. Although, again like Lewald, he was allowed to keep his place in the GOC, he was promptly fired from his job at the Hochschule.

Diem had unrealistically applied for a new position in the Nazi sports bureaucracy—that of Reichssportführer. The job went instead to Hans von Tschammer und Osten, a tough SA leader from Dessau in Saxony, whose primary qualifications for the position seem to have been his knack with foreign languages (he had interpreters' certificates in French and English), his lack of squeamishness regarding the use of violence (his SA thugs had beaten to death three working-class athletes and a thirteen-year-old boy in a Dessau gymnasium), and absolute loyalty to the Nazi system. Tschammer sat a horse well, but otherwise he was neither much of an athlete nor very knowledgeable about sports. Those who knew him joked that in giving him the job of Reichssportführer the regime must have gotten him confused with his older brother, who actually did know something about athletics. Over the years Tschammer has had his defenders in Germany, who have argued that he tried his best to "protect" his bailiwick from Nazi penetration. But of course he was himself a devoted Nazi, and as we shall see later on, he was fully prepared to apply Nazi principles to sport.

Tschammer's position as Reichssportführer gave him considerable influence over Olympic planning and organization, though it took him some time to make his presence felt. He had a seat on the organizational committee for the Berlin games and assumed the presidency of the National Olympic Committee, the official governing body of Germany's Olympic community.

But the Hitler regime by no means relied solely, or even primarily, on Tschammer to exert its control over the orchestration of the 1936 games. With time Goebbels's Propaganda Ministry, the Reich Interior Ministry, the Wehrmacht, and even the SS took over crucial aspects of the Olympic operations. Just as Hitler would come during the war to consider Nazi Germany's engagement on the field of battle too important to be left to his generals, the Reich's commitment to "peaceful" competition on the field of Olympic play shaped up as much too significant to be left to mere sports bureaucrats, let alone the athletes themselves.

Boycott Berlin!

▲

▲

I N 1936, for the first time in modern Olympic history, a protest movement of international scope was mounted against a designated host city, Berlin. The protest of course did not take shape until Berlin had become the capital of the Nazi Reich, but once this happened, various anti-Nazi groups and individuals around the world appealed to the IOC to move the games elsewhere. Short of that, the protesters called for a boycott of the 1936 German games.

The international boycott movement had its origins and greatest resonance in the United States, a nation whose professed commitment to equality of opportunity in sports was not diminished by its actual discriminatory practices. But whatever the element of hypocrisy here, the American boycott effort came within a hair of succeeding. And had the Americans decided to shun Berlin, there was a chance that other Western democracies, most notably Britain and France, might have done so as well. Britain's and France's decision to stay home would very likely have prompted a host of other no-shows, with the result that the 1936 games, if they were held at all, would have looked like a slightly expanded version of those purely German *Kampf-spiele* of the 1920s.

Unfit to Host the Olympics

America's Jewish community had reacted with alarm to the Hitler government's anti-Semitic pronouncements and measures. In the wake of the government-orchestrated boycott of Jewish businesses across Germany on

April 1, 1933, Jewish representatives in the United States began appealing to leaders of the American Olympic movement to raise the possibility of moving the 1936 Summer Games out of Berlin.

In mid-April 1933, K. A. Miller, the editor of the *Baltimore Jewish Times*, asked AOC president Avery Brundage to take a stand against holding the games in the German capital. In his reply Brundage ducked the issue by noting that questions of venue were the province of the IOC, which planned to review the matter at its next annual meeting in Vienna in June 1933. At the same time, however, Brundage offered his personal opinion that "the Games will not be held in any country where there will be interference with the fundamental Olympic theory of equality of all races. The Olympic protocol provides that there shall be no restriction of competition because of class, color, or creed." Grateful for what he thought was a clear stance against the "Nazi games," as the '36 Olympics were already coming to be called, Miller published Brundage's reply.

What Miller did not know when he lodged his appeal to Brundage was that the AOC president, despite his programmatic affirmation of Olympic principles, was dead set against moving the games out of Germany, or, for that matter, boycotting the contest should they remain there. Time and again he would justify this stance on the grounds that "politics" and "sports" occupied independent realms, and that the Olympic movement in particular could survive only if politics were kept out of it.

This argument seems so disingenuous that one is tempted to think that Brundage must not actually have believed it. But apparently he did. His romanticized and frankly naive conception of the Olympic movement seems to have derived, oddly enough, from his professional career in the extremely corrupt and anything but "unpolitical" Chicago construction business. The product of humble origins and genteel poverty, Brundage worked his way to a degree in engineering at the University of Illinois and then went on to become a millionaire in a business milieu in which kickbacks and bribes were as commonplace as voting "early and often" in elections. One of his biographers, Allen Guttmann, writes with some plausibility that Brundage was so shocked by this rampant dishonesty that he looked to sports for an alternative world where ability and hard work were all that counted. His own very positive experiences in sports, especially as a member of America's Olympic team at the Stockholm games of 1912, apparently reinforced his idealization of amateur athletics and the Olympic movement.

Brundage's dedication to Olympism was so intense that he interpreted any opposition to what he considered best for the games as an attack on the games as such, and as the product of some perversity of character. The fact that the primary opposition to an Olympiad under Hitler came from Jews proved significant, for Brundage quickly began to see in this opposition a diabolical Jewish plot to subvert the entire Olympic enterprise.

In April 1933 the Germans did not yet realize that they had a friend in Avery Brundage: They took his statement regarding the imperatives of racial equality in the Olympics as a sign that the AOC might push to remove the 1936 games from Berlin. The German press reacted heatedly, one paper thundering: "Brundage hasn't the least cause to utter opinions such as were published. In the new Germany nobody in a position of authority has attempted to change the form of the Olympic Games."

Deeply worried about the American stance, Theodor Lewald convinced the Hitler government to issue a statement on April 20 promising to respect the Olympic charter and to welcome to Germany "competitors of all races." The regime added a significant caveat, however: The composition of Germany's own team was nobody's business but Germany's. Having made this "concession," the Germans could only hope that the IOC would put a quick end to any talk of moving the games out of Berlin.

IOC President Henri Baillet-Latour held views similar to Brundage's in regard to the relationship between the Olympic movement and politics. He believed that the IOC should avoid taking any "political" positions except in the case of communist penetration of the games, which he thought must be prevented at all costs. While he despised communism he had a certain respect for the Nazis, commenting in a confidential letter to his predecessor, Baron de Coubertin, that at a time when everything in Europe was "falling apart" due to governance by "mediocrities, arrivistes, and profiteers," at least the Nazis had an effective "plan and method." Baillet-Latour was astute enough to see a threat to Olympic principles in the Nazi regime's open racism, but he also believed that if the racism was confined to the German domestic scene, the IOC had no right to interfere.

Hence in late April the IOC president issued a public statement saying that the agency was holding fast to its 1931 decision to hold the 1936 Summer Games in Berlin, provided that "every people and every race would be allowed to participate in complete equality." The requirement of equality, he was quick to add, did not mean that the IOC could concern itself with Germany's internal affairs.

Baillet-Latour's insistence on religious and racial equality at the games, and repeated promises from German Olympic officials that all foreign competitors and guests would be "cordially welcomed" in Berlin, did not reassure Jewish groups in America. They insisted that the Nazis' persecution of German Jews and their practice of racial discrimination in sport made Germany unfit to host the Olympics. If Berlin *did* remain the host for 1936, the American Jewish Congress (AJC) publicly called on the three American members of the IOC—William May Garland, Charles Sherrill, and Ernest Jahncke—"to take a firm stand against America's participation under the existing circumstances and conditions."

Publicly pressured as they were, the American IOC members found themselves in a tricky situation. On the one hand they knew the IOC wished to keep the games in Berlin; on the other they worried that if Germany continued to deny German Jews equal access to the Reich's Olympic program, American Jewish pressure groups would lobby hard against American participation in the German games.

Looking for guidance, William May Garland turned to Gus Kirby, the influential treasurer of the AOC, for advice. In a letter to Brundage, Kirby said he would advise Garland to insist that the Games be "open to all amateurs irrespective of race, creed, or color," and that Berlin should have "no more right to impose a condition against the Jews of Germany than it would against the Jews of the United States or France or any other country." But Kirby also believed Hitler was beginning to "soften" on the Jewish question and that therefore pressure from the IOC would "do much to have Germany change its attitude, not alone toward the Olympics but toward the world."

Like Garland, Charles Sherrill, a member of the IOC since 1922, received cables from the AJC demanding a hard line against Berlin. Sherrill, a blustery, mustachioed former United States ambassador to Turkey and Argentina, was a well-known figure in the American sports world, having been a top sprinter at Yale, a pioneer in the use of the crouch start, and captain of America's track team at the 1900 Paris games. His political perspective was perhaps best evidenced by his frequent praise for his "friend" Benito Mussolini, whom he described as "a man of courage in a world of pussyfooters." Although Sherrill would also come to admire Hitler and eventually argue that America had no right to instruct the Germans on racial matters, he apparently relished the prospect of putting the Germans' feet to the fire at the upcoming IOC meeting in Vienna. Accordingly he informed AJC president Bernard Deutsch that the group could "rest assured that I shall stoutly maintain the American principle that all citizens are equal under the laws."

Meanwhile, because various figures in the German sporting world were continuing to boast of applying racial principles to athletics, Baillet-Latour began to wonder if the games could stay in Berlin after all. Hoping to resolve this problem privately, he warned Lewald and Ritter von Halt that the Olympic movement could not tolerate "German games," meaning games run on Nazi racial principles.

Lewald dutifully forwarded Baillet-Latour's letter to Hitler, no doubt expecting a favorable response, since the IOC was really asking only for a programmatic declaration that did not go substantially beyond the promises of good behavior that various German Olympic officials had already made. Hitler, however, was incensed at being pressured in this way, and he let Lewald know that he, Lewald, should have rejected Baillet-Latour's "impertinent" letter out of hand. Lewald apologized to Hitler for Baillet-Latour's "inappropriate" missive as abjectly as if it had been his own.

And yet Lewald, Ritter von Halt, and the rest of the pro-Olympic faction in Berlin well knew that if Germany did not make *some* visible concession in the matter of racial equality for the Olympics, including at least a theoretical opening to German Jewish athletes, the IOC might yet feel obliged to pull the games from Berlin.

Assuming that Hitler himself did not want this to happen, Lewald and Halt, along with officials of the Interior Ministry (which controlled Germany's Olympic planning from behind the scenes), took the bold step of simply leaving the Führer out of the Olympic loop. Lewald and Hans Pfundtner of the Interior Ministry agreed on a statement to be delivered at the Vienna IOC meeting that was designed to put an end to the international pressure. The statement, duly presented in Vienna by the German delegates, declared that Lewald was being retained as president of the GOC and all provisions regulating the Olympic Games would be observed. In a crucial concession, the Germans also promised that Jews would "not be excluded from membership in German teams."

No sooner was this promise made, however, than Reichssportführer Tschammer undercut it by declaring, in an address to a Nazi audience in Berlin, that Germany had no intention of changing its ways: "We shall see to it that both in our national life and in our relations and competitions with foreign nations only those Germans shall be allowed to represent the nation against whom no objection can be raised."

Tschammer's backsliding notwithstanding, the German IOC delegation's timely concession at the Vienna meeting was a milestone in the German effort to keep the 1936 games in Berlin. With Germany's promise of good behavior in hand, the IOC voted unanimously in Vienna to reaffirm its 1931 decision to hold the 1936 Summer Olympics in Berlin. At the same time it announced that the 1936 Winter Games would be held in Garmisch-Partenkirchen, the Bavarian alpine site proposed by the GOC.

"There Will Be No Discrimination in Berlin Against Jews"

Among Jewish groups opposing the 1936 Berlin Olympics, the prospect of an American-led boycott of the festival had always been a fallback position in case Germany was allowed to keep the games without ending its persecution of German Jews. The Nazis' failure to match promises with practices in the months following the Vienna meeting moved that boycott threat to the front burner, forcing it to a boil on the eve of the annual meetings of the AAU and the AOC in late November 1933.

The AAU, whose position was crucial because it certified track-and-field athletes for the Olympics, was known to be considerably more critical of Nazi Germany than the AOC. Gus Kirby, who planned to introduce frank admonishments to the Germans at both meetings, tried hard to get Brundage and AOC secretary Frederick Rubien to see matters his way. In early November he complained to Brundage that he could "not understand" Brundage's attitude regarding a stiff warning to the Germans, since by all accounts they had done absolutely nothing to improve the situation of German Jews. Although it might in general be wiser to "let sleeping dogs lie," he said, in this case the "dogs are not sleeping, they are growling and snarling and snipping and all but biting."

Brundage, however, opposed taking any official position on the German situation for the time being. "In my opinion," he told Kirby, "there is no necessity for immediate action since the Games are not until 1936 and there may be and probably will be many changes in the next three years." By this point, moreover, the AOC president was becoming highly irritated by the

Jewish pressure to take a stand against German racism. He suggested to Rubien on November 5 that Deutsch of the AJC was using the Olympic issue to promote Deutsch's own political career (he was running for an alderman post in New York City). Following Deutsch's election to that seat, Rubien concurred in Brundage's analysis, declaring, "The representatives of the Jewish organizations made full use of our work and gained a great deal of publicity for themselves thereby. Now that the election is over, perhaps they will not be so keen to keep stirring the matter up."

Brundage and Rubien were hardly alone in their irritation over the Jewish protests and in their concern over possibly alienating the Germans through a sharp public rebuke. The IOC, having extracted a promise of good behavior from the Germans at Vienna, was content to let the matter rest. Writing in his idiosyncratic English to Brundage, Baillet-Latour spelled out his own views regarding the Germans' behavior and Jewish protests:

> I do think like you that it is most important to work together hand in hand, while we are handling this difficult question. One might expect the Germans to carry [out] the promises made to the IOC last June, but it would be unwise to believe all that is said by the other side. . . . I know [the Jews] shout before there is no reason to do so and I have always been struck by the fact that all the horror which took place in Russia for instance, much more barbarous than anything which took place in Germany, has never excited public opinion in the same way. Why? Because the propaganda was not made as cleverly.

Although the American reporters who covered the Olympic controversy were aware of growing anti-German sentiment within the AAU, there was considerable surprise in the American press when Kirby presented his sharply worded resolution at the AAU meeting in November and had it adopted with only three abstentions. According to its new resolution, the AAU would not certify any American athletes for the German games "until and unless the position of the German Olympic Committee . . . is so changed in fact as well as in theory as to permit and encourage German athletes of Jewish faith or heritage to train, prepare for, and participate in the Olympic Games of 1936." The *New York Times* article reporting this action was headlined "AAU Boycotts 1936 Olympics Because of Nazi Ban on Jews," as if the boycott were a reality rather than a threat. In actuality a proposal to set a date of January

1, 1934, for German compliance was rejected on the grounds that this did not allow the Germans enough time. Nonetheless the AAU resolution was certainly a powerful shot over the German bow—enough to inspire the British Olympic Association, which theretofore had taken no position on the issue, to consider following the American AAU's example. Meanwhile the AAU, which had a strong voice in the AOC, urged that body to adopt a similarly tough resolution.

In an AOC Executive Committee meeting in November, Sherrill, with support from Brundage, was able to water down a statement put forth by Kirby so that it came out as a mere slap on the wrist. In it the AOC expressed "regret" over conditions in Germany and its "ardent hope" that "Dr. Lewald and his associates" would be able to remove "all disabilities affecting the rights and privileges of Jews in training, competing for and being on German sports teams." Defending his role, Sherrill told Congregation B'nai Jeshurun in New York that although he considered the Nazis' treatment of the Jews "outrageous and hideous," an Olympic boycott would not only fail to help the Jews in Germany but very likely provoke "anti-Semitic feeling in the United States."

Many members of the IOC were caught off guard by the persistence and vehemence of the American boycott movement. They thought they had settled everything in Vienna. J. Sigfrid Edstrøm, an influential Swedish delegate who would become president of the IOC in 1946, dispatched a plea to his friend Avery Brundage to let him know "what is happening over there," complaining:

> It seems there is some agitation from the American Jews. . . . I cannot understand the reason for this agitation. I understand it is on account of the persecution of the Jews but as to the sport this persecution has not been allowed. Already at the Congress of Vienna in June last year the International Olympic Committee was assured from the highest German authorities that there would be no trouble for Jewish athletes in connection with the Olympic Games. Even German Jews would be allowed on the German team. . . .
>
> It is too bad that the American Jews are so active and cause us so much trouble. It is impossible for our German friends to carry on the expensive preparations for the Olympic Games if all this unrest prevails. . . .
>
> As regards the persecution of the Jews in Germany I am not at all in favor of said action, but I fully understand that an alteration had to take

place. As it was in Germany, a great part of the German nation was led by the Jews and not by the Germans themselves. Even in the USA the day may come when you will have to stop the activities of the Jews. Many of my friends are Jews so you must not think I am against them, but they must be kept within certain limits.

The Germans, for their part, were watching American developments closely, and while they may have taken some solace in the AOC's temporizing they were profoundly alarmed by the tough line coming out of the AAU. Hoping to obscure ugly reality with positive rhetoric, Lewald dashed off a telegram to the AAU claiming that the Germans had lived up to all the promises they had made at Vienna. But in a letter to Pfundtner, Lewald warned that the IOC might still yank the games from Germany if the Americans went through with their boycott. Italy and Japan, he noted, were waiting eagerly in the wings should the IOC need an alternative venue.

Meanwhile, acting as if the matter had been resolved by earlier promises, on December 20, 1933, the GOC sent formal invitations to fifty-three nations, including the United States, to participate in the Eleventh Olympiad in Berlin. The German ambassador to Washington followed up with a note to Secretary of State Cordell Hull saying his government would "especially welcome" American participation, which would allow Germany to repay the hospitality America had shown in 1932.

Now confronted with the choice of formally accepting or rejecting the German invitation, the AOC, with characteristic flabbiness, sidestepped the issue by turning the question over to its executive committee and proposing that this body might come up with a final decision after one of its members, presumably Avery Brundage himself, had had a chance to travel to Germany and personally assess the situation.

While the AOC was dithering, the ongoing effort to prevent American participation in the Berlin games, which had been essentially a Jewish phenomenon in its earliest phase, broadened to include a wide spectrum of organizations and individuals. On March 7, 1934, at a mass anti-Nazi rally in New York's Madison Square Garden, opposition to an American presence at the 1936 German Olympic Games meshed with a diverse protest campaign against Nazi political and racial policies. Sponsored by some twenty groups, including the Amalgamated Clothing Workers Union, the American Civil Liberties Union (ACLU), the American Federation of Labor (AFL), and the

National Committee to Aid Victims of German Fascism, the Garden rally featured addresses by Senator Millard Tydings of Maryland, former Governor Al Smith of New York, New York City mayor Fiorello H. La Guardia, and the AOC's Gus Kirby, who spoke on Nazi Germany's discrimination against Jewish athletes. According to the *New York Times*, boos followed Kirby's mention of the Nazi swastika fluttering over athletic fields, while applause greeted his call for an American boycott of the Berlin games unless Jews were permitted to try out for Germany's Olympic teams.

In a revealing move Brundage had tried hard to talk Kirby out of attending the Garden rally. Having learned that the AOC treasurer intended to "speak at the mass meeting arranged by the New York Jews to protest against conditions in Germany," he warned Kirby, "We must be careful about involving the AOC in this controversy." Later, on receiving newspaper reports about the rally, Brundage repeated his mantra about political neutrality, adding: "We have protested that they [the Germans] were not carrying out their promises, and they assured us that they were. The burden of proof seems to be on us, and I have seen no direct evidence that they were not living up to their pledges." Of course such direct evidence might be gathered through an inspection trip of the sort proposed by the AOC, but Brundage opposed this idea. As he told Kirby, "It would . . . be obviously impossible for anyone to make an exhaustive survey of conditions [in Germany] in a brief visit to that country. . . . If the IOC is satisfied that the terms of the pledge are being carried out, there is little for the AOC to do."

But while the IOC might have been satisfied, dissatisfaction remained strong in many American circles. Taking issue with the German assurances, Deutsch of the AJC called on the AOC "to make an impartial investigation of conditions in Germany as they are likely to affect Jews who might compete in the Olympics." Kirby privately pleaded with Brundage to make a study trip to Germany, including a visit with Hitler, so that the AOC would have "first-hand" evidence on which to act. "As the matter now stands," he warned, "I doubt if any Jew who makes our team would be willing to go to Germany as a member thereof." The AAU made it clear that it would not certify any American athletes unless the president of the AOC could give Germany a clean bill of health on the basis of a personal fact-finding tour.

At a meeting of the AOC on June 4, 1934, Brundage agreed to make the proposed study tour of Germany following his attendance at an International

Amateur Athletic Federation (IAAF) conference in Stockholm in August. Although this decision was greeted with much applause by Brundage's supporters, his critics feared that he had already made up his mind about Germany, since before leaving for Europe he had written an article for the *Olympic News* urging American athletes to begin preparing immediately for the 1936 games, and predicting that in Berlin the Americans would encounter "the forebear of a race of free, independent thinkers accustomed to the democracy of sport." Indignant, Samuel Untermeyer of the Non-Sectarian Anti-Nazi League accused Brundage and his colleagues of "glossing over the race discrimination issue," while Emanuel Celler, U.S. Congressman for the tenth District of Brooklyn, warned Brundage that a preordained verdict would be unacceptable: "The American public demands that you at least withhold your judgment until you know all the facts."

As it turned out, Brundage's fact-finding journey amply confirmed doubts regarding his impartiality: The only "facts" he gathered were ones fed to him by his German colleagues. Throughout his six-day excursion his old drinking buddy, Ritter von Halt, who had handpicked all his German interlocutors, accompanied him. One of those he questioned was the Nazi sports boss, Tschammer, whom Brundage said he "liked very much." Since Brundage knew little German, Halt did the translating when the American interviewed German officials. At the Kaiserhof Hotel in Berlin, Brundage made a point of interviewing Jewish sports leaders, but he raised no objection to the presence of Arno Breitmeyer, the deputy Reichssportführer, who appeared dressed in his full SS regalia. As if to put his Nazi hosts at ease, Brundage let it be known that his own men's club in Chicago barred Jews. This policy, he added, was a product of the American belief in "separate but equal treatment," an approach he believed was consistent with Olympic ideals. Apparently forgetting entirely his earlier reservations about the usefulness of a whirlwind fact-finding tour, on his return to America he submitted a report to the AOC Executive Committee full of praise for the German effort to be inclusive in its Olympic sports program. He then told the press that German officials had given him their word "that there will be no discrimination in Berlin against Jews. You can't ask for more than that and I think the guarantee will be fulfilled."

On September 26, 1934, the day after Brundage's return, the AOC voted unanimously to accept the German invitation to participate in the 1936 games. To the press the AOC explained that it took this action only after agreeing "to divorce entirely from its discussion anything pertaining to the anti-Semitic situation in Germany other than sports."

Germany was quick to applaud the AOC's decision, with some papers crowing over a "defeat of the Jews." Aware of Brundage's crucial role in this affair, Lewald sent him a congratulatory telegram. In a letter to Halt, Brundage acknowledged the congratulations but warned that "radical Jewish organizations" were still threatening "to carry on the agitation against [American] participation in 1936," and therefore he pleaded that there should be "no untoward occurrences to disturb the situation."

With the AOC's formal acceptance of the German invitation, opposition to American participation in the German games focused on getting the AAU to make a declaration in the opposite direction. Specifically Wise and Deutsch appealed to the AAU to refuse once and for all to certify American athletes for the 1936 games at its upcoming meeting in Miami. Prior to this meeting, however, Charles Sherrill returned from a fact-finding trip of his own to Germany, where he met with German Olympic officials and government figures, including Foreign Minister Konstantin von Neurath. The Germans, reported Sherrill, had assured him that they had sent out invitations to seventeen Jewish athletes, inviting them to begin training for Olympic tryouts.

Believing that the highly publicized interventions by Brundage and Sherrill made prospects for a proboycott vote at the December 1934 AAU meeting unlikely, Jewish members of that organization, most notably Charles Ornstein, who represented the Jewish Welfare Board, decided not to press for a formal resolution. With the concurrence of its thirteen Jewish delegates, the AAU elected not to reissue, much less harden, its earlier ultimatum to the Germans. Yet Ornstein and his Jewish colleagues in the AAU were careful to leave the door open for a new boycott push should further scrutiny of conditions in Germany reveal that the situation was not as rosy as Brundage, Sherrill, and the Germans themselves claimed. Moreover, the AAU elected as its new president (to replace Brundage) one Jeremiah T. Mahoney, a former Olympian and New York State Supreme Court judge who had come to share Ornstein's perspective. With time Mahoney would emerge as the most serious threat in the American sports establishment to Brundage's proparticipation agenda, but his challenge did not fully materialize until the summer and fall of 1935. In the meantime the boycott movement fell into a lull, and it appeared to most observers that the Yanks were as good as on their way to Berlin.

The Apogee of the American Boycott Movement

While the German Olympic organizers continued to profess their good intentions regarding racial equality at the 1936 games, the Hitler government, by sharpening and expanding its anti-Jewish campaign in 1935, ensured that American efforts to boycott the German games came alive with a vengeance in the second half of that year.

Munich, the birthplace of Nazism and self-proclaimed "capital of the [Nazi] movement," witnessed a series of ugly anti-Jewish actions in spring 1935. SA thugs sprayed acid and racist graffiti on Jewish shops, smashed store windows, and assaulted Jews in the streets in broad daylight. The fact that Munich, famous for its *Gemütlichkeit*, was scheduled to host most of the larger social and cultural functions connected to the Winter Olympics in nearby Garmisch-Partenkirchen was clearly no deterrent to the local zealots. Seeing an obvious threat to their Olympics project in such impolitic behavior, Lewald and Halt appealed to Hans Lammers, head of Hitler's Reich Chancellery, to halt the anti-Jewish actions.

Even more troubling in its implications for the Nazi-hosted games was a spate of anti-Semitic violence on Berlin's Kurfürstendamm—the "Champs-Elysées" of the German capital. Between June 13 and 19, 1935, Nazi thugs attacked Jews and "Jewish-looking" people up and down that elegant street, even smashing women in the face. One outraged observer saw in this action the beginning of an effort to "cleanse" Berlin of its Jews, adding: "Nobody came to their aid because everyone is afraid of being arrested."

In response to the Kurfürstendamm violence the AJC and the American Jewish Labor Committee (AJLC) held an emergency meeting, calling once again for an Olympic boycott. In a sign of rising anti-Nazi sentiment in New York, five thousand demonstrators boarded a German ship in the harbor, pulled down the swastika flag, and pitched it into the Hudson River.

In terms of the potency of America's anti-Olympic boycott movement, the most important consequence of the latest upsurge in anti-Jewish violence in Germany was the transformation of Jeremiah Mahoney, the new AAU president, into an active opponent of American participation in the 1936 games.

Previously Mahoney had not publicly supported a boycott, but within a few days of the Kurfürstendamm rioting he openly stated his personal opposition to American participation. He added however that he could not speak for the entire AAU, which would not meet again until December 1935, by which time the issue might be "amicably resolved."

Mahoney's declaration, albeit unofficial and tentative, infuriated Brundage and his supporters, who felt they had been betrayed. (The Germans were equally indignant: Guido von Mengden, press secretary of the GOC and chief of staff of the Reichsbund für Leibesübungen, denounced the Irish Catholic judge as a "powerful Jewish financier.") Brundage ascribed Mahoney's intervention to personal ambition, suggesting that he was trying to curry Jewish favor for his bid to become New York City's next mayor.

What Brundage failed to see was that, with the involvement of personalities like Mahoney, La Guardia, Al Smith, and Governor James Curley of Massachusetts, the boycott movement was adding a significant Catholic dimension to its core Jewish backing. This became even more evident when *Commonweal,* one of the most influential Catholic organs in the United States, came out solidly against American participation in the German games. Noting that, contrary to its Concordat with the Vatican in 1933, Hitler's government was disbanding Catholic youth groups, *Commonweal* denounced the Nazis as "not merely anti-Semitic but pagan to the core." Given this reality, the magazine declared, "In the interest of justice and fairness we suggest that no Catholic, and no friend of the sport activities of Catholic institutions, ought to make the trip to Berlin."

Some progressive American Protestants now added their voices to the proboycott chorus. Protestant intellectuals like Reinhold Niebuhr and Harry Emerson Fosdick spoke out on the issue. In mid-August a self-described "group of fair-minded Protestants" launched an "Olympic Protest Letter" in support of the boycott. Most important, *Christian Century,* the chief voice of liberal Protestantism in America, ran a series of editorials sharply critical of the "Nazi games." The paper's publisher, Charles Clayton Morrison, argued that a boycott would send a message to the Nazis that their racial policies were intolerable.

The secular Left jumped on board the boycott train via an editorial in *The Nation* and a sharply worded column by famed sportswriter and social activist Heywood Broun. Broun, citing Brundage's touting of German pledges of good behavior, noted that "German pledges are not the highest-ranking currency in the world," and faulted the AOC president for ignoring American public opinion, which Broun insisted was "overwhelmingly against sending a team [to Germany]."

It would have been more accurate to say that American public opinion was deeply split on this issue. A Gallup poll taken in March 1935 registered 43 percent in favor of a boycott and 57 percent against. Polls of the sports and political editors of major newspapers around the country revealed a similar division. A number of leading figures in American sports came out *against* a boycott, among them William J. Bingham, the athletic director at Harvard. The German consul in Boston was especially gratified by Bingham's stance, interpreting it as the "official position of Harvard University."

Although the American public did not clearly favor keeping U.S. Olympians out of Berlin, there was certainly enough of a boycott groundswell to alarm Brundage. In late August 1935 he wrote his Swedish friend, Edstrøm, with the troubling news that, because of "anti-Nazi bias" in the "Jewish-controlled press of New York City," Americans were becoming more vulnerable to the "clever" anti-Olympic propaganda of the Jews. Moreover, he noted, Catholics were being "aroused" by Judge Mahoney, who in his race for mayor of New York City had announced that he would do "everything in his power to keep the United States teams from Germany, thus dragging the AAU into politics in the most unwarranted fashion." If Mahoney managed to persuade the AAU to refuse certification of American athletes for the German games, Brundage was prepared, he told Edstrøm, to ask the IOC and the IAAF to accept certification solely from the AOC.

Of course Edstrøm was fully in sympathy with his American colleague in his battle against the New York Jews. In an earlier letter Edstrøm had confided that he himself had "the Swedish Jews after me," and he complained that the German Jews were becoming uppity "owing to [their] too prominent position in certain branches of German life and [their] misuse of their positions." He added, however, "Our mutual friend Dr. Karl von Halt told me that the Jewish athletes would be treated just as the other German athletes."

German assurances of equal treatment for Jewish athletes were undercut by a steady stream of reports from the Reich that Jews were being denied access to the best training facilities and coaching, and were not allowed to practice with or compete against their "Aryan" counterparts. Much attention was focused on the case of Gretel Bergmann, a high jumper of international stature, who because of her Jewish origins was kicked out of her sports club in Ulm, denied a place in Berlin's Deutsche Hochschule für Leibesübungen, and forbidden to compete in the German track-and-field championships of 1935. The official reason for barring her from the competition was that her new sports club, the Jewish *Schild*, was not a member of the German Track and Field Association.

Nazi Germany's unequal treatment of its Jewish citizens, an ongoing practice since early 1933, was codified in September 1935 through the infamous Nuremberg laws. These laws officially reclassified German Jews as "subjects" rather than as citizens, deprived them of basic political rights, and—in the interest of "defending German blood and honor"—prohibited them from marrying Aryans or even from having sexual relations with them.

Even the IOC, which, like the proverbial see-no-evil and hear-no-evil monkeys, was doing its best to overlook racial injustice in the Third Reich, understood that the Nuremberg laws provided additional ammunition for the advocates of a boycott against a Nazi-hosted Olympic festival. Again the repercussions were likely to be most damaging in the United States, where boycott groups and newspapers were busy adding the Nuremberg legislation to the growing list of reasons why America should shun Germany in 1936.

Charles Sherrill also felt personally responsible for delivering American teams to Germany in 1936; unlike his countryman Brundage, however, he was ultimately able to use the American indignation over the Nuremberg laws to convince the Germans that they had to do something fairly dramatic to undercut the boycott advocates.

Sherrill traveled to Germany just prior to the 1935 Nuremberg Party Rally with the hope of persuading the Reich authorities to name at least one Jew to the German Olympic squads for 1936—a kind of athletic fig leaf. On August 24 he discussed the matter personally with Hitler in Munich, proposing that Germany add a Jewish athlete to its team for the Berlin games, a symbolic gesture he compared with the American tradition of "the token Negro." He warned that if Germany did not do this, America might boycott Berlin. To reinforce his point, he reminded Hitler of the Jews' tremendous influence in America, especially in New York City, where he said "the Jew La Guardia" (La Guardia's mother was Jewish) was cultivating "anti-Nazi sentiment" to promote his own political fortunes. But Hitler flatly rejected such tokenism, insisting there could be no Jewish participation on the German teams, period. If the IOC insisted on polluting Germany's teams with Jews, he said, he would call the whole damn thing off and substitute "purely German Olympic Games" for the international festival.

But would he really have done this? Hitler knew that German-only games would not have been useful in terms of propaganda, nor would they have provided a world stage for the grand architectural display he envisaged. Nonetheless Sherrill, who had described himself to Hitler as "a friend of Germany and of National Socialism," came out of the meeting confident that the Führer would give way in the end. On returning to his hotel Sherrill wrote self-importantly to his friend Col. Edward M. House, a presidential adviser from World War I until well into the 1930s: "My hour as personal guest of Hitler was wonderful. I hope and believe I did some good and reported it to Mr. Roosevelt at Hyde Park."

The Führer subsequently invited Sherrill to be his personal guest at the upcoming Nuremberg Party Rally, an invitation Sherrill cheerfully accepted. Just before attending the rally Sherrill wrote a letter to President Roosevelt's secretary bragging that he had won over Hitler by asking him how Bismarck might have handled the Olympic question. "It was dreadful nerve for me to tackle him in his own Munich home," he wrote, "but I am only a private citizen, and he can't eat me." In his privately published autobiography Sherrill had this to say about the time he spent with Hitler in Nuremberg: "I was Hitler's personal guest for four days in mid-September 1935. . . . It was beautiful! You could almost hear the [Nazi] units click, as each fitted into place, exactly on time."

After the rally Sherrill discussed his one-Jew proposal with Tschammer, specifically mentioning the brilliant high jumper Gretel Bergmann as a suitable prospect for the German team. Her earlier exclusion from Olympic contention had been duly noted and lamented in the American press. Fully appreciating that what Sherrill had in mind was a bit of strategic window dressing, Tschammer agreed to a partial concession: Bergmann would be named to the German Olympic *training* team and allowed to compete in the regular qualifying events. After inviting Bergmann to return to Germany from her exile in England, Tschammer assured Sherrill that "the Jewess will be treated in exactly the same manner as all German Olympic candidates."

It soon turned out, however, that the Germans had no intention of giving Bergmann, a full Jew according to the Nuremberg laws, a fair shot at the Olympics. Although she had won the Württemberg championship on June

27, 1936, with a jump of 1.60 meters, she was not allowed to compete in the German track-and-field championships in July 1936, which served as the qualifying event for Berlin. Her absence from the qualifying competition meant that she had no chance of being named to the German Olympic team.

Bergmann was not officially informed that she would not be named to the German team until the American athletes were ready to depart for Berlin. At that point Ritter von Halt told her that her "inadequate qualifying performance" precluded her from participating in Berlin. As compensation he offered her complimentary tickets to the track-and-field events at the Berlin games.

Bergmann did not accept this offer. Instead she immediately emigrated to America, where she won the U.S. women's high-jumping crown in 1937 and 1938. Of course she might also have won in Berlin had she been allowed to compete there: The winning jump turned out to be 1.62 meters, well within her range. (Fifty years later the seventy-two-year-old Bergmann turned down another compensation offer from the Germans: an invitation to attend the fiftieth anniversary celebration of the Berlin games in 1986. She replied, "Although fifty years have passed since my exclusion from the German Olympic team in Berlin, my disappointment and bitterness have only slightly abated.")

In his talks with German Olympic officials, Sherrill also put forth another Jewish athlete for consideration on the German team in case Bergmann proved unacceptable. This was Helene Mayer, a fencer who had won a gold medal for Germany in the 1928 Amsterdam games. Mayer had also competed for Germany in Los Angeles in 1932, taking fifth place. Following the LA games she had stayed in the U.S. to study at Scripps College and to teach German at Mills College in Oakland, California. While in the United States she won the American fencing championships in 1933, 1934, and 1935.

For German purposes it was significant that Mayer, unlike Bergmann, was only half Jewish, since her mother was an "Aryan." According to the Nuremberg laws, Mayer could still be considered a German citizen. Moreover, although her fencing club in Offenbach had expunged her name from its ranks in 1933, she still spoke in positive terms about the new Germany and expressed a desire to compete once again for the Reich in the upcoming Berlin Olympics. According to the German consul general in San Francisco, she had turned down an invitation to participate in a local protest rally against the Berlin games. She also made clear that she did not subscribe to the Jewish faith, had no contact with Jewish organizations, and in fact did not think of herself as Jewish at all.

Seeing Mayer as someone who would not embarrass the Reich, Tscham-mer invited her on September 21, 1935, to return to Germany and to join the national fencing team. At the same time he officially pronounced this green-eyed, blond-haired Valkyrie an "honorary Aryan." Reassured by Tschammer that her German citizenship was intact, Mayer accepted the invitation. Before sailing back to Germany she wrote an admiring letter to Avery Brundage saying, "I very much look forward to meeting you in Berlin."

Germany later added a half-Jewish ice hockey player named Rudi Ball to its team for the Winter Games in Garmisch-Partenkirchen, but this decision was made not to appease the Americans or the IOC but to improve the prospects of the German hockey team, which hoped to medal in Garmisch as it had in Lake Placid. Having been instrumental in Germany's taking the bronze in Lake Placid, Ball was such a valuable asset that the Germans saw fit to overlook his "tainted" ethnicity. He was invited back to Germany from his exile in Switzerland and placed on the German hockey team on January 15, 1936, the last day for naming team rosters for the Winter Games.

Sherrill returned to the United States convinced that with the Mayer concession he had dealt a fatal blow to the boycott movement. "I went to Germany," he announced at a press conference, "for the purpose of getting at least one Jew on the German Olympic team and I feel that my job is finished. As to obstacles placed in the way of Jewish athletes or any others in trying to reach Olympic ability, I would have no more business discussing that in Germany than if the Germans attempted to discuss the Negro situation in the American South or the treatment of Japanese in California."

SHERRILL'S mention of "the Negro situation in the American South" is interesting in light of the fact that antiblack racism in the United States was fast becoming an issue in the debate over whether America should participate in the 1936 games—and whether, if America did participate, African Americans should be part of the U.S. team.

The American black community took up this question when it became evident that blacks were likely to constitute a significant component of the team America sent to Berlin, especially in track and field. With Germany undeniably racist toward blacks as well as toward Jews, the question was: Should the African American community join the American Jewish community in boycotting the Berlin games?

Many black-owned newspapers pointed out that it was hypocritical for American sports officials to demand equal treatment for German Jews when they tolerated, indeed practiced, discrimination against black athletes at home. Yet at the same time, the black press, along with the National Association for the Advancement of Colored People (NAACP), strongly opposed Nazi racial policies and, in light of the openly expressed hostility toward blacks in the Nazi press, worried about how Negro athletes would be treated were they to compete in Germany.

In October 1933 Roy Wilkins, assistant secretary of the NAACP, wrote to the three American IOC members expressing his organization's "increased apprehension [over] the reiterated emphasis on color and race" emanating from Germany. "We are particularly concerned," he went on, "that there shall be no discrimination against colored athletes who may be chosen to represent the United States of America and other countries." He asked the American members of the IOC to make inquiries in Germany on this point, warning: "Unless Germany gives unqualified and unequivocal assurance of fair play to those possible colored competitors, we respectfully request the American members of the International Olympic Committee to refuse to permit Americans to compete at Berlin."

As the American boycott debate wore on, with Jewish organizations putting considerable pressure on the black community to come out firmly against American participation in Berlin, the black press split on this issue, a few papers endorsing the boycott, many others opposing it. One prominent black paper that endorsed the boycott was the *New York Amsterdam News*, which in August 1935 published an open letter to track star Jesse Owens and other prospective black members of the American team, urging them not to go to Berlin. "As members of a minority group," the paper editorialized, "whose persecution the Nazis have encouraged, as citizens of a country in which all liberty has not been destroyed, you cannot afford to give moral and financial support to a philosophy which seeks the ultimate destruction of all you have fought for."

In November 1935 the NAACP officially called upon American Negro athletes "not [to] participate in the 1936 Olympics . . . under the present situation in Germany." In sending news of this resolution to the American Jewish Committee, however, Roy Wilkins admitted to a certain ambivalence about the decision, for he too saw advantages in watching American blacks put the lie to the Nazi doctrine of racial superiority on the athletic field.

"[The fact that] the United States Olympic team will be decidedly brunette in composition gives us a great opportunity to strike a blow at all that Hitler stands for and to do so on the high plane of sportsmanship."

Not surprisingly the response of most black athletes to the suggestion that they refuse to participate in the Olympic Games was anything but positive. They had trained hard to reach the level of Olympic competition and were anxious to show off their skills to the largest possible audience. Moreover, some of the American athletes had participated in competitions in Germany without encountering any discrimination. Ralph Metcalfe, a sprinter from Marquette University, declared that he and other American Negro athletes had been "treated like royalty" during a track meet in Germany in late 1933.

"Royal treatment" in Germany, of course, contrasted sharply with the treatment that black athletes often received at home. Neither Jesse Owens nor the black high jumper David Albritton, who like Owens attended Ohio State University, was allowed to live in on-campus housing. Black athletes could not compete alongside whites in university-level competition across the South. And none of the Olympic qualification events could be held in the South because of a ban on interracial competition.

Despite widespread reservations in the black community about holding Germany accountable for iniquities that were present also in America, Jesse Owens, the most prominent black track-and-field athlete of all, initially came out in favor of boycotting the Berlin games. Owens had in one hour broken three world records and tied another at the 1935 Big Ten track championships in Ann Arbor, Michigan. Expected to be a shoo-in for the American Olympic team, he was hounded to say where he stood on 1936. During a radio interview in November 1935, Owens declared: "If there is discrimination against minorities in Germany, then we must withdraw from the Olympics."

Owens's declaration won him an immediate letter of gratitude from Walter White, the secretary of the NAACP. In congratulating Owens on his stand, however, White, like Wilkins before him, confessed to being "somewhat divided" on the boycott issue. On the one hand, seeing Nazi racial policy as "a duplication of what we Negroes have suffered for three centuries in America," he believed that American blacks should stay away from Berlin. On the other hand, as he told Owens, "because of the preeminence of athletes like yourself, Eulace Peacock, [Ralph] Metcalfe, [Cornelius] Johnson and others, the American team next year will be decidedly brunette in complexion [that quaint expression again]. There have been times when I have felt that there might be a certain psychological value in having blond Nazis run ragged by yourself and others." Yet on balance, White considered the position Owens had just taken "a much finer one," and he asked the athlete to tell him more about how he felt on the matter.

Owens did not reply, and for good reason: He was in the process of changing his mind. Larry Snyder, Owens's coach at Ohio State, was flabbergasted by his charge's proboycott declaration and immediately set about getting him to reverse it. This proved not terribly difficult to do, for Snyder had a powerful influence on Owens, and the athlete himself was not really committed to a boycott, his radio comments notwithstanding.

Like his colleagues Owens truly looked forward to competing in Berlin, where he confidently expected to win. He was especially anxious to shine on the international stage because he had recently been snubbed at home. After a booster at Ohio State had secured him dubious summer employment as an honorary page, his name was removed from the list of finalists for the Sullivan Memorial Award honoring the year's best amateur athlete. Moreover, like other black athletes he had not been invited to the Sugar Bowl track meet in New Orleans, where a strict Jim Crow policy prevailed. As Coach Snyder put the issue: "Why should we oppose Germany for doing something we do right here at home?"

Along with five other top black athletes, Owens announced in December 1935 that if selected for the American team he intended to go to Berlin after all. In support of this decision, a black journalist writing in the *New York World* pounced on the issue of double standards: "One wonders if, by chance, the next Olympics were to take place in Atlanta, Georgia, or almost any one of the states below the Mason-Dixon Line, would 'the powers that be' remove signs in the railroad stations reading, 'Whites on this side, Colored on that side'? Would the fine hotels, some of them built especially to accommodate visitors to the games, extend their hospitality to all comers, regardless of race?"

DEEPLY worried about the growth of the boycott movement in America, Baillet-Latour made a personal appeal on October 5, 1935 to his three American IOC colleagues, asking them to do their best to counter the anti-Berlin agitators. Calling on their "devotion to the Olympic idea," Baillet-Latour said it was up to Sherrill, Garland, and Jahncke to "convince your people that the

IOC has upheld the rights of everyone concerned and the unanimous decision [to keep the games in Berlin] was the only wise one."

Sherrill and Garland replied that they would do their utmost to get the Americans to Berlin, but the third American IOC member, Ernest Jahncke, delivered a very different response—a flat rejection of the German games and a blistering condemnation of the IOC for endorsing them. Just who was this contrarian, and what motivated his action?

Ernest Lee Jahncke was the scion of a prominent New Orleans family. His father had made a fortune in shipbuilding, and Jahncke continued with the business, building it into one of the largest firms of its type in the South. A passion for rowing and yachting brought him fame as a sporting gentleman, and in 1927, recommended by Charles Sherrill and President Calvin Coolidge, he was named to the AOC and the IOC. Service as assistant secretary of the navy under President Herbert Hoover, however, kept him from being a very active participant in the Olympic movement. He rarely attended IOC meetings.

Coming from German American stock, Jahncke grew deeply concerned over what was happening in his ancestral country following Hitler's seizure of power. He was especially shocked by the Nuremberg laws and by the steady reports that the Nazis were denying Jewish athletes any reasonable chance at a place on the German Olympic teams. This violated his sense of fair play and chivalry. Moreover, as a Southerner, he bristled at comparisons between America's "private" racism (which he deplored) and the Nazis' state-sponsored persecution. Used to saying exactly what was on his mind, he wrote a sharp rejoinder to Baillet-Latour, along with an equally blunt letter to Lewald.

Judging from Baillet-Latour's correspondence files in the IOC archives, Jahncke's letter was probably the least reverential missive the Belgian aristocrat ever received. Citing Baillet-Latour's invoking of the "Olympic idea," Jahncke said it was "precisely [his] devotion to the Olympic idea" that caused him "to do just the opposite of what you so confidently ask of me." He would, he said, "do all I can to persuade my fellow Americans that they ought not to take part in the Games if they are held in Nazi Germany." Arguing that the Nazis had "violated and are continuing to violate every requirement of fair play in the conduct of sports," he insisted that no foreign nation could participate in the Nazi games "without at least acquiescing in the contempt of the Nazis for fair play and their sordid exploitation of the Games." Jahncke did not shy away from a personal rebuke of the IOC president: "You remind me of my duty as a member of the IOC. Therefore, I feel sure you will not consider me presumptuous in reminding you of your duty as president of the IOC. It is plainly your duty to hold the Nazi sports authorities accountable for the violation of their pledges. I simply cannot understand why, instead of doing that, you are engaged in formulating and spreading 'arguments' to show why those of us who still believe in the Olympic idea should take part in the Games of Nazi Germany." Insisting it was still not too late to maintain the Olympics as "a school of moral nobility and purity" (Coubertin's phrase), he urged Baillet-Latour to move the games from Germany. "Let me urge upon you that you place your great talents in the service of fair play and of chivalry instead of brutality, force and power. Let me beseech you to seize the opportunity to take your rightful place in the history of the Olympics along-side of de Coubertin instead of Hitler."

Jahncke's eloquence was lost on Baillet-Latour, who in reply chastised the American for acting in "willful ignorance of the true state of affairs," which was that the IOC had sanctioned the German games not on the word of the Nazi authorities but on the basis of "proofs" of acceptable contact provided by outside investigators and Jewish groups in the Reich. Baillet-Latour accused Jahncke of misleading the public, "who is not aware that you know very little of Olympic Things and nothing at all about the XI. Olympiad's problem, as you have never been present at any meetings of the Council." Jahncke's invocation of Coubertin especially galled Baillet-Latour, since the great Frenchman had on this important question "the same opinion as all members of the IOC." And he concluded: "The blame you put in your letter on [the IOC] is so severe and unjustified that I believe that nothing but your resignation can be expected."

Jahncke was not the only thorn in the IOC's side, of course. On October 20, 1935, Judge Mahoney, who had already announced his opposition to the German games, wrote an open letter to Lewald questioning the latter's asser-tions that Germany had lived up to its promises to give German Jews an equal shot at participating in the games. He listed all the ways in which Germany was violating the Olympic rules. The letter took on a painful personal note when Mahoney told Lewald that he feared the "non-Aryan" official lacked "any real authority" and was shamefully allowing himself to be "used as a screen to conceal your government's flagrant violations of the Olympic ideal of fair play." He called on Lewald to resign immediately from the GOC and IOC. At the same time Mahoney called on Baillet-Latour to remove the games from Berlin. If the IOC did not do so, he warned, he would push for an American boycott of the festival.

Baillet-Latour chose not to respond directly to Mahoney, but he urged Brundage to go on the offensive with a public campaign of enlightenment about the "true conditions" in Germany. If national AAU chapters nonetheless refused to certify athletes for the games, Baillet-Latour promised Brundage that "the IOC would inform the International Federation that, exceptionally, the signature of the National Olympic Association will be considered to be sufficient." Brundage, as we have seen, had already proposed this option, and by accommodating him Baillet-Latour showed that the IOC was willing to suspend its own rules to ensure America's presence at the German games.

Brundage took Baillet-Latour's advice to go on the offensive. In late October 1935 he drew up, with the assistance of his publicity expert Clarence Bush, a lengthy pamphlet titled *Fair Play for American Athletes*. The AOC distributed some ten thousand copies of this publication to sports and civic groups around the nation. In *Fair Play* Brundage set the tone with the opening statement, which smeared boycott advocates with a wide red brush: "In 1932 there was a concerted effort by Communists both here and abroad to wreck the Los Angeles Games. Many of the individuals and organizations active in the present campaign to boycott the Olympics have Communist antecedents. Radicals and Communists must keep their hands off American sport." Asking, "Shall the American athlete be made a martyr to a cause not his own?" the pamphlet pounded home the message that the boycott effort was alien and un-American, little short of treason. It also carried a warning to Jewish opponents of the German games: "Certain Jews had better understand that they cannot use these Games as a weapon in their boycott against the Nazis." Additionally *Fair Play* advised the U.S. government not to interfere with the right of American athletes to go to Germany: "Will any of our athletes thank leaders who lose their heads in an argument having nothing to do with athletics and deny them the privilege of striving to maintain unbroken [the] tradition of American supremacy in world sport?" The pamphlet even invoked George Washington, citing his advice that America refrain from "meddling" in European affairs. "In all the history of the United States, we have disregarded this advice only once—'to make the world safe for democracy' [by entering World War I]—and we have not recovered from the after-effects."

With the publication of *Fair Play*, Brundage and the AOC sought to win over the public by playing on familiar chords of nativism, patriotism, anti-communism, and, of course, anti-Semitism. While it is impossible to know how effective this campaign was (no more public opinion polls on the subject were taken), it certainly prompted a barrage of approving letters to Brundage, congratulating him on "protecting" American sport from the predations of Communists and Jews.

A Conspicuous Silence: The Roosevelt Administration and the Boycott Movement

The battle over the Olympic boycott naturally included efforts by both sides to involve the government in Washington, especially the president. The government did not make the official decision on Olympic participation—that was the prerogative of the AOC and AAU—but everyone knew that if Washington came down solidly on one side or the other, this would probably decide the matter. The proboycott forces were especially hopeful about an intervention from President Roosevelt, believing that a man of his integrity and liberal conscience would have to see the issues as they did.

If the question had been left up to Washington's embassy officials in Berlin, the United States would certainly not have participated in the 1936 games. Beginning with the earliest phase of the discussion, two key American consular officials in Berlin, Chief Consul George Messersmith and Vice-Consul Raymond Geist, kept the State Department and White House apprised of the ugly situation in Germany regarding Jews and sports.

Their reports were frank and hard hitting. In late November 1933 Messersmith reported that Jews were being systematically excluded from sports clubs and high-level competition. Presciently he suggested that the Hitler government might make some concessions regarding Jewish access to the Olympic program, but these concessions would simply be camouflage designed to obscure ongoing iniquities. "It is not impossible that . . . a few Jews may be allowed to train and to figure on teams; but I think it should be understood that this will be merely a screen for the real discrimination that is taking place." With respect to the protestations of innocence voiced by Theodor Lewald, Messersmith insisted that the German official could not be trusted, for he was "not a free agent," having been allowed to retain his post only at the price of doing the Nazis' bidding. Believing it important that the AOC not have "the wool pulled over their eyes," he urged his superiors in Washington to forward his critical dispatch to the committee. Above all, he said, the AOC should be advised not to sanction American participation until it had reliable information that Germany was changing its policies regarding Jewish participation in Olympic tryouts. Barring that, he offered his personal view that it would go against the "American sporting tradition if American athletes were to participate in the Olympic Games of 1936."

Similarly Raymond Geist informed the State Department on December 15, 1933, "In the realm of sport . . . discrimination against Jews continues." Jewish youth were forbidden to wear the special buttons required of all young athletes belonging to official sporting organizations. Like Messersmith, Geist opined that foreign pressure and the fear of losing the games might induce the Nazis to "drop certain restrictive measures taken against the Jews," but these gestures would undoubtedly have no lasting significance.

The American consuls, especially Messersmith, eventually became deeply frustrated over what they saw as a systematic undercutting of their critical analyses by the activities of Brundage and Sherrill, whose "fact-finding" missions invariably exonerated the Germans of all wrongdoing. Messersmith considered Sherrill a self-infatuated blowhard whose desire to be at the center of things clouded any critical faculties he might have possessed. He complained to a colleague that Sherrill was willing to "whitewash" German misbehavior "in his eagerness that we participate."

In a last-gasp effort to counter Sherrill's "whitewash," Messersmith sent a long cable to Secretary of State Cordell Hull in December 1935, urging that he take a firm stand against America's participation in the German games. By then Messersmith was stationed in Vienna, but he still kept a watchful eye on conditions in Germany. Reminding Hull of his reservations about American participation two years earlier, he stated flatly, "Everything that has happened [since then] has been in the direction of showing that American participation is undesirable." Nazi control over all dimensions of public life had hardened. While the oppression still focused primarily on Jews, dissident Catholics, Protestants, professors, artists, and intellectuals were also targeted. Sport had been as thoroughly "coordinated" as any other public activity: "All German sport is today directly controlled by the Government and is professedly an instrument of the Party for the shaping of youth into National Socialist ideology." As for the prospective Olympic Games of 1936, these were understood by the regime to be a useful instrument for "consolidating the position of the Party among the youth of Germany." The regime had also recognized that "the decision of the American Olympic Committee would play a predominant part in determining to what degree there would be foreign participation in the Games." Hence the Germans were doing everything in their power "to convince the American Olympic Committee that there was no discrimination against the Jews" in German sports. Their campaign of dissimulation included enlisting the highly respected half Jew, Theodor Lewald, as a conduit to the AOC, which tended to swallow Lewald's blandishments whole. Messersmith related that he had privately "reproached [Lewald] for misusing the confidence which his American friends put in him," to which he replied that he had had no choice but to go along with the regime. "To this, I merely remarked that there were times when, in order to maintain one's self-respect and the confidence of one's friends, one must accept the consequences which come from doing right."

Messersmith further believed, as his report to Hull made clear, that sponsoring the 1936 Olympics had become even more crucial to the Nazis in the last two years because of the party's increasing dependence on the support of German youth, who needed to be convinced that National Socialist prestige was gaining ground outside Germany. "To the Party and to the youth of Germany, the holding of the Olympic Games in Berlin in 1936 has become the symbol of the conquest of the world by National Socialist doctrine. Should the games not be held in Berlin, it would be one of the most serious blows which National Socialist prestige could suffer within an awakening Germany and one of the most effective ways which the world outside has of showing to the youth of Germany its opinion of National Socialist doctrine."

Given the availability of "ample data" showing the continuation of anti-Jewish discrimination and the thorough politicization of sport in Nazi Germany, Messersmith found it "inconceivable" that the AOC could go on insisting there was no reason for America to shun the Berlin games. But if America insisted on taking part, he argued, other nations, "waiting for a clear signal from the United States," would undoubtedly take part as well, since American participation would presage a German success. A success for Nazi Germany in this realm would, Messersmith believed, have profound implications not just for the internal strength of the Hitler regime but also for the political future of Europe as a whole. "There are many wise and well informed observers in Europe who believe that the holding or non-holding of the Olympic Games in Berlin in 1936 will play an important part in deter-mining political developments in Europe. I believe that this view of the importance of the Olympic Games is not exaggerated."

Like Messersmith and Geist, William E. Dodd, Washington's ambassador in Berlin since 1933, hoped to derail the Nazi Olympic express—or at least to prevent American athletes from joining the passenger list. A report he dis-patched to Hull on the issue of American participation in the Olympics in November 1935 contrasted the oft-repeated claims of good behavior from Theodor Lewald with the statements of an (unnamed) German Jewish sports authority whom Dodd had managed to interview privately in the embassy. According to Dodd the official spoke of "flagrant discrimination" against Jew-ish athletes, including an exclusion from open competition and public sports facilities. The admission of a few Jews to Olympic training camps, insisted this official, was simply a ploy to ward off international pressure, and once in the camps the Jewish athletes were subjected to psychological pressures designed to hamper their performance. The official added that any Jewish athlete who openly called attention to the true conditions in which Jews were obliged to train would be thrown into one of the regime's new concentration camps. Obviously Dodd, like Messersmith and Geist, hoped that information like this would find its way to the American Olympic authorities and shape their final decision on U.S. participation in the German games.

There was, however, little chance of this happening. Messersmith received only one acknowledgment from within the State Department of his report-ing on the athletic situation in Germany. Nor is there any indication that the State Department passed the consular reports on to the AOC or the AAU. Given the mind-set at the AOC, the sobering commentary from Berlin might not have made much difference anyway, but it could have had an impact at the AAU, which was deeply divided on the question of sending American teams to Germany. As for Dodd, he had little chance of influencing Hull, who believed that the ambassador had no feel either for the intricacies of American German relations or the domestic political constraints under which the president had to work. In any event Hull was determined to keep the State Department out of the boycott debate.

But if Hull chose to remain silent, what about the president? FDR was known to sympathize with the plight of German Jews and apparently had pri-vate reservations about sending an American team to Berlin. Both the pro- and antiboycott factions hoped that FDR might take a clear stand on this issue, but in fact the prospects for this were no better than for a State Department intervention.

A consummate politician, FDR certainly understood that throwing his weight behind either position carried more risks than taking no position at all. Personal feelings aside, he was aware that a proboycott stance might be especially costly because his administration already had the reputation of being too "Jew friendly" among right-wing elements at home, which opposed doing anything to upset the Germans. Even one of his trusted Jewish advisers, Judge Samuel I. Rosenman, advised him against backing the boycott after consulting with Sherrill, who insisted that this would be a "grave mistake."

FDR also resisted being publicly identified with the proparticipation camp. When the German-American Olympic Fund Committee included his name on the masthead of a letter soliciting donations for the American team, the White House sharply protested to the AOC, under whose auspices the German American group operated. What particularly perturbed the White House was a line in the solicitation letter urging a contribution so that "American athletes after competing at the Olympic Games in Berlin could return home as apostles of truth and justice [and as advocates] for the promotion of friendship between our great countries." Although hesitant to offend the Hitler government, FDR hardly wanted to be identified with anything smacking of pro-Nazi sentiment, which the German-American Olympic promotion clearly was.

In the end, however, the president's conspicuous silence on the boycott question was not equally damaging to both sides. The proboycott faction suffered more for want of his endorsement, for it had always faced an uphill battle against Brundage and would have gained a tremendous boost from Roosevelt's backing.

A Narrow Defeat

The boycott battle came to a head at the 1935 AAU Convention, held at the Commodore Hotel in New York City on December 6–8, 1935. The final showdown was bitter and full of personal animus, since the chief contenders, Brundage and Mahoney, thoroughly despised each other. Once again, Brundage used dubious tactics to intimidate the opposition, implying in remarks to the press that a Mahoney victory would stimulate anti-Semitism in the

United States. "There are [sic] maybe five percent of the population which is Jewish. A study of the records of the Olympic Games shows about one-half to one percent of the athletes are Jewish. There is a larger percentage of Jewish delegates here than that. And responsibility for actions of this kind, right or wrong, would be charged to the Jews, I think."

In the end Brundage managed to win this showdown, albeit very narrowly: the AAU voted 58.25 to 55.75 against a resolution calling for yet another on-the-spot investigation of German conditions. The defeat of this amendment paved the way for the adoption of a resolution by Kirby that approved AAU sanction of American participation in Berlin, with the weak caveat that this action should not be interpreted as support for the Nazis. At the end of the meeting, Brundage's supporters elected him to displace Mahoney as AAU president, thus cementing his domination of American amateur athletics.

Immediately following the AAU meeting, Sigfrid Edstrøm, Brundage's Swedish ally on the IOC, cabled his American friend to congratulate him on having outmaneuvered "the dirty Jews and politicians." Edstrøm added, "I hope to see you in Berlin this summer as a colleague on the CIO [Comité Internationale Olympique—IOC]." Sure enough, in July 1936 Brundage became a member of the IOC—a reward, in part, for having helped squelch the American boycott effort. (In 1938 Brundage received another token of gratitude for his work against the boycott: a contract to his construction company to build a new German embassy in Washington. The outbreak of World War II prevented the embassy from being built.)

The Brundage victory, of course, came as very welcome news to Baillet-Latour, who dashed off a letter to the American congratulating him on "the issue of your struggle with the Mahoney group. You have fighted [sic] like a lion and deserve great praise for your achievement." Writing to Baillet-Latour, Charles Sherrill expressed delight that Brundage had "won a revenge for Mahoney's defeat of him last year, plus a high office."

Brundage was anything but magnanimous in victory. He demanded that the AAU members who had opposed American participation resign at once from the organization. Mahoney did so, but Charles Ornstein refused, obliging Brundage to force him out on the technicality that he had missed two meetings in a row. In a postconference assessment of the AAU action, Brundage congratulated the body "for its strength and fortitude in resisting pressure unprecedented in the annals of sport government in this country."

But in order to avoid having the body subjected ever again to pressure from "organized minorities," he urged that thenceforth all prospective members be carefully screened to ensure that their views were in accord "with the ideals of the AAU."

Brundage's victory at the AAU meeting did not spell an end to his anxieties over getting a solid American team to Berlin. Now his main problem was raising funds for the American effort, which had suffered because of the boycott controversy. Brundage's hopes of infusing new life into the fund-raising campaign were promptly undercut by the Germans, who in the aftermath of the AAU vote announced plans for an exhibition during the games that would trumpet the Nazi system, along with an Olympic film to be directed by Leni Riefenstahl, the same director who had recently produced *Triumph of the Will*, the documentary celebrating the 1934 Nuremberg Party Rally. In exasperation Brundage had his publicity manager, Clarence Bush, instruct the German organizers to stop trying "to capitalize [on Brundage's] success for the benefit of Nazi propaganda."

Brundage himself, however, tried to capitalize on his victory to squeeze contributions out of the Jewish-American business community, arguing that the Jews would do well to be generous now that their efforts to sabotage the German games had failed. In March 1936 he wrote a heavy-handed letter to the advertising magnate Albert Lasker, advising him that the best way for the Jews to atone for their sins and to combat anti-Semitism at home was to get on board financially for Berlin: "The great and growing resentment in athletic circles in this country against the Jews because of the activities of certain Jewish individuals and groups in seeking to prevent American participation in the Olympic Games next August, should be offset by some action on the part of prominent organizations or individuals of your race. . . . My suggestion now is that . . . some Jewish group or committee assists the American Olympic Committee in its campaign to finance the American team. If the record showed contributions from $50,000 to $75,000 from Jewish sources, it might be useful in the future."

Lasker, to his credit, refused to be blackmailed, responding: "As an American, I resent your letter and your subtle intimations of reprisals against Jews. You gratuitously insult not only Jews but millions of patriotic Christians in America, for whom you venture to speak without warrant, and whom you so tragically misrepresent in your letter."

The Boycott Movement in Britain and France

If the possibility of an American boycott of the 1936 Olympics posed the most serious threat to the Nazi games, a boycott by Britain would have been almost as devastating, for that nation was (in the words of the *Manchester Guardian*) "the mother of sport and the final arbiter of sportsmanship."

From the outset Britain keyed its own boycott debate to developments in the United States. In the wake of the American AAU's November 1933 decision to postpone certification of American athletes for the 1936 games, the British Olympic Association (BOA) let it be known that it too had doubts about sending athletes to Germany. The BOA cabled the AAU asking for details on its action, adding that it regarded any ban "on athletes from training on account of race or religion . . . as just as much a violation of the Olympic rules as the preventing [of such athletes] from competing." When the BOA discussed the boycott question a few days later, however, it decided to put off any action pending further developments in Germany. The British embassy in Berlin also followed the American boycott debate closely, noting in a report to the Foreign Office that the threat of a U.S. withdrawal was putting the fear of God into the Hitler government. "The German government are simply terrified lest Jewish pressure may induce the U.S. government to withdraw their team and so wreck the festival, the material and propagandistic value of which, they think, can scarcely be exaggerated."

In Britain, just as in America, Jewish groups and major labor organizations issued calls for a boycott of the games. Walter Citrine, head of the Trades Union Council (TUC), decried the Nazis' success in bringing all German sport "under the heel of Hitler," politicizing and militarizing sport in a manner totally incompatible with the Olympic spirit.

Clearly concerned that the Germans were not living up to the promises they had made at Vienna, Lord Aberdare, head of the BOA, wrote Lewald in early 1934 inquiring about the fate of three athletic officials who had reportedly been dismissed from their positions on grounds of their Jewish race or leftist politics. Aberdare also wanted to know "whether German cyclists of Jewish origin" had been barred from participation in that sport, and whether the German Boxing Federation had expelled Jewish boxers. Finally he asked whether it was true that a noted German Jewish tennis player, Dr. Daniel Prenn, had been "excluded on grounds that he is of Jewish origin."

In reply Lewald repeated earlier blanket assurances that the Germans were complying with Olympic regulations, while insisting that the specific cases cited by Aberdare had not involved racial or political discrimination. Further, he noted, many German sports clubs had been banning Jews for more than fifty years, a practice hardly unique to Germany. "I suppose this matter has been treated in a similar way in England," he added.

Aberdare, it turned out, did not need a lot of convincing to come around to the German point of view, although he continued to press for more gestures from Germany that would help him sell their case in Britain. "I have great hopes that all will be well," he wrote Lewald in February 1934, "and I hope that some of our Jewish supporters and Olympic athletes will also feel confident that they will be able to go in safety and with pleasure to watch the Games." Aberdare later warned that "a strong body of opinion" in Britain still wanted signs of a "change in spirit" in Germany, adding it "would be a splendid thing" if Lewald could send him notice that "some eminent Jew" who had been dismissed from his post in German sports had been reinstated, or that some young Jews were "joining with others in the preparation for the Olympic Games of 1936."

If the BOA was looking for reasons to send Olympic teams to Germany in good conscience, the British government was also hoping that disagreements over sport, including the Olympics, would not jeopardize London's efforts to stabilize relations with the Nazi Reich. In the Anglo-German Naval Agreement of June 1935, Britain risked antagonizing its own allies, most notably France, in order to promote goodwill with Berlin. Moreover, British leaders were opposed to using sport as a political weapon, which would have violated their country's hallowed tradition of the independence of athletics. Britain's punctiliousness here worked to the advantage of the Germans, who of course harbored no compunction at all about mixing sport with politics, even while mouthing the usual platitudes concerning the sanctity of athletics.

Germany's willingness to use sport as a weapon in its ongoing effort to woo the British came to the fore during a much-publicized football match between Germany and England in December 1935, a moment when the BOA was still toying with the idea of an Olympic boycott. When the British Football Association extended an invitation to the German national soccer team to come to London to play against the English team, Tschammer accepted immediately on behalf of the Germans, seeing the match as an ideal opportunity to promote German-English relations. He informed the British that Germany would come "in homage to the inventors of football." Along with the team would come ten thousand German supporters "as ambassadors of goodwill."

Needless to say, however, news of the upcoming match prompted cries of alarm from anti-Nazi groups in Britain, who envisaged an invasion of slogan-screaming, swastika-banner-waving thugs. In addition, the British press was full of reports that during a recent German Polish football match in Upper Silesia a Polish Jewish player had been beaten to death by Nazi fans. (The German government hotly denied the story, which turned out to be false.) British unease was heightened by the plan to hold the match at White Hart Lane stadium, home turf of London's Tottenham Hotspur football club, whose supporters included many Jews living in the area. Opponents of the match warned of violent clashes between residents and the visiting Germans, who reportedly planned to march through Jewish neighborhoods on their way to the game. Citing the likelihood of violence, and decrying Nazi intentions to "use this match for political propaganda," a leader of the National Association of Railwaymen demanded that the Foreign Secretary intervene to cancel the match.

The Foreign Office, while appreciating the danger of violence, refused to intervene, insisting that this was "a Home Office affair." Such buck-passing masked the Foreign Office's disinclination to take a position that might have injured relations between Britain and Germany at a very sensitive juncture. The Home Office, for its part, batted the issue around for some time before deciding that it, too, should not risk "the political trouble" that would attend a cancellation of the match.

As it happened the game turned out to have just the effect the Germans intended. There was no violence, largely because the German fans behaved with utmost decor. The German players did their part by chivalrously losing 3–0, their every missed tackle and errant shot an action for the greater good of the Reich. The British players were touched by the Germans' demonstration of "fair play," and the match turned into a kind of lovefest, full of hand-shaking and mutual congratulation.

At a gala dinner after the game Tschammer spoke of the "blue sky of friendship between the two Nordic countries." That friendship was even more pointedly celebrated the following evening at the inaugural dinner of the Anglo-German Fellowship, an avidly pro-German organization. Lord

Mount Temple, the group's spokesman, took this occasion to criticize the British government for being too gentle with those who had tried to prevent the British-German football match. "I would have told them to mind their own damn business. . . . The Germans have always been our good friends. They always fought fair in the war, and I hope we did the same. If another war comes . . . well, I hope the partners will be changed."

Although the British-German football match obviously did not lead to a new alignment of Germans and Britons against Russians, French, and Americans, it did help undermine the ongoing British boycott effort. That effort was further hindered by the British government's continuing disinclination to do anything to provoke the ire of the Germans. Also, Foreign Office officials privately harbored skepticism that a British boycott would be of any significant benefit to the German Jews. As early as October 1935 Baillet-Latour, who had fretted over the possibility of a British boycott, could write with relief to Baron Peter Le Fort, the secretary of the Winter Games organizing committee, that "the influence of the Jewish campaign in England for a boycott has waned."

WHILE the growth of appeasement sentiment in Britain militated against the success of an anti-Nazi boycott in that country, France might have been expected to take a firmer stance against its eastern neighbor and indeed to lead the European nations in a boycott of the 1936 games. After all, Paris had led the crusade to bar Germany from the 1920 and 1924 games. Now, in the mid-1930s, France was directly threatened by the new Nazi Reich, which openly pushed for overturning the Versailles treaty. Yet in the end France proved a great disappointment to all those who hoped that Paris would deal a severe blow to Nazi prestige by boycotting the 1936 games.

Opposition to the 1936 German games had surfaced in France immediately following Hitler's assumption of the German chancellorship, but efforts to give this opposition organizational coherence foundered on old divisions within the French sports community between its bourgeois and working-class components. The modern Olympic movement had been warmly embraced by most of the bourgeois sports clubs but largely spurned by the socialist and communist athletic clubs, which had sponsored their own "Workers' Olympics" since 1925. Some of the bourgeois clubs had reservations about the 1936 games but were disinclined to join with workers' groups in a boycott. In general they fell back on the old argument that the Olympics must remain "above politics."

French Jews, who might have been expected to combine with workers in opposing a Nazi Olympiad, failed to do so in significant numbers because most identified with the bourgeois parties and feared being lumped together with the left. True, a few prominent Jewish sports officials—most notably I. P. Levy, president of the Paris Racing Club, and Jules Reimet, head of the Comité National du Sport—came out against the Berlin games, but they did so as individuals, not as representatives of their associations.

France's most influential sporting publication, *L'Auto*, accepted the GOC's claim that it was following Olympic rules and even praised Germany's preparations for the games. Enthusiasm in France for the games was not observably diminished by the announcement in November 1935 that two French bobsled champions, Philippe de Rothschild and Jean Rheims, both Jews, would not compete in the Winter Games because of Germany's racist policies.

Despite the endorsement of bourgeois sports associations, France's ability to prepare for the 1936 games required an additional infusion of cash from the government. Following an initial meager outlay in June 1934, the Chamber of Deputies failed for months to give approval to another, much larger, budget request from the FOC for nine hundred thousand francs.

On the eve of the vote on that request, scheduled for mid-December 1935, boycott sentiment in France reached its zenith, with protest marches and demonstrations across the country. On November 7, 1935, *Sport*, a journal close to the Socialists, called attention to this "wave of protests" in editorializing against the "Hitlerian Olympic Games." A little later, noting the continuing persecution of Jews in Germany as well as the forced dissolution of Catholic and Protestant youth groups, *Sport* put forth the slogan, *"Pas un sou, pas un homme pour Berlin!"* (Not a penny, not a man for Berlin!) In early December about three hundred former athletes formed the Committee Against the Hitlerian Games, which called on athletes around the world to boycott Garmisch and Berlin.

Most of the objections to Nazi-sponsored games raised by the protest movement were eloquently summed up by the Socialist deputy Jules Longuet in a speech to the Chamber demanding the rejection of the nine-hundred-thousand-franc subsidy for France's Olympic teams. Arguing that the Olympics had hitherto been "a demonstration of international brotherhood," Longuet decried the Nazis' intention "to marshal the sportsmen and sportswomen of the world under their swastika flags [in a spectacle] that will have nothing in common with previous traditions." Averring that "we have always been attracted to the Germany of Goethe and Schiller, of Beethoven, Kant, Marx and Liebknecht," Longuet insisted that the "France of the Rights of Man, of [Jules] Michelet and Victor Hugo and [Jean] Jaurès" could have no truck with Hitler's Germany, which had "applied its despicable ideas to sport."

The legacy of Michelet and Hugo notwithstanding, Longuet's resolution went down to defeat 410 to 161, having found support almost exclusively on the Left. Two months later France duly sent a team to the Winter Games in Garmisch-Partenkirchen, which proved to be important less for France's athletic success (which was minimal) than for the signal it sent regarding the country's probable participation in the summer festival in Berlin.

OLYMPIC Games have traditionally provided smaller countries a chance to enjoy a moment of glory, so it is not surprising that there was little enthusiasm for a boycott from this quarter. Nonetheless opposition to participation in Hitler's spectacle surfaced in a number of smaller states, including Switzerland, home of the IOC, as well as such sport-besotted nations as Canada and Australia. In faraway India a group of Bombay students demanded that their nation withdraw from the Berlin games to protest Nazi persecution of the Jews and Hitler's racist slur that the British had "had to teach the Indians how to walk." In the end, with the notable exceptions of Italy and Japan, virtually every nation that participated in the 1936 games did so over some measure of domestic protest.

Personal Boycotts

While all the nations (excepting Spain, about which more below) that were invited to the 1936 games managed to overcome whatever scruples they may have had regarding an appearance at Hitler's spectacle, some prominent individual athletes, most of them Jewish, took a personal stand against the Nazi games either by withdrawing from their nations' Olympic trials or quitting their national teams.

One must stress that these actions did not constitute a broader trend.

Despite an appeal from the Maccabi Union to all Jewish athletes worldwide to refrain from going to Germany, there was no mass Jewish boycott. Many teams, including those from Poland, Britain, Czechoslovakia, Hungary, and, yes, the United States, included Jewish competitors. Harold M. Abrahams, the famous Jewish sprinter who had won the one-hundred-meter dash in the 1924 games, worked effectively to discourage British Jews from boycotting. Six Jews joined the American teams for the 1936 games over the impassioned objections of the American Jewish Congress and other Jewish groups. This number might have been larger had not two Harvard track stars, Milton Green and Norman Cahners, elected to withdraw from the U.S. track-and-field trials at Randall's Island in New York City after discussing Nazi racial policy with their Boston rabbi. Herman Neugrass, a Tulane University sprinter who was considered a likely candidate for the American team, refused on principle to try out for the American squad after learning of the Nuremberg laws. As he told the *New Orleans Times-Picayune*: "I feel it to be my duty to express my unequivocal opinion that this country should not participate in the Olympic contests, if they are held in Germany."

In addition to the above-mentioned French bobsledders who sat out the Garmisch games, a highly respected French fencer, Albert Wolff, withdrew from his country's squad for the Berlin games. Another prominent boycotter from the democratic West was Yisrael "Sammy" Luftspring, Canada's top-ranked lightweight boxer. He told the *Toronto Globe* that it would have been unconscionable for him to compete in a land "that would exterminate [the Jews] if it could."

Perhaps the most prominent boycotters in 1936 were three Jewish swimmers from Austria: Judith Deutsch, Ruth Langer, and Lucie Goldner. Despite growing anti-Semitism in their country, all three had been named to the Austrian team by virtue of their performances in the Austrian national championships. They all quit to protest anti-Jewish persecution in Germany. As Judith Deutsch put the matter in a July 1936 letter to the Federation of Austrian Swimming Clubs:

> I ask that my withdrawal be excused for the following reasons: For me the principles I accepted upon taking the required oath for Olympic training still hold. I cannot as a Jew participate in the Olympic Games in Berlin because my conscience forbids it. I declare that it is my own decision, freely made and unchangeable. The seriousness of this decision

is fully apparent to me because I am aware that I hereby forego the highest sporting distinction—the chance to compete at the Olympic Games. I ask for understanding for my position, and that I not be pressured to act against my conscience.

The Austrian authorities showed no understanding for the position of the swimmers, who were banned from further competitions in Austria and stripped of their records "due to severe damage to Austrian sports" and "gross disregard for the Olympic spirit."

A final resister of conscience worthy of mention is Gustav Felix Flatow, a German Jew who, along with his brother, Alfred, had won five gold medals in gymnastics for Germany at the first modern Olympics in Athens in 1896. Surprisingly Gustav Flatow was invited by Carl Diem to be an honored guest of the GOC at the 1936 games. He refused the invitation. Eight years later, having been arrested by the Germans in occupied Rotterdam, he was deported to the Theresienstadt concentration camp, where he died of starvation. His brother had died in the same camp two years earlier.

Those who chose individually to boycott the 1936 games, and those who fought hard for national boycotts, clearly believed that such action was morally imperative. But, beyond ruining Hitler's party, what would a large-scale boycott have meant for the host country? Here of course we can only speculate, but it seems obvious that it would have amounted to a black eye for the Hitler regime, stamping it as a pariah state. Such a development would have been no small setback for a regime that in its early years depended on foreign policy successes to consolidate its power at home.

We should remember that in 1933–36 the Nazi dictatorship was still a work in progress, despite the Enabling Act and the purge of political opponents. In the last parliamentary elections that Hitler had allowed, those of March 5, 1933, the Nazis, even with all the intimidation they imposed on voters, had not managed an absolute majority, winning 43.9 percent of the total vote Reich-wide and in Berlin only 34.6 percent. The effects of the Great Depression were still very much evident, with unemployment running high. Secret reports compiled by the Nazi Party and regional police documented considerable dissatisfaction in the German population over joblessness and shortages of consumer goods. Many ordinary Germans also worried that Hitler's rearmament program would draw the country into a new war. The Olympic Games were important to the Nazis because by hosting a successful festival the Reich could come across as a peaceful nation that was making economic progress at home and winning respect abroad. By deciding to show up in Berlin despite reservations about Hitler's policies, the world's democracies missed a valuable opportunity to undermine the regime's stature not only in the eyes of the world, but also—and ultimately more important—in the eyes of the Germans themselves.

IV

The Winter Games

▲

▲

WHEN it came time for the twin Bavarian villages of Garmisch and Partenkirchen to host the Fourth Winter Olympic Games in February 1936, the winter athletic festival was still the neglected stepchild of the modern Olympic movement. According to Avery Brundage many Olympic officials, himself included, considered the Winter Olympics a "mistake," since this spectacle lacked any ties to antiquity and, as an outgrowth of the winter sports industry, was highly vulnerable to the abuses of professionalism.

For the Germans, however, the winter festival was of crucial importance, for it provided the opportunity to show off their organizational skills and to dispel any lingering doubts regarding Germany's suitability as the host for the much larger summer festival to come. During the Winter Games the German organizers tested procedures relating to security, crowd control, transportation, hospitality, advertising, and media coverage that would be employed later on in Berlin. For the Garmisch-Partenkirchen region, a patch of beautiful alpine landscape near the Zugspitze (Germany's highest mountain), about sixty miles southwest of Munich, the games could be expected to bring a moment in the international limelight and excellent prospects for future tourism. Hosting this show, however, also entailed a weighty responsibility. "For those of us living near the Olympic sites," wrote one Garmisch booster, "these Games mean nothing less than a great national undertaking, which we have assumed in the interest of our fatherland's reputation and greatness." As with the upcoming Summer Games, the GOC hoped to make the Fourth Winter Games the largest and best organized ever.

"Gapa" Gets the Games

The Fourth Winter Olympic Games were awarded to Garmisch-Partenkirchen by the IOC at the latter's June 1933 meeting in Vienna. This was the same meeting at which the committee confirmed the Summer Games for Berlin, following promises by the German organizers to abide by all Olympic regulations. In giving the winter festival to the same country scheduled to host the Summer Olympics, the IOC was following procedures then in place, but it was not obliged to award the Winter Games to a German site, and in making the award *after* Hitler had come to power, the committee, whether it admitted it or not, was handing the Nazi regime a much-valued endorsement in the crucial early years of its existence.

The GOC had been thinking about the Garmisch area as a site for the Winter Games even before Berlin won the Summer Games. Writing in February 1931, two months before the Summer Games award, Theodor Lewald pleaded with Bavarian Minister-President Heinrich Held to support a Reich financial subsidy for Germany's participation in the 1932 Los Angeles games on grounds that if Germany failed to show up there for lack of funds, Berlin would have no chance of getting the '36 Summer Games, and Garmisch would accordingly be shut out of the winter spectacle. This would be a genuine loss for Bavarian tourism, warned Lewald. After all, as he noted, some three to four thousand visitors had attended the 1928 Winter Games in St. Moritz, a figure that, given the increased interest in winter sports, Garmisch should be able to surpass. Lewald estimated a profit of one million marks for the Garmisch-Partenkirchen area alone, supplemented by an additional windfall for nearby Munich, since most of the games' visitors could also be expected to stop off in the Bavarian capital. "Quite apart from the worldwide recognition redounding to the Bavarian winter sports region," prophesied Lewald, "the advantages to the Bavarian economy would certainly outweigh the relatively small costs accruing to Bavaria in connection with Germany's Olympic bid."

At least initially some key Bavarian officials were unenthusiastic about hosting the Winter Games. In February 1931 the minister for education and culture stated flatly that he did not think revenues from the games would cover their costs (he turned out to be right). If the games did end up in Bavaria, he said, that state should do all in its power to ensure that the Reich government, not the people of Bavaria, footed most of the bill.

The question of funding remained somewhat premature until the venue for the 1936 Summer Games had been definitely established. But even after Berlin had been awarded the summer festival in April 1931, Garmisch-Partenkirchen was not absolutely assured of getting the Winter Games. There remained the outside chance that the IOC, concerned about Depression-ridden Germany's capacity to take on too great an Olympic commitment, might turn again to St. Moritz, which had done a good job with the 1928 games. Nor was it certain, despite Lewald's push for Garmisch, that the GOC would select that site to put before the IOC. Some members of the committee were thought to prefer winter resorts in the Erzgebirge near the German-Czech border or the Harz Mountains in central Germany to Garmisch-Partenkirchen. Apart from regional patriotism, the main reason for this was that the Garmisch region, while undoubtedly blessed with the best terrain in Germany, was not known to be especially hospitable toward outsiders—"outsiders" being defined as anyone who did not live in that little corner of Bavaria. During a GOC discussion in June 1931 regarding an appropriate Winter Games location, concerns were raised that the folks in Garmisch were all too likely to use the Olympics as an occasion to "fleece" foreign visitors. The mayor of Munich, Karl Scharnagl, addressed this delicate issue at a meeting in Berlin with Carl Diem, insisting that he would use his influence to ensure that there would be no gouging in Garmisch. He also promised to roll out the red carpet in Munich. Munich's Chamber of Commerce and Industry joined in the fray, urging the Bavarian government to put its financial and political weight behind Garmisch so as to counter the influence of any anti-Bavarian "Prussians" in the GOC.

In the end the Bavarians' fears proved groundless. Even the Prussians agreed to present the Bavarian site to the IOC as Germany's choice for the 1936 Winter Games. The IOC's decision to give the games to Garmisch-Partenkirchen (or "Gapa," as the place came to be called by cognoscenti after the twin villages were administratively united on January 1, 1935) was unanimous.

Preparations

It was one thing to be awarded the games, quite another to prepare adequately to host them. Because the area lacked up-to-date bobsledding, ski-jumping, and ice-skating facilities, much new construction was necessary. Moreover the building would have to be done quickly given the very short lead time before opening day in February 1936. (Actually, because the organizers hoped to test the Olympic facilities during the 1935 German Winter Sports Championships, the lead time was even shorter.) In view of the amount of needed work, local officials in Garmisch and Partenkirchen made it clear from the outset that they expected substantial financial help from Bavaria and the Reich. Taking up the financial issue in October 1933, the GOC estimated total construction costs at eight to nine hundred thousand reichsmarks, of which three to four hundred thousand might be recouped by ticket sales and other revenues. The committee proposed that the Reich and Bavarian governments immediately put up two hundred thousand reichsmarks each, and that the twin villages raise another two hundred thousand through a bank loan. As it happened, however, Munich and Berlin were so slow to come up with their subsidies that the Organizing Committee for the Fourth Winter Games, which the GOC established to oversee preparations, warned in March 1934 that construction would have to be halted entirely unless more funds were forthcoming.

For the winter festival planners, the situation was all the more vexing, since on Hitler's personal orders, building was already proceeding at full throttle for the Berlin games, with lavish funding from the Reich. Hitler clearly had not taken an equal interest in the Winter Games, no doubt because they did not provide a similarly impressive stage for monumental construction and political theater. In early 1935, after several more appeals from the Winter Games committee, Munich agreed to put up its share of construction costs, but it also insisted that the Reich do the same, warning that a failure in Gapa would cast a pall over Berlin. "The Winter Games in Garmisch-Partenkirchen constitute the curtain-raiser for the German Olympic Year of 1936," wrote a Bavarian official. "The whole world will assess the prospects for a successful Olympic year according to our preparations for the winter event. The German government and the entire German people have a stake in the successful management of the Winter Games." Fearing an embarrassing Alpine debacle, in late 1934 the Reich treasury duly began making regular contributions to the preparations, and when the final accounts were tallied, much to the Bavarians' delight, Berlin ended up paying a little more than one-half the total cost of 2.6 million reichsmarks.

The Winter Games organizers did not intend to pay for the festival solely through government subsidies and ticket sales. With the backing of the IOC, they decided to sell advertising rights to various companies, agreeing to share the profits with Lausanne. This was not the first time in Olympic history that advertising had been allowed, but the Germans granted far more commercial concessions than any of their predecessors, and the German games ended up setting new standards in the marketing of the five rings.

Well before the games opened, billboards blighted the new "Olympic Road" between Munich and Garmisch-Partenkirchen. Among the most prominent of these roadside ads were signs for Coca-Cola, which, as a result of a generous donation to the IOC, became an "official sponsor" of the German games. Coke was already a veteran Olympic advertiser, having begun its association with the games in Amsterdam in 1928. "The Olympic Games and Coca-Cola are kindred spirits, forged through a rich history of continuous support for the noble ideas of the Olympic movement," boasted the Atlanta-based company in later years. In frigid Garmisch, however, the ubiquitous signs commanding *Trink Coca-Cola—Stets Eiskalt!* (Drink Coca-Cola—Always Ice-Cold) may not have been the best marketing concept.

While spectators at the Winter Games would have plenty of opportunity to drink Coke, the "official drink" for the athletes, courtesy of a separate deal with the GOC, was a concoction named *Ovomaltine*, made by a German company called Dr. Wander Pharmaceuticals. Dr. Wander's contract with the GOC allowed his salespeople to take photographs of prominent German athletes drinking his product. Although Peter Le Fort, who handled the negotiations, expressed confidence that *Ovomaltine* would be very popular with athletes, the stuff turned out to be so vile that none of them would drink it.

In yet another money-raising gambit, the organizing committee licensed the manufacture and sale of an "Official Pin of the Fourth Winter Games." When the company producing this pin delivered a supply of them to Jewish-owned stores in the Garmisch area, Le Fort sent the firm a warning stating, "Under no circumstances should Jewish stores be allowed to carry the Olympic pin."

Once construction for the games commenced, it became clear the most difficult and expensive project would be the bobsled run. The outmoded course on Lake Riesser had to be completely rebuilt, with tighter curves, a water-pumping plant, communications and timing equipment, spectator seating, and loudspeakers. Working at a pace befitting a bob run, the builders managed to have the course ready in time for the World Four-Man Bob

Championships in January 1934, which served as a test run for the Olympics. Although some of the drivers had trouble with the tight curves—one sled flew off the course entirely—the competitors and sports journalists gave the new course a hearty thumbs-up.

Work also proceeded rapidly on a towering new ski jump at the foot of Gudiberg Mountain outside Partenkirchen. The new jump made the older one next to it look like a child's slide. An expert from the International Jump Hill Commission certified the facility for trial jumps in January 1934. Eleven jumpers completed three heats with nary a wipeout. With its spacious grandstands, chalet-style Olympia Restaurant, and spectacular setting, the ski stadium was tabbed as the site for the opening and closing ceremonies at the Winter Games.

To accommodate the figure-skating and hockey events, the organizers planned for a new ten-thousand-seat skating rink to go up on a site in Garmisch near the train station. Bringing this project to fruition severely taxed the relations between the two villages, which were competing with each other for the best Olympic venues. Because officials in Garmisch tarried over putting in a new street to the stadium site, organizational secretary Baron Le Fort threatened to shift the skating stadium to Partenkirchen, thus sparking a no-confidence vote in him from the Garmisch town council, which accused him of bias toward Partenkirchen. The no-confidence vote was later rescinded when, following Garmisch's promise to put in the necessary street, Le Fort dropped his threat to shift the stadium location. This spat may seem trivial, but it was emblematic of the extent to which the upcoming games were inspiring a scramble for profit and profile among the locals. As for the stadium itself, a Munich firm rushed it to completion quite efficiently; the facility turned out to be one of the great successes of the games. It still stands today.

Athletic housing required no construction, since, in contrast to the Olympic Village planned for Berlin, the Winter Games competitors were to be quartered in boarding houses and private homes. Proudly the German organizers promised to provide food and lodging to the national teams at the amazingly low cost of only eight reichsmarks a head (about two dollars) per day. Visiting IOC officials, on the other hand, were assured "a most comfortable and agreeable sojourn in the finest hotels." Most of the VIPs ended up staying at the Alpenhof, the region's top hostelry.

Although constructing an advanced winter sports complex in a timely fashion presented a major challenge to the organizing committee, ensuring a congenial and harmonious atmosphere for the athletes and spectators constituted an even tougher one. As we have seen, the GOC was worried about a possible mass fleecing of Olympic visitors. Having alerted local officials to the dangers of price gouging, the German organizers promised the IOC in May 1934 they would ensure "that prices for board and lodging during the Games will not exceed normal levels." This proved an impossible promise to keep. A year later the GOC discovered that one hotel owner in the region was demanding an 80 percent increase over his usual rates for the period of the games. The Olympic Tourist Office of Garmisch-Partenkirchen, which took control over the assignment of lodging for the games, likewise complained that many local innkeepers were setting prices well over the maximum stipulated by the agency.

This problem had to be addressed immediately, warned the tourism officials, since, as everyone knew, there were plenty of anti-German elements around the world looking for reasons to discourage attendance at the "Gapa" games. At Bavaria's request the Reich Commission for Price Control put the full power of the Hitler government behind the effort to hold down lodging prices for the games. Innkeepers and hotel owners who tried to skirt the pricing regulations were threatened with severe penalties. But in the end, not even this threat worked, and many Winter Games guests found themselves paying highly inflated rates for their rooms.

Fortunately for the games' organizers, many of the Olympic guests were expected to stay in Munich rather than in Garmisch-Partenkirchen itself. Having for decades hosted massive bacchanals like the annual Oktoberfest, Munich was used to hoards of visitors and boasted extensive hotel space, much of it reasonably priced. However, since the Winter Games coincided with Munich's Fasching (Carnival) season, there would undoubtedly be pressure on hotel space in the capital as well. Nonetheless Munich's tourist board assured the GOC it would do everything it could to take care of Olympic guests, thereby validating Munich's reputation as "the most hospitable city in Germany."

The expected influx of visitors represented a potential bonanza not only to the Bavarian hospitality industry but also to street vendors, con men, pickpockets, and prostitutes. In an effort to provide a "safe and healthy" environment for the Olympic guests, authorities in Munich and Upper Bavaria rounded up a number of known swindlers, along with a host of "young runaways, beggars and vagabonds." (This precaution seems to have had some effect: During the games about thirty pickpocket incidents were reported each day, a figure the police considered low given the available prey.) Additionally the Bavarian police established a centralized registry of wanted criminals to facilitate the apprehension of such miscreants if they showed their faces during the games. Like the tourism officials, the police felt they had to be especially vigilant because hostile elements abroad were allegedly looking for ways to discredit the Garmisch games. The Bavarian Political Police (BPP) even claimed to have heard that someone belonging to the Committee for Fair Play in Sports in America had suggested, "It would be useful if an American athlete were found stabbed to death in the Alps." Accordingly the BPP urged local authorities to be on the lookout for "anyone making unusual advances toward foreigners," and the agency assigned officers to secure all the competition venues and training facilities against possible sabotage.

Another major worry of the Winter Games organizers was that Olympic visitors might be subjected to open displays of anti-Semitic sentiment, a development that would also provide ammunition to those hoping to reignite the boycott movement against Berlin. There were certainly good reasons for concern on this score. Garmisch-Partenkirchen was known to be a hotbed of anti-Semitism even by National Socialist standards. And just over the mountain was Oberammergau, site of the notorious passion plays depicting the "murder of Christ by the Jews." The Hitler movement had done especially well in the "Gapa" region in the elections leading up to the Nazi seizure of power, and since that time local leaders (both mayors were members of the NSDAP) had committed themselves to making the twin towns "Jew-free." In 1935 Nazi members of the newly merged "Gapa" town council submitted a bill calling for the expulsion of all Jews. The council passed this ordnance but decided to delay putting it into effect until after the Olympic Games. In the meantime local Nazis held a rally calling for vigilance against Jews and townspeople put up signs saying "Jews Not Wanted Here" and "No Jews Allowed." Vending cases containing copies of *Der Stürmer*, a viciously anti-Semitic newspaper, stood prominently on street corners. Finally some local innkeepers let it be known they would not rent rooms to "Jewish visitors" (presumably, anyone the hoteliers thought looked Jewish or who had a Jewish-sounding name), claiming that if they did so they would be kicked out of the Nazi Party.

Carl Diem was appalled by the pronounced anti-Semitic atmosphere in

Garmisch-Partenkirchen during a reconnaissance visit to the area in April 1935. He immediately alerted Ritter von Halt to the problem, warning that if German and foreign Jews were subjected to indignities during the Winter Games, "not only will a shadow fall over the Winter Olympiad but the Summer Olympiad will be endangered as well."

Halt duly made an inspection trip of his own to the region and was shocked to find the place boiling over with anti-Semitic agitation. During his brief stay there a local official made a speech calling for "the disappearance of everything Jewish" from the area and personally threw "a Jewish-looking man" out of the post office. Halt saw anti-Jewish placards and graffiti everywhere.

Fearing like Diem for the fate of the German games, Halt immediately took this matter up with his colleagues in the GOC, only to be told by Tschammer and Secretary of State Hans Pfundtner that they "did not want to hear anything more on the Jewish question." Halt therefore expressed his concerns to Hans Ritter von Lex, the official in the Interior Ministry responsible for the 1936 Winter Games. Halt's letter to Lex deserves extensive quotation, for it shows that while he was genuinely concerned about anti-Semitic displays, he was motivated by tactical considerations, not by doubts about racist dogma:

> The people here have apparently forgotten that Garmisch-Partenkirchen is to be the site of the 1936 Winter Games. All the nations have been invited and all have accepted. [Lewald, Tschammer and I] have explicitly promised the IOC and the leaders of the foreign athletic associations that nothing will be tolerated that might impair participation in the Games by Jewish athletes from other nations. But if the [anti-Jewish] propaganda continues, by 1936 the people of Garmisch-Partenkirchen will be so agitated they're likely to attack and injure any Jewish-looking person they encounter in the street. Thus it might well transpire that Jewish-looking foreigners who aren't even really Jews are mistreated. It might even happen that a Jewish or Jewish-looking member of the foreign press corps is attacked, and [if that transpires] the worst consequences are to be feared. . . . In fact, if the smallest disruption occurs in Garmisch-Partenkirchen, the Olympic Games won't take place in Berlin, since all the nations will retract their registrations. Yesterday the [national Olympic representatives] at an international

conference in Brussels explicitly made this standpoint clear to me. For us Germans, this would represent an incredible loss of prestige, and the Führer would certainly hold accountable those responsible.

Dear Lex, you know my point of view. You know very well that I'm not expressing these concerns in order to help the Jews. My sole concern is with the Olympic idea and the Olympic Games, to which I've devoted all my free time on a voluntary basis for many years. For me it would be the greatest disappointment of my life if, for the above-cited reasons, the Olympic Games were not carried out in Germany. I've expressed my views openly to you here in hopes that you will do all you can to ensure that appropriate steps are mandated by the relevant authorities.

In the same letter Halt informed Lex that he had prevailed upon Friedrich Döhlemann, the financial head of the Winter Games committee, to appeal to Adolf Wagner, the *Gauleiter* (Nazi regional leader) of Munich and Upper Bavaria, to clean up the situation in Garmisch-Partenkirchen. But for months thereafter nothing much happened, obliging Halt to warn Wagner's office that further foot-dragging would cause the Winter Games Organizing Committee to resign en masse. He also threatened to make a personal report to Hitler about the obstructionism in Bavaria.

Halt's threats, which were backed by similar warnings from Interior Minister Frick, got the Bavarians' attention, and Wagner's office promised to take action immediately. Yet even *Gauleiter* Wagner's word seems not to have had much effect, at least not right away. In September 1935, just five months before the Winter Games were set to begin, the responsible Gestapo official informed the BPP about reports in the British press regarding ongoing anti-Jewish actions in Garmisch-Partenkirchen. According to these reports Jews were being expelled from the towns and subjected to constant harassment. Visitors were confronted with signs outside public places saying "Jews Not Allowed Here." The head of the BPP duly dispatched an "urgent" communication to "Gapa": "In light of the upcoming Winter Olympiad I believe that public actions against Jews traveling to the region are inappropriate. Such actions are likely to strengthen calls for a transfer of the 1936 Berlin Olympiad to another metropolis. I therefore implore the responsible agencies of the NSDAP and the populace of Garmisch-Partenkirchen to desist from all actions against Jews, and to remove all [anti-Jewish] signs from public places. I wish also to remind you that the Führer expects total obedience and absolute discipline in this matter."

The reality of the situation, however, was that Hitler had not yet intervened personally in this business, which is perhaps why local Nazis and townsfolk were continuing to behave according to their own lights. This state of affairs did not change until Hitler was forced by none other than Baillet-Latour to make an intervention.

Paying a pregames visit to Munich and Garmisch-Partenkirchen in November 1935, Baillet-Latour encountered numerous anti-Jewish signs on the road between the Bavarian capital and the Alps. He was especially horrified to see that the speed-limit markers on dangerous turns included explicit exemptions for Jews, thereby encouraging them to kill themselves. Concerned that such displays could damage the Olympic image, he arranged for a personal meeting with Hitler to discuss the matter. According to Avery Brundage, who got the story from Baillet-Latour himself, the meeting between the two men proceeded as follows: "After the customary courtesies, President Baillet-Latour said, 'Mr. Chancellor, the signs that greet visitors to the Games are not in conformity with Olympic principles.' Hitler answered with a question, 'Mr. President, when you are invited to a friend's house you don't tell him how to operate, do you?' Baillet-Latour thought a minute and replied: 'Excuse me, Mr. Chancellor, when the five-circled flag is raised over the stadium, it is no longer Germany, it is Olympia and we who are masters.'" Thereupon Hitler promised to give an order to remove the signs. Indeed, citing the Führer's order, on December 3, 1935, Frick demanded the immediate removal of "all signs and posters relating to the Jewish question," as well as the *Stürmer* cases, from public places and roadways in the "Gapa" area. Summing up this development, Brundage wrote: "The IOC was probably the only organization that could have obtained such a concession, another tribute to the power of the Olympic movement."

No doubt Hitler did make this concession to avoid last-minute difficulties with the IOC, but it is important to note that Baillet-Latour never actually threatened the Führer with a loss of the games in case of Germany's noncompliance in the anti-Semitic-sign issue. Describing his meeting with Hitler to the three American IOC members, Baillet-Latour in fact praised the chancellor for his "fine gesture," adding that the IOC had a right to *ask* for concessions of this sort but no authority to *insist* upon them. Baillet-Latour said further that Hitler was now fulfilling all his obligations to the IOC, and that any continued opposition to the German games must be considered purely "political" and therefore not in the best interests of the Olympic movement.

Baillet-Latour was not the only foreign Olympic official concerned about Garmisch-Partenkirchen's unfortunate taste in Olympic decoration. Writing to Le Fort in late December, Charles Sherrill urged him "to carry out the Führer's agreement with Baillet-Latour that those anti-Jew signs in the Garmisch-Partenkirchen parks, etc. be taken down *before* the American team arrives. If not, there is a serious risk that many of the American team will leave, and then Berlin will lose out, and Garmisch will be blamed for that by Berlin!"

In mid-January, as the American team arrived in Garmisch, Baron Le Fort reported to Sherrill that there was no cause for worry: The anti-Semitic signs had been entirely removed, and all foreign guests, regardless of race or creed, would be "looked upon as our friends." But in fact not all the anti-Semitic displays *had* been removed, even at that late date. On January 13, 1936, Franz Ritter von Epp, the *Reichsstaathalter* (Nazi-appointed governor) of Bavaria, conceded that although most of the offending signs within Garmisch-Partenkirchen had come down, the *Stürmer* cases were still abundantly in evidence around the villages, and there were still anti-Semitic signs on the roads leading into the region. The British consulate in Munich could report on January 14 that the German authorities were still wrestling with the *Stürmer* problem, adding: "It is anticipated that when the Olympic Games are over and the visitors have been able thoroughly to satisfy themselves that the stories about Jew-baiting in the foreign press are grossly exaggerated or entirely untrue, the anti-Jewish notices will be replaced." Two weeks later, on the very eve of the games, the Reich Interior Ministry dispatched an urgent letter to the Bavarian Interior Ministry demanding that the sign removal must encompass the entire region and all Olympic sites.

The signs finally came down just as the games opened. The difficulty encountered by the Hitler regime in getting the citizens of "Gapa" to desist, even for a short period, from open displays of anti-Semitic sentiment can serve to remind us of how deeply entrenched racial intolerance was among ordinary Germans in many parts of the Reich. And of course, the British consul in Munich turned out to be right: Once the games were over the anti-Jewish signs returned, along with open anti-Semitic oppression. Martin Bormann, future Nazi party secretary, then deputy to Hitler's secretary, Rudolf Hess, spelled out the Nazi regime's true intentions on this score when he reminded party officials in February 1936 that "the aim of the NSDAP, to shut out Jewry bit by bit from every sphere of life of the German people, remains irremovably fixed."

Anti-Semitic decor was not the only cause for worry as the Olympic teams and guests began arriving in Garmisch. It seems that some of the local SS men were cursing and even assaulting "Jewish-looking" foreigners in the streets, their targets including dark-skinned members of the Spanish delegation. When reprimanded by their superiors for this behavior, the men claimed to have been "provoked" by the visitors. Furthermore, they said they had thought their victims were Jews rather than "ordinary foreigners."

Alarmed by these incidents, the SS command in Munich warned its cadres that they must not be taken in by "foreign provocateurs" trying to bring discredit to Germany. If insulted or otherwise provoked by outsiders, the SS men must turn the other cheek. Actual violations of the law by foreigners should be reported to the local police rather than dealt with on the spot. "Mistreatment of foreign visitors," concluded the SS command, "invariably brings undesirable international complications that are difficult to smooth over." When even the SS inveighed against displays of anti-Semitism, it was clear that the situation had become dire indeed!

FORTUNATELY for the German organizers, none of the local Nazi thugs seems to have attacked any of the large number of foreign journalists pouring into town to cover the Winter Games. The organizers were understandably anxious to make a good impression on the foreign reporters, especially on the Americans, whose verdict was perceived as crucial not just for Garmisch but also for Berlin. Thus the Olympic Press Office was quick to provide additional press passes to the American journalistic contingent, which turned out to be larger than originally stipulated. The Foreign Ministry sent down an official from Berlin whose sole job was to cosset the American scribes.

One American journalist who was accorded a rather different treatment, however, was CBS's man in Berlin, William L. Shirer, who had long been a sharp thorn in Nazi flesh. Commenting on the anti-Semitic signs around Garmisch in early January, Shirer wrote (rightly, of course) that the Nazi authorities wished to remove them only to shield Olympic visitors from "the kind of treatment meted out to Jews in this country." Goebbels was not amused. According to Shirer, a representative of the Propaganda Ministry called him to his office and accused him of writing lies about the condition of German Jews, while a Nazi zealot on German radio denounced him as "a dirty Jew trying to torpedo the Winter Olympic Games at Garmisch with false stories about the Jews and Nazi officials there." (Shirer was not Jewish.)

DURING the last days before the scheduled opening of the games on February 6, everything seemed finally to be in place. Streets and buildings were festooned with Olympic flags, emblems of the participating foreign nations, and swastika banners. By order of the Bavarian police, however, restaurants, pensions, and hotels owned by Jews could not display the German colors during the games. Many residents had touched up the frescoes depicting scenes from Scripture on their homes and barns. Locals also made a point of walking around town in their folkloric finery, replete with feathered hats, bone-buttoned loden coats, and long-stemmed pipes. A complicated traffic plan had been instituted to deal with the expected onslaught of cars and trucks, and additional busses had been brought in to ferry guests from site to site.

There was one crucial ingredient missing, however: snow. As if determined to achieve what the boycott movement had failed to manage—the ruin of Hitler's Olympic party—the weather gods had dropped nothing but rain in the "Gapa" area for several weeks. In order for the skiers to be able to train, fifteen hundred Labor Servicemen had hauled snow from higher elevations to the Olympic slopes, but the thin coverage was not suitable for the actual races. By February 2 the situation looked so grim that Tschammer asked Baillet-Latour for provisional permission to postpone the opening day until February 8, by which time he hoped "true winter weather" might have returned.

But apparently the weather gods were only trying to give Hitler a little scare. Starting on February 5 a blizzard swept in and turned the green hills white. Later, Germans would come to call a stretch of warm sunny days "Hitler weather." This time the "Hitler weather" was full of clouds and snow—enough snow to paint the Führer's mustache white when he arrived in Garmisch for opening day, which did not have to be postponed after all.

Hitler's decision to attend the opening of the games—a decision he had kept putting off—prompted a last-minute scramble of preparatory work by the organizers and Nazi officials. The Führer insisted on "first-class security," and Himmler himself took over the arrangements, delegating their implementation to SS officers Hans Rattenhuber and Sepp Dietrich. Hitler was to travel to "Gapa" from Munich by special train, arriving at the Kainzenbad station close to the ski stadium. Greeted there by Frick, War Minister Werner von Blomberg, Wagner, Tschammer, and local dignitaries, he would then walk to the stadium along a route sealed off in advance by his personal bodyguard, the Leibstandarte Adolf Hitler. The BPP was in charge of searching the area for bombs, monitoring the crowds, and mounting ski patrols in the hills above the stadium. Accredited photographers would be permitted at the train station but could not accompany the Führer on his brief walk to the stadium. By the standards of Hitler's usual security arrangements in the early years of his reign, these measures were particularly stringent. They reflected the Nazi dictatorship's real concern about the possibility of sabotage or assassination at the Winter Games. And they anticipated the even tighter security regime for the Summer Games in Berlin.

A "Fairy Tale" in the Alps

"One doesn't quite know how to describe it. The Olympic world was so beautiful! We swore to be forever thankful that fate had allowed us to be present at this Festival of Olympia, which could not have been more magical had it been a fairy tale."

Thus began Germany's official account of opening day at the Fourth Winter Olympic Games. Given the organizers' Herculean efforts to mask the uglier realities of life under Hitler with an elaborate display of good cheer and open-armed hospitality, a "fairy tale" was in fact what was on offer here. There were not even many Nazi uniforms in evidence around "Gapa" (though this would later change); hoteliers, per instructions from the organizing committee, said "*Grüss Gott*" to guests rather than "*Heil Hitler*"; and every Nazi official held forth on the regime's "love of peace." Echoing the German hosts, Frederick Birchall of the *New York Times* wrote of the opening-day setting: "It comes as near to perfection as could be expected in an imperfect world."

The opening ceremony began, as protocol dictated, with the march into the reviewing area by the athletes and their representatives. The first team to enter was Greece's—accorded this honor as the originator of the Olympic idea. Because the rest of the parade proceeded in alphabetical order (except for the host country, which always came last), Australia followed Greece. This was Australia's first appearance at a Winter Olympiad, its presence a testament to the German organizers' determination to put on a truly global show. Despite having only one entry, a speed skater, Australia hoped to use the Garmisch games to show the world that Down Under wasn't just about swimming, boating, and competitive beer drinking. As the Australian Olympic Federation explained to the GOC: "Australia may be widely perceived as a tropical land, but we have winter sports facilities that are the equal of those in Europe and America." Not far behind Australia came Great Britain. Members of the British team wore black armbands in honor of the recent death of King George V. Next to last came the American team, the third largest contingent after Germany and Austria. Among its ranks were six women.

After entering the reviewing area the teams marched past the ski stadium's restaurant, on whose balcony stood Adolf Hitler, flanked by his top Nazi satraps, IOC dignitaries, and members of the GOC. As was customary, most of the flag bearers dipped their national colors on passing the assembled dignitaries; the two exceptions were Italy and the United States. The Italians made up for this possible slight by raising their right arms to Hitler in a brotherly fascist salute. The Americans, for their part, complained after the opening ceremony that their reception by the crowd "lacked cordiality." Observing this contretemps, the British ambassador to Berlin informed London that the "dissatisfaction in the American camp" had "caused great concern in Berlin," prompting the German Foreign Ministry to send an emissary down to Garmisch "to pacify the Americans, possibly assuming the role of Cheer Leader on the American model."

While the Italians clearly rendered the "Hitler salute" at Garmisch, most of the other national team members opted for the "Olympic greeting," which had been introduced in 1924. This gesture involved holding the right arm forward and horizontal from the body, with palm down. Needless to say, this saluting business was a source of some confusion, for it certainly *looked* as if the athletes of the world were honoring the German Führer with a Nazi salute. Many in the crowd of sixty thousand interpreted the gestures in this fashion, which is why they screamed in delight when the French athletes held out their right arms on passing the reviewing stand.

The only foreign team receiving a louder ovation than the French squad was the large Austrian contingent, whose raised-arm salute was gleefully interpreted as a sign that the Austrians were anxious to "come home to the Reich." (The head of the Austrian delegation insisted later that the gesture in question had been the Olympic greeting.) Some German spectators claimed to have heard members of the Austrian team yell "*Heil Hitler!*," although Austrian officials vehemently denied this as well. Whatever the Austrians may have done on entering the stadium, on leaving it, according to an American reporter, they "unmistakably" gave the Nazi greeting, causing the Führer to gaze wistfully in the direction of his former homeland. "It was a little drama without a word spoken that did not go unnoticed and was a subject of comment later."

Apart from the entry and exit processions of the athletes, the most theatrical moment during the opening ceremony involved the ceremonial lighting of the Olympic flame. The Garmisch games marked the first time this was done at a Winter Olympiad. After the flame had been lit, German ski champion Willy Bogner swore the Olympic oath on behalf of all the assembled athletes. While taking the oath, Bogner held his right arm outstretched and with his left hand touched a swastika banner. Then Hitler officially opened the games with the ritual invocation: "I hereby declare these Fourth Winter Games, held in Garmisch-Partenkirchen, open." It was record brevity for the Führer.

ON opening day, and indeed for the rest of the games, the German press was under strict instructions from Goebbels's office to be upbeat and to avoid mentioning anything that might unsettle foreign visitors or embarrass the hosts. For this reason guests at the games learned nothing from the German press about a tragedy that occurred in Munich just as Hitler was opening the winter festival. It seems that two Luftwaffe training aircraft collided over the city; one of the planes fell into the center of town, killing four people and injuring many more. Police immediately cordoned off the area, and witnesses at the scene were warned to keep silent about the incident on pain of arrest.

The German press received similar cautionary instructions regarding a considerably more explosive story that was unfolding as the games opened. On the night of February 5 a Jewish student named David Frankfurter assassinated a leader of the Nazi movement, Wilhelm Gustloff, in Switzerland. This was not the kind of thing that could easily be hushed up, and the Hitler government had no intention of doing so. Nonetheless the German press was instructed to downplay its coverage of the Gustloff murder, putting it on the second and third pages for the duration of the games. The press gave more prominent coverage to Gustloff's funeral in Schwerin on February 11, attended personally by Hitler, who ordered that a new passenger ship originally scheduled to be named for him instead be christened the *Wilhelm Gustloff*.* Most important, Nazi leaders elected not to demand acts of revenge against the Jews for the Gustloff murder, as they would infamously do in November 1938 following the assassination by a Polish Jew of a Nazi official in Paris—the pretext for the brutal "Kristallnacht" pogrom. As the *New York Times* observed just after the Gustloff murder, "The party authorities are anxious to avoid anti-Jewish excesses, especially during the Olympics."

The IOC was relieved that the opening ceremony had taken place without any major mishaps. At a dinner party hosted by the GOC shortly after the opening, Baillet-Latour thanked Halt and his colleagues for ensuring that "despite some difficulties, the Winter Games have gotten off to an encouraging start. I thank you from the bottom of my heart for managing to prevent the encroachment on these Games of anything that might have demeaned the Olympic spirit."

The Competitions

The Fourth Winter Games boasted more athletes (688) and more events (seventeen) than any previous Winter Olympiad. Most of the competitions proceeded smoothly enough, but, contrary to the image of perfect harmony and efficiency cultivated by the German press, the Garmisch games were hardly without their share of snafus and protests. Indeed, the troubles began even before the games got under way. The bobsledding had to be postponed because of poor conditions on the course. The figure skaters complained about lack of practice space. The skiers lamented the lack of snow.

Most important, the Canadian ice hockey team almost withdrew from the games over the presence on the British team of two top players who, though born in Britain, had spent their entire competitive lives playing in Canada.

---

*On January 30, 1945, the *Wilhelm Gustloff*, crammed with more than ten thousand German refugees fleeing the Red Army onslaught in northeastern Germany, was torpedoed by a Soviet submarine in the icy waters of the Baltic Sea. More than nine thousand people, many of them women and children, perished. In later years the *Wilhelm Gustloff* became a potent symbol in Germany of the tragic fate that befell millions of German refugees and expellees at end of World War II and its immediate aftermath.

Commenting on the fact that Britain had recruited and repatriated the players under the noses of Canadian officials, the president of the Canadian Amateur Hockey Association denounced British hockey as "an unsportsmanlike racket" that lived off the importation of Canadian players. He indicated that Canada might leave the games if the IOC did not declare the two players ineligible. Seeing an opportunity to improve America's hockey prospects at the games, Avery Brundage supported the Canadian protest, declaring that the United States would prefer having to face only "one team from Canada." The British responded indignantly that the makeup of their team was nobody's business but Britain's. The IOC initially took the Canadian side and disqualified the two players. However, the vehemence of the British reaction, which ignited fears of a *British* withdrawal, prompted the officials to reinstate the players. Canada ultimately agreed to suspend its protest for the duration of the games because an early exit would have eliminated any chance for the gold medal the country so confidently expected.

Canada, which had won the gold medal in hockey in every Winter Olympiad so far, looked unbeatable once again as it rolled over Latvia 11–0 in the opening round. The burly American team, regarded as Canada's primary challenger, also advanced to the second round by beating Switzerland 3–0.

As the competitions progressed, the hockey action continued to provide some of the more dramatic and controversial moments of these Fourth Winter Games. During the France-Hungary match a nasty fight broke out between the two teams, and as the players rolled around on the ice one of the Frenchmen bit a Hungarian on the forearm, removing a good bit of flesh. "This raises the question whether hockey is a game really suited to the Latin temperament," commented an American reporter. Additional grounds for this query were provided by an Italian journalist who had to be restrained from throwing his typewriter at a referee who had disallowed an apparent Italian goal against Switzerland. The Italians lost that match, and they also lost to Germany 2–1. The major excitement in the German-Italian match was provided by Rudi Ball, the half-Jewish player whom the Germans had added to their team at the last minute to improve their chances for a medal. Much to the delight of the German fans, who did not seem to mind having a player who was not fully "Aryan" on their team, Ball scored the winning goal. The German press was under strict orders not to mention the race issue when discussing Ball, but some foreign papers made much of the fact that a "Jew" was the best player for the *Herrenvolk*.

Unfortunately for the Germans, Ball was injured in a match against Hungary on February 11 and had to sit out the rest of the games. In their team's next game Germany managed a draw with Britain after three overtimes. This long game was marred by so many brawls that one observer said he was reminded of World War I. That comparison would have been even more apt in regard to Germany's match against Canada, in which the players spent almost as much time whacking each other as they did the puck. Without Ball, Germany did not have much of a chance against Canada, but that did not prevent the German fans from practically rioting every time Germany took a shot on goal. When appeals for calm from the referees proved ineffectual, Göring and Goebbels both took to the microphone and begged the fans to remember that the Canadians were Germany's guests. Canada proved an ungracious guest, trouncing Germany 6–2.

Canada might have gone on to win another hockey gold medal in Garmisch had it not been for those "unsportsmanlike" British, who, it turned out, actually had *six*, not just two, members on their team who had grown up in Canada and learned the game playing in the Canadian amateur league. With these ringers all skating brilliantly, Britain defeated the favored ex-colonials, 2–1. The German crowd, mindful of Canada's threat to leave the games, cheered wildly for the Brits, giving them a roar of *Heils* when they won. By trouncing the Hungarians and also the Czechs, Britain ended the competition with the highest number of points, giving them the only gold medal they have ever won in Olympic ice hockey.

Canada, of course, was livid over the hockey results. Their Olympic officials launched a new protest with the IOC over the decision to award the gold medal on points rather than on a final play-off match between the two top teams. When this protest was rejected they threatened anew to walk out of the games and, for good measure, to cancel a post-Olympic match with Britain in London. In the end they backed off from these threats, but they remained deeply embittered over their treatment in Garmisch.

Alpine skiing, one of the glamour sports of the Winter Games, had, like hockey, been beset by a flurry of protests even before the competition in Garmisch got going. In May 1935 the IOC decreed that professional ski instructors would not be allowed to participate in the Fourth Winter Games because, having been paid to teach skiing, they were not true amateurs. This ruling affected many of the best skiers in the world, especially those from Switzerland and Austria, whose major ski areas already boasted top-notch ski schools. News of the ban inspired a spirited protest from the Swiss and Austrians, who, in hopes of forcing the IOC to relent, petitioned the Fédération International du Ski (FIS) to hold rival World Alpine Ski Championships at exactly the same time as the Olympic Games. The FIS refused to do this, but it did register a protest of its own with the IOC over the ban on ski instructors. Even the Council of Ski Clubs of Great Britain, hardly a hotbed of ski talent, threatened not to enter any British skiers if the instructors were banned.

Despite all the protests the IOC held firm. In response, the men's alpine ski teams from Switzerland and Austria elected to boycott Garmisch en bloc, thereby depriving the competitions of the major stars of the sport. Among those missing was the Austrian skier Heinrich Harrer, a Nazi zealot and SS member whose flight to Tibet from a British prisoner-of-war camp in India in 1944–45 became the subject of a 1997 Hollywood film, *Seven Years in Tibet*, starring Brad Pitt as Harrer. At the Garmisch games, Hitler pledged a gold medal to the first conquerors of the north face of the Eiger, which was ultimately claimed by Harrer and his team. Justifying their decision to boycott the Winter Games, the Austrians pointed to an "overly subtle" distinction that allowed Nordic ski *trainers* from Norway to participate in the Olympics while banning the alpine *instructors*. As for the British, they ultimately did send alpine skiers to Garmisch, but their performance was so poor that insiders questioned the measly four hundred pounds spent on their training.

The absence of the Swiss and Austrian skiers in the men's alpine competition was a boon to the skiers from Germany, who took full advantage of the weaker field. The winner of the men's alpine combined (downhill and slalom) was a carpenter from Berchtesgaden named Franz Pfnür. His first place in the slalom and second place in the downhill gained him the overall title. A devoted Hitler backer, Pfnür became a member of the SS in 1937 and ended up working for the SS Main Office for Matters Concerning Race and Settlement. Another member of the German team, Ludwig "Guzzi" Lantschner, won silver. A native Austrian, Lantschner had been a member of the Nazi Party since 1931 and had become a naturalized German citizen only in January 1936, one month before the games. Between 1930 and 1939 he worked as a cameraman for Leni Riefenstahl.

While talented skiers like Pfnür and Lantschner made the best of the Swiss-Austrian absence, the lone alpine skier from Egypt, Erces Resat, probably did not notice the difference. It took him 22:44.4 minutes to finish the slalom run that Pfnür completed in 4:51:8. One wonders what the poor fellow was doing up there.

The Garmisch games included the first women's alpine competition in Olympic history. In this competition, which consisted of one slalom event, Christl Cranz, a German woman, took the gold. Cranz, who in her long career won fourteen world championships and twenty-four German national titles, was so dominant that the American coach considered her the equal of the best German men. She was certainly similar to them in her politics. A devoted National Socialist, she later gained much attention by donating her skis to the German troops on the Russian front.

As expected, Scandinavians, especially Norwegians and Swedes, starred in the speed skating and Nordic skiing events. The most dominant athlete at the Garmisch games—and indeed one of the greatest competitors in Winter Olympics history—was Norwegian speed skater Ivar Ballangrud. He took gold in the five hundred-, five thousand-, and ten thousand-meter races, slipping (barely) to silver in the fifteen hundred behind his teammate Charles Mathisen. This feat was not surpassed until America's Eric Heiden won five gold medals in 1980.

The diminutive, baby-faced Norwegian Birger Ruud won the special ski jump by a wide margin, starting a trend of little-guy conquests of big hills. Amazingly Ruud also turned in the fastest time in the men's downhill event and would have gotten a gold for that performance had a separate medal been awarded for it (this practice did not begin until 1948). Ruud continued to compete successfully after 1936, but when he refused to enter events during the German occupation of Norway in World War II, the Nazis sent him to a concentration camp.

In Nordic ski racing, Swedes and Finns prevailed over the Norwegians. Eric-August Larsson, a coal miner from Sweden, won the eighteen-kilometer Nordic race. A religious fundamentalist, Larsson gave his medal to his church. A fellow Swede, Elis Wiklund, took gold in the grueling fifty-kilometer race, the Winter Games equivalent to the marathon. Finland won the forty-kilometer Nordic relay due to an incredible performance by Kalle Jalkonen, who on the last leg of the race overcame a huge Norwegian lead to win by six seconds. "Tonight," said one enthusiastic commentator after the race, "[Jalkonen's] name is in every conversation and he has become a public figure."

SOMEONE who had long been a public figure in winter sports was Norwegian figure skater Sonja Henie, and she was by far the best-known competitor in Garmisch-Partenkirchen. Having won golds at St. Moritz and Lake Placid, she reigned as "Queen of the Ice." She also was a queen of fashionable society, frequenting all the right nightspots with her various beaux and even hobnobbing with King Haakon VII of Norway, who regarded her as a national treasure.

It seems that Henie had accumulated considerable treasure of her own via her many skating exhibitions around the world, which called into question her amateur status. In an indignant letter to Avery Brundage, a representative of the United States Figure Skating Association (USFSA) claimed that Henie received "50% of the receipts from the exhibitions she gave in Norway," and that she brazenly went by the title "the Greatest Professional Amateur in Europe."

In passing this letter on to Ulrich Salchow, the president of the International Skating Union, Brundage, a stickler on the issue of amateurism, stated that there was undoubtedly "some truth" to the rumors about Henie's professionalism. However, if the Americans were disturbed by Henie's frequent flouting of the Olympic amateur code, no one else in Garmisch seems to have cared, least of all Adolf Hitler, who made a point of being photographed frequently with the skater. Hitler seemed so smitten with the button-nosed, blond-haired Norwegian beauty that local paparazzi could not help speculate whether the white corsages she habitually wore around Garmisch "came from *him*."

When it eventually came time for Henie to move from the fashion stage to the ice rink she needed more than the Führer's cheers to prevail, for she faced unexpectedly stiff competition from a young English newcomer, Cecilia Colledge. The English girl placed a very close second to Henie in the compulsory school figures, prompting a temper tantrum from Henie, who claimed she had been cheated. Colledge's masterful performance in the free-skating program, which preceded Henie's, caused many in the crowd to wonder if the Norwegian queen might finally be dethroned. Sonja however responded like the pro she was, answering Colledge's spins and leaps with a high-risk double "Axel Paulson" jump that had never been executed before in Olympic competition.* Managing to land on her skates, Henie ended her

---

*Axel Paulson was a legendary Norwegian skater of the late nineteenth century who invented the jump executed by Henie in 1936. In this maneuver the skater vaults forward into the air from one foot, rotates one and a half revolutions, and lands backward on the opposite foot. The jump is now known simply as the axel.

performance with a (voluntary) split and her patented cover-girl smile. As they had done so often before, the judges gave her first place.

This was Henie's last victory as an "amateur." After the Garmisch games she launched a film and ice-show career that earned her a fortune of forty-seven million dollars, some of which she used to amass one of the world's most impressive diamond collections. She immigrated to America in 1937 and became a U.S. citizen in 1941. During World War II she refused entreaties from her former countrymen to contribute financially to the Norwegian resistance fighting the German occupation, an "act of betrayal" for which many Norwegians never forgave her.

ANOTHER crowd-pleasing event at Garmisch was pairs figure skating. As in the women's solo competition, an unexpected duel erupted here, this one between the highly favored German champions, Ernst Baier and Maxi Herber, and an unheralded Austrian pair consisting of teenage siblings Erik and Ilse Pausin. Baier and Herber, who months earlier had supplied a film of their routine to a composer so that their moves could be perfectly synchronized with the musical score, turned in a near-flawless performance. The capacity crowd, however, learned the difference between programmed artistry and genuine spontaneity as soon as the young pair from Austria began their program, which they skated to the accompaniment of (what else?) a Strauss waltz. "In a moment they were off like dragonflies," rhapsodized an American reporter, "skimming over the surface of the ice with the tempo, verve, and abandon that the crowd had been waiting for. The two children went flying through their figures so easily and joyously, spinning and pirouetting furiously from one end of the ice to the other, that they brought the spectators half out of their seats." When, nonetheless, the nine judges ultimately chose to give the gold to Baier and Herber rather than to the Austrian kids, the crowd, though predominantly German, booed and hissed. What made this display all the more noteworthy was the fact that Hitler was in the audience. He registered obvious displeasure with the catcalls, as if reading a political message in them.

AT Lake Placid four years earlier an American couple had taken the silver medal in pairs figure skating, one of the many American medal performances in that home-court Olympics. But on foreign ground in Garmisch the Americans generally proved weaker than the Europeans, much to the dismay of Avery Brundage and the AOC.

One of the few bright spots for the Americans in Garmisch was two-man bobsledding, in which the USA finished first and third. The bobsled course was exceptionally treacherous, its infamous "Bavaria curve" having been the doom of several sledders during practice runs and the early rounds of competition. An Italian driver who failed to negotiate the curve suffered crushed ribs and a broken nose, while a French brakeman had the misfortune of falling off his sled and being dragged for fifty meters, which cost him his leg. Unlike the Europeans, who purchased their sleds from a Swiss maker and drove them more or less as they came from the shop, the Americans drove souped-up rigs built to their own specifications. This did not help the Americans' number one four-man sled, piloted by a daredevil Bronx mortician named (oddly, for a man) Donna Fox. Driving recklessly, Fox injured an arm so badly on his first run that he had to sit out the rest of the games. With a substitute driver, USA number one finished fourth. "I felt terrible to have to let down the Bronx," Fox told reporters. America's chances in the two-man bob competition looked promising because, as one reporter noted, this event featured "rich men from all sides," and the Americans were even richer than the Europeans. The driver of USA number two was Gilbert Colgate, of toothpaste fame. Colgate's sled ended up third behind a Swiss sled piloted by the son of the former president of Switzerland. The gold medal winner was USA number one, driven by a wealthy Adirondack sportsman named Ivan Brown. Brown's winning run provided some balm to injured American pride, but, as the *Times*'s man on the scene archly observed, "the American team isn't expecting to get a brass-band welcome on its return [to the States]. There is a rumor that a quiet entry by way of Quebec is being considered."

PERHAPS the most politically significant competition at Garmisch—military patrol skiing (now the biathlon)—was not even on the official program; it was a "demonstration event." Prior to the games the Norwegian Ministry of Defense turned down Germany's invitation to participate in this event, claiming that such races were not practiced in Norway. This was patently untrue. The real reason for Norway's decision undoubtedly lay in the Oslo Labor government's disinclination to be part of an event that it regarded as militaristic, and that the Hitler regime viewed as a measuring rod of military prowess. The presence of a Norwegian team in Garmisch did not prevent the left-leaning Norwegian government from sanctioning a small "alternative winter Olympics" in Oslo organized by local labor unions. The conservative press in Norway, which had hoped to see the national team shine against rival Scandinavian squads and the Germans, protested the no-show vigorously, as did Norway's envoy to the Winter Games, who left his post in protest. German officials were also angered over Norway's action, which Berlin's ambassador to Oslo rightly attributed to "political grounds." All one can say here is "Hurray for the Norwegians!" Their refusal to take part in the military patrol race turned out to be the only *politically* motivated team boycott in the entire 1936 Winter Olympiad. The Norwegian stance is all the more praiseworthy because Norway had traditionally dominated military patrol skiing and probably would have won in Garmisch. As it happened, *Italy* managed to come out on top. So much for military skiing as an index of military prowess.

THE winner of the unofficial national medal count in the 1936 Winter Games was Norway, with seven gold, five silver, and three bronzes. Germany followed with three golds and three silvers. The Americans and the Canadians were the big losers, America managing only one gold and three bronzes, Canada one lonely silver. Austria, which ended up with one gold medal, one silver medal, and two bronzes, undoubtedly would have done better had its top alpine skiers been in the competition. (Austrian skiers cleaned up at the World Alpine Championships, held eight days later in Innsbruck; revealingly the German winners at Garmisch elected not to show up for that event.) To add insult to Austrian injury, the band at Garmisch played what sounded to many in the crowd like the *German* national anthem when Austria's lone gold medal winner, figure skater Karl Schäfer, received his award. In fact this was not a mistake. Nazi Germany had appropriated the music of Austria's "Emperor Hymn," (based on an old folk song and employed by Haydn in his *Kaiserquartett*), for its own new anthem, "Deutschland, Deutschland über Alles." Soon, of course, Nazi Germany would appropriate Austria as well.

The Social Scene

The modern Olympic Games had from the outset been about more than sports; they were also occasions for rigorous partying and socializing among the world's plutocracy and what was left of its aristocracy. And of course the Olympics afforded the hosts the opportunity to preen before the entire world. The Germans did not intend to miss this opportunity either in Garmisch or Berlin.

Because the Winter Games were act one in Germany's "Olympic Year" drama, the organizers hoped to attract a large and cosmopolitan audience. They were confident that their visitors would come away impressed by what they had seen of the new Germany. As *Gauleiter* Wagner stated prior to the games: "Olympia is a great German undertaking. . . . To Germany will come the entire world, visitors from every corner of the globe, journalists, states-men, etc., [many of whom] will come into contact with National Socialism for the first time in their lives. . . . As they return home, these foreigners will act as propagandists for Adolf Hitler throughout the entire world."

The overall attendance figures for the Garmisch games turned out to be impressive enough: the best estimates put the figure at roughly 650,000 for the eleven-day period. Whatever the exact count was, it was certainly far higher than the measly 14,000 who had showed up at Lake Placid. However, *foreign* attendance fell considerably short of projections; only about 4,400 for-eign guests are estimated to have stayed in Garmisch-Partenkirchen and sur-rounding towns during the games; a few hundred more stayed in Munich. Winter sports, it seems, had not yet attained the global reach they would after World War II. No doubt the foreign gate was also hurt by the fact that the event was held in a fascist-ruled country, though there is no way of knowing how many foreigners chose to stage their own personal boycotts of the games.

Among the thousands of Germans who filled the seats and lined the courses at "Gapa," the vast majority came from the surrounding region—Bavarian day-trippers. Each day the German organizers also brought in by special tram some 59,000 workers belonging to Kraft durch Freude (Strength Through Joy), a Nazi leisure-time organization catering especially to the laboring classes. They were fed en masse in a large wooden shed erected near the train station. One way or another organizers saw to it that the Olympic venues were packed with warm bodies.

The relatively low number of high-paying foreign guests meant that the economic return from the Winter Games was less than hoped. According to the final financial report, total income amounted to 2,415,368 reichsmarks, while expenditures totaled 2,618,259 reichsmarks. The problem of reduced revenue from foreign visitors was compounded by the fact that the Hitler government, in order to give an impression of prosperity, dispatched extra supplies of meat and fat to the "Gapa" region. This ruse required increasing Germany's food imports from abroad, which was very costly. As many other Olympic hosts would later learn, putting on a grand show could amount to running up a significant deficit.

While the organizers failed to bring in large numbers of foreign guests, they did manage to attract a fairly respectable sampling of bluebloods and moneyed globetrotters. One conspicuous absentee in the blueblood department was the new king of England, Edward VIII, who as Prince of Wales had regularly skied at Kitzbühel in Austria and was known to harbor pro-German views. Early on the German organizers had hoped to see the prince grace the Garmisch games, but even before his accession to the throne German planners had concluded it made no sense to invite the future Duke of Windsor because, according to a confidential Foreign Office report, he had had a rotten time during his last season in "Kitz" and was temporarily down on winter sports. In the end the Germans settled for lesser nobility, such as the crown prince of Sweden, the former crown prince of Prussia, and Crown Princess Juliana of the Netherlands, who despite traveling incognito was assigned a bodyguard by the BPP.

Among the VIPs arriving from England were Lord and Lady Londonderry. A cousin of Churchill's and confidant of King Edward VIII, Londonderry was the most prominent figure in the group of English aristocrats who expressed sympathy for Hitler and Nazi policies. He had been secretary of state for air between 1931 and 1935—the first (and ultimately only) Cabinet member openly to back Hitler. Londonderry particularly admired Air Minister Hermann Göring, who was a fellow aviation enthusiast. The British marquess had tried unsuccessfully to meet Göring during his tenure in the Cabinet.

Londonderry's formal invitation to the Garmisch games probably came from Hitler's foreign policy adviser, Joachim von Ribbentrop, a sometime guest at the Londonderrys' elegant Park Lane mansion in London. On their way to the games Londonderry and his wife stopped briefly in Berlin, where Göring hosted a banquet in their honor, using the occasion to urge eternal friendship between the "Nordic" nations of Britain and Germany. Hitler invited the Londonderrys to dinner at the Reich Chancellery. In Garmisch, Göring personally took the couple under his wing, introducing them to Sonja Henie and securing them seats in Hitler's box for the hockey matches. At the games Lord Londonderry was struck by the enthusiasm shown by the German fans for Hitler and Göring every time the Nazi leaders made an appearance.

Lord Londonderry seems to have gotten the message his German hosts intended him to, for in a speech on his return to London he praised the Germans' peaceful intentions, claiming that the last thing they wanted was a military confrontation with France or Britain. These comments caused the *Manchester Guardian* to suggest that it was a very good thing that Londonderry was no longer in the government. Of Londonderry's jaunt to Germany, British diplomat and man of letters Harold Nicolson wrote archly in his diary: "Now I admire Londonderry, in a way, since it's fine to remain [mired in] 1760 in 1936; besides, he is a real gent. But I do deeply disapprove of ex-Cabinet Ministers trotting across to Germany at this moment. It gives the impression of secret negotiations and upsets the French."

Lady Londonderry was equally impressed by what she had witnessed in Garmisch and Berlin. Hitler in particular had entirely bowled her over:

I saw him drive to the opening of the Olympic Games in Garmisch. He went in an open car, he stood, an open target. More than 100,000 people were there to acclaim him. [In fact, of course, he had walked to the opening ceremony, surrounded by bodyguards.] He gave a dinner party for me and my husband at his house in Berlin. I sat next to him. I beheld a man of arresting personality, a man with wonderful, far-seeing eyes. I felt I was in the presence of someone truly great. He is simple, dignified, humble. He is a leader of men.

The Londonderrys, we might add, eventually paid for their fawning over Hitler and the Nazis. Churchill made sure his errant and somewhat dim-witted cousin remained on the political periphery when he took over as prime minister during the war. In a fitting irony German bombs crashed down on the Londonderrys' mansion during the Blitz, reducing it to a "pitiful sight."

Visitors to the Winter Games, whatever their lineage, needed to be kept entertained when they were not attending the competitions. This was not an easy task in "Gapa," which in the mid-1930s did not boast the plethora of après-ski amenities it has today. The area did have a few rustic restaurants and bars, however, where Olympic visitors could drink far into the night because the usual midnight closing hour had been suspended for the duration of the games to enhance revenues. The watering hole of choice for the well-heeled was the bar at the Alpenhof, where Avery Brundage and most of the IOC members stayed. (Incidentally, the owner of the Alpenhof tartly refused a request from Baron Le Fort to create a folksier atmosphere by relaxing his rigid dress standards. He'd be damned, he said, if louts in ski attire would be admitted to dinner in *his* hotel.) As the festival progressed, athletes who had finished with their competitions hit the bars for so-called letdown parties—bouts of sustained drinking designed to make up for the months of privation suffered during training. According to one witness a letdown party for the alpine skiers at the Hochland Restaurant would "long be remembered for its abandon and general joyousness."

Given "Gapa's" limited resources, most of the important socializing, especially involving VIPs, went on up in Munich, a city famous for its well-lubricated conviviality. The town boasted mammoth beer halls like the legendary Hofbräuhaus, a multistory affair where the beer came in one-and-a-half-liter steins. Tschammer hosted a *Bierabend* for journalists and Olympic officials in the Hofbräuhaus's vast Banquet Hall. Because the games coincided with the annual pre-Lenten Fasching, the city decided to lay on a special Carnival with significant "cultural-artistic" dimensions. Also in the interest of supplementing inebriation with edification, the city's vaunted art museums mounted special exhibitions and extended their hours. Munich's opera house was the scene of a special ballet performance titled "The Olympic Rings," with music by Richard Strauss. Five of Germany's most famous ballerinas, dressed in frilly tutus, sought dutifully to capture the spirit of the occasion by entwining themselves with one another in the fashion of the Olympic symbol.

The official reception for the IOC and other prominent personages took place in the Congress Hall of the cavernous German Museum in Munich. This was "the biggest and most representative reception of an illustrious international gathering so far attempted by the Nazi regime," noted one foreign observer. Following a plan worked out well in advance by the GOC, the roughly one thousand guests sat at twenty tables according to rank. Professor Ernst Buchner of the Academy of Applied Art personally handled decorations at the head table. Alfred Walterspiel, owner of the luxury hotel Vier Jahreszeiten, catered the dinner. Between courses a group of singers from the Munich State Opera entertained the diners. As a souvenir of the evening, each guest received a fine porcelain sculpture from the famous Nymphenburg Porcelain Factory. For most of those present the only letdown of the evening was Hitler's failure to show up; he sent Goebbels in his place. Welcoming the guests, Goebbels declared: "It is true that the Olympic Games are not political in spirit or in idea, but this gathering of men and women of all countries sounds a political note in a higher sense. There is afforded here an opportunity for all, beyond all political differences and differentiations, to get to know one another and thus to promote understanding among nations."

Goebbels's oily blandishments by no means reassured everyone in the room. Austria's chief representative in Germany, who worried (with good reason) that the Reich's idea of getting to know Austria was to absorb it, cabled the following cautionary observation to the Foreign Office in Vienna: "As much as one would like to believe the German leaders' constant assurances of peace, one is tempted to say with Faust: 'I hear the message well enough, but I just cannot believe it.'"

Finally Munich was also the site for an elaborate banquet and ball for all the Olympic officials and athletes that took place just after the games ended. In addition to prodigious amounts of food and drink, the guests were treated to various themed entertainments designed to show the Germans' jocular and witty side. Thus, to start the evening, there was a tableau entitled "*Die Meistersinger von Gudiberg. Ein Olympisches Spiel mit Gewitter und 300 Darstellungen,*" followed by a "*Schneeflocken-Ballett.*" As if this were not enough hilarity, at midnight the revelers were subjected to a "*Mitternachtswirbel! (eine Ode an die Weisswurst* [an ode to White Sausage])" and, at 2:00 A.M., a rousing "Can-can for Twelve."

Whether the German efforts to show the Olympic visitors and athletes a good time paid off in positive impressions and happy memories is hard to say with any precision. Foreign journalists managed to interview only a few of the visitors, and the German press's claim that virtually everyone went away full of enthusiasm cannot be taken at face value. In any event the relatively small number of foreign guests (only about five hundred Americans showed up) would have limited the effect of any word-of-mouth propaganda.

Not surprisingly the IOC officials professed complete satisfaction with what had transpired in "Gapa," as did Avery Brundage, who had enjoyed a convivial tête-à-tête with Hitler during his stay. After returning to America, Brundage wrote a glowing assessment of the games to the German ambassador: "The Fourth Winter Olympic Games at Garmisch-Partenkirchen were a huge and unqualified success in every particular. The splendid arrangements, the delightful setting, the brilliant competition, the friendly courtesy and good sportsmanship which one found in Garmisch-Partenkirchen left unforgettable memories. Everyone who witnessed the wonderful spectacle and enjoyed the charming hospitality has a warm spot in his heart for his German hosts."

As for the athletes, despite complaints about this or that snafu or inadequacy, most of them seem to have come away impressed by their hosts' efficiency and courtesy. This is not surprising: The athletes cared almost exclusively about the conditions under which they competed, not about the political and social environment of Nazi Germany. The Norwegian ski jumper Birger Ruud may be taken as a case in point. Sixty years later he could still find nothing bad to say about the Garmisch games (even though, as noted, he had been imprisoned by the Germans during World War II): "We came to participate in sport," he told an interviewer. "Everything else was insignificant to us." Some of the American athletes showed themselves to be not the best of losers: The skaters shouted "Veal, Veal, Veal!" at the owner of the Hotel Hussar in retaliation for having been served Wiener schnitzel night after night, while the hockey team tore up the Hotel Stubl "as a farewell gesture." But in general, according to *Washington Post* reporter Paul Gallico (future author of *The Snow Goose*, *The Poseidon Adventure*, and many other novels and short stories), the Yanks "found the Germans friendly" and the games well run. This was also the verdict of the Gestapo agent who had shadowed the U.S. team. The American athletes, he reported, "displayed little interest in politics," and, despite some quibbles about conditions, "were surprised and touched by the friendliness, order and cleanliness" they found in Germany. According to AOC secretary Fred Rubien, the American athletes he contacted after the games "expressed the view that the Fourth Olympic Winter Games just completed were the nearest approach to fulfilling the ideas of the founders of the modern Olympic Games than any heretofore held."

Reporting and Recording the Winter Games

Of course the German hosts did not rely solely on Olympic visitors to spread the good word about Nazi Germany abroad; they welcomed an unprecedented number of foreign print and broadcast journalists—some five hundred in all. They also commissioned a film about the games for international distribution. With respect to the foreign journalistic coverage, the regime saw in the games "an opportunity to convince the world once again of the will for peace harbored by the German people and their Führer." But the hosts certainly did not take positive coverage for granted. In an ambitious effort to shape the image of Germany coming out of Garmisch, Reich press officials did everything they could short of dictating copy. Foreign journalists were treated like VIPs—provided with state-of-the-art communication facilities, multilingual secretaries, free food and drink, and guides to show them around.

The foreign journalistic accounts of the games often did read or sound like the Nazis themselves had produced them. Frederick Birchall's commentary for the *New York Times* was a case in point. This journalist, who in 1934 had won the Pulitzer Prize for "unbiased reporting on Germany," assured his readers that he found "not the slightest evidence of religious, political or racial prejudice" at the Games. "Anti-Jewish signs have been removed from villages," he reported. "The *Stürmer*, the anti-Semitic newspaper, is being kept out of sight. A Jewish hockey player has even been drafted for the German team. In short, politics is being kept out of a sphere in which it has no place. Only sports count and nobody thinks of anything else." Elsewhere Birchall proposed that the tourists who had been at the games would invariably go home averring that Germany was "the most peace-loving, unmilitaristic, hospitable and tolerant country in Europe." While not going so far as to endorse this Pollyanna assessment himself, Birchall made no effort to look under the surface of the Nazis' "efficient propaganda" to point up the discrepancies between reality and show.

The press office of the Winter Games Organizing Committee put together summaries of the foreign commentary proving, in the words of the chief press officer, "The entire world press agreed that the Fourth Winter Games were a tremendous achievement made possible only because a great statesman stood behind them."

In the end, however, German assertions of a uniformly positive foreign-media response to the Garmisch games were no more valid than their claims of a completely harmonious atmosphere. The notion that "everything worked" in "Gapa" was certainly not endorsed by the Austrian press. "In many respects," complained a reporter from Vienna, "the organization here has failed entirely. No one knows the lay of the land in Garmisch-

Partenkirchen. Peace officers hailing from other parts of Bavaria can provide no reliable information about the local scene, and even the Garmisch folks know nothing about Partenkirchen and vice-versa." The British press bristled with reports about inadequate housing, poor food, and pushy Bavarian day-trippers.

The American press—Birchall's work in the *Times* notwithstanding—offered some of the most critical commentary of all, especially in the latter phase of the festival. As the games drew to a close, *Time* magazine's reporter called attention to a collapse of goodwill: "Last week, long before any significant results had been recorded, a series of major and minor brawls in sad contrast to the gay opening made it clear that, in competitive ill-will, as well as in size, beauty of scene and dignity, the Winter Olympics of 1936 will outclass all their predecessors."

William Shirer, who (as noted) had fallen afoul of the Nazi press bureaucracy even before the games began, found his stay in Garmisch "a more pleasant interlude" than he had expected due to the beautiful scenery, exhilarating mountain air, "bone-breaking" competitions, and "rosy-cheeked girls in their skiing outfits." But in the end Shirer interpreted all the pleasantries as an artful snow job designed to blind foreign guests to the realities of Nazi policy. Alarmed that a group of visiting American businessmen seemed to have been totally taken in by the Nazi blandishments, Shirer invited them to a luncheon in Garmisch with an American embassy official, Douglas Miller, who had been sent down from Berlin by Ambassador William Dodd to set the Americans straight about conditions in Germany. Instead, to Shirer's dismay, the businessmen spent the entire luncheon telling Miller how charming the Nazis were.

During his brief stay in Bavaria, Shirer teamed up with another American correspondent, Westbrook Pegler of the *Chicago Daily News*, in a strenuous effort to reveal the dirt beneath the snow at Garmisch. Describing a Hitler-attended event in the skating rink, Pegler wrote:

Thousands of people were herded this way and that in the snow who had bought tickets or were trying to buy tickets to see the sport event, and thousands were shunted off and away from the enclosure by long cordons of officers, beefy young Nazis in various kinds of uniforms whose only duty was to flatter the house painter who had become the head man of the Third Reich. It was a magnificent display of strong-arm authority wholly corroborating the old tradition that the German people's favorite sport is to be shoved around by men in uniform.

Pegler, a curmudgeon who later became a favorite of America's political right, continued to harp on the theme of militaristic menace behind the Bavarian bonhomie throughout his coverage of the Winter Games. The German organizers were indignant that America's Olympic press corps, which they had pampered so assiduously, could contain a critic like Pegler. Bill Henry, a former *Los Angeles Times* journalist who later became press secretary of the AOC, was also appalled by Pegler's reporting, opining, "It's a shame to have sports written by those who have no understanding." Shortly after the games, Ritter von Halt inquired of the AOC "whether it intends to provide a press pass for the Summer Games to Westbrook Pegler, after he has reported in such a hateful way on the Winter Games." It turned out that the AOC had no intention of approving Pegler for Berlin, but in case he tried to come anyway, Germany's ambassador in Washington instructed all the consuls in America to deny him a visa.

IMAGES of the Winter Games in "Gapa" were also conveyed to the world via a feature-length film, *Jugend der Welt*. Now largely forgotten, the film gained considerable attention at the time. Produced and financed by the Ministry of Propaganda, and directed by a Goebbels favorite, Hans Weidemann, the movie was ultimately shown some 750,000 times in forty countries around the world.

Originally Leni Riefenstahl was supposed to have directed *Jugend*. Riefenstahl was the natural choice for this assignment because she had become Hitler's favorite filmmaker by virtue of her work on *Triumph of the Will*, her brilliant documentary on the 1934 Nuremberg Party Rally. Riefenstahl also had plenty of experience working in the mountains, having acted in Arnold Fanck's alpine movie *Der heilige Berg* (1926) and in 1932 directed and acted in *Das blaue Licht*, another mountain film. Although not a classic Nordic beauty—her dark hair and rather prominent nose fed rumors that she was part Jewish—Riefenstahl exuded a powerful sexuality. Despite being the obvious choice to lead the Winter Games film project, Riefenstahl decided to beg off on the grounds that she was also scheduled to direct the film on the Summer Games in Berlin and could not undertake two Olympic projects in one year. "Besides," she later wrote, "the Summer Olympics [film] was more important to me."

Riefenstahl did, however, drop in at the winter festival in order to develop ideas for her summer project and to be part of the social scene in the Alps. An avid skier herself, she loved to schuss down mountains in her bathing suit. The cover of *Time* for February 17, 1936, has her just so attired, looking like a cross between Christl Cranz and a bathing beauty. Having had no connection with the production of *Jugend der Welt*, Riefenstahl was dismissive of it as a work of serious sports cinematography. Later on she also sought to discredit the film by emphasizing its connection to the Propaganda Ministry (as if her own film, *Olympia,* did not share that same tie). As she wrote in her *Memoirs*: "The Goebbels film on the Winter Games, heavily subsidized by the Ministry of Propaganda, was unsuccessful, even though I had to make available some of my best cameramen, such as Hans Ertl, to Herr Weidemann. Despite some fantastic shots, it was hissed and booed at the Olympic Village when it was first screened to the athletes there in July 1936: which shows how hard it is to make a good sports film, even with the best cameramen and all kinds of technical aids."

Riefenstahl's self-serving dismissal of *Jugend* is unfair. Although a bit kitschy in places, the film, which was edited by Carl Junghans, one of the best in the business, demonstrated precisely the sort of technical virtuosity that Riefenstahl would emulate so famously in *Olympia*. In *Jugend* the political drama of the opening procession was effectively captured by cameramen following the athletes on motorized sleds, careful to frame their outstretched arms against a backdrop of fluttering swastika flags. A camera placed strategically close to the end of the fifty-kilometer ski race mercilessly recorded the pained expressions on the racers' snot-covered faces. Another camera, located above the notorious "Bavaria curve" on the bob run, caught three bone-breaking wrecks in slow motion. Astoundingly Ertl even managed to give viewers a puck's-eye view of the hockey action by affixing a tiny camera to a player's stick in the Canada-Britain match. The film may indeed have elicited some derision in the Olympic Village when it was shown there, but on the whole its reception was quite positive, especially in Germany. Appearing initially on a double bill with the fairy tale *Hans im Glück* at Berlin's Ufa-Palast am Zoo, *Jugend* quickly elbowed *Hans* aside to run for four months on its own.

THE Fourth Olympic Winter Games ended with a nighttime closing ceremony that was even more elaborate than the opening pageantry—and also more ominously militaristic. Hitler returned to bring down the curtain, assisted this time by elements of his new draft army, the Wehrmacht, which was about to march into the Rhineland to remilitarize that region for Germany. Wehrmacht soldiers carrying flaming torches ringed the ski stadium. Artillery salvos reverberated from peak to peak across the valley. Huge searchlights pointing straight up produced the majestic "cathedral of light" effect that Albert Speer had pioneered at the 1934 Nuremberg Party Rally.

Witnessing this impressive but eerie sight, Paul Gallico commented in the *Washington Post*: "Your correspondent could not help but feel the irony of the artillery salutes as fine young kids, border neighbors, stood beneath their gay trooped colors and those horrible guns banged as they will some day bang again with erstwhile Olympic sportsmen on the opposite sidelines dying to each detonation."

On to Berlin

THE success of the Winter Games more or less guaranteed that the Summer Games would go on in Berlin as planned—with a full complement of participants. It would have been rather awkward for a nation that had gone to Garmisch to bow out of Berlin, whatever the Germans' fears in this regard. Yet Hitler's Germany did not suddenly become a model international citizen in order to waylay any possible last-minute reservations about participation in the Berlin games. In March 1936 Hitler remilitarized the Rhineland in violation of the Versailles treaty, and in July he began assisting General Franco's rebellion against the Spanish government. At home the Nazi regime continued to harass and persecute Jews in an effort to force them out of the country.

With respect to the impending Berlin Olympiad, the period between the Winter and Summer Games saw the rush to completion of the largest building program to date in Olympic history. This was also the time when the GOC put on a final push to advertise the games at home and abroad. In addition to the Olympic torch relay, the organizers conceived a host of promotional ventures whose ambitious scope was unprecedented in the history of the modern games.

"He Who Dares Nothing Wins Nothing!"

Hitler had not confined himself to welcoming the world to Garmisch on the opening day of the Winter Games. He also held secret discussions with his military entourage regarding his plan to remilitarize the Rhineland, a key part of his broader campaign to throw off the "yoke of Versailles." He was obviously not troubled by the fact that he was preparing a military stroke against a backdrop of peaceful athletic competition and invocations of international harmony. Indeed, if his guests were lulled into complacency by the talk of Olympic peace, so much the better.

While the opening of the Winter Games provided ideal camouflage for a discussion about remilitarizing the Rhineland, this was by no means the first time the matter had been mooted by Hitler and his aides. The Nazi leader considered the 1919 peace settlement's prohibition on German fortifications and troop installations in the Rhineland intolerable. Once Hitler achieved power, the question was not *if* this restriction would be cast aside, but *when*. The issue of timing was crucial because sending troops into the Rhineland was akin to sticking a bayonet into the heart of the European security system; even a risk taker like Hitler understood that a strike of this sort needed to be executed at the proper moment. He had raised the matter with his military advisers in 1934 and again in 1935. The military men had counseled caution. Most German diplomats had also advised against precipitous action, insisting that Germany wait at least until after the Summer Olympics. But Hitler was getting impatient. The longer he waited, he believed, the more likely it would be that his adversaries would resist his strike.

Benito Mussolini, that other restless tyrant in search of a grander role on the world stage, made it easier for Hitler to move in the Rhineland by launching his invasion of Ethiopia in 1935. Before his push to become a new Caesar in Africa, Mussolini had placed himself among the opponents of Germany's campaign to revise Versailles, seeing this as a threat to Italy's post–World War I absorption of the ethnically German South Tyrol, which previously had been part of the Austro-Hungarian Empire. But the African adventure, which occasioned sanctions against Italy on the part of the League of Nations, alienated Mussolini from his Western partners, driving him toward his "brutal friendship" with Hitler. Italy's departure from the German-containment equation meant that if Hitler were to remilitarize the Rhineland he need not worry about a two-front opposition; he would have to face only France (Britain, he was pretty sure, would not intervene). And, in contrast to some of his timorous generals, Hitler was confident that France would not parry his strike with a military response of its own. Contemplating the Rhineland move while he watched France's Olympic team parade before him in

Garmisch, he apparently concluded that if he struck soon he might strike with impunity.

Still, Hitler did not come to a final decision on the Rhineland action until two weeks after the Winter Games. Obviously he could not move *while* the Garmisch games were going on; this would have been too brazen even for him. Moreover, he was continuing to receive cautious advice from most of his top aides, including Goebbels, who believed that Germany should not move until France had ratified a new friendship pact with Russia, which would give the Reich a diplomatic pretext for action. Yet Goebbels, as always, swung firmly behind his Führer when, on March 1, Hitler announced that he was ready to strike. "It's another critical moment, but now is the time for action," Goebbels wrote in his diary. "Fortune favors the brave! He who dares nothing wins nothing!"

The date for the Rhineland action was set for March 7. As far as the Olympics issue was concerned, although March 7 was less than four months before the Summer Games were scheduled to open, the Nazi leadership clearly hoped that this was enough time for any indignation over the action to subside.

Hitler did not publicly announce his Rhineland decision until his troops were already moving into the region. On the evening of March 7 he went before his rubber-stamp Reichstag to inform the delegates, and with them the world, about the Rhineland operation. This news came as more of a shock to the Germans than to the Western powers, whose agents in Germany had been warning for some time that such a drive could be expected. Recovering from their shock, the brown-shirted parliamentarians leaped up in unison and thrust out their right arms to their Führer.

Having detonated his bombshell, Hitler was quick to reaffirm his peaceful intentions, offering France a non-aggression pact. He also included the Olympic Games in his arsenal of rhetorical reassurance: "During the Winter Games," he said, "I disallowed any expressions of hatred against France in the German press. I tried, certainly not without success, to instill in our youth an understanding for reconciliation. A few weeks ago, when our French guests paraded into the Olympic stadium, they were able to see that the German people had undergone an internal transformation in their thinking. This inner willingness to search for reconciliation is certainly more important than the calculated attempts by statesmen to envelop the world in legal nets and impenetrable pacts."

Hitler was correct in predicting a flabby response from France—and from France's allies. Believing that the French army was incapable on its own of forcing a German withdrawal, Gen. Maurice Gamelin insisted on asking the British for assistance. Britain, as Berlin sensed, had no intention of joining France in a military move against the Reich over the Rhineland, which many Britons believed Germany had every right to remilitarize. Britain's unwillingness to be part of any retaliatory campaign against Germany gave Gamelin the pretext he needed to advise the weak caretaker government then in power in Paris to take no military action. France contented itself with a diplomatic protest.

If Germany's remilitarization of the Rhineland did not prompt a retaliatory move from the French military, it did reignite that country's Olympic boycott debate, which had seemed moribund in light of France's participation in the Winter Games. In order to send a team to Berlin, France's Olympic committee required an additional subsidy of 1.8 million francs from the government, which still had not approved the grant when the Rhineland crisis occurred. Now, in the view of the proboycott forces, there was more reason than ever to shun the Berlin games. Germany's aggressive action in the Rhineland, they said, put the Reich's pacifistic rhetoric in Garmisch in a new light, revealing the insidious manner in which Hitler had exploited the Olympic ideals. Writing in *L'Intransigeant*, Claude Farrère, a member of the Académie Française, argued the Germans had used the Winter Games as a cover to hide their aggressive intentions in the Rhineland. Furthermore, he said, the French team's warm welcome at Garmisch had been designed to lull France into complacency. Now, he said, by staying away from Berlin, France could avoid being drawn into another deceptive maneuver that might mask even more ominous intentions. The influential newspaper *Paris Soir*, meanwhile, editorialized that a boycott of Berlin would constitute an effective economic sanction against Germany as well as a salutary diplomatic slap in the face.

In early May 1936, shortly after the Rhineland humiliation, France embarked on its experiment with a Popular Front government, which was elected in response to the threat from Nazi Germany and with the promise of far-reaching socioeconomic reforms at home. The advent of this new regime, led by the Socialist Léon Blum, gave additional hope to the boycott faction, which now stepped up its agitation for a rejection of the government subsidy for the Berlin games. *L'Humanité* and *Le Populaire*, the chief Communist and

Socialist organs respectively, editorialized passionately on the necessity of a firm French *non* to Berlin. In addition to citing the usual political arguments, *Le Populaire* opined that the team France planned to send to Berlin was so weak that its presence there would undoubtedly constitute a source of national embarrassment.

On June 6–7, 1936, the Committee for the Defense of the Olympic Idea sponsored an international gathering in Paris to bring further pressure on the Blum government. The keynote speaker was the German novelist Heinrich Mann (Thomas Mann's older brother), who had fled Germany for France in 1933. Mann accused the Western democracies of acting against their better judgment in supporting the 1936 games. "People know what the Nazi state is, and yet they are still going to the Olympics," he complained. Nonetheless this perversity could still be arrested at the last moment. "Working-class parties can in some countries confront left-bourgeois parties with the choice: Olympics or Popular Front. He who goes to Berlin deserts the Popular Front! Anti-Fascists, stand up and act! World public, protect the Olympic ideal!"

Preoccupied with a wave of strikes and factory occupations designed to force an implementation of the promised social reforms, Blum's fledgling Popular Front government did not take up the Olympics issue until June 19. Contrary to Heinrich Mann's hope, Blum and the Socialists did not confront their bourgeois allies with the choice of going to Berlin or leaving the Popular Front. To do so, Blum knew, would certainly alienate the middle-class Radicals in his coalition government. Such a confrontation would also, he further knew, add grist to the mills of the country's anti-Semitic Right, who already accused the Jewish premier of being part of an international Semitic conspiracy against the true France. Moreover, according to the British ambassador in Berlin, Blum was under pressure from his ambassador to Germany not to risk a boycott on grounds that such a step "would mean the end of any cooperation between France and Germany." France's man in Berlin further believed that a boycott, if exercised solely by France, would be "futile," not to mention a boost to the Soviet Union, which in his view was the secret guiding force behind the whole boycott effort.

Unwilling to risk a rift with Germany, and determined to keep the bourgeois Left in his coalition, Blum settled for a compromise solution on the Olympics issue that pleased no one. With parliamentary backing the government budgeted 1.1 million francs to support the French contingent in Berlin (significantly less than the French Olympic Committee had asked for), while setting aside six hundred thousand francs to support France's participation in the planned alternative games in Barcelona. Blum drew harsh criticism from the Right and from France's Olympic community for skimping on the Berlin team, while the leftist press protested that France would now be going to Berlin with a team more generously supported than the "peace-loving" athletes bound for Barcelona.

France's example had a strong impact on Spain, another country with a newly minted Popular Front government. On May 4, 1936, a delegation of leftist workers presented Premier Manuel Anzaña with a petition calling for the withdrawal of a four-hundred-thousand-peseta subsidy that the preceding government had granted the Spanish Olympic Committee for participation in the Berlin games. Anzaña replied that although he personally opposed sending a team to Berlin, he was obliged to respect Spain's international obligations and follow the lead of other democratic countries, most notably France. In fact, like Blum, Anzaña feared the wrath of the Right if he pulled the plug on Spain's trip to Berlin. Thus democratic Spain was fully intending to be part of the Nazi Games when the Spanish civil war broke out in July 1936. It was the chaos engendered by this brutal conflict, not a principled boycott decision on the part of the beleaguered Spanish government, which ultimately forced Spain to become the only nation invited to Berlin that actually did not send a team.

Building Olympia in Berlin

When Hitler first toured Berlin's prospective Olympic site on October 5, 1933, he made clear that he wanted a completely new stadium and adjoining sports complex rather than a mere renovation of the existing facilities, as the GOC had originally proposed. At subsequent meetings in December 1933 with Lewald, Tschammer, Goebbels, Frick, and the architects Werner and Walter March, Hitler held forth at length on the kind of facilities Germany needed to build and on why a uniquely impressive performance in this domain was imperative. "Germany finds itself in a difficult and unfavorable foreign-political situation and therefore must try to win world opinion to its side through great cultural accomplishments," he said. Germany, he went on, must be like Mussolini's Italy, a country to which people traveled not only to admire the great works of the past but also to see what the new order had achieved. When Lewald pointed out that Rome had bid for the 1940 games and that, if the bid was successful, Mussolini intended to build a stadium capable of holding 150,000 people, Hitler, his competitive juices stirred, declared that Germany would set a standard even the Duce could not match: a stadium of massive proportions covered in natural stone or marble—none of that dreary "gray cement" the Italians were so fond of. In addition to the new stadium, Hitler proposed a vast parade ground, where five hundred thousand people could gather for assemblies and military reviews. He also demanded an open-air theater modeled on those of ancient Greece, but of course much bigger. After checking off these imperatives Hitler asked Lewald if he knew of any place in the world possessing such a complex. Lewald said no, adding that he had not seen anything like this even in America. Pleased to learn he would be charting new territory, Hitler acknowledged that an undertaking of this magnitude could not be done on the cheap: Perhaps twenty million marks would be required. Such an expenditure, however, was "absolutely necessary in light of the impression this creation will make on the rest of the world." By way of further justifying the investment, Hitler noted that in recent years Germany had spent twenty million marks a year on unemployment support, an outlay that the Olympic building program could reduce by putting thousands of people to work. "That prospect fills me with special joy," he declared.

In October 1933 Hitler assigned the primary architectural work on the Olympic complex to Werner March, who was instructed to report directly to the Führer and to Interior Minister Frick—the Interior Ministry being the Olympic *Bauherr* (general contractor).

In some ways it is odd that March got the assignment to design what was by far Nazi Germany's largest construction project to date. He had not joined the NSDAP until July 1933, taking this step mainly for career reasons. Although he had excellent professional credentials he was not known to favor architectural grandiosity, and the modesty of his first designs for the Olympic complex made them unacceptable to the Führer. In the end March bent to Hitler's wishes and built big, but not quite as big as Hitler would have wished. The stadium as finally constructed turned out to be about the same size as the Los Angeles Memorial Coliseum, and the adjoining parade ground, the "May Field," could hold only 250,000 people rather than the 500,000 Hitler had wanted.

March's plan for what came to be called the Reichssportfeld echoed ancient

Greek and Roman models of athletic architecture. The stadium recalled the classical arena or coliseum; the parade field harked back to the forum; the Reich Academy suggested the Greek gymnasium. As a student of modern architectural practices, however, March initially sought to realize this conception by using the latest materials and techniques. For the stadium he favored a steel, glass, and cement structure with unadorned exterior walls—about as un-Greek as you could get.

Hitler was livid when he learned what March was up to during a tour of the building site on October 31, 1934. He reportedly said that he would sooner cancel the Olympic Games than have them take place in "a modern glass box" of the type March envisioned. At a hastily called meeting with the architect and other officials, Hitler insisted that the building be dressed in natural stone and that the columns ringing the structure be widened to convey a greater sense of power. March drew up new plans conforming to the Führer's wishes. But now Hitler was sufficiently mistrustful of March that he called in his favorite architectural *Wunderkind*, Albert Speer, to consult on the Olympic project. Speer quickly drew up a sketch showing how a more powerful feel could be obtained by adding massive cornices, and how the steel skeleton could be clad in limestone. This was a favored building material in the Third Reich because it connoted rootedness in the native soil, durability, strength, and power—the ideals of the Nazi worldview.

The construction went ahead with extensive use of limestone from Germany's own quarries. The decision to go with this material, however, occasioned a new problem: There was not enough limestone available for the plethora of Nazi building projects requiring the use of this patriotic stone. The biggest competitor was Speer's own Nuremberg Party Grounds project, which was going up at the same time. Because the Olympics complex absolutely had to be ready by summer 1936, March's project received precedence over Speer's in the allocation of resources. Speer may have wished that he had kept his mouth shut about using limestone to build Olympia in Berlin.

The Reichssportfeld also had priority over all other projects in the allocation of labor; even the Autobahn took a backseat. But the need for large numbers of workers—some 2,600 on the stadium alone—did not mean that just anybody could find a job on the Olympics projects. The regime insisted that only German citizens of Aryan background be employed; furthermore no one who had been involved in a strike or shown anti-Nazi tendencies could be hired. Tschammer recommended that, whenever possible, firms give Olympics work to down-on-their-luck former athletes. When it was revealed that Werner March had brought in a Hungarian Jew to work as a statistician, Hans Pfundtner insisted that the man be fired forthwith.

Because time was of the essence, work went forward at a breakneck pace on the Reichssportfeld and other Olympics venues. There were many accidents at the various building sites around Berlin. On August 20, 1935, nineteen laborers were killed by a cave-in at an excavation site near the Brandenburg Gate for the expansion of the North-South Railway, one of the Olympics projects. It turned out that in order to meet its deadline there the construction company had tunneled too close to the surface and ignored elementary safety procedures.

Despite the frantic pace, work on the Reichssportfeld fell behind schedule. Warning in late 1934 that a failure to complete the Olympics construction on time would constitute "a humiliation of National Socialist Germany in the eyes of the entire world," Pfundtner ordered that any firm failing to keep pace be replaced immediately by one that could do the job on time. However, since not all laggards could be replaced without disrupting production, the Interior Ministry eventually contented itself with imposing fines of one thousand reichsmarks a day on companies not meeting their deadlines.

The rapid pace and ambitious scope naturally brought an escalation of costs. In the end, Hitler's projected twenty million marks for all Olympics construction proved far too modest. By June 1934 it was apparent that an initial governmental outlay of eight million marks for the stadium and 6.5 for the surrounding sports forum would be woefully insufficient. Pfundtner initially tried to cope with the looming deficit by calling on German corporate leaders to make private contributions. The first to do so was Gustav Krupp von Bohlen und Halbach, who had helped to finance the first "Olympic" stadium in Berlin back in 1916. Krupp's 550,000-mark donation inspired Pfundtner to establish an "Olympics Fund of German Industry," designed to squeeze additional donations from the Reich's largest firms. How much the corporations actually kicked in remains unclear, but the amount was certainly insufficient to meet the rising costs. In the end, the organizers had to cover the deficit by diverting some 7.5 million marks from a fund designated for the construction of air-raid shelters in Berlin.

So how much, finally, did the Berlin Olympics construction cost? We know from surviving records that the stadium alone cost at least 27 million marks, and that several more millions went into other Reichssportfeld structures, but we cannot state precisely the total price for all the Olympics-related building in Berlin because ancillary projects like street and transportation improvements were not included in the Olympics spending reports. Estimates place the total cost of hosting the games at more than 100 million marks, certainly a record to date. (Hitler boasted during a series of World War II informal conversations with his aides and hangers-on (later published as "Table Talks") that the stadium itself had cost 77 million marks to build, but this was just another case of the Führer sounding off to his cronies.) The city of Berlin, financially weak then as now, needed support from the Reich government to pay for all its Olympics upgrades. Once again, Reich officials insisted that the extra expenditure was fully justified because the Olympics provided "a unique opportunity to showcase before the entire world National Socialist Germany's will and capacity to build."

As the Olympics facilities were going up Nazi officials argued among themselves over how the various structures should be officially designated. Hoping to highlight the Germanic and Nazi dimensions of the Berlin games, Frick proposed the stadium be named Die Deutsche Kampfbahn (the German Stadium); he further suggested that the bell tower rising above the May Field be called Der Führerturm (Führer Tower) and the entire complex carry the name Adolf-Hitler-Feld (Adolf Hitler Field). Hitler himself vetoed the Nazi nomenclature, opting instead for the more neutral Olympia-Stadion, Glockenturm, and Reichssportfeld, respectively. He also endorsed naming the south side of the stadium Coubertin-Platz. The Führer agreed, however, that the open-air theater be christened Dietrich-Eckart-Bühne in honor of the poet-publisher who had helped the Nazis in their early years of struggle. An exhibition hall beneath the bell tower was designated Langemarckhalle in tribute to a group of German students who, according to patriotic legend, had joyfully sacrificed their lives for the fatherland at the Battle of Langemarck in 1914.

If Nazi mythos was only partially evident in the Olympics venues' nomenclature, it was certainly obvious in the artistic decoration of the buildings and grounds at the Reichssportfeld. All the entries in the Reich-wide competition through which the freestanding sculptural pieces and reliefs were chosen went through an arts committee chaired by Hans Pfundtner. Not surprisingly the winning designs came from artists close to the regime: Georg Kolbe, Arno Breker, Josef Thorak, Willy Meller, and Joseph Wackerle. Pfundtner's committee carefully vetted each piece, suggesting "improvements" here and there.

Thus, regarding Kolbe's *Resting Athlete*, it advised: "The positioning of the crossed legs should not be conceived in such a loose and easy fashion." Wackerle was advised to make the raiment covering his *Horse Rider* hang in "simpler and more disciplined folds." Overall the dominant aesthetic emerging here was one of heroic monumentalism: big, blocky, stilted knockoffs of ancient athletic statuary. A prime case in point was Breker's *Zehnkämpfer* (Decathlete). A tour de force of bulging muscles and straining tendons, this piece referenced Myron's *Discus Thrower* but had none of that work's classical balance or restraint; it was pure "Aryan man," an icon of buffed-up brutality. Revealingly, when Hitler saw the *Zehnkämpfer* in preparation he declared to the artist, "Henceforth you work only for me." And in fact Breker went on to become the Führer's private Michelangelo.

The target date for the completion of the Reichssportfeld complex was April 1, 1936, but by mid-1935 it had become clear that the harried contractors would not be able to meet this deadline even by instituting around-the-clock shifts. In July 1935 Frick ordered that guided tours of the building site be stopped because they were delaying work. The regime had to call off a dedication ceremony scheduled for May 1, 1936, because even then the facilities were not yet ready. Finally, in mid-July 1936, just two weeks before opening day, Werner March pronounced the project complete.

IN addition to building the largest and most technically advanced competitive facilities in Olympic history, the Germans were also determined to set a new standard in athletic housing for the games. Here the relevant precedent was the Los Angeles games of 1932, which had provided an elaborate "Olympic Village" for male athletes. (There had been a "village" for athletes at the Paris games of 1924, but it was a rudimentary affair.) The German organizers decided to emulate the Los Angeles example, while of course improving on it in every way. (Berlin's Olympic Village included on its grounds a model of one of the LA dwellings, so the athletes could see for themselves just how superior their German-built quarters were.)

The Olympic Village for the Berlin games was situated in the town of Döberitz, some fourteen kilometers west of the Reichssportfeld. This town was known primarily for its sprawling army base, the launching point in March 1920 of the so-called Kapp Putsch, in which a group of military rebels had tried to overthrow the young Weimar Republic. Döberitz remained a hive of military activity under the Nazis, and it was in fact the Wehrmacht that built the Olympic Village on the edge of the existing military base. The military was also responsible for the village's administration. As soon as the games were over, the army reclaimed the complex.

Given the army's role here, it is not surprising that the village had a certain martial feel about it, although the builders took considerable pains to produce an attractive and comfortable environment for the athletes. The complex consisted of 142 residences, plus a few larger buildings for dining, training, and recreation. The residences, partitioned into two-man sleeping quarters each with a shower, washbasin, and toilet, could accommodate between sixteen and twenty-four men. Each of the dwellings bore the name of a German city. Revealingly, one of the "German" cities so honored was Danzig, which the Versailles treaty had constituted a "Free City" so that Poland might have an outlet to the sea. The Australians, much to their amusement, ended up in a house named "Worms." The GOC commissioned art students from all over Germany to decorate the interior walls of the houses with frescoes depicting landmarks of the cities for which they were named.

Because the athletes were to be sequestered in the village when not competing, the organizers tried to provide for every need. The complex had its own cinema, shops, full-size gymnasium, running track, soccer field, swimming pool, and even a rustic Finnish sauna. Athletes were treated—if that is the right word—to variety shows and daily open-air concerts by an army band. Tellingly the movie fare included a film illustrating the value of sport in war. Located as it was in a bucolic birch forest dotted with lakes and ponds, the village boasted a resident population of rabbits, squirrels, deer, and waterfowl, to which the army added a flock of exotic decorative ducks. (The Australian team brought as their mascot a frisky kangaroo, making the menagerie even more exotic). A year prior to the games army chemists eradicated all the mosquitoes in the vicinity by spraying every lake and pond.

Unlike the Reichssportfeld, the Olympic Village was completed well before the games were set to begin, which enabled the Wehrmacht to use it for some quite un-Olympic purposes. The largest of the lakes, it turns out, briefly served as a secret underwater-warfare-training center. As the athletes began to arrive they noticed busloads of men in civilian clothes hastily departing. The "civilians" in question were members of the Condor Legion, a secret air force unit that had been living and training in the village prior to decamping for the Spanish civil war.

One other episode relating to the Wehrmacht's role in building and administering the Olympic Village needs mention here. The officer in charge of running the complex, Capt. Wolfgang Fürstner, was suddenly dismissed from his post a few weeks before the games opened. Another officer, Col. Werner von und zu Gilsa, replaced him. The reason for Fürstner's dismissal, though this was never officially admitted, was the discovery by Nazi officials that he was half Jewish. To avoid a scandal Fürstner was allowed to stay on as an assistant to Gilsa, which he loyally did for the duration of the games. However, on August 18, 1936, rather than attend an Olympic farewell dinner, Fürstner stayed home and put a bullet through his head. German newspapers announced that the officer had died in an automobile accident, but the American press got wind of the true circumstances surrounding the case and reported extensively on the suicide.

Not all the male athletes stayed at the Olympic Village out in Döberitz. Because the rowing events were scheduled to take place in Grünau, in the far southeastern corner of Berlin, the rowers bunked at an old castle in nearby Köpenick. (The men competing in the yachting events up in Kiel were quartered in private homes in that area.)

As for the female competitors, they ended up in quarters significantly less desirable than those for the men. In Los Angeles the women had been put up in one of the city's better hotels, but in Berlin they had to settle for a Spartan dormitory, Friesenhaus, that normally housed students of the Reich Sports Academy. The dorm was adjacent to the Reichssportfeld, which allowed the women to train at the Olympic facility without having to commute through the city. This arrangement allowed the athletes' German minders to keep a close eye on them. The chief chaperone was Baroness Johanna von Wangenheim, a stout Prussian martinet who proved completely insensitive to any complaints about the living conditions. With its tiny rooms and inadequate sanitary facilities, Friesenhaus became a source of many complaints by the female athletes, especially the Americans.

Construction for the 1936 games was not limited to the facilities specifically designated for Olympics use. As is now almost de rigueur for Olympics venues, large-scale infrastructural improvements affecting the entire city accompanied the buildup for the Berlin games. A new subway line to the Reichssportfeld was installed, along with a special "Olympia Station." To ease rail transportation through Berlin, the expansion of the North-South Railway was rushed to completion. The new rail line was conceived as the first step in a vast makeover of the city that, according to the Nazi grand plan, would transform Berlin into "Germania," capital of the world.

Building the rail line necessitated, among other demolition measures, cutting down all the linden trees on Unter den Linden, Berlin's most famous avenue. Although the trees were subsequently replanted, at the time of the games flagpoles and light stanchions rather than leafy lindens dominated the street. Berliners joked that the avenue should be renamed "*Unter den Laternen.*" Unter den Linden formed the main eastern extension of the so-called Via Triumphalis, a ten-mile route running from Alexanderplatz in the east to the Reichssportfeld in the west. Like the Linden, the central and western parts of the route sported flagpoles every few meters, many of them topped with swastika banners. Businesses and residences along the route also put up flags, although, as in Garmisch, Jews were prohibited from flying the Reich colors anywhere in the city. Jewish-owned stores could fly the colorful Olympic pennant-chains sold in local stores only if they removed the tiny swastika flags.

In addition to the large-scale construction projects, the regime undertook a number of smaller beautification measures designed to impress visitors to the games. The Bahnhof am Zoo, where most of the foreign visitors would arrive, was refurbished to look more welcoming. Private homes along the main arteries in the city were spruced up by order of the government, and vacant shops were filled with subsidized renters to convey an image of prosperity. Because many foreign visitors to the games were expected to take advantage of their trip to Germany to travel around the country, the Reich government put out an order that cities and towns across the nation must "display themselves to their very best advantage." Responding to this call, the nation's hundreds of spa towns announced their intention to give extra pampering to Olympic visitors, so that, while taking the waters, the guests would come to understand "the tender and soulful side of Adolf Hitler's Germany." The city of Nuremberg hired multilingual guides to give foreign visitors tours of the new Party Rally Grounds. And, lest visitors to that city's German Museum (which rivaled Munich's) get a skewed idea of the German character, the museum director ordered the nasty spikes removed from the "iron maiden" medieval torture device on display there. Regional authorities set to work clearing roadsides of litter and derelict structures. To further spare visitors unsettling images, the government ordered that, during the period between July 1 and September 1, no convict laborers could be employed along the roads and rail lines. The SS decreed that no concentration camp inmates would be sent out for road- or fieldwork during this same period. Two months prior to the games, agents of the Propaganda Ministry toured the country to ensure that the beautification/sanitization projects had been completed and that every- thing was in place "to show foreign visitors a good time."

Publicity and Propaganda

A key part of the preparations for the Berlin games was an elaborate interna- tional and domestic publicity and propaganda campaign. This proved to be the most ambitious and expensive promotional program the Olympic movement had yet seen. It also constituted a violation of Olympic regulations circumscrib- ing governmental involvement in promotion, inasmuch as the domestic com- ponent of the campaign was run by Goebbels's Propaganda Ministry rather than by the GOC.

The Germans put considerable energy into promoting the Berlin Olympics abroad because they were worried that all the controversy over the Nazi games might inhibit foreign attendance even if there was no formal ath- letic boycott. As of December 1935 only about 50 percent of America's quota of special passes and all-inclusive tickets had been applied for. Advance sales in Britain were moving slowly, and in France they were not moving at all. In late 1935 Tschammer and Diem, likening themselves to the "Messengers of Elis" who had traveled through the Greek world to announce the ancient games, undertook promotional trips around Europe, giving speeches about the upcoming festival and touting the Nazi government's dedication to peace. For this purpose Lufthansa German Airlines provided an airplane with the motto "XI. Olympiade 1936" painted on the side. During his visits to Lon- don and Paris, Tschammer extended personal Olympic invitations from Hitler to British prime minister Stanley Baldwin and French premier Pierre Laval. Neither ended up accepting the Führer's hospitality.

The Reich Railway Central Office for Tourism, which was responsible for Olympic advertising and travel, launched additional publicity efforts abroad. The agency sent out posters and promotional brochures to more than forty countries. Its agent in New York, Ernst Schmitz, issued a barrage of press releases describing the preparations for the Berlin games and promising a bril- liant spectacle. On October 11, 1935, for example, Schmitz announced,

"Preparations for the Games have reached a stage where one is amazed at the magnificence of the projects that are being carried out by the authorities. Whole streets have been torn up and widened to make room for the broad avenues which are to lead to the great Olympic Park called the Reich Sport Field, where the Games will be held." Schmitz, like his colleagues in other foreign cities, also subsidized promotional junkets to Berlin for friendly journalists and sports officials. In Chicago the Germans hired a stunt flyer to advertise the games, and in London they had men bearing Olympic placards walk through the crowded streets and Underground stations. Lufthansa did its part with a "By Air to Olympia" campaign. The airline dispatched 10,000 copies of its Olympic advertising brochures to the United States alone. Even the famous German Zeppelins helped out by carrying promotional messages about the Olympics to South American countries during the airships' regular postal runs between Germany and Buenos Aires.

By March 1936, with foreign advance-ticket sales finally starting to pick up (and this despite the Rhineland remilitarization), the German organizers were convinced that they had made a positive impact with all their elaborate promotional efforts. Friedrich Mahlo, deputy chairman of the GOC's Publicity Commission for the Olympic Games, claimed: "The fact that there is no longer serious resistance anywhere in the world to holding the Olympic Games in Germany is a testament to the excellent propaganda and enlightenment work of the foreign branches of the Reich Railway Central Office for Tourism, which, following the guidelines of the Publicity Commission for the Olympic Games, has carried the Olympic wakeup call to the entire world."

The games' organizers were also determined to send an Olympic wake-up message to their own people, for they believed that a successful show depended on widespread enthusiasm at home. In October 1934 Pfundtner sent out an appeal to the *Reichsstaathalter* to do their best "to deepen appreciation for Olympic sports among the German people." He instructed the officials to set up Olympics volunteer groups in every town with more than five hundred inhabitants. Nazi Party affiliates were ordered to promote the idea that pursuing sports was a vital part of being a good National Socialist.

To generate enthusiasm for the games, and at the same time to underscore Germany's claim to be *the* preeminent steward of the Olympic idea, Diem and his associates mounted two major exhibitions on Olympic history. The first, focusing on the modern games, opened in February 1935 in Berlin, where it stayed for six weeks before moving on to other German cities. This exhibition combined photographs and memorabilia of the modern games with specific German artifacts, so as to emphasize Germany's central place in the modern Olympic experience. Among the artifacts on display was Goethe's carriage, which, in a promotional stunt, had been pulled by a team of horses all the way from Weimar to Berlin. Germany's greatest poet was also featured in an essay competition on "Goethe and the Olympic Idea," which asked entrants to "shed light on Goethe as a fencer, swimmer, rider, ice-skater and mountain hiker, thereby establishing a connection between this great voice of our people and the Eleventh Olympic Games." In a speech at the ceremony opening the exhibition, Goebbels declared that the show was "not only a testament to the new Germany but also a statement about the great Germany of the past—in short, a documentation of the Eternal Germany."

The second exhibition, "Sport in Hellenic Times," brought together under one roof significant sport-related classical artworks from German museums, along with bronze casts of artifacts from many foreign museums. This was undoubtedly the most complete exhibition of its kind ever mounted. Diem was justified in praising the "overwhelming" perspective it offered on ancient sport. But of course the point here was not just to document the achievements of the ancients but also to highlight contemporary Germany's role in preserving and illuminating these treasures. To this end the organizers assigned the keynote speech at the opening ceremony to Professor Theodor Wiegand, the aged excavator of Pergamum. Noting that the show encapsulated a long German tradition of collecting "works that represent ancient life in its care for the body and sporting competition," Wiegand went on to praise the Nazi state for reviving and popularizing the Greeks' concept of "the harmony of body and soul as a vital force."

While the Olympic art and history exhibitions catered primarily to educated audiences in the big cities, a traveling show labeled *Der Olympia-Zug* (The Olympic Train) aimed at enticing the broad masses, especially in rural areas. As organized by the Propaganda Ministry, the "train" was in reality a truck caravan consisting of four Mercedes-Benz diesel tractors each pulling two huge specially made exhibition trailers with removable sides. The convoy traveled the length and breadth of Germany, stopping for two or three days in more than five hundred towns and villages between early 1935 and July 1936. Once strategically parked around a town square, the trailers' sides were opened and an awning spread out to create a 560-square-meter tented enclosure capable of holding two hundred people. The display under the tent

focused less on the ancient games than on recent developments and preparations for the 1936 festival. Plaster-of-Paris scale models of the Garmisch venues, the Reichssportfeld, and the Olympic Village illustrated the magnitude
of the undertaking. There were photographs of Hitler and Tschammer discussing preparations for the games and of laborers erecting Olympia in
Berlin. Visitors to the show could also see short films and hear sound clips
relating to Germany's past Olympic successes and athletic preparations for the
coming games. The theme running through all this was that the Berlin games
were a "national task for the German people."

Another promotional venture with a patriotic message involved the transport of a nine-and-one-half-ton "Olympic bell" from its foundry in Bochum
to the Olympic site in Berlin. This bell, which was the brainchild of Theodor
Lewald and a gift to the GOC by its Bochum founders, was a unique contribution by the German organizers to Olympic theatricality. The monster
Glocke bore on one side a picture of the Brandenburg Gate and on the other
a rendition of the Reich eagle with the Olympic rings in its talons. Around
its rim in Gothic script ran the phrase "*Ich rufe die Jugend der Welt*" (I sum-
mon the youth of the world). Berlin was the only Olympic festival in history
to feature a totemic symbol of this magnitude: The cute and cuddly Olympic
"mascots" of later games are but a weak echo. The Germans did their best to
commercialize the big bell by selling porcelain miniatures of it at the games.
Costing 4.50 reichsmarks apiece, the souvenirs were advertised as a perfect
way "to keep the Olympic ideals fresh and to preserve memories of the
Eleventh Olympic Games."

The massive bell began its ten-day journey from Bochum to Berlin on January 16, 1936. Lewald and Diem had hoped to use this odyssey to advertise
the games to their fellow Germans, but in the end the venture turned out to
be far more successful than even they could have imagined. As the bell moved
across the land at a stately twelve-mile-per-hour pace, people turned out in
their thousands to cheer it on. In advance of the bell's arrival in their towns
and villages, local authorities organized patriotic fêtes, replete with brass
bands, black-red-and-white bunting, and the inevitable long-winded
speeches. On its arrival in Berlin the *Olympia-Glocke* trundled across town to
Kaiser Franz Josef Platz, where its makers officially handed it over to the
GOC in an elaborate ceremony. In order to maximize the bell's exposure to
the Berliners, the object was displayed for several days at a time in four other
city squares before finally being taken to the May Field on May 11 and

hoisted to the top of the Glockenturm. This last task was conducted in deep secrecy in case of a mishap, but everything went smoothly.

Athletic Preparations

In announcing his ambitious building program for the 1936 Berlin games, Hitler declared, "Buildings alone will not suffice to guarantee a showing by our athletes that is commensurate with Germany's world importance. More decisive here is the nation's unified commitment to pulling together the best *Kämpfer* [athletic warriors] from all regions, and then schooling and hardening them, so that we [as a nation] can perform honorably in the upcoming competition." By performing "honorably" Nazi Germany could show the world that its commitment to breeding and training a new elite of athletic warriors was rendering the entire nation physically and spiritually superior to the "soft and decadent" Western democracies.

Work on putting together a world-beating team for 1936 began as early as 1933, when, through the "coordination" of sporting organizations the regime was able to pit the nation's top athletes against each other for purposes of Olympic selection. In early 1934 the chief Nazi organ, the *Völkischer Beobachter,* called on the SA and SS to drop their traditional antagonism toward competitive team sports and to identify young men in their ranks who were likely candidates for Olympic training. At the same time a committee of experts under newly appointed "Olympic Inspector" Christian Busch launched athletic competitions called "The Days of the Unknown Athlete."

Athletes selected for the Olympic training teams received a host of privileges, including an "Olympic passport," free travel, food, housing, medical treatment, and compensation for lost wages. For all practical purposes, therefore, the German Olympians of 1936 were "state amateurs"—their status both an echo of the ancient games, where competitors were often extensively subsidized by their respective city-states, and an anticipation of the post–World War II games, in which ideals of amateurism were often honored more in the breach than in the observance.

Also presaging future controversies, the medical treatment afforded the German Olympic trainees probably included certain forms of pharmacological enhancement. (Here, too, there was an ancient precedent: Some competitors in the original games illegally fortified themselves with wine, while others resorted to special diets of herbs, dried figs, and mushrooms.) In the 1920s, Germany's medical and physiological journals had touted the benefits of phosphates for improved athletic performance, and a commercial phosphate additive called Recresal became all the rage in German sporting circles. The drug continued to be used widely in Germany in the 1930s. Another popular product, Dallkolat, consisting of a combination of crushed kola nuts and cocaine, had arrived in Germany via the United States, where athletes spoke enthusiastically of its near-mystical powers. Then there was "oxygen priming," the inhaling of pure oxygen. This practice took on cult status in Germany as a result of rumors that the Japanese swimmers had used it to perform so brilliantly in the Los Angeles Olympics. Finally another American import, ultraviolet radiation baths, became widely used in German athletic circles following reports that the Yale crew had been "irradiated" by its trainer before decisively defeating archrival Harvard. After Hitler came to power Nazi sports officials grasped at UV treatments as a necessary equalizer in their impending showdown with the Yanks in Berlin. They claimed, however, that this practice could not be construed as an unnatural form of performance enhancement since it simply involved a technological version of solar energy.

Because the 1936 games would test female as well as male athletes, the German organizers did their best to assemble a credible body of women warriors. While Diem and Lewald had never objected to the inclusion of women in high-level competitive sports, the very idea of female sports ran sharply contrary to traditional Nazi doctrines regarding the proper place and role of women in society. As the SA sports leader Bruno Malitz had put the matter in 1933: "We oppose women's sports. . . . Women should remain womanly. . . . Look at the girl athletes who have reached the age of thirty. They look like *fifty*: manly, the spirit of battle written on their faces, bony and bare of womanhood." Nazi health experts contended that strenuous athletic competition could damage the female reproductive organs. To the chagrin of Nazi true believers, however, in Germany's Olympic trials the female candidates performed extremely well, attaining results previously thought possible only by men. And as we shall see, in the Berlin games the German women would end up outperforming their male counterparts in track and field, a domain that at the Olympic level had only recently been opened to women.

Members of Germany's Olympic training squads were obliged to swear an oath promising fidelity to the principles of sportsmanship as set down by Reichssportführer Tschammer und Osten. On December 16, 1934, one hundred athletes, acting as representatives for all the trainees, took the following highly charged oath in a public ceremony aired on German radio:

> I will voluntarily follow the call of the Reich Sport Leader to enter into the ranks of a German youth cohort determined to commit itself to the German cause, which is also my cause. I swear to conduct myself in accordance with the requirements of a German Olympic combatant. During the period of training I will forswear all of life's pleasures, keeping as my sole goal the task of schooling and hardening my body, so that I may be worthy of fighting nobly for my fatherland. I subordinate myself fully to the Reich Sport Leader and to his cadre of trainers, who are my helpers on the way to this goal. I will follow their teachings and training guidelines exclusively. I promise to remain silent regarding the measures that have been taken and will be taken in the future.

The concluding promise of silence was necessary because parts of the German training program, such as compensation for lost wages, violated Olympic regulations on amateurism.

Germany, of course, was not the only nation whose athletes were throwing themselves into preparations for the Berlin games. Fascist Italy, whose state-controlled sports program constituted a model for the Nazis, worked hard to produce a team that might perform as impressively as Italy's contingent had in Los Angeles. Indeed, directly following the LA Games Mussolini himself admonished Italy's Olympic trainees: "Four years lie before you. Use the time to prepare well. In Los Angeles you were second. In Berlin it's necessary to be first!" Later *Il Duce* instructed the Italian team that it was imperative not only to win but to win "*nel modo più degno* [in the most dignified manner]." Italy's confidence was greatly boosted when, in June 1933, Primo Carnera beat Jack Sharkey for the world heavyweight boxing championship, and Italy's national soccer team defeated Czechoslovakia to win the 1934 World Cup. As had been the case before the LA games, Italy's team for Berlin was lavishly subsidized and provided with everything it needed in terms of training facilities. Leaving nothing to chance, Italy even brought in a coach from Germany and a trainer from Finland.

Japan's Olympic training squad also lacked for nothing. The Japanese military, which increasingly set the nation's political and social agenda, instituted a policy of physical fitness designed to aid Japan's expansionist designs in Asia.

Olympic success was seen as an integral part of Japan's push for national glory and imperial conquest. "Japan has set as its primary mission for 1936 the goal of astounding the world through its superior performances," announced the team's chief trainer. In 1933 the government built a sports medicine facility to screen candidates for the national team and to help those selected prepare for the coming combat. Government subsidies for Japan's Olympic program increased from sixty thousand yen ($17,400) in 1928 to one hundred thousand yen ($29,000) in 1932 and three hundred thousand yen ($87,000) in 1936. The emperor himself donated ten thousand yen to the Japanese team headed for Berlin.

In comparison to Japan's 178-athlete team bound for Berlin, China's squad of 55 seemed paltry, as did its government subsidy of ten thousand dollars. Yet China's commitment to Berlin amounted to a great leap forward following its very tentative Olympic debut in Los Angeles, and the country's athletic officials worked hard to put together a credible team in order to show the world that the Republic of China was a virile and disciplined young nation, not simply a plaything of foreign powers. (Tellingly a Chinese sports official rendered the alien concept "Olympiad" in Mandarin as "*Won eng bi ya*"—literally, "I can compete!") China's Olympic authorities put on a two-month summer training camp at Shandong University in July–August and brought in four German coaches to supplement the native coaching talent. The country's soccer team and boxers traveled around Asia during the year before the games to hone their skills and raise money for their trip to Germany. The Chinese were ecstatic when Howard Wing, a Dutch bicycle racer of Chinese ancestry then living in Amsterdam decided to ride for his "motherland" rather than compete for the Netherlands.

Next to China's pre-Olympic enthusiasm, the European democracies' commitment to Berlin seemed almost blasé. Certainly their funding was inadequate. The French Olympic Committee (FOC) requested substantial subsidies following the LA games for team trials and training but received only a fraction of the requested sums. As a consequence training programs were scaled back, as was the size of the team France sent to Berlin. Fearing a debacle, French trainers complained bitterly over the "small-mindedness" of the government and warned that a poor showing in Berlin could be interpreted by France's enemies as a sign of weakness across the board.

Following the LA games, in which the British Olympic team had not exactly covered itself in glory, the *British Olympic Journal* dared hope that

Britain might do better in Berlin if sufficient funding were available to "undertake serious training over the next four years." Because the British Olympic Council did not rely on government subsidies to support its programs, the monies would have to be drummed up from private contributors. The BOC set a fund-raising goal of between £10,000 and £15,000, but proved unable to reach this target. In the end the council had to settle for £9,034, of which almost a third came from two private benefactors, Lord Portal and Lord Nuffield. The *News of the World* coughed up another £250, Imperial Tobacco £210, the Greyhound Racing Association £157, and Horlick's Malted Milk £52.

Modest as they were, however, the private contributions raised in Britain turned out to be more than sufficient for the nation's Olympic needs. Having set their sights far lower than the Germans, Italians, and Japanese, the British ended up spending remarkably little on training and equipping their Olympic squads for 1936. The total bill for the British Berlin expedition came to just over £4,000, and since the BOC had spent only £259 on its Garmisch contingent and £831 on office expenses, it finished up with a surplus of nearly £4,000. It seemed, in short, that by the 1930s Britain's once-vaunted Olympics program was as much caught up in the muddle-along mentality as was the nation as a whole.

And what about the Americans? All the controversy surrounding the boycott movement certainly threatened the AOC's fund-raising effort. On April 13, 1936, less than four months before opening day, the AOC announced that it needed "money and needs it soon." Avery Brundage specified that a total of $350,000 was needed to transport, equip, and house the four to five hundred athletes who would represent the United States in Berlin. In June Brundage wrote Sigfrid Edstrøm that the AOC was "in the midst of a strenuous campaign" to raise money, "always a tremendous task for an organization of volunteers," and made even more difficult by "the continuing opposition of the Jews." He was confident however that "we will be able to send most of our team on the *SS Manhattan*, which sails from New York City on July 15."

Fortunately for the AOC, the German American Olympic Fund Committee continued aggressively to solicit contributions from German Americans despite the above-mentioned flap over including FDR's name on its letterhead. Fund chairman Dietrich Wortmann's latest solicitation letter tried to capitalize on Jewish lack of support for the American team: "The Olympic

Games will be held in Germany this year and I earnestly appeal to you to help the American Olympic Committee raise the necessary funds to send a full American team to make up for the withdrawal of financial support of certain parties. More than ever do we need the united moral and financial support of all German Americans to answer the anti-Olympic propaganda [and to promote] friendship between our two great countries." Ernst Schmitz of the Reich Railway Central Office for Tourism helped coordinate the fund-raising campaign among German Americans. Commenting on the importance of getting the Americans to Berlin and thereby helping Germany bring off a successful Olympiad, the German-language *Chicago Sonntagsboten* editorialized: "A successful Olympics in 1936 will also constitute a success for the German community abroad and simultaneously a defeat for all those rabble-rousers and boycott-advocates who malign our people and fatherland."

The AOC also made an effort to tap into the African American community. Noting that some Chicago Negroes had established a radio program to raise money for American blacks' participation in the 1936 games, Clarence Bush, the committee's publicity director, proposed that the AOC get "one or two of the Negro stars on the program," so they "could tell of their thankfulness for the chance to pursue sports on the basis of equality which they find in no other avenue of life." Bush suggested a similar program for Harlem. "This racial enthusiasm will be valuable in contrast to another racial [that is, Jewish] boycott," he predicted.

All these efforts notwithstanding, by early July the funding still looked questionable. Gus Kirby, the AOC treasurer, announced on July 5 that to completely fund the American team some $150,000 was still needed. On the same day Henry Penn Burke, chairman of the American Olympic Rowing Committee, admitted that the rowers needed another $10,000 to get to Berlin. For the rowers part of the task of raising the necessary cash fell to the University of Washington crew, which had won the American trials in the heavyweight eights. The Huskies held a bake sale. They were not alone in their self-reliance. The AOC ordered athletes and coaches in all the competitive divisions to help raise money for the Olympic effort by hitting up their churches, city governments, and friends. The American press helped out by publishing inspirational articles about needy athletes. One story told of a runner who had hitchhiked across the country to get to the Olympic trials; another related the saga of a female competitor who had pawned her engagement ring to finance her Olympic dream.

In the end, just as the *Manhattan* was getting ready to sail, the AOC finally came up with the necessary funds, largely through last-minute individual contributions and by revenues from ticket sales at the various Olympic trials events. Once the *Manhattan* was under way Brundage could confess that he had actually *turned down* a contribution of $100,000 from "a breakfast food concern," which had offered the money on the condition that the company could advertise its product as the preferred breakfast food of American Olympians. (The breakfast food concern was undoubtedly General Mills, which had started promoting its *Wheaties* brand as the "Breakfast of Champions" in the early 1930s.) "I had a check in my hand for $10,000 and the balance was promised in nine installments," said Brundage. "Although tempted to accept this means of solving most of the money worries, the committee finally rejected the offer on the ground that it would be unethical and set a precedent injurious to sport." How quaint such qualms seem today!

The Olympic trials may have helped to raise money for the American team, but their primary purpose was of course to select the athletes who would represent the United States in Berlin. Describing the track-and-field trials, which were held at New York City's Randall's Island on July 11–12, Brundage declared grandiloquently:

> Sport flourishes particularly in democratic America because, after all, sport is a great democratic institution. The same qualities that led to the conquering of the wilderness, the founding of the Great Republic, and the development of science and invention and business and industry to the high levels of modern America, are responsible for the supremacy of American athletes. These boys [*sic*] realize that their success depends on their own efforts. With fair rules impartially administered, they know that all have an equal opportunity for victory. The winner will be congratulated and cheered on his way in a sporting spirit by those who are not so fortunate. This is the essence of staunch, sturdy, true old Americanism.

The sturdy Americanism celebrated by Brundage did not, in fact, mean equality for all competitors, male or female. None of the Olympic trials could take place in the Deep South because the southern states would not allow blacks to participate in events with whites. Even states bordering the South could be a problem in this regard. At a regional trial held in College Park,

Maryland, four black athletes were barred from competing by the director. Rather than insist on black participation in the meet, national Olympic officials dodged the issue of racial discrimination by automatically qualifying the four athletes for semifinal tryouts to be held later in Cambridge, Massachusetts. Jesse Owens, who, as expected, qualified in the sprints and long jump, was fortunate that the track trials were held in New York and not in his native state of Alabama.

The Olympic trials produced what looked to be a powerful American team once again. Yet there were worries about how the team would fare in Berlin—worries that had cropped up in the wake of America's miserable showing in Garmisch. As the *Washington Post* noted in late February 1936, America's rivals in Europe and Asia had come on strong in the last few years, ensuring that the US was likely to be "severely tested in Berlin this summer." The *New York Times* spoke ominously of "a massed European attack on American athletic supremacy" pending in Berlin. By "European attack" the *Times* meant mainly a *German* attack. "Sports has become a part of what is known to the Germans as *Kultur*," explained the paper. "A cult of brawn, and, for that matter, just good clean, athletic living, is spreading. In its militaristic or semi-militaristic phase it has become one of the near-religious ecstasies indulged in by the youth of dictatorially governed nations."

Preamble in the Ring

American concerns about European, especially German, challenges to the Yanks' traditional athletic superiority were greatly heightened by an event in June 1936 that was not directly connected with the Olympics, but which seemed at the time to presage a possible changing of the guard in the realm of international sporting prowess. That event was the surprising heavyweight boxing victory by Max Schmeling over Joe Louis on June 19, 1936. Although two years later Louis would get his revenge by smashing Schmeling to the canvas in less than one round, their first bout represented a stinging humiliation for the "Brown Bomber" and a shock to his American supporters, most of whom had never considered the German a serious threat to Louis.

Schmeling, fancifully nicknamed by his manager "the Black Uhlan," had won the heavyweight crown in a controversial battle with American Jack

Sharkey on June 12, 1930, as a result of being fouled by a low blow. He was the first European to hold the heavyweight title. Up to the moment of the foul in the Sharkey match, Schmeling had been losing badly and he was only half conscious when the controversial decision was announced. Once he fully came to, he realized that the way he had won the crown was not likely to make him popular in America. His short reign as champ did nothing to improve his stature. He defended his dubious crown successfully against William Young Stribling in 1931, but did not enter the ring again until June 1932, when the New York State Boxing Commission essentially forced him to accept a rematch with Sharkey. This time it was Schmeling who believed he was denied a rightful victory, for, after fifteen rounds of outboxing his American opponent, he saw a split decision go to Sharkey. "We wuz robbed!" yelled Max's Jewish American manager, Joe Jacobs, in a phrase for the ages. "The great Sharkey-Schmeling controversy now stands at one steal apiece," wrote Paul Gallico, in another memorable line.

Schmeling returned to Germany, where, despite the loss to Sharkey, he was considered a hero for having put his nation on the map in the American-dominated world of professional boxing. Exploiting his celebrity status, he married the Czech-born film star Anny Ondra, with whom he promptly made a stinker of a movie called *Knockout!*

During the Weimar era Schmeling had cultivated friendships with leftist artists like George Grosz and Heinrich Mann—he liked to think that boxing, too, was an art—but once the Nazis came to power the boxer showed some fancy footwork in adapting agilely to the new political order. In truth the Nazis made matters easy for Schmeling because they sensed his symbolic value as an Aryan tough guy. The regime did not even make much of a fuss over the fact that Schmeling had a Jewish manager, for even the Nazis understood that the cigar-chomping Jacobs was a valuable asset in the Jewish-dominated world of New York boxing. (Jacobs helped out here by claiming, after a trip to Germany in 1933, that all the talk of Jewish persecution under the Nazis was so much baloney.)

Even after Schmeling had lost his crown, Adolf Hitler remained a fervent admirer, granting the boxer private meetings and sending him fan mail. The Führer was therefore deeply disappointed when Schmeling, attempting a comeback, was defeated in 1933 by the American Max Baer, who, in a testament to the preeminent role of Jews in American boxing, claimed to have a

Jewish father, though his dad was actually a gentile pig farmer from California. Fully cognizant of the fight's broader implications, Baer drummed up interest in the bout by declaring: "Every punch in the eye I give Schmeling is also one for Adolf Hitler." Baer wore a Star of David on his trunks and, on examining his puffed-up nose in the mirror after the Schmeling bout, quipped: "They thought I was a Hebe and now I look like one."

Not long after the Baer fight Schmeling lost to American Steve Hamas and could struggle only to a draw against the undistinguished Spaniard Paulino Uzcudun. Now it looked as if the German was washed up for good. Nonetheless, pushed on by Jacobs and his diehard supporters in Germany, he continued to fight.

In 1935 Schmeling managed to avenge his defeat by Hamas by almost killing the American in Hamburg, and then he went on to beat Uzcudun, signaling that he was definitely back in the game. Jacobs, who had an excellent eye for the broader social and racial issues that had been a vital, if ugly, aspect of professional boxing since the great Jack Johnson had become the first black to hold the heavyweight crown, now began to sense that a bout between Schmeling and the powerful new American contender, Joe Louis, might be the perfect vehicle to highlight the old divide between black and white, as well as the newer rift between democratic America and Nazi Germany. The approach of the Berlin Olympics made the timing perfect, there being much talk about an impending showdown between America's blacks and Hitler's Aryans.

With the upcoming Olympics in mind, the Nazi regime and the GOC sought to use Schmeling as a kind of goodwill ambassador to America, where the Nazis (incorrectly) thought the German boxer had real popularity and influence. In December 1935, just before Schmeling left for New York to watch Joe Louis fight Paulino Uzcudun, Tschammer took him aside and asked if he would "exert a positive influence on the right people" regarding America's participation in the Berlin games, which the Reich government still worried might still be questionable. Schmeling promised to talk with AOC officials. Learning of Schmeling's agreement with Tschammer, Theodor Lewald prevailed on the boxer to carry a personal letter from him to Brundage, in which Lewald reiterated all his earlier promises regarding fairness and hospitality for American athletes.

Schmeling duly met with Brundage at New York City's Commodore Hotel shortly after his arrival in America. According to Schmeling's account of this meeting in his autobiography, Brundage produced some newspaper clippings about the harassment of Jews in Germany and asked whether Jews and blacks on America's Olympic team might have to fear similar mistreatment in Berlin. Schmeling replied that the German athletes themselves would not allow any discrimination against their fellow Olympians. In his memoir Schmeling admitted that it had been "naive" of him to make such a guarantee, but he also claimed that his intervention had saved the day for Germany, prompting "the Olympic committee to vote by a slim margin to attend the Games." This of course is nonsense: The AOC had already voted to accept Germany's invitation. It was the AAU, not the AOC, which was voting in December 1935, and there is no evidence whatsoever that Schmeling's "word" played any role in their deliberations. In any event Avery Brundage, who ran the AAU meeting, did not need Schmeling to convince them that, whatever the Germans might be doing to their Jews, the United States must be present in Berlin.

Shortly after his meeting with Brundage, Schmeling and Joe Jacobs sat down with Joe Louis's handlers and worked out the details of a bout between the Black Uhlan and the Brown Bomber. The fight was set for June 18, 1936, in Yankee Stadium.

While Max Schmeling struck many fight fans in America as a has-been, or even as a never-had-been, by the mid-1930s Joe Louis had emerged as the dominant figure in professional boxing even though he had yet to claim the heavyweight title. Since turning pro in early 1934 he had won twenty-four straight bouts, twenty by knockouts. His meteoric rise was duly noted by boxing's premier promoter, Mike Jacobs (no relation to Joe), who, in time-honored fight-game fashion, took control of Louis's career in order to "protect" the young fighter.

In early 1933 Jacobs arranged for Louis to fight Primo Carnera, the Italian strongman who would go on in that same year to take the heavyweight crown from Sharkey. It was actually Louis who should have gotten that shot at Sharkey, for in his bout with Carnera, nicknamed "the Ambling Alp" because of his enormous size, Louis made the mountain man look like a hillock, knocking him out in the sixth round. Many Americans, especially African Americans, saw Carnera as a pugilistic stand-in for *Il Duce*, who was at that very moment beating up on the black African kingdom of Ethiopia. Following the fight, kids ran through the streets of Harlem shouting, "Let's get Musso next."

Not long after the Carnera fight, Louis put down Max Baer with brutal efficiency in a contest that Jacobs cleverly promoted as a battle pitting his "Dark Destroyer" against the white-skinned Baer, the "Clown Prince of Boxing." Louis's lucrative draw potential was evidenced by the fact that this was the first million-dollar gate since the glory days of Jack Dempsey and Gene Tunney.

Louis's vaunted skill as a boxer was not the only source of his popularity among the largely white American fight audience. This son of Alabama sharecroppers who had migrated to Detroit and worked in an auto plant before becoming a professional fighter was known to be a clean-living, modest, soft-spoken young man who (in contrast to the uppity Jack Johnson) "knew his place." He carefully followed a list of rules set down by Jacobs, which forbade his consorting with white women, hanging out in nightclubs, gloating over his victories, or putting on airs before the media. The white press generally embraced him as a "credit to his race," which did not prevent sportswriters from trotting out all their demeaning alliterative wit at his expense. In addition to "Brown Bomber" and "Dark Destroyer," he was labeled "Chocolate Chopper," "Dusty Downer," "Mocha Mauler," "Mahogany Maimer," the "Panther with the Pin Cushion Lips," the "Tan Tarzan of Thump," the "Murder Man of the Maroon Mitts," and "KKK (Kruel Kolored Klouter)." Moreover, although even the southern press was less condescending toward Louis than it was toward most black athletes, Dixie sportswriters harbored considerable ambivalence regarding Louis's domination over a succession of "Great White Hopes."

So could Schmeling succeed where so many white boxers before him had failed? Few thought so. The smart money was all on Louis's side, the odds running as high as 14 to 1 in favor of the Bomber. Even the Nazi leaders, all their talk of Aryan racial superiority notwithstanding, were not so sure that Schmeling could hold his own with Louis, and, initially at least, several Nazi journals sought to minimize in advance the potential damage from a possible defeat. The *Reich Sports Journal* insisted that there was "not much interest" in Germany in a contest involving a black man. The *Völkischer Beobachter* strategically tried to make Schmeling's cause the cause of all whites, including American whites, so that a Schmeling loss would not be exclusively a blow to German pride. "In America," said the paper, "the racial factor is strongly placed in the foreground, and it is hoped that the representative of the white race will succeed in halting the unusual rise of the Negro. In fact there is no doubt that Max Schmeling, when he enters the ring, will have the sympathy of all white spectators on his side, and the knowledge of this will be important moral support for him." By the time Schmeling was ready to depart for New York, his Nazi backers had decided to put on a more confident game face, arguing that their man's superior intellect and discipline would surely prevail over Louis's brute strength. Goebbels's newspaper, *Der Angriff*, carried advertisements for cruises to New York for the fight.

Whatever Goebbels and company thought about Schmeling's chances, the boxer himself was confident that he could beat Louis. When watching the Bomber fight Uzcudun, Schmeling had noticed that Louis sometimes briefly dropped his left hand after throwing a left jab. This made him vulnerable for a split second to a well-placed right cross, which was Schmeling's best punch. "I zee zomezings," he reportedly said in explaining how he thought he could beat Louis.

The big fight had to be postponed by one day because of rain. It is a myth that Schmeling blessed the heavens for giving him a day's reprieve from an expected pummeling; he was actually anxious to get into the ring with Louis, which made him perhaps unique among the Bomber's opponents. Louis himself claimed later to have noticed something "peculiar" about Schmeling as he climbed into the ring: He didn't look scared. Once the fight began Schmeling proved unusual also in his ability to take Louis's opening barrage of lightening-fast lefts without any sign of distress, save a bloody lip. "I never see so many left hands," Schmeling later admitted.

But he also saw, in the third round, the chance he had been waiting for: a momentary opening created by Louis's lowered guard. Schmeling immediately crossed with a hard right that landed smack on the side of Louis's jaw. Louis won that round, as indeed he had won the first two, but both Schmeling and his trusted cornerman, Max Machon, knew that the Bomber had been badly hurt. "*Du hast ihm da einen Schönen geholt,*" ("You gave him a good one there") confirmed Machon during the pause between rounds three and four. Schmeling later claimed that he had "won" the fight in the third round. In fact, in subsequent rounds he was able to score frequently with his powerful right cross because Louis was increasingly unable to defend himself. "Ach, the path to his chin looks more wide than Unter den Linden, now that the Lindens are gone from it," Schmeling told reporters after the fight. One of his rights dropped Louis to the canvas in round four, the first time this had happened to the Bomber in his professional career. According to the *New York Times* reporter covering the fight, that historic punch was the beginning of the end for Joe: "Louis never recovered from that blow, nor from the countless other right-hand punches Schmeling rained on his jaw with the unerring accuracy of the true marksman through each succeeding round until the finish."

The finish finally came in round twelve, when Louis hit the canvas for good after a savage series of head blows from Schmeling. Although Louis was probably not aware of it, he had by now lost the largely white and very fickle crowd, which, putting racism over patriotism, now became "delirious with joy" at the sight of Louis's impending defeat. The crowd shouted itself hoarse while Louis, after being counted out, was carried to his corner and slowly resuscitated by his handlers.

Louis was understandably devastated by the loss. When, back in his hotel room, he was finally able to talk, he allowed that he "felt awful because I let my friends down."

Louis's "friends," especially in the black community, were indeed desolate over the loss. At least four of his elderly black supporters died of heart failure while listening to the radio broadcast of the fight. A teenage black girl in Harlem tried to poison herself. In Chicago and New York, young black men ran amok in the streets, breaking windows and torching cars. Immediately after the fight one white man was kicked unconscious outside Yankee Stadium, while another was wounded by gunfire. Later, reports in the black press insisted that Louis had been "drugged" before the fight by white doctors.

Although initially shocked by Louis's loss, some white commentators took this occasion to consign the Bomber to the dustbin of boxing history, and also to praise Schmeling for having restored the upstart Negro to his proper place in the racial pecking order. Davis Walsh of the International News Service congratulated "the white master" Schmeling for having made "the black avenger revert to type and become again the boy who had been born in an Alabama cabin." Former champion Jack Dempsey, who had bragged that he would never fight a black man, hailed Schmeling's victory as "the finest thing to happen to boxing in a long time. . . . The big bubble broke tonight. Joe Louis will be licked by every bum in the country."

In Germany, where because of the time difference the fight was broadcast in the early morning hours, Schmeling's fans across the nation went wild over his triumph over Louis, who was now described by one German paper as "the poor defeated Nigger-boy." Schmeling received twelve hundred telegrams on the day after the fight, most of them from German fans. One of the congratulatory

Adolf Hitler greeting crowds as he is driven to the opening ceremony of the 1936 Winter Games at Garmisch-Partenkirchen. (*Olympic Study Center, Lausanne*)

Members of Britain's controversial gold-medal-winning ice hockey team at the Garmisch games. (*Olympic Study Center, Lausanne*)

Norway's Sonja Henie, "Queen of the Ice," at Garmisch-Partenkirchen. (*Olympic Study Center, Lausanne*)

Housing units for athletes at the Olympic Village outside Berlin.
(*Olympic Study Center, Lausanne*)

The "Olympic Train" truck caravan that traveled through Germany in
the months before the Olympics to generate enthusiasm for the games.
(*Olympic Study Center, Lausanne*)

Adolf Hitler, IOC president Henri de Baillet-Latour (on Hitler's right) and German Organizing Committee president Theodor Lewald enter the Olympic Stadium at the opening of the 1936 Summer Games. (*Olympic Study Center, Lausanne*)

Athletes giving the "Olympic salute" as they march into the Olympic Stadium during the opening ceremony. (*Olympic Study Center, Lausanne*)

The Olympic torch being carried through Berlin's Brandenburg Gate en route to the Olympic Stadium for the opening ceremony of the 1936 Summer Games. (*Olympic Study Center, Lausanne*)

Jesse Owens with Lutz Long, the German long jumper who befriended Owens during the jumping competition in Berlin. (*Olympic Study Center, Lausanne*)

America's Glenn Morris, winner of the 1936 Olympic decathlon (and, briefly, paramour of filmmaker Leni Riefenstahl). (*Olympic Study Center, Lausanne*)

Britain's intrepid Harold Whitlock, who set a new Olympic record in the fifty-kilometer walk despite having to stop several times during the race to vomit. (*Olympic Study Center, Lausanne*)

Marathon winner Kitei Son and second-place finisher Ernest Harper running by his side. Although Son wore the Rising Sun of Japan on his jersey, he was a passionate Korean nationalist and felt ashamed to be running for Japan. (*Olympic Study Center, Lausanne*)

Fencing medalists Helene Mayer of Germany (left), Ellen Müller-Preis of Austria (center), and Ilona Schacher-Elek of Hungary. All were of Jewish or part-Jewish ancestry, and Mayer was added to the German team to undercut the international movement to boycott the Nazi games. (*Olympic Study Center, Lausanne*)

Germany's soccer team giving the Nazi salute during the Berlin games.
(*Olympic Study Center, Lausanne*)

Leni Riefenstahl presiding over shooting during the making of her documentary
of the Berlin games. (*Olympic Study Center, Lausanne*)

messages came from Goebbels, who had invited Schmeling's wife to the Propaganda Ministry to listen to the broadcast: CONGRATULATIONS! I KNOW YOU FOUGHT FOR GERMANY. YOUR VICTORY WAS A GERMAN VICTORY. HEIL HITLER! In his diary the propaganda minister exulted: "Wonderful! Schmeling fought for Germany and won. White over Black, and the White was a German!" Hitler, that avid student of pugilism, likewise dashed off a congratulatory cable to Schmeling.

Two days after the fight, Schmeling, his face still puffy and bruised, was able to rush back to Germany on the sold-out *Hindenburg* zeppelin, courtesy of one of the airship's officers, who ceded his cabin to the boxer. On the way to Germany the craft dipped low over Doorn, Holland, home of exiled former Kaiser Wilhelm II. Looking out his cabin window, Schmeling could actually see the old man tip his hat in homage as the craft passed over. On disembarking in Frankfurt, Schmeling received an invitation from Hitler to attend a reception in his honor at the Reich Chancellery. There Hitler formally thanked the boxer for his victory in the name of the German people. He also insisted on an immediate screening of a film of the fight that Schmeling had brought back with him from New York. Soon a dubbed version of the film, entitled *Max Schmelings Sieg—Ein Deutscher Sieg*, was playing in cinemas across the Reich.

Exciting as Schmeling's victory was, however, it had to compete with the buzz that was building over the impending Olympic Games. In fact, during the Schmeling reception talk quickly turned to the Olympics, about whose commercial success the Nazi leaders were now much more confident. All of Berlin's hotels were already booked for the duration of the games, reported Goebbels. This news allowed Hitler to "guarantee" that the "70 million marks" [*sic*] spent on the sports stadium would be made back "several times over." With respect to Germany's athletic prospects in the Games, Schmeling's experience in New York had shown, Hitler believed, that the Germans need not fear the Americans and their legions of black gladiators. Olympia '36 promised to be a great "*deutscher Sieg*" in every regard.

On the Eve of the Games

About one month after Max Schmeling returned to Berlin, the United States Olympic Team set off from New York to Hamburg on board the SS *Manhattan*.

The mood on the ship was festive—indeed, a little too festive in the opinion of the AOC chaperones accompanying the team. According to reports from the vessel, some members of the field hockey, fencing, and women's swimming teams were engaging in such brazen violations of training regulations that the committee was considering dropping them off in Cobh, Ireland (the port of Cork). The most egregious offender, it seems, was swimmer Eleanor Holm Jarrett, a twenty-two-year-old beauty who had won the one-hundred-meter breaststroke in the LA Games and was expected to repeat that feat in Berlin. In 1933 the swimmer had married bandleader Art Jarrett, with whose ensemble she liked to appear in a bathing suit, high heels, and cowboy hat singing "I'm an Old Cow Hand." On board the *Manhattan* she spent most evenings drinking champagne and playing dice with sportswriters like Joe Williams, who labeled her "the glorious Brooklyn mermaid." Shipboard gossip also had her involved in "an all-night party" with playwright Charles MacArthur, who was traveling without his wife, actress Helen Hayes. On one occasion Jarrett reportedly got so drunk that she collapsed on her way back to her cabin. After discussing her case with fellow AOC members, Avery Brundage dismissed her from the team, citing the need to protect the image of American Olympism. He stuck to his ruling despite a petition from Jarrett's teammates pleading that he reinstate her.

Jarrett did not go quietly. When she arrived in Berlin she issued a statement asserting that the AOC had known in advance she was a girl who liked her champagne but had said nothing to her about her habits. Moreover, she noted, she was hardly the only athlete to have broken the rules, and even the officials accompanying the team had not exactly set an example of moral probity. Cocktail parties had been "a nightly occurrence," she said, and Gus Kirby had presided over a mock wedding ceremony that was "so shocking that many athletes had walked out of the social hall." In short, the officials had singled her out "to distract attention from their own misdeeds and their laxity in maintaining discipline."

To the AOC's horror Jarrett decided to stay on in Berlin and cover the games for Hearst's International News Service. She let it be known that her former teammates had sent her a box of handkerchiefs with a note saying "Keep Your Chin Up!" But Jarrett needed no such advice. She plunged into the Olympics party scene, attending receptions held by Hitler, Goebbels, and Göring. The last gave her a silver swastika pin, which she brandished proudly on her right breast. (Later, after divorcing Jarrett and marrying the Jewish impresario Billy Rose, she tactfully had the pin redone in gold with a diamond Star of David.)

It turned out that Jarrett was not the only athlete to be dropped from the American team on the eve of the Berlin games. On July 29 featherweight boxer Joe Church and welterweight Howell King, both top candidates in their respective divisions, reboarded the *Manhattan* to return to New York. The explanation given by the AOC for their sudden departure was "homesickness." This explanation satisfied no one, but the committee would not elaborate. Eventually it came out that the two athletes had been apprehended while trying to steal a camera from a Berlin shop, and that they had been sent home immediately to avoid a scandal. King, who was black, later claimed that he had been framed with the theft accusation because he had dared complain about racial discrimination on the American team. He said the white boxer had been sent home with him "to cover up any racial angle."

The Americans, of course, were not the only athletes pouring into Berlin after lengthy passages to Germany. The Australians had arrived a month earlier than the Americans in order to have more time to recover from an exceedingly long ocean voyage. Complete with their kangaroo mascot, the Aussie team was greeted, according to the *Sydney Herald*, "by high officials of the Nazi party" and treated to a propaganda film about Hitler. The Japanese also arrived early, after a twelve-day trip on the Trans-Siberian Railway, for which they had to get special dispensation from the Soviet government.

The Chinese team showed up in Berlin after a twenty-five-day ocean voyage from Shanghai to Venice and a two-day rail trip that included a stopoff in Munich, where the mayor took them on a personal tour of the sites connected to the birth of Nazism. In Berlin the team was greeted by three hundred Chinese residents and students chanting "Long Live the Republic of China" and waving the national flags that local Chinese restaurants had been distributing for weeks. According to one of the Chinese athletes, the Berliners were extremely impressed by the discipline and smart appearance exhibited by the athletes as they marched out of the station. "They thought that Chinese men wore little hats and Chinese women had little bound feet, but we came out wearing Western suits!"

The British, for their part, arrived at the last minute after a short trip on the boat train from London. There were no fans at the station waving Union Jacks, and the athletes repaired immediately to their quarters. It turned out that the Olympic Village houses reserved for the British were named after

Ruhr Valley industrial towns—the very towns, as chance would have it, that the British army would occupy after World War II.

As they settled into the Olympic Village, most of the athletes, whatever their nationality, found it to their liking. They were especially impressed with the food, for the German organizers, taking a cue from Los Angeles, saw to it that every national taste was accommodated. The North German Lloyd Shipping Company, which got the provisioning contract based on its long experience with picky passengers, provided special menus including underdone steaks and milkshakes for the Americans; medium-done grilled meat and boiled vegetables for the British; steak tartare and raw liver for the Germans; mushrooms, anchovies, white bread, and wine for the French; lots of pork for the Czechs; rye bread and blueberries for the Finns; vegetarian dishes for the Indians; raw fish and soy sauce for the Japanese and Chinese.

The athletes' chief complaint about the village was its isolation. They could take special buses into central Berlin, but the round trip consumed so much time that it was hard to fit into busy training schedules. While resident in the village the athletes had little contact with the outside world, for the Gestapo ensured that only "authorized" guests were allowed into the compound. One of those visitors was Max Schmeling, who took special care to meet Jesse Owens, telling the American that he expected him to win several gold medals. After the meeting Owens, loyal to his friend Joe Louis, allowed that Schmeling was "all right," but insisted, "Joe'll whip him next time." (Owens, of course, was right about this, but what he did *not* tell Schmeling was that he had bet on him to defeat Louis in the first fight.)

Other "visitors" to the village included handsome young women especially selected by the Gestapo to supply the athletes—but only the *white* athletes— with sexual favors. According to Swiss Olympian Paul Martin, a retired physician in Lausanne, the athletes met their assigned paramours in a secret wooded area on the edge of the village, informally known as "the Love Garden." Recalls Martin:

The Olympic athlete in Berlin was elevated to a godlike creature. . . . The Germans had even reserved a sort of heavenly forest for those gods. And there the prettiest handpicked maidens would offer themselves to the athletes – to the good Aryan types. . . . The maidens were usually sports teachers or members of Hitler's *Bund deutscher Mädchen* and they had special passes to enter the Village woods and mingle with the athletes. It was a lovely birch forest which had a pretty little lake, and the place was tightly ringed by Schupos [Berlin city police] so no one could disturb the sportive couples. It was interesting that before submitting to the Olympic god of her choice, the girl would request her partner's Olympic badge. In case of pregnancy, the girl would give this information to the state or Red Cross maternities to prove the Olympic origin of her baby. Then the state would pay for the whole works."

Ordinary German prostitutes also tried to work the Olympic Village, but they had to stay outside the tightly guarded security fence. The authorities were particularly eager to prevent any acts of so-called *Rassenschande* (miscegenation) between the German prostitutes and "non-Aryan" Olympians.

During their excursions into the city the athletes had only limited opportunities to socialize with local women because here, too, police agents shadowing the men had orders to prevent contacts that might lead to unauthorized sexual encounters, especially between the races. On the eve of the games the Gestapo issued warnings to fifty-two German women for, as the police put it, "approaching foreigners, particularly colored foreigners, in an undignified manner."

IF the Olympic Village presented a relatively tranquil image on the eve of the games, the city of Berlin emphatically did not. Although the number of foreign visitors showing up for the festival proved fewer than expected, with the American turnout especially disappointing, Berlin was overflowing with visitors because Germans from other parts of the Reich were arriving in huge numbers. Old-line Berliners insisted that they had never seen so many people parading up and down Unter den Linden and other central streets. Out near the Olympic Stadium thousands of German visitors guzzled beer, ate sausages, and listened to brass bands in the "Strength Through Joy Olympic Village," which consisted of six straw-roofed halls capable of serving 24,000 people at a time. The Strength Through Joy Village had its own temporary train station, where twenty to thirty special trains arrived each morning bearing twenty thousand German workers for day trips to the games. These excursions, like the Strength Through Joy holiday cruises and recreation camps, were designed to give the impression to the working classes that the Hitler state was *their* state, despite its suppression of the left-wing parties and independent unions.

As they had during the Winter Games, the German organizers went out of their way to make the foreign visitors to Berlin feel welcome and well cared for. The GOC brought in five hundred specially trained guides and translators to help the foreigners get around. The Berlin police held classes for its officers in English, French, and Spanish. Large hotels like the Adlon, Eden, and Excelsior hired additional translators and guides of their own. Frau Margarete Frick, wife of the interior minister, set up a committee to advise guests on places to visit. Multilingual guidebooks were made readily available. The GOC pleaded with ordinary Berliners, who had a reputation for rudeness, to show patience with outsiders and to give up their seats on the subway to foreign visitors.* As *Der Angriff* put the matter: "We are not only going to show off the most beautiful sports arena, the fastest transportation, and the cheapest currency: we are also going to be more charming than the Parisians, more lively than the Romans, more worldly than the Londoners, and more efficient than the New Yorkers."

In tandem with the GOC, the Hitler government was determined to "prove" to its Olympic guests from abroad that the Nazi capital was not the hotbed of racism and repression that many foreign newspapers claimed it to be. On the racial front the regime was able fairly quickly (more so than in Garmisch) to remove most visible signs of anti-Semitism. Most notably, the vending boxes containing Nuremberg *Gauleiter* Julius Streicher's Jew-baiting paper *Der Stürmer* disappeared from street corners for the duration of the games.

While *Der Stürmer* became hard to find in Berlin, many foreign papers, hitherto repressed by the regime, were suddenly available all over town. Similarly Berlin's bookstores, which theretofore had carried only politically acceptable volumes, now displayed some of the very titles that had been thrown on the pyres in the infamous book burnings of May 1933. The regime had been intending in June 1936 to revoke the citizenship of novelist Thomas Mann, who had fled Germany and spoken out against the Nazis;

---

*Some seventy years later, in preparation for the Beijing games of 2008, Chinese authorities launched a similar campaign aimed at improving the manners of the city's notoriously discourteous inhabitants, hoping to discourage them from their habitual hawking, spitting, cigarette-butt-throwing, and line-jumping behavior.

given the writer's international stature, however, this decision was put off until after the games.

Before the Nazis had come to power, Berlin had been famous for its avant-garde art scene, and now, in preparation for the games, city museums brought out of storage their modernist pieces and put them prominently on display. The Kronprinzenpalais on Unter den Linden featured paintings of the Blaue Reiter group. This was the kind of work that would not be seen again in Germany until the Nazis' infamous "Degenerate Art" exhibit in 1937, where viewers were invited to mock these "un-German" works in anticipation of their destruction (or sale to foreign dealers).

Visitors to the games could also partake of another Weimar-era cultural staple that had been under attack by the Nazis: jazz. The Nazi leaders decried jazz, with its roots in black American culture, as the ultimate in musical barbarism, but they had never banned it entirely. Rather they had sought to tame it by expelling the most innovative players (who were often foreign) and by censoring performances in the few jazz venues that were allowed to stay open. They even experimented with the ultimate in oxymorons—Nazi jazz—concocted by a state-sponsored band called the Golden Seven, but this experiment was quickly dropped when legions of young Germans practically broke the knobs off their radios tuning back to the BBC to hear genuine American jazz. As the Olympics approached the regime allowed some of the city's nightclubs and hotels to bring in "American-style" combos. The "jazz" in question, however, was extremely tame, typified by the pallid stylings of Swiss "swingmeister" Teddy Stauffer and His Original Teddies, who performed at the Delphi Palast. No black jazz groups were allowed in Berlin, even during the games. The likes of Duke Ellington, Louis Armstrong, and Coleman Hawkins would not be heard in Germany until after the Nazi defeat.

Another bit of Americana on hand in Berlin was Coca-Cola, which, as we have seen, had also been on the scene at the Winter Games in Garmisch. Coca-Cola Company president Robert Woodruff made a special trip to Berlin to secure a place for his product at the Summer Games. As it turned out, that place was not quite as prominent as Woodruff would have liked. Because the GOC had already granted an exclusive "Olympic beverage" concession to a popular Berlin brewery, Coke could not be sold within the Olympic facilities and had to settle for sidewalk stands outside the official venues. Moreover, Nazi health authorities insisted that a warning about Coke's caffeine content be placed on every bottle. On top of that an anti-Coke pamphlet circulating in Germany on the eve of the games described the beverage as "a soft drink made of South American herbs"—a reference to its use of Andean coca-leaf extract—and insisted that the company was a "Jewish-owned enterprise" whose secret purpose was to corner the German soft drink market for the benefit of big American capital. When it came to nonalcoholic beverages, said local patriots, good Germans must drink "Olympia," a soft drink produced by Franz Seldte, the founder of the right-wing Stahlhelm veterans' group, or confine themselves to one of the domestic seltzers, as did the Führer himself. Perhaps due to all the restrictive measures and the local anti-Coke agitation, Coke reported only "middling sales" during the Berlin games.

Still the Olympics introduced many Germans to America's subtly addictive cola concoction, and the caffeine additive undoubtedly proved to be a plus with the coffee-crazed Germans in the long run. During the games Woodruff met with Hermann Göring, chief of the Reich's Four-Year Plan, and after some hard bargaining (and perhaps a bribe), he secured the right to keep Coke flowing into the Third Reich. The American firm continued to advertise at German sports events, and Woodruff even managed to get Göring himself to pose chugging a bottle of Coke. By the end of the 1930s sales had climbed to 4.5 million cases annually. Beer, move over!

During the Weimar era Berlin had also been famous for its anything-goes approach to sex. As Christopher Isherwood declared: "Berlin Means Boys." Isherwood's friend W. H. Auden, who like him had fled stuffy London for the relative openness of Berlin in the late 1920s, described the city as "a bugger's daydream," with "170 male brothels under police control." Catering to heterosexual tastes was an army of some 25,000 registered female prostitutes, backed up by thousands of part-timers, including legions of preteen girls who patrolled the seedy Friedrichstadt district. The Nazis had shut down most of this rampant sex scene shortly after taking power, but in the interest of showing Olympic visitors a good time and projecting an image of openness, the authorities reinstated seven thousand prostitutes whom they had previously banned from Berlin. The government also announced that local women would be allowed to wear their hemlines five centimeters higher than theretofore permitted.

Moreover, just in time for the influx of Olympic visitors, the authorities ordered the reopening of a number of shuttered nightclubs and quietly permitted the reappearance of homosexual bars. Himmler himself instructed the

Gestapo to obtain his written permission before arresting any foreign gentlemen for violating paragraph 175 of the penal code, a nineteenth-century regulation outlawing homosexual acts that had been expanded in 1935 to include any behavior that merely aroused homosexual desires. It is noteworthy that Himmler's caveat applied exclusively to *foreign* men. The police continued to arrest German men for homosexual acts during the period surrounding the Olympics; the number of such arrests reached 5,321 in 1936, up from 938 in 1934.

The Nazis were astute enough to realize that if many foreign visitors to Berlin might be put off by finding too little avant-garde culture or "decadent" sex, they would be equally dismayed by encountering too much militarism in the streets. The GOC had toyed with the idea of opening the Reichssportfeld with a military-sport competition but abandoned this idea on Hitler's own orders. Interior Minister Frick put out the word that members of Nazi organizations should wear sporty civilian clothes rather than their uniforms at Olympic events. Himmler commanded Hitler's bodyguard not to wear their usual sidearms while on duty at Olympic venues. The Germans rejected an offer from Mussolini to send a squadron of military stunt flyers to entertain the Olympic visitors. Even military music, theretofore ubiquitous on state-controlled radio, was scaled back somewhat in favor of traditional classical fare.

Arriving in Berlin in late July to cover the Olympics, *The New Yorker's* Janet Flanner wrote:

Berlin is now a handsome, hustling place to be at home in. The past year has been closer to physical prosperity and farther from political nervousness than any Germany has known since the war, and its capital city shows it. Kurfürstendamm, which is the new *Gemütlichkeit* center, is crowded with restaurants and cafés. At the government's request, fresh house paint and fuchsias at windows brighten every boulevard, especially those leading to the sports stadium. The lovely old linden trees on Unter den Linden have been cut down to make way for the new subway; even dendrologists would admit that that handsome highway now shows its best points for the first time. The elegant Wilhelmsplatz and the more popular Lustgarten have also both been deforested, as part of the Reich's plan to pattern important squares on Roman forums, useful for public meetings. Probably the only blot on Berlin's beauty will be the still unoccupied new American Embassy, discolored, drab, three windows broken and boarded, a solid, homey reminder of American depression amid Germany's prosperous facades.

On July 29 the IOC opened its thirty-fifth congress in the auditorium of Berlin's Friedrich Wilhelm University. On behalf of the Führer, Rudolf Hess welcomed the delegates. Tschammer and Lewald extended a welcome from the GOC, the Reichssportführer thanking the members for "guarding the noble fire of sport," a not-so-subtle reference to the IOC's stance against the boycott effort. Accepting the Germans' greetings and congratulations, Baillet-Latour patted himself on the back for having kept "politics and religion" out of the games. He also took this occasion formally to propose Coubertin for the Nobel Peace Prize, an initiative that had actually come from the Germans. (This effort failed, the Nazis having little clout with the Nobel committee. The peace prize in 1936 went to the imprisoned anti-Nazi German journalist, Carl von Ossietzky.)

During its three business sessions the IOC adopted Richard Strauss's *Olympic Hymn* as the official festive music for 1936, turned down a last-minute appeal from Russian exiles to participate in the games, and confirmed that the next Summer Games, those of 1940, would be held in Tokyo. Finally, in an especially telling move, the IOC unanimously accepted a motion from William May Garland that Ernest Jahncke, the only American IOC member to have criticized the Nazi games, be summarily expelled from the body. Technically Jahncke was excluded for having habitually missed IOC meetings (he was not present in Berlin either), but everyone knew that the real reason was his open defiance of his colleagues in the matter of the German games. In fact, in a private letter to Jahncke, Baillet-Latour told him that the IOC had removed him because he was "a traitor to its interests."

To add insult to the injury of expulsion, the IOC replaced Jahncke with Avery Brundage. This was doubly insulting because the committee, if it was determined to appoint Brundage, should by all rights have brought him in to replace not Jahncke but Charles Sherrill, who had died suddenly on June 25, 1936.

Aside from Jahncke, the other injured party in the IOC reshuffling was Gus Kirby, who had lobbied hard for a place in the group for himself. But

Kirby, despite his eventual championing of American participation in the Berlin games, had by his earlier questioning of this decision made himself persona non grata with the IOC. As for Brundage, he started his long tenure on the committee by proposing that all women athletes competing in the Olympics be subjected to thorough physical examinations to make sure that they were "100% female."

VI

"Holy Flame, Burn"

The Ceremonial Games

▲

▲

CEREMONY and ritual had been part of the modern Olympic experience from the outset. For Coubertin, the presence of solemn rites distinguished the Olympics from ordinary sporting championships. The amount of ritual, however, had varied considerably from Olympics to Olympics. Much to Coubertin's dismay, there was no official opening ceremony in the 1900 Paris games. Coubertin was also sharply critical of the 1920 Antwerp games for being too long on mere sport and too short on symbolism.

The Berlin Olympics of 1936, by contrast, left nothing to be desired in the realm of cult and culture—except possibly restraint. The prominence of rite and ritual in the Berlin games stemmed from the broader importance of cultic practices in the Third Reich. For the Nazis ritual was intended not merely for propagandistic effect—it reflected the movement's sense of itself as a kind of political religion. The 1936 Olympic Games amounted to a one-time extravaganza pulling together and magnifying such typical annual shows as the Nuremberg Party Rallies, celebrations of Hitler's birthday, and commemorations of the Beer Hall Putsch. While the purpose of the annual rituals was to capture the hearts and minds of the German masses, the Berlin Olympiad was designed to show the entire world that when it came to the sacralization of sport, nobody could do it better than the National Socialists. And here, too, the Germans claimed to be walking firmly in the footsteps of the ancient Greeks.

"A Victory for the German Cause"

Opening day of the 1936 Summer Olympic Games constituted the grandest party Germany's young capital had ever seen—grander even than the celebration in June 1871 marking Germany's inauguration as a new empire. That occasion had been rife with military symbolism, and so too was the Olympic opening, despite the professedly peaceful nature of the event at hand and the gestures at scaling back military display.

The day began at 8:00 A.M., when, with Prussian punctuality, the band of the Berlin Guards Regiment played a *Grosses Wecken* (grand reveille) in front of the Hotel Adlon, where the IOC officials were staying. Promptly at 9:30 cars arrived to ferry the dignitaries to religious services at the Berlin Cathedral (for the Protestants) and Saint Hedwig's Church (for the Catholics). As the IOC members were praying, thousands of Berlin schoolchildren marched to recreation fields around the city, where they engaged in group gymnastics, obstacle races, and synchronized club twirling. According to the German *Official Report*, the point of this show was "to provide a comprehensive picture of the many athletic pursuits of Berlin's schoolchildren." The show also, however, offered a picture of a highly regimented and militarized youth.

Military reverence was more obviously on display at a midmorning ceremony in front of the Neue Wache, a former Prussian guardhouse on Unter den Linden that now served as Germany's primary shrine to the soldiers who had died in World War I. Amassed at the monument were honor guards from the Wehrmacht as well as uniformed Hitler Youth detachments. Baillet-Latour, whose nation had been invaded and pillaged by Germany in 1914, deposited a wreath on behalf of all foreign sportsmen at the Tomb of the Unknown Soldier. The inspiration for this gesture came from Carl Diem, who had always seen Olympic competition as a form of war by other means. No doubt he also intended to suggest reconciliation among the former warring nations, but it was telling that he would make the cult of military sacrifice an important part of Berlin's Olympic ritual.

While the Neue Wache ceremony was still in progress, thousands of SA men and Hitler Youth gathered at the Lustgarten across from the Royal Palace to help welcome the arrival of the Olympic torch in central Berlin after its long journey from Olympia. Just getting these masses to their appointed places was a major logistical operation. The IOC members, fresh from their wreath-laying ceremony, were welcomed at the Old Museum by Hermann Göring, resplendent in a sky blue air force uniform. For their part, the committee delegates sported heavy gold chains spangled with medallions representing ancient Greek athletic events. The chains were yet another contribution from Diem, who believed that the IOC, as the "supreme senate of physical culture," must quite literally carry the burden of their august office. Following Göring's reception, the dignitaries assembled on the museum steps to witness a series of rituals designed to welcome the Olympic flame. As flags went up around the square the Hitler Youth sang the *Flag March*: "Hoist up our flags in the wind of the morning / To those who are idle, let them flutter a warning." Reich Youth Leader Baldur von Schirach addressed the multitudes: "We, the youth of Germany, we, the youth of Adolf Hitler, greet you, the youth of the world." There followed more communal singing and windy oratory by Tschammer and Goebbels, who, in anticipation of the Olympic torch's arrival, concluded his peroration with the words: "Holy flame, burn, burn, and never go out."

No sooner had Goebbels pronounced his ominous invocation than a sound of cheering arose from down the avenue, indicating the approach of the torch runner. On reaching the Lustgarten, the runner jogged down the center aisle, lit a flame at the Old Museum, and then ran back across the square to ignite another sacred flame at the Royal Palace. Both "flames of peace" would burn for the duration of the games. With the flames duly lit, Baillet-Latour stepped forth to thank Hitler in the name of the IOC for "the stupendous preparations which Germany has made for the Olympic Games." With specific reference to the torch ritual, he added: "All those who appreciate the symbolism of the sacred flame which has been borne from Olympia to Berlin are profoundly grateful to Your Excellency for not only having provided the means of binding the past and present, but also for having contributed to the progress of the Olympic ideals in future years." In response Hitler thanked the IOC for the opportunity to host a festival whose purpose was "the strengthening of human understanding." As further proof of Germany's commitment to the traditions and ideals of Olympism, Hitler announced that the German government would resume and conclude the excavations at ancient Olympia that German scholars had undertaken between 1875 and 1881. He called this undertaking "a permanent memorial to the Festival of the Eleventh Olympiad, Berlin, 1936."

Following a lunch for the IOC members at the Royal Palace, hosted by

Hitler, the dignitaries convoyed by car down the Via Triumphalis to the Reichssportfeld for the official opening of the games. The entire route was guarded by members of the National Socialist Motor Corps, the SS, the SA, and special units of the Berlin police. Tens of thousands of spectators stood patiently behind the guards, awaiting the chance to cheer their Führer. Among the crowds was the American novelist Thomas Wolfe, who, in his novel *You Can't Go Home Again*, provided a verbal snapshot of Hitler's passage:

> At last he came—and something like a wind across a field of grass was shaken through that crowd, and from afar the tide rolled up with him, and in it was the voice, the hope, the prayer of the land. The Leader came by slowly in a shining car, a little dark man with a comic-opera moustache, erect and standing, motionless and unsmiling, with his hand upraised, palm outward, not in Nazi-wise salute, but straight up, in a gesture of blessing such as the Buddha or Messiahs use.

The stadium gates had opened at 1:00 so that all spectators would be seated before Hitler's arrival, which was scheduled for 3:58 sharp. Security was extremely tight. During the previous evening police had swept the premises for possible bombs and had cleared the area of unauthorized vehicles. Guards were stationed at all entrances to the stadium, and plainclothes policemen patrolled the grounds. Vending booths were closed, and the sale of all items except for programs and guidebooks was prohibited. Even the restaurants and bars remained shuttered.

While the spectators were filing into the stadium, 170 buses brought the athletes from the Olympic Village to the sports complex, a process that was completed by 3:00. To keep everyone entertained during the long (and dry) hours before Hitler's arrival, the huge Olympic Symphony Orchestra, which was composed of the Berlin Philharmonic and the National Orchestra, supplemented by the Bayreuth Wagner Festival choir, presented a concert. Among the selections were the overture to Wagner's *Meistersinger* and Liszt's tone poem, *Les Préludes*.

Another source of entertainment was the giant airship *Hindenburg*, which cruised back and forth above the stadium trailing an Olympic banner from its gondola. The enormous zeppelin was perhaps the preeminent symbol of German inventive genius and an object of considerable national pride. Having gone into service only five months prior to the Berlin games, it had already crossed the Atlantic several times, including one speed-record passage of forty-nine hours from Lakehurst, New Jersey, to Frankfurt.

Hitler arrived at the Reichssportfeld precisely as scheduled. His first stop was the Bell Tower, where, accompanied by Blomberg and members of the IOC, he reviewed the athletes, who were assembled by national team on the May Field. With Blomberg he then entered the Langemarck Hall, there to commune silently for a few minutes with the spirits of the German war dead.

Escorted by Baillet-Latour and Lewald, Hitler passed through the Marathon Gate into the stadium, his entry announced by a trumpet fanfare and the hoisting of the *Führerstandarte*, a red swastika against a purple background. Upon glimpsing their Führer the German spectators leaped from their seats and emitted a giant roar. The cheering gradually gave way to Wagner's "March of Honor" as Hitler and his entourage began walking across the broad arena in the direction of the Honor Loge. In the middle of the field Hitler stopped briefly to accept a bouquet of flowers from little blond-haired Gudrun Diem, the five-year-old daughter of the GOC general secretary.

At the moment when Hitler finally took his place in the Honor Loge next to Hess, Blomberg, Frick, Baillet-Latour, and Crown Prince Umberto of Italy, the orchestra struck up the German national anthem, while the flags of all the participating nations were raised slowly up fifty-two flagpoles. Then the giant Olympic bell began to ring—its deep tolling the signal for the traditional march-past of the Olympic teams. Revealingly Diem entrusted the command of the march to a Wehrmacht major whose regular duties included choreographing all the military reviews in Greater Berlin.

First to enter, as always, was Greece, the historic birthplace of the Olympics. At the head of the Greek team and carrying the blue-and-white Greek flag was the 1896 marathon winner, Spiridon Louis. Behind Greece came the rest of the teams in alphabetical order, with Ägypten (Egypt) first, followed by Afghanistan. The Egyptians had participated in the games before, but this was the first appearance for Afghanistan.

As in the Winter Games at Garmisch, the parade of athletes in Berlin became a source of confusion and controversy because the "Olympic salute" rendered by most of the teams looked very much like the Nazi salute. The Austrians, again as in Garmisch, received a huge cheer from the largely German audience for giving what most in the stadium misinterpreted as the *Hitler-Gruss*. A hearty cheer also went up for the French, although the warm reception they received could be read as a sign of amity toward an old adversary with whom the German masses hoped to live in harmony. According to Speer, who stood near Hitler during the opening ceremony, the Führer was not pleased by the cheers for France, sensing in them "a longing for peace and reconciliation with Germany's western neighbor."

Great Britain, which followed France, garnered much less applause because its athletes chose to eschew the salute in favor of a snappy eyes-right. The Turks, by contrast, held their salute for the entire procession, while the Bulgarians saluted *and* goose-stepped. Italy, in honor of its new friendship with Germany, not only gave the Fascist salute but dipped its flag to Hitler, which it had not done in Garmisch.

The United States athletes, entering as the penultimate team before the host Germans, elicited a chorus of catcalls because, on passing the Honor Loge, they placed their boater hats over their hearts while gazing steadfastly at their unlowered flag. This business with the flag was not a specific insult to Hitler. It had been a custom for American Olympians to keep their flag high since the 1908 London games, when the Yanks had not wanted to appear to kowtow to the British king. That tradition was confirmed in 1928 by Douglas MacArthur, then president of the AOC. Nonetheless the Americans were later chastised by the GOC for failing to show due respect to Hitler. As AOC Secretary Rubien acknowledged to Secretary of State Hull, "We were the only one of the fifty-three [*sic*] nations to fail to dip our flag."

Disgruntlement over the Americans' haughty behavior gave way to mass ecstasy as the huge German team, decked out in white suits and jaunty yachting caps, swept into the stadium "like a great machine" behind a fluttering swastika banner. The Olympic Orchestra contributed its part to the symbolic merger of the German state and Nazi Party by striking up, back to back, the national anthem and the "Horst Wessel Lied." Carrying the German flag was Hans Fritsch, a discus and javelin champion who, like a sizable number of his teammates, was a member of the German military. (When Fritsch failed to medal in the games, he was forced to devote himself full-time to his military duties.)

Once the athletes had assembled on the playing field the scratchy sound of a recorded human voice trickled from the loudspeakers. It was the voice of Coubertin, the old man present "in spirit" if not in body. Coubertin's message was innocuous enough—his standard refrain that the important thing about the Olympics was to take part rather than to win, just as the crucial thing in life was to struggle nobly rather than to conquer—but the delivery of this platitude at a Nazi-hosted festival could not have been more bitterly ironic.

While the primary motive behind the Coubertin recording was to co-opt further the founder of the modern Olympics for the Nazi cause, the rationale behind the next piece of aural theater, an overlong speech by GOC President Theodor Lewald, was to cast Hitler as the man of the hour and to reassert Nazi Germany's "blood" ties to the ancient Greeks. After lionizing Hitler as the "protector of these Olympic Games," Lewald had this to say regarding the upcoming torchlighting ceremony in the stadium: "In a few minutes the torch bearer will appear to light the Olympic fire on his tripod, where it will rise, flaming to heaven, for the weeks of this festival. It creates a real and spiritual bond of fire between our German fatherland and the sacred places of Greece founded nearly 4,000 years ago by Nordic immigrants." Lewald then turned the microphone over to Hitler, inviting him to open the games. Following protocol, the Führer stuck to the prescribed simple declaration: "I announce as opened the Games of Berlin, celebrating the Eleventh Olympiad of the modern era."

Hitler's brief announcement was the signal for a new onslaught of ceremonial bombast and ritual. Sailors standing in the center of the infield raised a giant five-ringed Olympic flag to the accompaniment of trumpet fanfares and a twenty-one-gun salute. At the same time, Hitler Youth members opened cages to release twenty thousand carrier pigeons. The birds swept up over the stadium in a widening spire, dung-bombing some in the crowd. Watching the birds vanish into the sky, the spectators probably could not have been aware that this traditional symbol of peace also had a military side to it: The pigeons in question belonged to the German army.

Nor were the crowds aware of the behind-the-scenes wrangling shadowing the next piece of ritual: the performance of the *Olympic Hymn*. The IOC had originally proposed that the hymn composed for the Los Angeles games should also be used in 1936, but Lewald insisted that Germany, as *the* music nation par excellence, must provide its own anthem. In fall 1931 he approached Germany's greatest living composer, Richard Strauss, with a request to compose the music.

Strauss agreed, provided he had an adequate text to work with. To come up with a suitable text the GOC sponsored a national competition in 1934 that generated reams of patriotic kitsch, including one entry celebrating

Siegfried as "the first master of sport." Finally the judges found what they considered an acceptable work by an unheralded "poet of the people" named Robert Lubahn. Lubahn's initial effort, however, did not pass muster with officials of the Propaganda Ministry, who objected to its lack of a true "National Socialist spirit." The officials proposed specific revisions, which Lubahn reluctantly accepted. The phrase "*Peace* be the Games' slogan" was changed to "*Honor* be the Games' slogan," while the line "*Rule of law* shall be the highest" became "*Loyalty to oath* shall be the highest." The revisions may have been small in number, but they turned what had been a standard ode to Olympic idealism into a celebration of principles dear to the Nazis.

Strauss's part in this project also presented problems. He demanded an honorarium of ten thousand reichsmarks, which was out of the question for the GOC. When informed by Lewald that his demand was unacceptable, Strauss agreed to do the work for free, which is what the GOC had in mind all along. No doubt the fact that Strauss had recently been named president of the Reich Chamber of Music influenced his decision here, for his new job carried with it responsibilities to the Reich. Lewald thanked Strauss profusely for his "gift," which he said was "the greatest and most beautiful" the GOC had ever received. He hoped, he added, that the IOC would make Strauss's work the "Olympic Hymn for all time," and he proposed that Strauss himself conduct the piece on opening day.

Strauss received Lubahn's amended libretto in late September 1934 and managed to complete a score by early December, which suggests that he did not take undue pains with the work at hand. Indeed, as he told one of his regular librettists, the Jewish writer Stefan Zweig, "I'm killing time during the slack Advent season by composing an Olympic hymn for the proletarians." Despite his disdain for this project, however, Strauss proposed to Lewald that he be permitted to preview his hymn personally for the Führer. Behind this request was an apparent desire on the part of the composer to ingratiate himself with Hitler and the Nazi leadership. Lewald endorsed Strauss's request, and on March 29, 1935, the composer performed his hymn at the Reich Chancellery for Hitler and Göring.

Yet for all his apparent anxiousness to flatter Hitler, Strauss harbored a highly ambivalent view about his role in the Nazi regime. By reemploying Stefan Zweig as the librettist for his new opera, *Die schweigsame Frau*, he showed an impolitic disregard for Nazi regulations regarding the exclusion of Jews from German cultural life. Goebbels only very reluctantly allowed the opera to premiere in Dresden. Shortly thereafter Strauss was forced to step down from his presidency of the Reich Music Chamber because the Gestapo discovered he had written Zweig to say that he had taken the Nazi post only to prevent worse things from happening. Now it looked as if he might not be able to conduct his hymn at the opening ceremony of the Berlin Games, which in his vanity he very much wanted to do. Lewald intervened with the Reich Chancellery on Strauss's behalf, pointing out that the composer's huge international reputation made him the perfect candidate for this job. Aware that having the grand old man at the podium would indeed be a coup for the Reich, the government relented.

The crowd cheered lustily when the white-haired composer mounted the rostrum to lead the huge Olympic orchestra and chorus in a rousing rendition of his *Olympic Hymn*. No one seemed to notice that this was among the weakest pieces Strauss had ever written. Certainly the IOC did not notice, or care, for it formally endorsed Lewald's proposal that the 1936 hymn be declared the "Olympic hymn for all time." Fortunately for future generations of Olympic spectators, this decision did not outlast the collapse of the Third Reich and the tainting of Strauss's reputation by his association with the Nazi regime. For the 1948 London games the IOC recycled the 1932 hymn; and in 1956 it commissioned a new one, a practice it has followed ever since.

While the audience inside the stadium was absorbed in all this grand ritual, outside, on the Via Triumphalis, the final stages of the torch relay, from the Lustgarten to the Reichssportfeld, were in progress. Just as the *Olympic Hymn* ended, a white-clad, flaxen-haired youth bearing the sacred flame appeared atop the steps at the East Gate of the stadium. The figure in question was Fritz Schilgen, a twenty-nine-year-old Telefunken employee who a few years previously had been among Germany's best middle-distance runners. After a brief pause Schilgen loped through the ranks of athletes amassed on the infield and mounted the steps below the Marathon Gate. At the top of these steps he paused again, and then touched his torch to a brazier mounted on a bronze tripod. The flame that would burn above the stadium for the next sixteen days leaped to life.

The torchlighting moment in the stadium, while certainly the high point of the opening-day ceremony, was not the end of it, not by a long shot. Spiridon Louis, the ancient marathoner, now tottered up to the Führer's box and presented him with an olive branch plucked from a tree growing in the ruins at Olympia. Louis had been invited to Berlin by the GOC, which paid all his expenses, including, according to his German guide's account record, 33.40 reichsmarks for "beverages" and 6 reichsmarks for cigarettes. Obviously Louis was on hand so that the Germans might stake yet another symbolic claim to the tradition begun by Coubertin forty years earlier. According to the *Official Report*, Hitler replied to Louis's gesture "with words of deep gratitude." Another German account said of the moment: "Past and present shook hands, as the great ideals of mankind bridged the millennia." (Louis, a lifelong heavy smoker, died of a heart attack on March 26, 1940, a year before Germany invaded his homeland.)

With past and present successfully bridged, it remained only for the athletes to swear their Olympic oath and march out of the stadium. For the oath swearing, the flag bearers of the various nations formed a semicircle around the speaker's platform while weightlifter Rudolf Ismayer, a German medal winner from the 1932 games, took the oath on behalf of all the assembled athletes. Like his counterpart in Garmisch, he clutched a swastika flag while doing so. This task completed, the athletes filed out of the stadium to the music of Handel's *Hallelujah Chorus*.

One would have thought, as the athletes trooped out of the stadium, that the German organizers had packed enough ceremony into one day, but there was still another event to come that evening—a performance of *Olympic Youth*, a five-act pageant written especially for the occasion by Carl Diem and directed by Hanns Niedecken-Gebhard, a former stage director of the Metropolitan Opera in New York. Most of the music was composed by Werner Egk, a young German maestro whose first opera, *The Enchanted Violin*, had won him fame "second only to that of Richard Strauss." The inspiration for this project was a request from Coubertin to work the choral section of Beethoven's Ninth Symphony—based on Schiller's *Ode to Joy*—into the opening-day ceremony. Diem and Niedecken-Gebhard managed to do this, though the *Ode* almost got lost in the process.

Advertised as a celebration of romantic youth, the pageant began just after nightfall with trumpets sounding the "Welcome Song." Five thousand little girls in white dresses and nine hundred boys clad in the five Olympic colors entered the stadium and began to dance to the tinkling of glass chimes. They eventually formed the Olympic flag. The chimes gave way to a recording of the bells of the Potsdam Garrison Church, burial site of Friedrich the Great and the place where, in 1934, Hitler had presented himself to President Hindenburg as the embodiment of German conservative virtue. When the bells ceased tolling, two choruses stepped out of the darkness to sing *Eternal Olympia*, a hymn by Egk. Now the children left the area to be replaced by two thousand older girls, who were presently joined by five hundred more girls from a Berlin gymnastics club. Together they performed a rhythmic dance number until "The Voice of the Mother" sounding from the loudspeakers admonished them to be serious and solemn. The next scene involved groups of boys from many nations playing games around a series of bonfires blazing away on small handcarts. At the sound of a trumpet the fires were whisked away, and a spotlight focused on the Marathon Gate, picking out twelve hundred youths descending the steps carrying the flags of all nations. The Swiss flag bearers in the lead put on a demonstration of synchronized flag twirling. When the flag bearers reached the center of the stadium they raised their arms in the Olympic salute and sang another hymn.

This was followed by Diem's pièce-de-résistance—a sword dance involving two armor-clad warriors who slew each other in rhythmic agony. The moral here was supposedly the futility of war, but it was also an *homage* to the glory and beauty of death in battle on the part of young heroes gladly spilling their blood for a noble cause. As the young warriors were being carried off on their shields, eighty women belonging to a dance troupe headed by Mary Wigman, one of the preeminent choreographers of the era, presented a "Dance of the Mourners." All this transpired before the first notes of Beethoven's choral ode finally sounded. A chorus of one thousand belted out Schiller's famous lines while the thousands of performers who had appeared in previous scenes all streamed back into the stadium to join hands and embrace. Lighted torches formed a ring of fire around the outer edge of the stadium, and seventeen searchlights played across the sea of flags as a sign that the pageant was finally over.

Perhaps one had to have been there. The spectators who were present seem to have found the performance effective and moving, or at least gratifyingly noisy. Writing in *The New Yorker*, Janet Flanner observed that Diem's "novel application of cinema principles" had produced "a brilliant new nocturnal beauty." *Time* magazine spoke of a spectacle that made the Los Angeles opening ceremony seem "as quiet as a race between two trained fleas around the brim of a felt hat." The *New York Times* was positively rhapsodic: "[*Olympic Youth*] was the most ambitious and, in the opinion of many, the most beautiful pageant ever before attempted in any land." This show, the *Times* reporter opined, constituted a fitting climax to the most impressive opening-day ceremony in modern Olympic history. "These Olympic Games have had an opening notable even beyond expectations, high as they were. They seem likely to accomplish what the rulers of Germany have frankly desired from them, that is, to give the world a new viewpoint from which to regard the Third Reich. It is promising that this viewpoint will be taken from an Olympic hill of peace."

Goebbels, that connoisseur of political theater, was elated by all that had transpired on opening day. "A beautiful day, a great day," he wrote in his diary. "A victory for the German cause."

An Olympics of the Mind and Spirit (and a Little Flesh)

When founding the modern games, Coubertin had hoped that the festival would be as much about the intellect as the body. From 1912 on each of the Olympiads had included an "arts competition," but these affairs had been half-heartedly organized and were generally ignored by the press and public. This changed in 1936. Lewald and Diem fully shared Coubertin's vision of "a marriage of spirit and muscle." The Nazi regime, for its part, was anxious to give the impression that the Third Reich was a hotbed of cultural creativity. The Berlin games therefore featured an extremely ambitious program of artistic competitions, theatrical and musical performances, exhibitions, conferences, and other cultural events. By and large these affairs were well attended, and all received extensive coverage by the German and international press.

The impressive *quantity* of cultural activity, however, did not necessarily translate into a high *quality* of artistic expression. Given the ongoing exodus of Jews and political dissenters among Germany's cultural elite, many of the country's most respected talents either could not or would not be part of this *Kultur-Olympia*. Some foreign artists also refused to participate in protest against Nazi racial and political persecution. For example, in response to Goebbels's personal invitation to take part in the International Dance Competition, Martha Graham, leader of America's premier modern dance troupe, replied: "I would find it impossible to dance in Germany at the present time. So many artists whom I respect and admire have been persecuted, have been deprived of the right to work for ridiculous and unsatisfactory reasons, that I should consider it impossible to identify myself, by accepting the invitation, with the regime that has made such things possible. In addition, some in my dance group would not be welcome in Germany."

Like Graham, the American composer Charles Wakefield Cadman wanted no part of the Nazi games. Announcing his withdrawal from the committee charged with judging the music competition, he stated: "If I [initially] gave my consent to serve on such a committee, it was before I learned definitively and specifically of the attitude of Herr Hitler in regard to the persecution of racial and religious groups and the suppression of civil liberties." Taking up the theme of Nazi cultural persecution, the American magazine *Art Front* published a cartoon titled "Hitler as Art Patron," which showed a demonic-looking Führer holding up a mask of friendliness while extending an invitation to the Olympic Art Exhibition.

Moreover, just as anti-Nazi athletes protested the 1936 games by agreeing to participate in "alternative games," a number of artists organized an alternative art show to call attention to Nazi cultural oppression. Entitled "The Olympics Under Dictatorship," the exhibition took place in Amsterdam from August 11 to August 17, 1936. The show featured avant-garde prose and poetry, anti-Nazi broadsides, and some 270 paintings, posters, cartoons, and photographs by the likes of Robert Capa, Max Ernst, John Heartfield, Fernand Léger, Max Lingner, David Low, and Pablo Picasso. The German press condemned the exhibition as a hateful slur put together by "international Jewry, Marxists of all shades, and a clique of stateless émigrés." Hitler's government registered an official protest against the show, causing the Dutch authorities to close it down and to jail its chief organizer for "insulting the head of a friendly nation."

The official art competitions sponsored by the GOC during the 1936 games were closely monitored by the Propaganda Ministry and the various "cultural chambers" that controlled artistic expression in Nazi Germany. The "international" juries that judged the entries were made up primarily of Germans, and indeed, of Germans who had passed the regime's ideological muster. For example, chairing the Plastic and Graphic Arts jury was the painter Adolf Ziegler, who headed the Reich Chamber for Visual Arts (and who, because of his fondness for painting startlingly realistic nudes, earned the sobriquet *Reichsschamhaarpinsler*—official pubic hair painter of the Reich). Chairing the music competition was Peter Raabe, the new president of the Reich Chamber of Music, while Hanns Johst, a "Blood and Soil" novelist and president of the Reich Literary Chamber, headed the jury for literature.

The juries did not hesitate to favor works from the German-speaking realm and Fascist Italy. Of the sixty-two awards in the five arts categories—architecture, plastic and graphic art, sculpture, music, and literature—twenty prizes went to Germans, nine to Austrians, and eleven to Italians. Werner March, chief designer of the Reichssportfeld, won the gold medal in architecture; Werner Egk, the "Olympic Youth" composer, won first prize for orchestral composition; Arno Breker, Hitler's favorite sculptor, won a silver medal in standing sculpture; Felix Dhunen, a party hack, won gold in lyric poetry. Olympic visitors were able to see the prizewinning visual art at the German Reich Art Exhibition and could hear the music winners at a special Olympic concert performed by the Olympic Orchestra on the penultimate day of the games.

Fortunately for those Olympic visitors with a genuine interest in the arts, the cultural offerings on hand during the games went beyond the official events connected to the Olympic Arts program. Berlin had long been preeminent in opera, and it remained so despite boycotts by some international stars, most notably Arturo Toscanini. During the games the State Opera House on Unter den Linden did not put on any shows because the space was reserved for official receptions, but the German Opera in nearby Berlin-Charlottenburg mounted an "Olympic Richard Wagner Festival" featuring first-class productions of *Der Ring des Nibelungen*, *Die Meistersinger*, and *Rienzi*.

The new Dietrich-Eckart Open Air Theater provided a grand setting for a host of alfresco theatrical and musical performances. First in the lineup was Handel's oratorio *Heracles*, which was performed five times due to its supposed "inner attachment to the Olympic idea and its particular appropriateness for the Eckart Theater." Some one hundred thousand people witnessed the Handel production. This theater also offered lighter fare, such as a "Waltz Evening" and concerts by the official band of the Reich Chamber of Music.

The elegant Schauspielhaus in the Gendarmenmarkt was another prime location of Olympic entertainment, primarily of the elevated sort. On tap here were credible productions of Goethe's *Faust*, Schiller's *Bride of Messina*, Kleist's *Hermannschlacht*, Hebbel's *Gyges and His Ring*, Aeschylus's *Orestes*, and Shakespeare's *Hamlet*. The *Hamlet* claimed greatest attention because Gustav Gründgens, Germany's most celebrated man of the theater, directed the production and played the title role.

The German organizers understood that Shakespeare, Goethe, and Wagner were not likely to galvanize most visitors to the games, and so they also laid on a host of less demanding popular entertainments. At the Strength Through Joy Village near the Funkturm (a radio transmitter that was Berlin's answer to the Eiffel Tower), audiences could watch high-wire acts as well as the world's first large-screen television broadcasts. Strength Through Joy performers put on a nocturnal program at the Olympic Stadium entitled "Music and Dance of the Peoples," with a giant cast of German and foreign performers. Of a similar ilk was the Reich Labor Service's vaunted "Tree Trunk Exercise," in which burly men tossed around massive pieces of timber to the accompaniment of a harmonica band.

On another night in the stadium forty-five military bands with more than two thousand musicians staged the largest military music concert in history. For the duration of the games Hagenbeck's Circus came to town with a "Five-Ring Olympic Circus Festival" featuring a high-jumping bear and an elephant that could heave a shot with its trunk. The city's many cinemas catered to foreign visitors with Walt Disney cartoons and an English-language version of *Max Schmeling's Victory—A German Victory*. The Wintergarten Variety Theater showcased the "Hiller Girls," a Nazi-era takeoff on the famous Tiller Girls erotic dance show of the Weimar period. Dressed in eighteenth-century Prussian military uniforms, and trained by an army drill sergeant, the Hiller Girls sacrificed eroticism for a military precision that put the Wehrmacht to shame. For something rawer visitors could repair to the Café Aryan for transvestite reviews, although the entry fee of twenty American dollars meant that practically only fat-cat Americans could go.

AS noted above, the GOC had organized various exhibitions in advance of the games to awaken interest in the upcoming festivals. The exhibitions "Germany-Olympia" and "Sport in Hellenic Times" stayed open during the Olympics, and to these shows were added a number of new ones designed primarily for the festival visitors. The Museum of Ethnology mounted an earnestly didactic program on "The Sport of Non-European Peoples." Here visitors could learn that "the ancient Chinese were experts at pole-vaulting, the Negro races were good at the high jump, while the Polynesians excelled at water sports." The Kronprinzenpalais mounted an exhibit called "Contemporary Portraits of Great Germans"—the "great Germans" including composers like Bach and Beethoven (but no Mendelssohn), writers like Goethe and Schiller (but no Heinrich Heine or Thomas Mann); scientists like Robert Koch (but no Einstein).

Finally there was a monster attraction simply called "Deutschland," which covered some 40,000 square meters in eight indoor exhibition halls plus another 113,000 square meters of outdoor space. Interestingly enough, this show was put together by members of the Bauhaus, the avant-garde design school that had recently been shut down by the Nazis. There was, however, nothing avant-garde about the "Deutschland" exhibition, which amounted to one big advertisement for Germany, especially National Socialist Germany. Among the thousands of exhibits were original copies of the Gutenberg Bible and Luther's *Ninety-Five Theses*, and the manuscript of Hitler's *Mein Kampf.* There were also historical paintings of World War I and a display called "Die Frauen," which advocated keeping women at home. A presentation on eugenics called for sterilizing the unfit and expanding German living space abroad. Upon entering the "Deutschland" exhibit, visitors saw a photomontage titled "Der Führer and His Entourage," which depicted Hitler and his top henchmen leading the German people happily into the future.

The intellectual claims staked out by the Olympic exhibitions were reinforced by various high-minded lectures. Perhaps the most notable lecture was given by Sven Hedin, the famous Swedish explorer of Central Asia. Hedin was invited to speak at the Berlin games by Hitler, who in 1933 had sent the explorer a congratulatory telegram on the fourteenth anniversary of his first expedition to the Asian highlands.

Hedin was also admired by Himmler, with whom he shared the crackbrained theory that ancient Tibet was the cradle of the Aryan race. Upon his arrival in Berlin for his Olympic cultural mission, Hedin held a news conference in which he said exactly what his hosts wanted to hear. "I am convinced," he declared, "that the Olympic Games have much greater significance than the League of Nations." On the evening of the first day of competition at the Olympic Stadium, Hedin addressed a short oration to the youth of the world, containing such exhortations as: "Do not be content with what you are able to do. Strive to achieve what you are not able to do, and, if possible, the unattainable."

Hedin reserved his weightiest scholarly insights for his main Olympic presentation: a long disquisition on "The Role of the Horse in the History of Asia." Here he lavished praise on the great horses of the steppes, which had been instrumental to the Mongol conquests. His argument was later taken over by Himmler to help justify a wartime program to breed super–steppe horses for the Germans' ill-fated campaign in Russia. Hedin's ideas also helped inspire the three Tibet expeditions of an SS officer named Dr. Ernst Schäfer, who in a report to Himmler extolled the "racially pure" natives of that mountain kingdom as "brave, sturdy and fit." With Hedin's contribution, the 1936 Olympic festival added Tibet to ancient Greece as a progenitor of the modern German *Volk*.

No major cultural occasion in Germany could be complete without a scientific congress, and the German Olympics boasted three of them. The largest of the conferences—"The World Leisure and Recreation Congress"—was organized by the Strength Through Joy program and took place in Hamburg in late July. Hitler's deputy Rudolf Hess acted as patron of this event, which brought together more than three hundred experts on sport and recreation from sixty-one countries. Although billed as a purely scientific undertaking, the event had a clear ideological agenda. Strength Through Joy offered free room and board to ethnic German participants from regions outside the Reich who agreed to advertise their German ethnicity during the congress. The idea here was to document the spread of German blood, customs, and values around the world, and, by implication, to suggest the possibility of "bringing home" these European *Auslandsdeutsche* (foreign, or ethnic, Germans) to an expanded super-Reich. This design was so transparent that the parliament of Luxembourg, a country harboring a sizable ethnic German minority, passed a Socialist-sponsored protest against the congress and censured the scientists from Luxembourg who chose to attend.

Just as with the Olympic arts competition, some foreign scholars refused to involve themselves in the Germans' Olympic conferences. The British physiologist A. V. Hill, a Nobel Prize winner, turned down an invitation to attend an "International Sport Medicine Congress" held in conjunction with the games, writing: "I am sorry, for I have many German friends, but so long as the German government and people maintain their persecution of our Jewish and other colleagues, it will be altogether distasteful to me, as to most English scientists, to take part in any public scientific function in Germany."

Hamburg's Leisure and Recreation Congress was not the only big cultural event to take place outside the capital during Germany's Olympic summer. Munich, having hosted most of the major social and cultural activities during the Winter Games, was anxious to attract some of the Summer Games trade as well. Just prior to the games Munich celebrated "Five Hundred Years of Horse Racing in Munich" with a special running of the "Brown Ribbon of Germany," Nazi Germany's premier horserace. As Mayor Karl Fiehler explained to Baillet-Latour, during the period between July 15 and 29 Munich would become "the world-center of equestrian sports activity," with "historically oriented parades, popular festivals and other cultural offerings." Noting that Hitler himself had sanctioned the equestrian event, Fiehler invited Baillet-Latour to join the organizing committee. On August 16, the last day of the Berlin games, Reichsstaathalter Ritter von Epp opened a "Chess Olympia" in Munich's Old City Hall. The world's best players were invited to match wits at the chessboard. To honor the participants, the city sponsored a dramatic spectacle called "Chess of the Nations," held on the Theresienwiese, site of the annual Oktoberfest.

The Richard Wagner Festival in Bayreuth, held annually in the summer, also hitched its wagon to the Berlin games. Hoping to attract Olympic fans to Bayreuth, Winifred Wagner (Richard Wagner's daughter-in-law and the then-director of the festival) elected on Hitler's advice to divide the Bayreuth festival into two parts, one just preceding and one directly following the Berlin games. Winifred cast the 1936 Wagner festival as a cultural melding of Bayreuth and Olympia. Reichssportführer Tschammer und Osten sought to reinforce this dubious proposition in a telegram to Winifred on the eve of the Bayreuth festival: "In this historic moment connecting the works of Richard Wagner with the Olympic idea, German sport greets you as the carrier of the great [Wagner] legacy."

Hitler, who was truly knowledgeable about Wagner, attended the first part of the Bayreuth festival, rejoicing in a new production of *Lohengrin* under Maestro Wilhelm Furtwängler. But Hitler's attention was not focused exclusively on Wagner. On the day before the festival opened, General Franco launched his coup in Spanish Morocco, hoping to carry his rebellion to the Spanish mainland. Learning of the coup from Goebbels, Hitler immediately decided to assist the Franco rebellion by sending logistical support for the general's crossing to Spain.

German assistance soon included the dispatch of the Condor Legion, which, as mentioned above, departed for Spain from the Olympic Village in Döberitz. By the end of part one of the Bayreuth festival, Franco's troops, having with German help gained the mainland, were making good progress in their rebellion. Hitler returned to Berlin to open the Summer Games in an ebullient mood. He provided free Olympics tickets to the Wagner family and the entire Bayreuth cast. Wagner's granddaughters Friedelind and Verena made use of the tickets and were the only women present at a lavish lunch hosted by Hitler at the Reich Chancellery on August 4.

The Social Scene

The Wagner women were among hundreds of VIPs, many of them from abroad, who attended the games in Berlin. As they did for the Winter Games, the organizers sought to lure large numbers of foreign dignitaries and celebrities to Germany in the hopes that once these foreigners had seen what Nazi Germany was "really like" they would influence opinion at home in Germany's favor. For their most prestigious guests, the Nazi leaders laid on grand receptions and parties.

Undoubtedly the most prominent American to visit Germany during the Olympic summer was the "Lone Eagle," Charles Lindbergh, whose pioneering solo crossing of the Atlantic in 1927 had instantly transformed him into one of the most famous men in the world. The chief purpose of Lindbergh's trip to Germany in 1936 was not to attend the Olympics (he showed up only for the opening ceremony), but to inspect the Reich's civil and military aviation facilities on behalf of America's Army Air Corps, in whose reserve component Lindy then served.

Although Lindbergh came as an official guest of the German Air Ministry and Lufthansa Airlines, his visit was the inspiration of Capt. Truman Smith, Washington's military attaché in Berlin. Smith believed that America needed to know more about Germany's aviation capacities and that Lindbergh was the perfect man to provide firsthand information. He thought that if Lindbergh consented to combine his inspection tour with an appearance at the Olympic Games, the Air Ministry would be certain to invite him to Berlin. "It was my impression," Smith wrote later, "that the German Air Ministry would like nothing better than to gain favor with Hitler by presenting the world-famous flyer as the special guest of the Luftwaffe at the Olympic Games. [It was] clear that the Nazis were seeking to attract to the Games celebrities from all over the world." Indeed Air Marshal Göring eagerly took up Smith's suggestion to invite Lindbergh to Berlin, stipulating that the flyer must attend the Olympics opening-day ceremony as his personal guest. Lindbergh consented to do this, albeit reluctantly, for he feared being hounded by the press.

When news leaked out that the Lone Eagle planned to visit Berlin, Roger Straus, cochair of the United States Conference of Christians and Jews, urged him to reconsider, arguing that the Nazis would interpret his visit as a form of endorsement of their regime. But Lindbergh, who in fact did sympathize with some of the things Hitler was doing, ignored Straus's entreaty. On July 22 he and his wife, Anne, flew to Berlin from London. The Lindberghs were greeted by Smith and members of Göring's ministry. On the following day Lufthansa hosted the flyer and his wife at a tea party to which William Shirer and other American journalists managed to gain entrée. Shirer observed in his diary: "The talk is that the Lindberghs have been favorably impressed with what the Nazis have shown them. [Charles Lindbergh] has shown no enthusiasm for meeting the foreign correspondents, who have shown a perverse liking for enlightening visitors on the Third Reich, as they see it, and we have not pushed for an interview." Bella Fromm, a society reporter for Berlin's *Vossische Zeitung*, was also present at the Lufthansa tea, and she, too, was struck by the extent to which Lindbergh seemed taken in by the Nazis. Fromm, who was soon to be fired because she was Jewish, recalled in her diary: "Lindbergh seems impressed. He appeared pleased when Secretary of State [Erhard] Milch . . . patted him on the shoulder. And when a genuine prince, Louis Ferdinand, linked arms with him, he beamed with happiness. I heard him say to Captain Udet: 'German aviation ranks higher than that in any other country. It is invincible.'"

During his eleven-day visit Lindbergh stopped briefly at the Olympic Village, where he posed for pictures with American athletes. He also took a turn around the running track. Most of his time, however, was spent touring aviation facilities and factories. At Tempelhof Airport he flew a Junkers JU-52, the Germans' new bomber. He was permitted to inspect the latest Stuka dive-bombers and fighters at two Heinkel factories. During a libationary luncheon with the Luftwaffe's Richthofen Fighter Wing, he charmed his hosts with a toast: "Here's to bombers, may they fly slower; and here's to pursuit planes, may they fly swifter." According to one bemused commentator, Lindbergh "learned enough German secrets to have him hanged ten times over had he been a Jew instead of the most popular of Nordics."

The Germans had hoped to impress Lindbergh with their growing aviation arsenal and in this they succeeded. At the conclusion of his inspection tour he gave a speech at the Berlin Air Club in which he warned that the destructive power of military aircraft had now "stripped the armor from every nation in war," creating a situation in which "all the institutions we value most are laid bare to bombardments." It was an argument that Lindbergh would later repeat in urging the United States to remain neutral even as the Germans ran roughshod over most of Europe.

Toward the end of Lindbergh's brief stay in Germany, Göring hosted a lavish luncheon for the flyer and his wife. Bon vivant Göring chatted about wine and opera with Anne Morrow Lindbergh, and then whisked Charles away to an anteroom for a man-to-man talk about flying. While they chatted Göring played with his pet lion until the beast peed on his pants leg, forcing a hasty change of clothes. After the change Göring treated both Lindberghs to a tour of his ornate study, lined with artworks he had confiscated from German museums. All in all the meeting gave Göring the chance to show his American guests the congenial and "cosmopolitan" side of the Third Reich.

On his last full day in Berlin, Lindbergh attended the opening of the Olympic Games as the guest of Göring. His seat was fairly close to the Honor Loge but, despite the best efforts of Truman Smith, he did not get the opportunity to meet Hitler. Shortly after leaving Berlin he wrote Smith:

> Our visit to Germany was one of the most interesting we have ever made, not alone because of the aviation developments but from many other standpoints as well. I think Germany is in many ways the most interesting nation in the world today, and that she is attempting to find a solution for some of our most fundamental problems. While I still have many reservations, I have come away with a feeling of great admiration for the German people. The condition of the country, and the appearance of the average person whom I saw, leaves me with the impression that Hitler must have far more character and vision than I thought existed in the German leader who has been painted in so many different ways by the accounts in America and England.

Lindbergh elaborated on his impression of Hitler in a letter to his friend Harry Davison at the brokerage firm J. P. Morgan: "With all the things we criticize, [Hitler] is undoubtedly a great man, and I believe has done much for the German people. He is a fanatic in many ways, and anyone can see that there is a certain amount of fanaticism in Germany today. It is less than I expected, but it is there. On the other hand, Hitler has accomplished results (good in addition to bad), which could hardly have been accomplished without some fanaticism."

Anne Morrow Lindbergh was every bit as enthusiastic as her husband about Nazi Germany and its Führer. She had loved the Olympic ceremony and found her entire stay in Berlin "perfectly thrilling." On August 5 she wrote her mother: "Hitler, I am beginning to feel, is a very great man, like an inspired religious leader—and as such rather fanatical—but not scheming, not selfish, not greedy for power, but a mystic, a visionary who really wants the best for his country and *on the whole* has rather a broad view."

As it turned out, Charles Lindbergh was virtually the only truly high-wattage American celebrity to show up in Berlin during the Olympic summer. Mrs. William Randolph Hearst made an appearance at the games, but her husband, the famous publisher, did not. Probably the most important figure from the American business community to attend the games was IBM president Thomas J. Watson, who admired Hitler and whose company later provided the cataloging technologies the Nazis used to process Jews for ghettoization, deportation, and annihilation. Watson's request to visit the Olympic Village was instantly granted. The majority of American visitors to the games, however, were distinguished solely by their interest in amateur sports and their financial means to travel to Europe in the midst of a severe depression.

The young American novelist Thomas Wolfe represented something of an exception to this rule; he was neither wealthy nor much of a sports fan. He was, however, enamored of Germany, and Germany seemed enamored of him. The German critics had recently hailed him as an "American Homer." His trip to Berlin in the summer of 1936 represented his second experience of Germany, the first having been an excursion to Bavaria in late 1928. Since then, of course, Hitler had come to power, and Wolfe—as he tells us in *You Can't Go Home Again*—had heard ugly reports about what was going on in the Reich. He did not want to believe these reports, and the Germans he met in 1936 reassured him that all was well and that "everyone was so happy." Arriving in Berlin in May he found the city truly glorious. "Along the streets, in the Tiergarten, in all the great gardens, and along the Spree Canal, the horse chestnuts were in full bloom. The crowds sauntered underneath the trees on the Kurfürstendamm, the terraces of the cafés were jammed with people, and always, through the golden sparkle of the days, there was the sound of music in the air." Once the Olympics got under way in August the city seemed "transformed into a kind of annex" of the magnificent stadium, which in his view was "the most perfect in its design that had ever been built." Wolfe stayed drunk for most of his time in Berlin. At one point he staggered down a street hugging the trees and pronouncing his admiration for all things German. He told a reporter for the *Berliner Tageblatt* that "if there were no Germany, it would be necessary to invent one." Yet befogged as he was by beer and fan adulation, Wolfe was shrewd enough to see that the Olympic Games, which he attended almost every day with his new German girlfriend, amounted to much more than a mere athletic event, and that the very meticulousness of the games' organization suggested something sinister about the hosts:

> The sheer pageantry of the occasion was overwhelming, so much so that [George] began to feel oppressed by it. There seemed to be something ominous in it. One sensed a stupendous concentration of effort, a tremendous drawing together and ordering in the vast collective power of the whole land. And the thing that made it seem ominous was that it so evidently went beyond what the games themselves demanded. The games were overshadowed, and were no longer merely sporting competitions to which other nations had sent their chosen teams. They became, day after day, an orderly and overwhelming demonstration in which the whole of Germany had been schooled and disciplined. It was as if the games had been chosen as a symbol of the new collective might, a means of showing to the world in concrete terms what this new power had come to be.

Wolfe did not, however, let his feeling of unease disrupt his enjoyment of the games, which brought out his patriotism. He rooted loudly for his American compatriots and, despite a prejudice against blacks, included Jesse Owens in his cheers. "Owens was black as tar," he conceded, "but what the hell, it was our team and I thought he was wonderful. I was proud of him, so I yelled." Wolfe was sitting in Ambassador Dodd's box, which was close to the Honor Loge, and at one point his cheers for Owens became so boisterous that Hitler looked over angrily to see who was making all the commotion.

In terms of their political importance to the German hosts, American VIP guests at the Olympics counted for less than the British, for at the time of the

Berlin games Germany, in the words of one scholar of Anglo-German relations, "started the greatest-ever propaganda campaign for an alliance with Great Britain." The Germans hoped to wean Britain from France and to gain London's support for their planned expansion in the East. The moment seemed propitious because British conservatives were alarmed over the advent of Popular Front governments in France and Spain and shared Berlin's hopes for Franco's success in the Spanish civil war.

Joachim von Ribbentrop, long an advocate of closer Anglo-German ties, was appointed Berlin's ambassador to London during the Berlin games. He, along with Hitler, Goebbels, and Göring, saw the Olympics as an opportunity to convince influential Britons that Berlin and London belonged in the same camp. Accordingly Ribbentrop blanketed the British upper crust with invitations to the festival. "From London alone," he wrote in his diary, "I expected something like a friendly invasion. Lord Monsell . . . had accepted, and so had Lord Rothermere and Lord Beaverbrook. . . . All our personal friends had been asked." The Führer himself hosted a party for the Anglo-German Fellowship, including Lord Rothermere and Lord Beaverbrook, during the games.

Significantly Germany's campaign to woo Britain focused not only on known pro-German figures but also on Britain's leading anti-Nazi diplomat, Sir Robert Vansittart. There was good reason for this: None of the pro-German crowd held governmental power at that moment, while Vansittart, as undersecretary for foreign affairs, had real influence over British foreign policy. (Vansittart had also opposed a British boycott of the Berlin games, but the Germans did not know this.) Aware that he could not get Vansittart to Berlin on an official state visit, Ribbentrop invited Sir Robert and his wife for a "private" visit to the Berlin Olympics. Surprisingly enough, Vansittart accepted, and he and his wife ended up staying in Berlin for the entire duration of the games.

During his time in the German capital, Vansittart was wined, dined, and squired about town by most of the major Nazi leaders. According to his confidential post-games report to the Foreign Office, the common theme of his discussions with the Germans was the Communist threat. "Indeed, they can think and talk of little else. The obsession is in any case endemic, but Spanish events have reinforced their thesis."

The Nazi leadership claimed to have thoroughly rooted out the "Red menace" at home and thereby to have transformed Germany into the Continent's most reliable bastion against the spread of Communism. To prove this Rudolf Hess drove Vansittart unescorted through the formerly Red districts of Berlin, managing to complete the excursion "without a sour look." Seeking to one-up Hess, Göring offered Vansittart a large wager that he could drive him alone to the very heart of former Red territory and then stroll about unguarded without being accosted. Vansittart declined the wager on the grounds that there was little point in betting on a certainty; even the most rabid Red would be unlikely to take on Hermann Göring! Ribbentrop, Vansittart's primary host, insisted on several tête-à-têtes with his guest, convincing himself in the process that he had won the Briton over.

Similarly Goebbels, supremely confident of his persuasive powers, invited Vansittart to his office for a chat on August 6. In his diary the propaganda minister described Vansittart as "an extremely nervous gentleman" who, though somewhat a prisoner of his anti-German prejudices, "could be without doubt won over to us." Accordingly Goebbels "worked on" his guest for an hour, focusing on the Communist threat to Western civilization. "He leaves deeply impressed. I have opened his eyes," concluded Goebbels. Three days later, after a dinner party hosted by British ambassador Eric Phipps, who was Vansittart's brother-in-law, Goebbels was even more confident that Vansittart's stay in Berlin had turned him into a convert. "He has changed radically. Berlin left a definite impression on him."

France's ambassador to Berlin, André François-Poncet, had observed the Germans working on Vansittart and concluded with some alarm that they indeed seemed to have made an impact. Vansittart and his wife had been "rather impressed by everything they had seen and heard," François-Poncet reported to Paris. "Without doubt they return to their country confused, and, if not fascinated, then at least intimidated by the mighty size and efficiency of the apparatus which has been constructed by the regime."

We know from Vansittart's own contemporary reports, and from his subsequent diplomatic activities, that, contrary to the Germans' hopes and François-Poncet's fears, the Englishman did not significantly change his view of Nazi Germany as a result of his stay in Berlin. True, he was impressed by the organizational skill and cordiality displayed by the Germans during the Olympics, praising to one reporter "the splendid spirit of sport which pervaded the Games." But his assessments of the Nazi leadership showed not the slightest awe or suasion. In the atmosphere of good feeling provided by the Olympics, Hitler, in Vansittart's eyes, generally came across as amiable and unintimidating, although even at the games there were moments when the Führer's "darker side" erupted with volcanic power. Then one saw in the German leader "the harder, more violent, mystically ambitious, hotly and coldly explosive traits which flare capriciously and keep everyone . . . in such a state of nervous tension that I more than once heard the stadium compared with a crater."

Of Goebbels, Vansittart wrote condescendingly: "I found much charm in him—a limping, eloquent slip of a Jacobin, quick as a whip in quotes and afterwards, I doubt not, as cutting." For Göring the British visitor had nothing but contempt, describing him as "a primitive, bounding creature with the limitless appetites of the true parvenu." The corpulent Göring was in Vansittart's view a low-class libertine who "enjoys everything, particularly his own parties, with the gusto of a Smith Minor suddenly possessed of unlimited tick at the school stores. The world is his oyster, and no damned nonsense about opening it!" Ribbentrop came off no better: "I fear that he is shallow, self-seeking and not really friendly. No one who studies his mouth will be reassured. . . . To him one has to listen without much chance of interruption . . . for he is guided by his command of English."

Ribbentrop would become even more insufferable in Vansittart's eyes over the course of his three-year tenure as German ambassador in London, a period when British appeasement of Hitler, after peaking under Neville Chamberlain, began finally to ebb following the ill-fated Munich Conference of 1938. During this entire period Vansittart played a prominent role in the antiappeasement camp—hardly the behavior of a convert to the German cause. Clearly in his case all that careful cosseting during the Olympics had not paid off.

Vansittart turned out to be the only high-level British governmental official to attend the Berlin games. Former prime minister David Lloyd George, who had long admired Hitler, did visit the Führer in 1936, but only after the games had ended. His subsequent description of Hitler as "unquestionably a great leader" and his insistence that the Germans had "definitely made up their minds never to quarrel with us again" hardly helped him regain the great influence he had once enjoyed.

In lieu of major British political figures, the Berlin games attracted a sprinkling of members of Parliament, the most notable being Henry "Chips" Channon, Conservative MP for Southend since 1935. Through his marriage to Lady Honor Guinness (of the beer family), the featherbrained

Channon gained a foothold in British high society, much of which in those days was distinctly pro-German. Channon's diary, full of breathless commentary on the social scene at the games, suggests that he had certainly fallen under the Nazis' ether. For all its airheadedness, however, Channon's commentary provides good evidence of how hard the Nazis worked to impress their high-society guests.

The Channons arrived in Berlin on August 5 as official guests of Ribbentrop. They were met by a personal aide-de-camp who installed them in "a magnificent suite of rooms" at the Hotel Eden.

> Berlin crowded with foreigners, and the streets beflagged. Honor and I went for a walk down Unter den Linden, an avenue of banners blowing in the breeze, and everywhere we heard the radio booming 'Achtung,' and then giving the latest Olympic results. About six, we went to the Bristol for a cocktail. . . . We dined with the Bismarcks, a party of over fifty in the Eden roof garden, and Otto, ever gauche, put German women on his left and right. It was a brilliant, cosmopolitan dinner of Viennese, German, and English. . . . Bed about 4, and we came for a rest!

The next day, Chips and Honor actually made it to the Reichssportfeld, but they found the games boring. Chips noticed that whenever the Germans won the band played the "Horst Wessel Lied," "which I thought had rather a good lilt." After an hour or so Hitler arrived at his box. It was Chips's first live sighting of the Führer, and he was ecstatic: "I was more excited than when I met Mussolini in 1926 in Perugia, and more stimulated, I am sorry to say, than when I was blessed by the Pope in 1920." That night the Channons attended a state banquet at the Royal Opera House.

> We were in evening dress and Honor in full regalia, with her rubies, but minus tiara. A hundred or so footmen in dix-huitième pink liveries and carrying torches in glass holders, lined the entrance. A reception took place in the foyer, and here Frau Göring, a tall, handsome, and seemingly almost naked, woman, was the principal figure and moved about amongst an obsequious crowd of Royalties and ambassadors. Berlin has not known anything like this since the war, and one was conscious of

the effort the Germans were making to show the world the grandeur, the permanency and respectability of the new regime.

Undoubtedly the British visitors who caused the greatest commotion in Berlin were Diana and Unity Mitford, who had already become infamous for their attraction to the fascist cause. Diana was married to the brewery heir Bryan Guinness, but the love of her life was British Union of Fascists leader Sir Oswald Mosley, whom she was to marry in October 1936 in a secret ceremony in Berlin. Her younger sister Unity had developed a personal fascination for Hitler in 1933, and a year later actually moved to Munich in hopes of meeting him. She lurked about in his favorite restaurant, the Osteria Bavaria, waiting to be noticed by him. With her perfect "Nordic" looks—golden hair, tall frame, fair skin and blue-green eyes—she stood out even in a German crowd, and Hitler eventually called her to his table. Unity became part of Hitler's retinue in Munich, though there is no evidence that she ever supplanted Eva Braun in his sexual affections, such as they were. "The greatest moment in my life," she later confessed, "was sitting at Hitler's feet and having him stroke my hair."

In spring 1936 Diana and Unity were eating at a restaurant in Cologne when Hitler happened to walk in and, seeing them there, promptly invited them to the Berlin Olympics. During the games the sisters resided in Goebbels's country house outside Berlin and were ferried every day by limousine to the Reichssportfeld. They found the sporting events so tedious, however, that they preferred to stroll about the stadium, socializing with other English visitors and nipping frequently from flasks of gin. The only athlete they bothered to watch was Jesse Owens, but they cannot have watched him very closely, for in a letter describing the games Diana had him defeating "a poor Indian," when in fact no Indians competed in any of his races.

Upon returning to England, Unity and Diana did their best to lobby for Nazi Germany, but their pro-Nazi antics occasioned more derision than admiration. Diana, who was one of the few people in the world to know both Hitler and Winston Churchill personally, suggested to the latter that he visit the Führer in Berlin. Churchill replied in alarm, "Oh, no, no!" Diana's liaison with Mosley increasingly turned her into a pariah even with the smart set, and in 1940, when Britain and Germany were at war, the Churchill government jailed her as a security risk, a fate she shared with her husband.

As for Unity, her practice of greeting everyone in her village with the Nazi salute caused considerable consternation, and in 1937 she returned to Munich to be close to Hitler. When war broke out Hitler instructed Unity to return to her native land, but, unable to bear leaving the man she loved, she shot herself in the head. The wound was not fatal, and Hitler managed to get her back to England, where she died in 1948.

AS the busy social schedules of visitors like the Mitfords and Channons suggest, parties and receptions meant more to many VIP guests than did the athletic competitions themselves. These high-society visitors were not likely to look behind the Nazi regime's Olympic curtain to see what was really going on in Hitler's Germany, but lest they be tempted to do so for want of alternative activities, their hosts kept them occupied with one bacchanal after another. As the Olympic party scene unfolded, it became apparent that the chief Nazi potentates were vying with one another to see who could throw the most opulent bash. The Berlin Olympiad of 1936, it seems, amounted not just to a contest of athletic prowess, but also of party-throwing bravura.

Ribbentrop, the former champagne salesman and Nazi foreign policy adviser who had just become ambassador to Britain, threw a dinner party at his villa in the posh Berlin suburb of Dahlem on August 11. The party was meant to celebrate, as François-Poncet noted, "both the Olympic Games and [Ribbentrop's] rise to the highest diplomatic position in the gift of the Reich. Champagne flowed like water; it was the best Pommery, a brand for which he had long been salesman and agent. Meanwhile he strolled from group to group under admiring glances of a family marveling at his brilliant fortune, his expression the picture of assurance and self-content."

Having seen what Ribbentrop could do by way of party hosting, and not about to be outdone by a man he considered a fool, Göring set out to top him with a lavish party in the garden of his city palace. Ambassador Dodd, who was appalled by ostentation of any kind, could not help noticing that Göring's palazzo was "far larger and more elaborately fitted out than the White House in Washington." The minister's nocturnal party was lit by spotlights stationed on neighboring roofs and by hundreds of lights suspended from trees. Underwater lights illuminated lilies and swans floating in a giant swimming pool. "There was hardly anything that modern inventors could have added," commented Dodd. Guests could stroll through a miniature eighteenth-century French village, replete with inn, bakery, post office, and craft shops. Göring and his wife, actress Emmy Sonnemann, received guests ensconced on a divan in front of a tea pavilion. Dinner entertainment was provided by the State Opera's corps de ballet, which danced on a stage lit only by moonlight. After dinner painted screens were swept aside to reveal the evening's pièce de résistance—a brightly lit full-scale alpine-theme carnival including shooting galleries, wine and beer stalls, and a merry-go-round, all staffed by actresses in low-cut peasant dresses. According to François-Poncet, Göring, the perpetual child, "rode the merry-go-round until he was breathless."

Naturally Chips Channon was present and could barely contain his enthusiasm for the carnival: "It was fantastic, roundabouts [the aforementioned merry-go-round], cafes with beer and champagne, peasants dancing and 'schuhplattling [a form of knee-slapping alpine folk dance],' vast women carrying pretzels and beer, a ship, a beer house, crowds of gay laughing people, animals, a mixture of Luna Park and Old Heidelberg and the Trianon. . . . [Max] Reinhardt could not have done it better. The music roared, the astonished guests wandered about. . . . Goebbels, it appears, as well as Ribbentrop was in despair with jealousy."

Goebbels exacted his revenge on Göring by hosting an even larger Olympic party. The setting was the beautiful Pfaueninsel (Peacock Island) in the Havel River west of Berlin, a former possession of the Hohenzollerns. Guests reached the island via a newly constructed pontoon bridge and then passed through an "aisle of honor" formed by seminaked young female dancers holding torches. The whole place was done up like a movie set and stocked with starlets from the UFA studio, one of whom, the Czech beauty Lida Baarová, was Goebbels's latest mistress.

After dinner there was a fireworks display on a scale that, in Chips Channon's view, "would have impressed the Romans, had they known about fireworks. . . . For half an hour the German Himmel blazed with coloured light, and the noise was deafening." Ambassador Dodd, again dutifully in attendance, was unsettled by the fireworks, which to him "suggested war," and he was shocked by the opulence of Goebbels's hospitality, which he guessed "must have cost 40,000 marks of government money." But whatever the cost, Goebbels would hardly have blanched at using a hefty chunk of government funds to impress the Reich's Olympic guests—and to one-up his rivals.

In the end, the Nazi regime's splurging on its most distinguished Olympic visitors seems to have had some of its desired effect. Many of the guests had been expecting to encounter open oppression and harsh conditions, which they did not find (of course, they did not look very hard). Some came away with the conviction that they had been sold a false bill of goods by anti-Nazi foreign correspondents and embassy officials. There is no evidence, however, that the favorable impressions of the Reich that the society visitors carried home significantly influenced their governments' policies toward Nazi Germany. Few of the VIPs attracted to the games had genuine clout. The aristocrats, celebrities, society lions, and minor royals who descended on Berlin for the games were simply not the movers and shakers of world politics in the mid-1930s.

Policing and Persecution

The fact that the vast majority of visitors to the games, distinguished or otherwise, saw little evidence of oppression during their visit does not mean that oppression did not exist. True, the Nazi regime, as it had during the Winter Games, sought during the Berlin games to temper public expressions of racial bigotry and did not carry out open assaults against Jews. More subtle forms of anti-Semitic persecution continued unabated, however. For example, just before the Games opened the regime ordered that Jewish doctors could no longer treat "Aryan" patients, and it proceeded without letup in its program of "aryanizing" Jewish businesses. Moreover the police did not hesitate to come down hard on other perceived "enemies of the Reich" or potential troublemakers. Carl Diem later claimed that the Olympics had constituted "an oasis of freedom" during the Nazi dictatorship, and many commentators have since spoken of an "Olympic pause" in the campaign of oppression, but this brief respite applied only to the most obviously visible measures of anti-Semitic harassment. In other areas the authorities actually *increased* measures of repression in order to preempt any possible disruptions to the festival. The atmosphere of peaceful harmony praised by so many visitors was secured through a draconian deployment of police power, though much of this was invisible to the average visitor.

It was not a coincidence that the Nazis opened a major new concentration camp, Sachsenhausen, just prior to the Berlin games. Located in the Berlin suburb of Oranienburg, the camp was a model incarceration center for political opponents as well as "asocial elements," such as unregistered prostitutes, homosexuals, and beggars. By September 1936 its inmate population already numbered more than 1,000. To counter charges in the foreign press that atrocities were being committed in the camp, the regime published a picture book on the institution showing rows of orderly barracks and fit-looking prisoners. The camp, insisted this book, had already achieved great success "in helping misdirected citizens to turn their lives around and recover their work-ethic."

Sachsenhausen, however, was not capacious enough to take care of all the "problematical elements" rounded up by the authorities in advance of the games. The Nazi authorities arrested an average of 170 "asocials" a month in 1936, quietly confining them in ad hoc jails like the Municipal Work and Detention House in Berlin-Rummelsburg, which in June 1936 counted 1,433 detainees.

In the Nazi perspective Gypsies constituted a threat to the social and racial order almost as serious as that of the Jews. Gypsy encampments in large cities like Hamburg and Berlin were decried as cesspools of vice, dirt, and crime— a "grave moral danger" to society. Various officials in Berlin had been demanding "cleansing" measures against the local Gypsies for some time, but it was the approach of the Olympic Games that provided the catalyst for drastic action in the summer of 1936. On July 16 some six hundred Gypsies in Berlin were rounded up by the police and moved to a temporary detention camp in the district of Marzahn—the so-called *Zigeunerlager* (Gypsy camp). The move was justified as a means to guarantee Olympic visitors a "clean" and safe environment during their stay. But the camp continued to function after the games were over. In September 1937 some 852 inmates were registered there, the majority of them women and children. By that time most of the adult males had been moved to regular concentration camps around the Reich, which themselves were way stations to later liquidation in the East.

The security agencies of the Reich took extensive measures to ensure that there would be no significant signs of political protest, much less acts of sabotage, during the games. Concerned that "foreign communists disguised as harmless Olympic visitors" might try to disrupt the festival in some way, the head of the Gestapo in Prussia instructed all his agents to be "on high alert." At the same time, however, the Gestapo chief cautioned that the relevant security measures must be carried out with utmost discretion so as not to alarm foreign visitors. "Under no circumstances must our Olympic visitors be given the impression they are under police observation, nor must our preemptive measures become a source of irritation to foreign guests," he decreed. In this spirit the spies who kept tabs on the comings and goings of the visiting Olympic teams operated under the guise of bilingual "student helpers." The Kriminalpolizei station at the Olympic Village was disguised as an "Information Center" and was staffed exclusively by female officers.

The files kept by the Gestapo on security operations during the games show that in general the painstaking vigilance paid off. Given the amount of hostility to the Nazi regime around the world, the volume of antiregime activity was quite low.

A special police postal inspection unit established at the Charlottenburg Post Office to inspect all the mail coming into the Olympic Village proved its value by intercepting hundreds of antiregime letters and cards addressed to foreign Olympians. On August 8, 1936, the unit intercepted seventy-four anti-Nazi messages from England disguised as good luck wishes to the British team. On the following day the office confiscated fifteen similar messages from Holland for the Dutch team and twelve from France. A letter posted in Paris addressed to the American Olympic Committee and signed by fourteen antifascist American artists pointed out that Germany was using the Olympic Games "to disseminate propaganda," something that would hardly have been news to the AOC.

Perhaps the most important interception, in Gestapo eyes, was a letter from England addressed to Jesse Owens advising him to spurn any medals he might win with the following protest declaration: "It was an honor for me to represent my nation here and a pleasure to compete against the best athletes in the world, but I must reject with contempt the prize offered me by a government that preaches racial hatred." (Leaving aside the fact that it was not the German "government" that presented the Olympic awards in Berlin, Owens would certainly never have acted on this advice had he been given the chance to receive it. But of course the Gestapo kept the letter.)

During the games the police had to contend with sporadic demonstrations of opposition to the regime, but these incidents were carried out by single individuals or very small groups and seem to have had little resonance. On August 4 someone set fire to a swastika flag hanging from a balcony in Berlin's Salzburgstrasse. Someone else painted "*Heil Moskau*" across pictures of Mussolini displayed on a train used by the Italian team. Another protestor taped communist slogans to a telephone booth on the corner of Kant- and Uhlandstrasse.

Anti-Nazis belonging to the Communist underground in Berlin distributed flyers protesting the huge expenditure on the games as a rip-off of the poor. The *Arbeiter Internationale Zeitung*, published in Prague, put out a special "Guide through the Land of the Olympiad," which pointed out, among other attractions, prominent concentration camps and political prisons. An eighty-four-page pamphlet, also printed in Prague by exiled Socialists, and disguised as an edition of the official *Olympic Magazine*, called for the liberation of German sport from Nazi ideology.

According to police reports the authorities arrested a tailor for yelling "Red front!" in a tavern; another man was jailed after he was overheard saying to his wife during the Olympic opening ceremony: "Now one must go after the Führer, just like they are going after the king of England" (presumably a reference to the pressure exerted on King Edward VIII to abdicate the throne because of his determination to marry the divorced American, Mrs. Wallis Simpson). At the stadium some German spectators remained seated and failed to give the Hitler salute during the playing of the "Horst Wessel Lied." Plainclothes policemen quietly arrested these miscreants as they exited the building.

The authorities came down especially hard on German citizens caught expressing antiregime sentiments to foreigners or engaging in "offensive" behavior toward Olympic guests. As the games opened, the People's Court in Berlin* sentenced a German journalist to life imprisonment for informing his foreign colleagues about the repressive reporting guidelines in effect for German scribes during the Olympics. Learning of a plan by members of the "Confessing Church" (a dissident Protestant faction) to print and circulate their moral objections to Nazi policy, the Gestapo raided the synod offices and confiscated the printing machines. The Gestapo arrested a group of German working-class women who dared discuss their actual living conditions in Germany with members of the Brazilian and Australian Olympic teams. For simply *threatening* to discuss Nazi labor policies with visitors, an unemployed worker named Hans Bräutigan was taken into custody. A Berlin salesman named Wilhelm Bote, who had a record of homosexual offenses, was arrested for making homosexual advances to two Argentineans. A thirty-seven-year-

*The People's Court (*Volksgerichtshof*) was established in 1933 by the Nazi government to try political offenses against the Third Reich. During World War II the court, under Judge Roland Freisler, handed down an enormous number of death sentences to opponents of the Hitler regime.

old German male was jailed for accosting a fifteen-year-old foreign boy at the Olympic swim stadium. On a rather different front, the Gestapo questioned the owner of the Hubertusquelle Restaurant near Potsdamer Platz after a complaint by a Greek Olympic visitor that he and his wife had been denied service by a waiter who mistakenly held them to be Jewish. The Gestapo reminded the restaurateur that during the games even "Jewish-looking" customers had to be served.

When it came to the expression of regime-unfriendly views by Olympic visitors, the authorities moved more cautiously than they did with errant German citizens. One of the Gestapo's omnipresent spies reported that a coach belonging to the Swedish team had criticized the policies of the German government and praised the Soviet Union during an excursion by the Swedish team to Schorfheide, a nature preserve north of Berlin. The Gestapo conducted an investigation of the incident and kept the Swedes under close surveillance, but for obvious reasons said nothing in public about the matter.

THE German security forces' greatest fear during the two-week Olympic festival was that someone might strike at the Führer. As mentioned above, security for Hitler was tight during the opening ceremony, and it remained tight for the duration of the games. To protect Hitler during his comings and goings at the games, a special Olympic *Führerschutz* was established to supplement his regular bodyguards. Led by SS Standartenführer Hans Rattenhuber and comprising forty experts from the Sicherheitsdienst (the security service of the SS), the group was authorized to call on 150 additional criminal police officers if the need arose. Hitler traveled to and from the sports complex in a convoy of ten armored Mercedes touring cars. The security police ordered landlords all along the Via Triumphalis to keep their premises free of unauthorized visitors while the Führer's cavalcade was in progress. Whenever Hitler walked around the Reichssportfeld he was flanked by seven uniformed guards and a host of plainclothesmen. His box in the stadium was protected by a bulletproof glass shield.

Yet there were surprising lapses in the Olympic security system. Hitler refused to vary the route his convoy took to the Olympics complex even though his aides pointed out that this regularity made him more vulnerable to potential assassins. Spectators entering the sporting venues, including the main stadium, were not systematically searched for weapons. It was possible to gain access to the Reichssportfeld grounds without undergoing any inspection. The shield protecting Hitler's box was only chest high, leaving him vulnerable whenever he stood up to cheer, which he did often. (We recall that Thomas Wolfe had sat close enough to Hitler to annoy him with his yelling. What if Wolfe had had murder rather than cheering on his mind, and had brought along a pistol rather than a flask of whiskey?)

Outside the stadium Hitler was even more vulnerable, despite his bodyguards. When he reviewed the athletes assembled on the May Field on opening day he passed so close to them that any one of them could have pounced on him. Fifty years later a London policeman who had wrestled for the British team in 1936 was still angry at himself for not dealing the Führer a deadly chop when he had the chance to do so: "If I'd just stepped forward and clobbered him then and there, what an incredible amount of life and trouble I would have saved!"

On another occasion, when Hitler was visiting the swimming stadium, an elderly American woman named Mrs. Carla de Vries suddenly embraced him and even planted a wet kiss on his cheek. Later she said she had merely wanted to get his autograph, but then decided he looked so nice that he deserved a hug and a kiss. At the time a startled Hitler put on a show of enjoying this bit of grandmotherly affection, but afterward he dismissed several of his guards for their lack of vigilance. And well he should have: Mrs. de Vries could easily have stuck a knife in his ribs.

IN a secret postgames assessment of Olympic police procedures, Count Wolf Heinrich von Helldorf, chief of the Berlin police, took pride in what his security forces had accomplished. "The success of the police measures taken on the occasion of the Olympic Games is . . . the best demonstration of the rightness of the struggle that we have been waging since the Party came to power against professional criminals, traffic offenders, profiteers and other enemies of the people."

The absence of any significant security crises during the games confirmed the Nazi authorities in their belief that draconian measures, including preventative incarceration and mass roundups of social and ethnic undesirables, constituted an effective and practical way to protect the state. And if the regime could do this when "the whole world" was present in Berlin, how much more could it do when the world went home?

Some critics of Nazi Germany sensed at the time that open persecution of the Jews in particular would resume with redoubled fury once the games were over. In a report on the Nazi government's Jewish policy, a Dutch journalist predicted that, on the conclusion of the Olympics, the Hitler regime, having during the festival led the world to believe it "wouldn't harm a hair on a Jewish head," would proceed with "a general liquidation of the German Jews." The diarist Viktor Klemperer, who because of his Jewish ancestry was stripped of his professorship in literature at the Dresden University of Technology in 1935, likewise predicted that as soon as the games were over the Nazis would "first of all take things out on the Jews." The danger that German Jews faced on conclusion of the Berlin games was perhaps most graphically illustrated in a nasty little ditty sung by the local SA: *Wann die Olympiade ist vorbei, / schlagen wir die Juden zu Brei.* (When the Olympics are over, we'll beat the Jews to a pulp.)

VII

"Darktown Parade"

Track and Field

▲

▲

THE anti-Nazi diarist Viktor Klemperer observed that the 1936 Berlin Olympics amounted to "an entirely political enterprise." This was true enough, but for the vast majority of athletes participating in the Nazi games, the unprecedented political controversy surrounding the affair meant little. Like their counterparts in Garmisch-Partenkirchen, they cared about the quality of the facilities and competition, not the ideological agenda of the host country. A partial exception here was the large German team. As in the Winter Games some of the German competitors in Berlin were convinced National Socialists who saw themselves as athletic soldiers of the Hitler regime. No doubt the presence of their Führer provided an added incentive to excel. In the end, however, the success achieved by the German athletes must be attributed to their rigorous training and well-honed skills, not to their patriotic motivation.

Track and field, the centerpiece of the modern Olympic Games, dominated the first week of competition. With the exception of the marathon and fifty-kilometer walk, all these events took place within the confines of the Olympic Stadium, which, in addition to a very fast track, featured a state-of-the-art photoelectronic timing system that essentially ruled out human error. Activated by the starter's pistol, the system produced slow-motion films of the races broken down into sixteen images a second. The starter's pistol also activated an immense stopwatch mounted on a tower next to the Marathon Gate. This monster clock, almost three meters in diameter, allowed audiences to see instantly just how fast the runners moved down the track. Observing this measuring machine, one journalist was moved to comment: "As a race starts, the watch writes, and once it has writ no luck-less runner can cancel its message."

Seven hundred and seventy-seven men and 111 women participated in twenty-nine track-and-field contests in Berlin. In the men's competition the powerful American team, as usual, garnered the lion's share of the medals. But there was something unprecedented in this particular example of Yankee supremacy. For the first time in Olympic history, the American dominance in men's track and field derived *primarily* from the presence of a sizable contingent of African Americans. Jesse Owens, of course, is the name everyone remembers, but he had plenty of company. There were seventeen blacks on the American men's Olympic team in 1936, and all but six of them competed in the track-and-field events (the American women's Olympic squad included two blacks, both in track). Black athletes so dominated the U.S. men's Olympic track team that a black reporter joked that in order for an "ofay" (white guy, and in pig Latin, "foe") to make the squad he would have to rub cork on his face. At the Berlin games, African American men ended up winning a total of thirteen medals in track and field, accounting for 83 of America's 107 points in that division. The American blacks' total in track and field was actually higher than that of any other national team at the 1936 games. The *Los Angeles Times* spoke with glee of Hitler's "depression" in the face of a "darktown parade."

Snubbed by the Führer?

The first day of athletic competition, August 2, began before the largest audience in the history of the Olympic Games. An overflow crowd of 110,000 spectators, thousands of them sitting in the aisles or standing on the stairways, jammed the Olympic Stadium. Fans not fortunate enough to be in the stadium could follow the developments live on the radio or hear the results blared over loudspeakers set up all around central Berlin.

The first event—elimination heats for the men's one-hundred-meter dash—generated particular excitement because Jesse Owens was scheduled to run. Even before his appearance in the Olympics, Owens had firmly established himself as "the fastest man in the world." Articles in the German press had brought fans up to speed regarding Owens's inspiring personal story. They related his birth in 1913 into a family of sharecroppers in tiny Oakville,

Alabama, and of his move at age eight to Cleveland, Ohio, where to assist his family he worked during his teen years loading freight cars and repairing shoes. There were stories about his crucial early mentoring by a junior high school track coach named Charles Riley, who taught Jesse to run as if he were dancing over a field of hot coals. Other reports chronicled his emergence as a track star at Cleveland East Technical High School and his spectacular world-record run of 9.4 seconds in the one-hundred-yard dash at the Interscholastic Championships in Chicago in 1933. Finally, like their American counterparts, German writers rhapsodized over Owens's "humility" and easygoing demeanor.

Jesse Owens was not the only focus of attention and excitement in that first one-hundred-meter elimination heat—at least for German fans. Germany's own speedster, thirty-three-year-old Erich Borchmeyer, offered an outside chance at victory for the home team. Borchmeyer had raced against Owens once before at an AAU event in 1932 in Los Angeles. On that occasion Owens had run the one-hundred-yard distance in 9.6 seconds, so impressing Borchmeyer that the German had gotten a signed picture from Owens that he still had in his possession in 1936, as if expecting to have it signed again.

Owens and Borchmeyer predictably won their respective heats, Owens with a 10.3 finish that equaled the existing world record. The sportswriters ransacked their repertoire of racially tinged superlatives: "black arrow," "black panther," "black blitz." Observing Owens directly after the heat, one German writer was astounded to see a calm and composed young man who looked as if he had merely gone out for a stroll.

Yet Owens was just getting warmed up. In the second round of heats, held in the afternoon, he ran a 10.2, which would have been a new world record had there not been a slight tail wind. Borchmeyer and Owens's teammate, Ralph Metcalfe, each won their second heats in the identical time of 10.5. Owens looked to be unbeatable in the one-hundred-meter semifinals and in the finals scheduled for the following day.

Meanwhile the remaining events of the first day offered plenty of excitement and gratification for the home fans. A German, Tilly Fleischer, won the first gold medal of the 1936 Summer Games in the women's javelin with an Olympic-record throw. This was not a great surprise—she had come a close second to the great Mildred "Babe" Didrickson in the 1932 Los Angeles games—but Fleischer was the first German woman *ever* to win a gold medal in the Summer Games, and the crowd went wild, screaming *"Til-ly!"* over and over.

Fleischer's medal turned out to be one of seven won by German women in track and field at the 1936 Games, the largest bounty of any of the female contingents. The German women won only two fewer track medals than the German men, although the men competed in twenty-three disciplines and the women in just six. "Thank God for our *women*," the Führer might have said, had he been inclined to acknowledge that Germany's overall victory in the Berlin Games was heavily dependent on its women.

Hitler did not personally witness Fleischer's victory, but he was on hand in the late afternoon for the Germans' second gold medal, an Olympic-record shot-put heave by Hans Wöllke. Like Fleischer's feat, Wöllke's victory charted new territory for Germany: it was the first Olympic gold in track and field for a German male. That Wöllke won at home in front of Hitler made the moment all the more special for the athlete, who was a member of the SS. Almost as gratifying to the home crowd was the bronze-medal finish of German Gerhard Stöck, while the favored American, Jack Torrance, finished a lowly fifth. Stöck, who belonged to the SA, later went on to win gold in the javelin. When his victory was announced in that event he snapped to attention in the middle of the field and gave the Nazi salute.

By all accounts Hitler was jubilant over the German victories on opening day. His pleasure was such that he showed no frustration over the Finns' sweep of the ten-thousand-meter run, an event in which the Germans were not expected to do well anyway. Hitler called the victors in the shotput, women's javelin, and ten-thousand-meter race to his box and personally congratulated them, shaking the hand of each. While it seemed innocuous at the time, Hitler's gesture on that opening afternoon soon took on added significance because of what was to happen later that evening and on the following days: his failure to congratulate American black victors, including, most famously, Jesse Owens.

The final event of the first day's competition—the men's high jump—took longer than scheduled and did not conclude until dusk had fallen. Fully twenty-two of the fifty entrants cleared the 1.85-meter threshold in the opening round and went on to the final. Among the qualifiers were three Americans, Cornelius Johnson, David Albritton, and Delos Thurber, plus two Germans. Johnson, a six-foot-five-inch beanpole from California, was black, as was Albritton, a teammate of Owens's from Ohio State University. After almost three hours of jumping, the two Germans fell out of the competition and only one European, a giant Finn named Kalevi Kotkas, remained to battle against the Americans. A German writer described the blue-eyed, blond-haired Finn as a "Siegfried" type. The Nordic Siegfried, however, could not keep pace with the Americans, who in the last stage of the event were jumping against themselves for the medals. Johnson, who had not bothered to take off his warm-up suit until the final rounds, ended up getting the gold medal with an Olympic-record vault of 2.03 meters; Albritton came in second, and Thurber third.

Accounts vary regarding Hitler's noncongratulation of the American winners in the high jump. The *New York Times* man on the scene had Hitler leaving the stadium five minutes before the award ceremony. A German eyewitness recalled him getting up and leaving just as Johnson and Albritton, apparently expecting his congratulations, mounted the steps toward the Führer's box. The historian Richard Mandell states that Hitler left the stadium "in the darkness and threatening rain" following the elimination of the German jumpers. Whatever the precise moment of his departure, he undoubtedly left not because of the lateness of the hour or the weather but because he was faced with the prospect of congratulating American blacks. Given his treatment of the other victors earlier that day, and his well-known tolerance for drawn-out functions, Hitler's behavior here must be seen as a deliberate snub. This is certainly how Baillet-Latour saw the matter. The next morning the IOC president had Ritter von Halt inform Hitler that it was not customary for heads of state publicly to congratulate Olympic medal winners, but if he insisted on doing so he must congratulate *all* of them without exception.

Undoubtedly fearing that more blacks would win medals, Hitler assured Halt that he would not congratulate *any* of the medal winners in public from then on. Of course only a few insiders knew about this decision at the time, which is why many observers, especially Americans, felt outraged when Hitler neglected to congratulate Jesse Owens and other black victors down the line. In reality *all* these athletes, not Owens specifically, were snubbed by the Führer.

The rain that had threatened to drench Berlin on the opening day of competition did so on the second day, making the track soggy and slow. The unfavorable conditions yielded relatively unimpressive times for the four-hundred-meter hurdle heats and promised tough going for the one-hundred-meter dash semi-final heats. Nonetheless the slow track did not prevent Owens from winning his heat in 10.4. In the other semifinal Ralph Metcalfe won in 10.5 over Martin Osendarp of the Netherlands (10.6) and Germany's Borchmeyer (10.7). The scene was now set for the final, scheduled for 5:00 in the afternoon.

At 4:58 the runners used small trowels to dig purchase holes in the cinder track at the starting line (starting blocks were not yet in use). Hitler, who clearly hoped his man Borchmeyer might yet pull off an upset, leaned over his box, tapping the railing impatiently. The starter, a portly Bavarian named Franz Miller who endeared himself to the crowd by bending his knees as he gave each command, called out *"Auf die Plätze!" "Fertig!"* and then fired his pistol. Owens was first off the line and was never seriously challenged, although Metcalfe put on a surge in the last twenty meters that brought him within a tenth of a second of the victor. The final results were: Owens, 10.3; Metcalfe, 10.4; and Osendarp, 10.5. Despite Hitler's cheers, Borchmeyer had not been a factor.

Like all the medal winners in the 1936 games, Owens was crowned on the victory podium with a wreath fashioned from oak leaves. In previous games the winners had received olive- or laurel-leaf crowns, which became the custom again after 1936. The Germans resorted to their oak-leaf deviation because the oak tree was a symbol of the pagan god Thor and represented strength and purity in Indo-Germanic mythology. Carl Diem declared that the oak-leaf crowns were a no less worthy reward than the olive-leaf garlands, seeing that "a great statesman" had defined the spiritual context for their use in 1936. It is probably safe to assume, however, that Diem did not have Jesse Owens in mind when he contemplated the Olympic heroes who would wear these sacred crowns.

In addition to the garlands Owens and his fellow gold-medal winners in the Berlin games received potted oak-tree seedlings that they were encouraged to plant in their homelands. Most of the athletes, including Owens, did so gladly. There are now full-grown oak trees all over the world that stand as living (albeit unacknowledged) symbols of the pagan-Germanic ideology surrounding the Nazi games.

If Owens expected congratulations from Hitler along with his other fruits of victory, he showed no sign of it at the time. Nor, of course, did Hitler encourage any approach from the black runner. We can only speculate on how Hitler would have behaved toward Owens had he not made his earlier face-saving concession to Baillet-Latour, but in all likelihood he would not have offered his hand. Hitler could no more abide blacks than he could Jews and was appalled by the very notion of physical contact with them. According to Nazi youth leader Baldur von Schirach, Hitler later declared in regard to Owens and other black athletes: "The Americans should have been ashamed of themselves for allowing their medals to be won by Negroes. I would never have shaken this Negro's [Owens's] hand." Schirach also relates that when he suggested that the Führer be photographed with Owens, Hitler screamed in indignation: "Do you really think I'd allow myself to be photographed shaking hands with a Negro?"

Interestingly enough, however, Owens himself had no inkling of any animosity toward him on the part of the Führer. He certainly never claimed to have been snubbed by Hitler. On the contrary, on his return to America after the Games he told an audience of one thousand blacks in Kansas City, Missouri, that it was *President Roosevelt* and not Hitler who had shown him disrespect at his moment of triumph in Berlin. "Hitler didn't snub me—it was our president who snubbed me. The president didn't even send me a telegram." Owens also claimed that while he had not managed to meet Hitler in Berlin, he had once caught the Führer's eye at the stadium, and that Hitler had gracefully acknowledged him. "When I passed the chancellor he arose, waved his hand at me, and I waved back at him."

In fact, no one else witnessed this putative Hitler wave, and even Owens's coach, Larry Snyder, doubted that it had actually happened. Snyder speculated that Jesse was trying "to take the sting out of Hitler's apparently rude behavior toward him and other American blacks." But why would Owens want to absolve Hitler of allegations of rudeness if he did not believe that he had been snubbed in the first place? Whatever the truth behind the wave story, Owens turned out to be something of a Hitler fan. Back in the US he chastised American journalists for having had the bad taste to criticize "the man of the hour in Germany." And in campaigning for Republican presidential candidate Alf Landon against FDR in 1936, Owens repeatedly praised Hitler as a "man of dignity," while condemning Roosevelt as a "socialist."

If Owens himself was not put off by Hitler's treatment of America's black Olympians, the American press, especially the black press, certainly was. HITLER SNUBS JESSE! shouted a headline in the *Cleveland Call and Post*; OWENS HUMILIATED IN HITLER'S LAND, proclaimed the *Chicago Defender*. In the view of the *Pittsburgh Courier-Journal*, Hitler revealed his own inadequacies in cold-shouldering America's black stars: "Hitler is an individual envious of talent, suspicious of high character, devoid of chivalry, bereft of culture, a cowardly effeminate, who proved incapable of being a gentleman even at the Olympic Games, where prejudice and politics are traditionally taboo." The Jewish War Veterans of New Jersey passed a resolution condemning the Hitler government and the German Olympic Committee "for their gross lack of sportsmanship and decency in affronting America's supreme colored athletes."

It should be noted, however, that American criticism of Hitler and the German organizers did not extend to the German fans in general, whose treatment of black athletes was seen to be respectful and friendly. Indeed, as many American athletes noted, the people of Berlin were as hospitable toward blacks as they were toward any of the other visiting athletes. John Woodruff, an American black who won a gold medal in the eight-hundred-meter race, stated after the games: "A lot of people asked me how the Germans treated us. They treated us royally. They rolled out the red carpet. They were very friendly, very accommodating, very gracious, very cordial. They were considerate in every respect."

The German fans could afford to be gracious toward Owens and company because they had their own stars to celebrate in the early days of the track competition. On the same day that Owens won his first gold medal a German named Karl Hein won the hammer throw with an Olympic-record toss of 56.59 meters. Reminiscent of the ancient Greek cities' custom of honoring their Olympic victors with landed estates, Hein's employer, a German cigarette company, presented him with a new house and garden. The silver medal in the hammer throw went to another German, Erwin Blask, while a Swede, Oskar Warngard, got the bronze. The hammer competition was enlivened by Hitler's arrival just before Blask took a temporary lead; reportedly both Blask and Hein drew inspiration in their mighty duel from the presence of the Führer.

"You Should Be Running for Germany"

Another German who put on a heroic show for the Führer was the gold medal winner in the women's discus, Gisela Mauermayer. Undoubtedly the most popular female athlete in the 1936 games (at least with the German fans), Mauermayer was a tall and strapping blond who wore her long hair in the tightly wound "snail-style" bun favored by the Bund deutscher Mädel (League of German Girls). As the world record holder in her event she was heavily favored to win, and win she did, with an Olympic-record toss of 47.63 meters, two meters farther than the effort of the second-place finisher, Jadwiga Wajsowna of Poland, and fully eight meters beyond that of her German teammate, Paula Mollenhauer, who took the bronze.

Mauermayer had joined the Nazi Party in 1932 and was an enthusiastic supporter of Hitler. In 1945, following the German defeat, she was barred from continuing her high school teaching career on account of her Nazi past. Interviewed in 1986 for the fiftieth anniversary of the 1936 games, she professed no regrets for having been, in the words of her interviewer, "a blond, Nordic advertisement for the Nazis at the Berlin Games." "It was an honor to be allowed to compete for Germany," she stated. Asked about the notion that Hitler had used the Olympic Games to mask his aggressive intentions, Mauermayer replied: "Hitler was no more aggressive than Churchill."

The Germans had hopes in the women's one-hundred-meter dash for their speedster Käthe Krauss, but the favorites in that event were Helen Stephens, an eighteen-year-old farm girl from Missouri, and the world-record holder, Staneslawa Walasiewiczówna, who ran for Poland but lived and trained in the United States under the more pronounceable name Stella Walsh. In one of the preliminary heats Stephens clocked in at 11.4, which, like Jesse Owens's amazing heat over the same distance, would have been a world record but for a tailwind. The contestants were so keyed up for the much-anticipated final that there were repeated false starts, much to the annoyance of starter Miller, who perhaps wished that he possessed the power of his counterparts in the ancient games to flog false starters. Finally the women were off, and even without a tailwind Stephens ran only one-tenth of a second slower than her fantastic heat time. She beat Walasiewiczówna/Walsh by two meters and set a new world record. Krauss came in a distant third.

Hitler was as impressed as anyone by Stephens's performance. He insisted on meeting her privately in the special enclosure behind his box in the stadium. According to Stephens's later account of the meeting, the enclosure was guarded by fifteen blackshirted soldiers carrying Luger pistols. "Why, it looked like an assassination squad!" she recalled. "When Hitler came in with his interpreter, he gave me a little Nazi salute, and I thought, 'I'm not going to salute you.' So I extended my hand and gave him a good ol' Missouri handshake. Well, immediately Hitler goes for the jugular vein. He gets a hold of my fanny, and he begins to squeeze and pinch and hug me up, and he said, 'You're an Aryan type. You should be running for Germany.'"

After the games Stephens, who was almost 6 feet 1 inch tall and quite flat-chested, was accused by a Polish journalist of being a man (presumably the journalist believed that only a man could beat the "Flying Pole," Walasiewiczówna). The AOC was quickly able to establish Stephens's female bona fides to the satisfaction of the German organizers and the IOC. What none of the officials knew was that—irony of ironies—Stephens's Polish rival, Walasiewiczowna/Walsh, *was* a man. This fact was not revealed during Walsh's lifetime. "She" continued to compete successfully as a woman until 1954 and was inducted into the U.S. Track and Field Hall of Fame in 1975. But when Walsh was killed by a stray bullet during a robbery at a Cleveland shopping center in 1980, an autopsy revealed standard male genitalia and male chromosomes.

Stephens anchored the American team in the women's four-hundred-meter relay, which came down to a hard-fought duel between the U.S. women and the favored German quartet, which had previously established the world record in that event. The Germans had a ten-meter lead at the beginning of the last leg, and though Stephens was faster than her German counterpart, Ilse Dörffeldt, the Germans would likely have taken the gold had Dörffeldt not committed the ultimate relay blunder by dropping the baton at the pass. The Americans went on to win in 46.9 seconds (well behind the Germans' earlier best time of 46.4), followed by Britain and Canada. After the race the tearful German girls were invited up to Hitler's private enclosure. Although reportedly furious over their defeat, the Führer assured them that he was positive they would have won had it not been for the botched pass. Göring sought to soothe the women's distress by inviting them to his garden party.

In the women's high jump the home team had a good chance at gold in the person of Dora Ratjen. Ratjen, however, failed to be among the three jumpers who cleared the bar at 1.60 meters. A jump-off between Ibolya Csák of Hungary, Dorothy Odam of Britain, and Elfriede Kaun of Germany resulted in gold for Csák with a 1.62-meter leap. Odam was second and Kaun third. The Germans might have done better in this event had the German Jewish jumper Gretel Bergmann been on their team, but as we have seen she was kept off the squad because of her "race." Bergmann's personal best was 1.64 and she had jumped 1.60 at the Württemberg championships in June 1936.

Intriguingly Bergmann had become suspicious of Dora Ratjen's sexuality at an earlier meet—with good reason, it turned out. The jumper was actually a man, though that fact was not officially clarified until October 1938 following Ratjen's victory in the European championships. It seems that on the train home after the meet Ratjen's traveling companions noted an unmistakable beard and turned the athlete over to the authorities in Magdeburg. A physical investigation revealed—as a secret SS report put it—"quite definite secondary male sexual characteristics." Further tests confirmed these findings. After the war Ratjen, now using the first name Hermann, claimed to have been compelled by his Hitler Youth Brigade to masquerade as a girl. He claimed also that his trainers knew of his true gender but forced him to compete as a woman "for the honor and glory of Germany." He offered no proof for these assertions, but it is hard to imagine that the trainers who worked closely with him would not have been aware of his actual gender.

There was no question about the gender of the winner of the women's eighty-meter hurdles, but the gold medalist, Trebisonda "Ondina" Valla of Italy, had to wait for an inspection of the photographic record of the finish to be declared the winner because four women seemed to have crossed the line at exactly the same time. It was, however, Valla's very appearance in these games, more than her photo-finish victory, which provided the real story here.

Resistance from Pope Pius XI had prevented Italy from entering any female athletes in the Los Angeles games. The fascist government did not emphasize female athleticism (a woman's job was to bear children and to take care of her husband), but Mussolini himself believed that a few crack female athletes could be a good advertisement for the strength and modernity of the fascist state. Accordingly in 1936 Italy sent seven female athletes to Berlin. In joining them, Valla had to overcome very strong opposition from her mother, who, in good Italian mama fashion, believed that it was unseemly for girls to participate in sports and that if Ondina went to Berlin she would never find a husband.

As it happened, Valla and her female teammates significantly outclassed the Italian male track athletes in Berlin. Valla's gold medal was the only top prize to be earned by an Italian athlete in track and field in 1936. Another Italian woman came in fourth in the eighty-meter hurdles, and the Italian women's team also finished fourth in the 4 x 100-meter relay. On her return to Italy after the games, Valla received the Italian Gold Medal for Sports Achievement from Mussolini and even the pope shook her hand. It was a great leap forward for Italian womanhood.

America's "Black Auxiliaries"

Enthusiastic as German fans were over the stellar performance of their women's track-and-field team, the central attraction continued to be Jesse Owens, about whom the only question seemed to be how many medals he might win. He won a second gold and established a new world record in the two-hundred-meter race with a time of 20:7. This result was almost a full second faster than Eddie Tolan's Olympic-record performance in Los Angeles in 1932 and just shy of the world record for the two-hundred-meter straightaway. Owens's black American teammate, Mack Robinson (Jackie Robinson's older brother), took the silver medal and Osendarp of Holland the bronze. (Osendarp, by the way, seems to have been as fleet-footed politically as he was on the track; when the Wehrmacht marched into Holland in 1940 he quickly adapted to the new dispensation and became a member of the volunteer SS and an employee of the Nazi Security Police, helping in the deportation of Dutch Jews.)

Perhaps Owens's most impressive performance came in the long jump, an event in which he already held the world record. In Berlin, Owens had a worthy opponent in a young German named, appropriately enough, Lutz Long. As the event got under way, however, it began to look as if there would be no Owens-Long duel, for Owens had surprising difficulty making it into the finals. Unaware that the actual competition had started, Owens made what he thought was his final warm-up jump, only to have the judges count it as his first qualifying attempt. It was well under the mark. Rattled, he blew his second qualifying effort by stepping over the starting board. At this point Long, who like many German athletes deeply admired Owens, went over to him and, in rudimentary English, assured the American that he was such a good jumper he could clear the qualifying distance even if he took off a few inches before the starting board.

Jesse accepted Long's advice and easily qualified on his third and final leap. Soon the expected duel was indeed on, for as the competition progressed only

Owens and Long were left in an epic battle for the gold, and the two jumpers traded the lead again and again. By the penultimate round both had surpassed the Olympic record. Long equaled Owens's best distance of 7.87 meters only to have Owens roar back with a 7.94. In a last desperate effort to defeat Owens, Long overstepped the starting board for a disqualification. Owens still had one more jump, and in his final effort, freed from any worries about who would get the gold, soared over the allegedly invincible 8-meter barrier to set a new world record of 8.06 meters. This mark would not be broken in Olympic competition until American Ralph Boston jumped 8.23 meters in Rome in 1960.

Comparing Owens's and Long's jumping styles, a German commentator put the matter in pseudoscientific racial terms: "In the person of the Nordic type, [we find] a well-thought-out style, a systematic working towards the outside edge of the takeoff point, in order to achieve an ever-better performance, a pulling together of the entire body. In the Negro [we find] an unsystematic upwards rush of the body, almost like the elegant and easy jump of an animal in the wild." This comment presaged the manner in which the Nazis would deal with the long parade of victories by America's black stars.

On the conclusion of their duel Long rushed over to Owens and embraced him. The two men then walked arm in arm along the track—a gesture that on the streets of Nazi Berlin could have gotten both of them arrested. Awaiting the awards ceremony, Long and Owens lay on the grass together, their warm feelings for each other obvious. The athletes kept their friendship intact in the years following the games, and after Long was killed fighting in World War II Owens took up contact with his family, taking pains to employ Long's son in a film about the Berlin games that he put together in the 1960s.

Jesse Owens could probably also have won the four-hundred-meter race in Berlin but the American team did not need him in order to prevail in that event. The United States had Archie Williams and James LuValle, two more "black auxiliaries," as *Der Angriff* infamously labeled the African American stars. Williams was a twenty-year-old sophomore at the University of California at Berkeley when he won his gold medal in Berlin. Asked after the games how he had prepared for the Olympics, he answered that he hadn't prepared at all because he was too busy working on his mechanical engineering degree. Initially he was a walk-on with the Cal track team, but he began shaving half seconds off his time with each race and won the Pacific-8 championships in the four-hundred-meter event in spring 1936 with a time of 46.8. At the

Chicago NCAA championships a little later that year he set a world record by clocking 46.1. In the U.S. Olympic trials at Randall's Island, where, in his words, "Everything [about the organization] was for shit," he ran slower but was still fast enough to win.

In Berlin, Williams waltzed through the heats and then hunkered down for the final. He and the other favorite, Britain's Arthur Brown, were in the two outside lanes, the least favorable ones in the four-hundred-meter race because the outside-lane runners cannot tell where they are sitting until the straightaway after the second turn. But Williams bolted fast out of the start and was three meters in front of Brown going into the straightaway. Brown almost closed the gap at the tape, which of course meant only that had the race been a bit longer he might have won. Williams clocked in at 46.5, Brown at 46.7, and LuValle, who took third, at 46.8. Pleased as he was to have won the gold, Williams was also excited to have beaten LuValle, an old rival from UCLA. The only thing better, said Williams, would have been to have beaten someone from USC, a "sports factory" where Coach Dean Cromwell had athletes "stacked up like cords of wood."

Williams also admired another of the "black auxiliaries," John Woodruff, a tall, lanky freshman from the University of Pittsburgh whose long loping strides were reputed to measure between nine and eleven feet. Of Woodruff, Williams said: "I was just a flash in the pan, whereas he was Mr. Consistency." In Berlin, Woodruff had the fastest time in the semifinals of the eight-hundred-meter race but got off to a rough start in the final, finding himself boxed in behind a group of relatively slow runners. After having to run—or, for him, almost walk—a good part of the race, he finally managed to get around the pack by moving to the far outside and, in an incredible burst of speed, pass everyone for the victory. His time of 1:52:9 was not brilliant, but, as one observer noted, he had probably run an extra fifty meters.

Owens's last gold medal came in the 4 x 100-meter relay—an event he was originally not even scheduled to enter, and that has been shrouded in controversy ever since. On August 4 the head coach of the American track team, Lawson Robertson (University of Pennsylvania), announced that Owens would not be entered in the relay because he had "done just about enough in one Olympics." Robertson added that he had not yet decided who would make up the relay team, but according to the *New York Times,* Marty Glickman (Syracuse), Sam Stoller (Michigan), and Foy Draper (USC) were considered "certainties on the basis of trials the last few days," and Frank Wykoff (USC) would probably be the fourth man.

Glickman and Stoller, the lone Jews on the American Olympic track team, had been personally assured by Robertson that they would run, and they had spent the first days of the games assiduously preparing for the event. Recalled Glickman: "For the ten days or so we were there before the race, we practiced passing the baton every day. Sam and I along with Foy Draper and Frank Wykoff. . . . Sam was the fastest starter. I had power down the straightaway, Foy could run the turn the best, and Frank was the seasoned veteran of the Olympic Games. That is the way we practiced and were coached."

At a team meeting on the morning of August 8, however, Glickman and Stoller were informed that they would not run in the relay and that the team would be composed of Jesse Owens, Ralph Metcalfe, Foy Draper, and Frank Wykoff. According to the *Times*, Robertson had made this decision the night before, on grounds that America had to have its fastest men on the track because the Dutch were a potent threat and Germany had "quietly built up a quartet that had been clocked in a sensational time." Just who these secret German weapons were and where they might be hidden Robertson did not divulge. Owens, when informed by Robertson that he would be running in the race after all, reportedly said: "That's swell news. I haven't known what to do with myself since Wednesday. I'll sure hustle around that corner." If Owens's hustle in fact helped the American team win, the black athlete would earn a fourth gold medal for himself, only one less than the great Paavo Nurmi's achievement in 1924. (In interviews later Owens insisted that he had urged the coaches to run Glickman and Stoller in place of himself and Metcalfe. Metcalfe, by contrast, recalled Owens lobbying hard for a chance at a fourth gold.)

Whatever Owens said or did not say, Stoller and Glickman were devastated at the news of their removal. Glickman recalls insisting that Owens and Metcalfe were not needed because *any* foursome the Yanks put together could beat the Germans by fifteen yards. "You can't hide world-class sprinters," he added, alluding to the rumor of secret German talent. Glickman also recalls reminding the coaches that he and Stoller were "the only two Jews on the track team," and if they didn't run there was "bound to be a lot of criticism back home." Stoller, for his part, was so angered over this turn of events, which he called "the most humiliating episode in my life," that he vowed on the spot never to run again. (He soon recanted this vow, going on to win the one-hundred-yard dash in the Big Ten Championships in 1937.)

Glickman and Stoller did not agree on the motives behind their ouster. In a diary he kept during the games, Stoller speculated that Robertson's decision to drop him and Glickman while keeping Draper and Wykoff was influenced by an intervention from assistant coach Dean Cromwell, who as the head coach at USC wanted to have his own men in the race. Asked later if he thought his being Jewish had anything to do with his being kept off the relay team, he replied: "I was given a raw deal. The real reason why Glickman and I were dropped [instead of Draper and Wykoff] was the influence of other coaches who wanted their pupils to run." Glickman, while not denying the possibility of college favoritism, believed at the time that anti-Semitism was the main motive behind his and Stoller's removal, and over the years he hardened this opinion. He was convinced that Avery Brundage had pressured the American coaches to drop the two Jewish runners so as not to "embarrass" the Germans by subjecting them to victories by Jews on top of the humiliation they had already received at the hands of American blacks. Brundage himself, not surprisingly, denied having had any role in this matter whatsoever, and there is nothing in his private papers to prove the contrary.

The four-hundred-meter relay turned out to be one of the American track squad's most convincing victories in the 1936 games. Led by Owens and Metcalfe, the quartet set a world record of 40 seconds in their heat and then won the final in 39.8—a record that stood until 1956. The "Dutch threat" evaporated because Martin Osendarp dropped the baton. No secret German weapons turned up, and the Reich squad, as Glickman had predicted, finished fifteen yards behind the Americans. The Germans' time of 41.2 earned them a bronze, while the Italians, with a time of 41.1, captured the silver. Given earlier training times by the original American quartet of Stoller, Glickman, Draper, and Wykoff, there is little doubt that this group could have won, though perhaps not quite so convincingly.

Although Americans naturally rejoiced at the U.S. victory in the relay, the removal of Glickman and Stoller stirred controversy in the American press and in Jewish circles (it was hardly mentioned in the German press). The *New York Times*, while not specifically broaching the question of anti-Semitism, predicted criticism from Americans who would understandably lament the fact that not all members of the U.S. national team got a chance to compete

(Glickman and Stoller were the *only* American Olympians in Berlin who did not get to participate in the games at all).

According to Glickman, Robertson told him privately after the race that he had made a mistake in not running him, but publicly the coach defended his decision to put the "best possible team" on the track. Both he and Cromwell denied that the issue of race had anything to do with their decision. Later on Brundage also weighed in on this question, insisting in his official *Final Report* that any charges of racial bias on the part of the American coaches were "absurd."

Even at this date it is impossible to know for certain why Glickman and Stoller were removed from the relay team. We still do not know exactly what Cromwell's role was in this affair or whether Brundage (his protestations notwithstanding) put any pressure on the coaches. It seems reasonable to speculate, however, that *all* the above-mentioned factors might have been involved. No doubt Robertson did not want to take any chances on winning the gold medal in the relay. Hence the addition of Owens and Metcalfe. At the same time, he might well have reasoned that since two of the original quartet had to be jettisoned to make room for the black stars, Glickman and Stoller were the most convenient candidates for expulsion. They could be dropped without aggravating the USC man Cromwell, who had a major role in running the team because Robertson was in ill health. Moreover, if a controversy were to arise over dropping the two Jewish runners, Robertson and Cromwell could be pretty certain of backing from Brundage and the AOC.

While the removal of Glickman and Stoller never bothered Brundage, it haunted the American Olympic establishment for decades afterward. In 1998, when Glickman was eighty (Stoller died in 1985), the United States Olympic Committee (USOC) sought to make amends for the 1936 decision by awarding Glickman the committee's first Douglas MacArthur Award. In making the award, William J. Hybl, president of the USOC, allowed that he had never seen written proof that Avery Brundage had kept Glickman off the relay team to appease Hitler. But he added: "I was a prosecutor. I'm used to looking at evidence. The evidence was there." (Exactly *what* evidence, he didn't say.) Glickman, who had gone on to become a much-beloved radio broadcaster for the New York (football) Giants and the New York Knicks basketball team, commented: "It was really remarkable, what [Hybl] said." Indeed it was.

THE spectacular success of the African American athletes in the Berlin Games naturally inspired jubilation in the black press back home. Much of the white press also saluted these performers, suggesting, as did the black papers, that the victories disproved the Nazi dogma of Aryan racial superiority. However, most southern papers chose to record the black victories without extensive commentary. The *Atlanta Constitution*, the most "liberal" of the southern papers, did not run a single photograph of Jesse Owens.

With the notable exception of the "black auxiliaries" slur, the German press generally treated the American blacks with kid gloves. At the beginning of the games the Propaganda Ministry instructed German journalists not to emphasize race in their reporting. "The racial standpoint should not be included in any way in the discussion of results; in particular, the sensitivities of blacks should not be trampled upon," said a ministry directive. Goebbels placed a specific ban on attacks against Jesse Owens. And in fact, one German paper, the *Kölnische Zeitung*, paid Owens the ultimate compliment by declaring that his "model" physique reflected "the ideals of the ancients."

Of course Nazi Germany's official efforts to downplay race during the games only masked the regime's entrenched conviction that the black athletes were little more than physically gifted freaks. According to Albert Speer, Hitler believed that blacks owed their victories to their "jungle inheritance," which gave them especially strong physiques. Hitler also told Speer that in his opinion blacks should be excluded from future Olympics because of their "racially conditioned athletic advantages." When Germany became the dominant world power, Hitler reportedly said, the Reich would take over the Olympic movement and hold future Summer Games in Nuremberg, where it could apply its own racial principles. Goebbels, his instructions to the German press notwithstanding, was privately disgusted by the presence of black athletes in Berlin. In his diary he opined that Owens's victory in the one-hundred-meter dash was "a day of shame for the white race," and that the American team should be "embarrassed" by it. Later on he reportedly tried to force Leni Riefenstahl to cut the extensive footage of Owens from her film on the Berlin games. Like Hitler and Goebbels, Heinrich Himmler attributed the successes of American blacks to their "primitive physicality" and to the motivating force of their view that they were engaged in a racial war with whites. The whites, he insisted, needed to take this race war more seriously so as to avoid future embarrassments. According to Martha Dodd, the daughter of America's ambassador to Germany, an assistant of Ribbentrop's expressed the view that Negroes were "animals, utterly unqualified to enter the Games." The official also stated that "if Germany had had the bad sportsmanship to enter deer or another species of fleet-footed animal, they would have taken the honors from America in the track events."

"A Great Keyboard"

The crew of German and international print journalists who covered the exploits of Jesse Owens and his colleagues at the Berlin games was the largest yet assembled for an Olympic festival, consisting of more than eighteen hundred newspapermen and 125 photojournalists from fifty-nine countries. Newspapers still constituted the primary prism through which Olympic contests were perceived, and the Nazis fully appreciated the importance of this medium. "Think of the press," advised Goebbels, "as a great keyboard on which the government can play." At the Berlin games Goebbels's men played this instrument with considerable verve, doing everything in their power to influence what the horde of print journalists wrote about the affair.

The roughly eight hundred German reporters present in Berlin presented no major problems to the regime because all of them belonged to the Reich Association of the German Press and were accordingly adept at toeing the party line. Every once in a while one of the local scribes wrote something the Propaganda Ministry found objectionable—the usual offense being that of tooting the German horn a little too loudly—and when that happened the offender was quickly called to account by the Press Conference of the Reich Government, which formally issued the German journalists with their marching orders on each morning of the games.

With one exception (an Austrian, Lothar Rübelt), all the photographers covering the games were German citizens and members of the Reich Commission of Photojournalists. They were the only commercial photographers allowed to enter the Olympic Stadium and other Olympic venues; each had to wear a numbered armband for easy identification by the police. Foreign journalists wishing to avail themselves of illustrations for their stories had to choose from among the images put on display by the official photographers at the Photojournalism Center in Berlin-Charlottenburg.

There is no evidence that any of the photographers tried to slip anything "subversive" into this collection, but some of the photojournalists certainly resented the strict rules under which they were obliged to operate. Because the GOC insisted that only photographers working for the big German press agencies could move about freely within the stadium, those without such credentials often were unable to get decent shots of the action. "Our disappointment was limitless," wrote one photographer. "Our mood sank to zero." Some of these nonagency men, including the Austrian Rübelt, responded to the restrictions by sneaking past the guards to snap the action they wanted. When the police arrested Rübelt for breaking the rules, he threatened to speak out publicly about the limitations on press freedom unless he was allowed to go about this business as he chose. The regime quietly backed down in his case.

Journalists received excellent seats, free of charge, in all the Olympic venues. The press facility in the main stadium was spacious and state-of-the-art, with fifty long-distance telephones, eighty writing cubicles equipped with typewriters, and plenty of translators and secretarial assistants. The Olympic Press Headquarters in downtown Berlin also offered comfortable writing desks, additional long-distance phone lines, and up-to-the-minute Olympic news handouts for those scribes who preferred to file their stories from the press center's well-stocked bar.

The Hitler government sought to influence foreign coverage of the games not only by providing generous amenities to reporters but also by imposing controls on the reporters' activities. To move about within the Olympic "security zones," which included the Reichssportfeld and the Olympic Village, foreign reporters had to avail themselves of special guides supplied by the SS. The foreign writers sensed that some of their German journalistic colleagues were actually government spies, sent to watch over them. The Berlin correspondent for the *London Daily Herald* complained in print: "Every day I see new faces in the press box. Not one of these newcomers makes any attempt to put pencil to paper. . . . Every [foreign journalist] is under suspicion."

So what kind of foreign press coverage emerged from the Berlin Olympic festival? Due in large part to the Nazis' own public claims regarding the international coverage of the games, a mythology has grown up attesting to a full-throated chorus of enthusiasm. The state-controlled German press published numerous excerpts from foreign papers, all of them full of praise for the organizational efficiency and cordiality of the hosts. But the regime's media functionaries knew full well that this selection was highly distorted. After the games the Propaganda Ministry conducted its own survey of the foreign press that revealed a much more nuanced picture. Encompassing twenty-nine states or regions, this survey showed that while there had indeed been plenty of positive commentary on the games and on Germany in general, there had also been plenty of negative reporting.

In particular, the American press coverage was far too mixed to satisfy the German propagandists, who had clearly hoped the anti-German commentary attending the boycott debate would not carry over into the coverage of the games themselves. In the case of America's most influential newspaper, the *New York Times*, early criticism of Germany did indeed give way to much more favorable views, with the *Times* reporter Frederick T. Birchall often sounding like one of Goebbels's hacks. The *Los Angeles Times* was also generally positive. As noted above, however, almost all the American papers were highly critical of Hitler's "snub" of American black athletes.

There was also considerable criticism of the Führer's strident partisanship (although Grantland Rice, the dean of American sportswriters, found Hitler's fan fanaticism more amusing than irritating: "Hitler was rooting for the Germans like a Yale sophomore at the Harvard Game. You could almost hear him saying, 'Block that kick! Hold 'em, Yale!'"). The *New York Herald Tribune*, in contrast to the *New York Times*, delivered a great deal of negative commentary, most of it from the pen of J. P. Abramson. He decried the opening ceremony as a "Germanized spectacle" that overshadowed the sporting events themselves. The Germans' fawning over Hitler during the games, he complained, constituted a breach of Olympic decorum. Overall the *Tribune* faulted the Germans for misusing a peaceful international competition for crass nationalistic purposes. It was ironic, said the paper, that the most brutal of the European dictatorships should be the one most skillfully to exploit the idealistic heritage of modern Olympism.

Great Britain's reportage on the games was on the whole more favorable than America's, but here too there were some very sour notes. The liberal *Manchester Guardian* chastised the Germans for turning the games into a "Nazi party rally disguised as a sporting event." Never before, said the *Guardian*, had the Olympic Games been used to promote the interests of a political party. Even the conservative *Daily Telegraph* saw in the Germans' stage-managing of the Olympics a clever but transparent effort to convince foreign visitors that the friendly scene they encountered in Berlin was typical of the political situation prevailing in Nazi Germany when the world wasn't watching.

In France the coverage ran the gamut from fawning praise for German efficiency and order to harsh condemnations of political manipulation and misuse. Jacques Goddet in *l'Auto* produced one of the most critical editorials about the festival to appear in any foreign paper. His attack, entitled "Les Jeux Défigurés," asserted flat out that no games in modern Olympic history had been so "profoundly distorted" as those of Berlin '36. True, he conceded, the Americans in Los Angeles had exploited the Olympics to promote tourism in a place "that had only climate going for it," but the Germans had misused the games to sell a rapacious and hateful regime. The Nazi games, in his view, represented a political scandal that cried out for a reassessment of the whole Olympic enterprise. Barring that, he quipped, it might be most appropriate to hold the next Olympic Games on Mars.

FORTUNATELY for Goebbels's propaganda keyboard artists, print journalism was not the only medium through which the world apprehended what was happening in Berlin. German engineers ensured that people around the world could receive live radio broadcasts in twenty-eight languages. (There had been no such live broadcasts from Amsterdam in 1928 or Los Angeles in 1932.)

Radio had been the Nazis' favorite instrument for the dissemination of propaganda since the seizure of power in 1933. In *Mein Kampf* Hitler wrote of radio: "It is a terrible weapon in the hands of those who know how to use it." No one thought he knew more about using radio for propaganda purposes than Joseph Goebbels, who loved the microphone the way most actors love the camera, and who took to the airways personally whenever he had a cause to promote. By arranging for the mass distribution of cheap radio sets called *Volksempfänger* (people's receivers), Goebbels made sure that ordinary Germans across the land had ready access to the government message.

The 1936 Olympics presented the Reich's radio functionaries with a new challenge—one not merely of filling German homes with "their master's voice" but also of organizing a global broadcast of a long and complicated sports spectacle. The Winter Games in Garmisch had provided German organizers an opportunity to try out their international broadcast system on a smaller scale. In July 1936 German radio engineers got additional experience by broadcasting parts of the inaugural torch relay, which called for the deployment of a special radio car, the world's first mobile broadcasting unit.

For the Summer Games in Berlin the GOC created a state-of-the-art broadcast facility at the Reichssportfeld, equipped with soundproof transmitting cabins and numerous long-distance phone lines. A huge switchboard under the Honor Loge in the Olympic Stadium directed transmissions around the world. One expert estimated that these broadcasts reached more than 300 million listeners worldwide, making the Berlin games the largest media event in history up to that point.

The 105 foreign radio reporters from forty countries covering the games received housing in Berlin courtesy of the Reich Radio Association, whose point man, Kurt Rathke, claimed to have inspected personally every lodging facility. Rathke's agency also provided the visiting radiomen with translators, guides, and the press credentials they needed to gain access to the Olympic venues.

The Nazi radio officials were generally satisfied with the crop of foreign radio broadcasters who showed up to cover the Berlin games. The radiomen were for the most part new to Germany and, unlike some of the veteran print reporters, possessed of little firsthand knowledge regarding the actual conditions prevailing in Hitler's Reich. From America, for example, came William Slater, Bill Henry, and Ted Husing—all novices to Germany who ended up greatly pleasing their German minders by sending back enthusiastic reports about the games. Bill Henry in particular went out of his way to praise the German organizers for "putting on the best Games ever."

Because international transmission was expensive, and foreign audiences' interest tended (then as now) to focus on events involving their own national athletes, none of the foreign broadcasters provided blanket coverage of the Berlin Olympics. The American radio reporters from CBS and NBC concentrated on the track-and-field and swimming events. Some of the Latin American radiomen showed up only for the soccer matches.

Germany's own broadcasters operated under the tight control of the Reich Radio Association and the Propaganda Ministry. Unlike the foreign broadcasters, they provided daily start-to-finish coverage of the competition along with hourlong recaps at 8:00 P.M. of each day's highlights. Another feature of the domestic broadcasts was a series of prerecorded "color" segments—precursors to the maudlin "up close and personal" clips that have blighted recent Olympic reportage in the United States. The 1936 segments included interviews with Jesse Owens and Tilly Fleischer, audio tours of the Olympic Village, and commentary on Olympic ticket swapping. The German broadcasters were particularly skillful at capturing for their listeners the look and feel of the events they were reporting, allowing millions of people across the Reich to "participate" in the spectacle even though they were far away from the action. As noted above, in Berlin itself, and in a few other major German cities, people could listen to the radio broadcasts over streetcorner loudspeakers as well as over their private receivers. The public loudspeakers were very useful for people on the go, since the private sets of the day were far too bulky to carry around. The downside of the loudspeakers was that drivers of cars and trucks, not just pedestrians, often stopped to listen to the broadcasts, creating a nightmare for the traffic police.

EVEN more innovative than the international radio broadcasts was Germany's experiment with televising the 1936 Summer Olympics. The technology involved was so embryonic, however, that the telecasts only hinted at the possibilities inherent in this revolutionary new medium.

Nazi-era engineers were not the first in Germany to experiment with television, some pioneering work already having been carried out in the Weimar period. Media savvy as they were, however, the Nazi leaders envisaged a great future for this new technology and did much to further its progress. Hitler himself backed the project, and in April 1935 Germany's first public reception center for television opened in the Reichspost Museum in Berlin (private sets did not become available until 1939). Here Berliners could see, or see after a fashion, images of people speaking into microphones in a studio—the original "talking heads." Not surprisingly Propaganda Minister Goebbels was quick to grasp the manipulation potential of this new technology. At a time when few politicians even knew what television was, Goebbels was boasting to a British media colleague about Germany's long-term plans to put the Führer's face in every German living room.

The Olympic Games afforded Nazi Germany a great opportunity to show the world how far the Reich had progressed with the new medium, and everyone connected with the country's fledgling *Fernsehen* industry was determined to put on a good show. By the time the games opened, Germany was experimenting with three different kinds of television camera, and all were put to use during the Berlin Olympics. The Telefunken company developed the so-called Ikonoscope, nicknamed "the cannon" because of its one-meter-plus length. It took three men to operate. Even more cumbersome was

Fernsehen A.G.'s monster machine, which used the design of American TV pioneer Philo T. Farnsworth and required *six* men to operate. The Telefunken cannon stood directly under the Führer-Loge in the Olympic Stadium, while Fernsehen A.G.'s apparatus looked out over the Marathon Gate next to the Olympic flame. A third camera, developed independently by the Reichspost, operated at the swimming stadium.

The world's first mobile television transmitting unit, a fourteen-vehicle "train" developed by Telefunken and Daimler-Benz at a cost of 250,000 reichsmarks, lumbered around the Reichssportfeld picking up images from the cameras and transmitting them to the "Paul Nipkow" central broadcasting studio in nearby Rognitzstrasse. From there the images were fed to twenty-five "television rooms" around Berlin, including one in the Hindenburg Assembly Hall at the Olympic Village. Because the different camera systems were not synchronized, blackouts ensued whenever the technicians switched from one system to another. Unlike the full-day radio coverage, the television network operated only between the hours of 10:00 to 12:00 A.M. and 3:00 to 7:00 P.M.

Given the experimental nature of the equipment at hand, the technicians involved in these first sports telecasts found their task extremely challenging, and it is not surprising that the operation was full of bugs and snafus. The cameramen cued their pictures to the audio commentary provided by radio broadcasters standing next to them, but the cameras were too slow and unwieldy to capture fast-moving events (it took two men several minutes just the change the Ikonoscope's three different lenses), so it often transpired that the announcer was enthusiastically describing one scene while the camera was focused on something entirely different. Inevitably the cameramen became very frustrated with the whole process. At one point the Propaganda Ministry issued a directive to the cameraman operating under Hitler's box to desist from his loud cursing because his profanity was being picked up by the radio microphone next to him.

Nonstop audio commentary was absolutely necessary, however, because the images that found their way to the various receiving stations were generally quite murky. (Early television was definitely not a case of one picture being worth a thousand words.) As a New York print journalist sniffed: "You cannot see the Olympics by television yet. All that you can see are some men dressed like athletes but only faintly distinguishable, like humans floating in a milk bath. Only the polo games show up fairly clearly when black or chestnut ponies are used. All white objects are divined, rather than seen, as vague blurs in milky mass."

The poor production quality of Germany's Olympic telecasts did not diminish the enthusiasm with which they were received by their (largely German) audiences. After the games the Reichspost reported that 162,228 viewers had watched the Olympics on television. So popular were the telecasts that it was sometimes harder to get into the television reception rooms than to obtain a seat at the Olympic Stadium.

Other Stars

The inadequacies of the Olympic telecasts, of course, did not concern the thousands of fans packed into the Olympic Stadium; they could actually *see* Jesse Owens and his fellow "black auxiliaries" burn up the Berlin track. But the track-and-field competition in 1936 was by no means an exclusive showcase for American blacks, dominant as they turned out to be. In addition to the above-noted German breakthroughs in the shot put, hammer, and javelin events, there was a typically powerful Finnish presence in the middle-distance races and a new challenge from the Japanese in the pole vault and marathon. There were also, to the relief of many observers, strong performances by some of Owens's white American teammates.

ONE of the notable American showings came in the most "classic" of all modern Olympic disciplines, the discus. Americans had often triumphed in this event in Olympics past, including the first contest in 1896, won by that Princeton man who had never even seen a discus before completing his victorious toss. But an American was not expected to win in 1936. A German, Willy Schröder, had emerged as the world's greatest discus thrower and was heavily favored to strike gold on his home turf in Berlin. Schröder, however, was often so energetic in his heaves that he pitched himself out of the ring, disqualifying himself. In his excitement over competing before Hitler in Berlin, Schröder made this mistake repeatedly, with the result that his best allowable toss earned him only a humiliating fifth place. The gold medal went to American Kenneth Carpenter, who, combining great power with perfect control, set an Olympic record with a mark of 50.48 meters. Another American, Gordon Dunn, took the silver.

Forrest "Spec" Towns won the 110-meter hurdles in 14.2 seconds and also set an Olympic record of 14.1 in his semifinal heat. Nicknamed "Li'l Abner" by his American teammates on account of the army boots he habitually wore, Spec also stood out among his peers as a chain-smoker of cigars. According to Archie Williams, the hurdler would typically put his cigar down on the starting line before a race, run the event, and then come back for his stogie on finishing. (Williams didn't know if Spec's cigar remained lit.) Like most of his teammates, Towns had no interest in the political aspects of the 1936 games. As he recalled later: "I think Berlin was the first big-time Olympic Games. They really went all out. We were treated about as well as anybody could be treated. Since then I've heard a lot of things said about those Games that I didn't know were going on then. . . . Of course, I did not participate in the politics of it. I went there to run and to do my thing, and that's what I did. I don't think any of the athletes got involved in the political side of things. If anybody was involved in politics, it had to be the officials of the Olympic Committee."

Glenn Hardin, the American favorite for the gold medal in the four-hundred-meter hurdles, duly won that event, but in a time that failed to match, let alone break, the Olympic record that he himself had set in Los Angeles. His problem in Berlin was a relatively weak field in the hurdles, the only track discipline in which that was the case.

The pole vault also featured an American favorite, Earl Meadows of USC, though his eventual victory proved much more difficult than Hardin's. Indeed, it capped the most grueling pole vault competition in Olympic history—an epic struggle of twelve hours. Meadows and two Japanese rivals, Shuhei Nishida and Suoe Oe, exchanged the lead as the competition dragged on and on into the night, the stadium eventually lit by floodlights and the thirty thousand remaining spectators shivering in the cold and rain. Finally, at 10:30, with the crossbar set at 4.35 meters, Meadows hurled himself up and over, touching the bar but not dislodging it. His opponents each failed to clear the bar, and Meadows could finally claim his gold medal with a new Olympic record. The two Japanese vaulters shared the silver and bronze medals—shared them quite literally, by cutting them in half.

Earl Meadows, like most of the participants in the 1936 games, was an athletic specialist, trained to excel in one or perhaps two events. There was, however, a competition in the modern games for sporting generalists who had to be good at ten different track-and-field events; this, of course, was the decathlon. Every four years it was said to answer the question of who was the best all-around athlete in the world.

In 1936 that man turned out to be Glenn Morris, a twenty-four-year-old automobile salesman from Denver. Morris's only serious competition came from two fellow Americans, Robert Clark and Jack Parker. "The way the United States dominated this event was utterly amazing," declared the *New York Times* at the halfway point in the competition. Clark led after the first day of the two-day event, but Morris was close behind, and since he was stronger in the second day's disciplines he was picked to win. He in fact passed Clark after nine events but, according to an announcement over the loudspeakers, he could not accumulate enough points to be guaranteed the overall victory without running under 4:32 in the last discipline, the fifteen-hundred-meter race. To achieve this feat Morris would have to run that distance sixteen seconds faster than his personal best—difficult under any circumstances but virtually impossible for a man who had competed in nine demanding events over the past forty-eight hours. Morris put everything he had into the race, and although it was said that he ran like a shot-putter he ended up clocking 4:33:3, only a little more than a second too slow. He and the crowd fell into gloom until the announcer came on again and explained that there had been a computational error; Morris had not needed to break 4:32 after all, and he was declared the winner with 7,900 points, a new Olympic record. Morris was not sure whether he wanted to thank or to strangle the German officials.

Morris was quite certain of what he wanted to do with Leni Riefenstahl, at least according to her. In her memoir she writes that he made his intentions abundantly clear when she met him in the stadium to film the decathlon victory ceremony: "The dim light prevented any filming of the ceremony, and when Glenn Morris came down the steps he headed straight toward me. I held out my hand and congratulated him, but he grabbed me in his arms, tore off my blouse, and kissed my breasts, right in the middle of the stadium, in front of a hundred thousand spectators. A lunatic, I thought. I wrenched myself out of his grasp and dashed away. But I could not forget the wild look in his eyes; and I never wanted to speak to him again, never go anywhere near him again." She did, however, see him again, because she needed his help in persuading the winners of the pole vault, whose last stage she had been unable to film, to vault again for her cameras. Morris complied with her request for help, and he and Riefenstahl went on to have a brief but torrid affair. "Never before had I experienced such passion," writes Riefenstahl.

After his return to America, Morris tried to parlay his Olympic medals into Hollywood fame, much as Buster Crabbe and Johnny Weissmuller had done (and like such later decathlon champions as Floyd Simmons, Bob Mathias, Rafer Johnson, and Bruce Jenner would attempt). Morris starred with swimmer Eleanor Holm Jarrett in *Tarzan's Revenge* in 1938—a film that did nothing for him but helped Jarrett get revenge on Avery Brundage for having kicked her off the U.S. Olympic team in 1936. He also "acted" in a comedy entitled *Hold That Co-ed.* Both of these films were universally and deservedly panned, prompting Morris to give up acting. While serving in the navy in World War II he suffered a severe psychological trauma from which he never fully recovered. He died in 1974 at age sixty-one.

With the parade of victories by Americans, black and white, the fans in Berlin had to hear the "Star-Spangled Banner" so often during the track-and-field competition that it was undoubtedly a relief when athletes from other lands climbed the victory podium, as was invariably the case after the middle- and long-distance races. The Finnish runners who swept the ten-thousand-meters had all trained under the great Paavo Nurmi, and this no doubt helped them win, but it might be noted that the gold-medal time by Ilmari Salminen in 1936 was fully 9.2 seconds slower than Nurmi's own mark in 1924. Finnish runners, as in previous Olympiads, also dominated the 5 K race, though for a while it looked as if a tiny Japanese runner named Kohei Murakoso, who had set a blistering pace and held the lead lap after lap, might pull off an upset. Instead Murakoso's role in the end was to spur Gunnar Hockert, another Nurmi product, to a gold medal in a world-record time of 14:22:2. The previous record holder, Lauri Lehtinen, another Flying Finn, was second, while the Swede Jon Johnson managed to edge out the exhausted Murakoso for third.

New Zealand fans found a hero to celebrate in the winner of the fifteen-hundred-meter race, or "metric mile." Often an exciting race, requiring a combination of endurance, speed, and strategy, the fifteen hundred in Berlin was especially dramatic. The favorites were the American ace, Glenn Cunningham, and the Olympic record holder, Luigi Beccali of Italy. Cunningham, who held the world record for the mile, was a legend in running circles, having overcome through numerous operations and years of physical therapy a horrific accident in which both his legs had been burned seemingly beyond repair. New Zealand was represented by a tiny runner named Jack Lovelock, then a medical student at St. Mary's Hospital in London. In his qualifying heat Lovelock was content to finish third, just enough to make the final, thereby displaying the restraint and canniness that made him such a great miler. In the final he also cleverly held back behind the front runners, Cunningham and Beccali, letting them battle each other with no thought about the little fellow in New Zealand black on their tail. Suddenly, three hundred meters from the tape, Lovelock made his move, blowing by the leaders and catching them completely off guard. They tried to recover but did not have enough in their legs to run down the New Zealander, who finished in an Olympic-record time of 3:47:8. Cunningham came in second and Beccali third.

Lovelock's performance, incidentally, later served as an inspiration for another London medical student, Roger Bannister, in his pursuit of the sub-four-minute mile in the early 1950s. While in New Zealand in 1950 to compete in the Centennial Games, Bannister made a pilgrimage to the village school that Lovelock had attended. There he noticed that the oak sapling which the gold-medal winner had received in 1936 had grown into a tree. Images of Lovelock ran through Bannister's head as he finally broke the four-minute mile in 1954.

Fortunately for their pride, English fans did not have to be content with medals won by representatives of their former colonies. Britain's men's sixteen-hundred-meter-relay team, consisting of Frederick Wolff, Godfrey Rampling, Bill Roberts, and Godfrey Brown was considered the strongest entry in that event because of the quartet's exceptional balance. After the first quarter mile, however, it looked as if the Britons' situation was hopeless, balance or no. Rampling, who ran the second lap for Britain, took the baton a full eight meters behind Canada's great black sprinter, Phil Edwards. And yet, in one of the most amazing performances of the 1936 games, Rampling managed to hand his team a three-meter lead at the conclusion of his lap. Britain went on to win in 3.09, eight-tenths of a second off the world record. Recalling his great feat fifty years later, Rampling attributed it to what athletes call "being in the zone." "On that day in Berlin I just seemed to float around the track, passing people without effort."

Effortless floating would hardly describe the performance put on in the fifty-kilometer walk by another intrepid Englishman, Harold Whitlock. The awkward heel-and-toe gait employed in this event made all the competitors look as if they were constipated, but Whitlock actually *was* constipated, and on top of that he was sick to his stomach for a good part of the race. He was supposed to have been met at the twenty-kilometer mark on the meandering course by a British team attendant with a shot of his special glucose drink, but the attendant did not materialize until the twenty-four-kilometer point, and then only with a ghastly sweet tea made with condensed milk. After thirty kilometers Whitlock, who had started last, managed to grab the lead, but his stomach was beginning to knot up along with his bowels, and soon he had to reduce his pace. Eventually he started vomiting copiously, which at least got rid of the tea. His bowels also finally opened, effusively, which had the advantage of leaving a trail of nasty obstacles for his pursuers. Swallowing his spit for hydration, he managed somehow to hold his lead to the end, but his margin of victory over Arthur Schwab of Switzerland, a holder of four world records, ended up being less than two minutes. With his display of stamina and courage, Whitlock, an auto mechanic by trade who was docked in pay by his boss for competing in Berlin, became a hero not only to British fans but to all defenders of true amateurism in high-level sports.

Apart from the fifty-kilometer walk, the only track-and-field event that took place mainly outside the Olympic Stadium was the marathon—another grueling test of staying power and sphincter control. Unlike the walk, however, the marathon was one of the glamour events of the modern Olympics, and this was especially so in 1936 because the German organizers kept calling it "the classic race" despite its complete lack of an ancient pedigree. About a million spectators lined the marathon course in Berlin, which meandered over fairly flat terrain through the leafy Grunewald Park and along the Avus Speedway before finishing in the Olympic Stadium, where it had started.

The race in 1936 was predicted by the *New York Times* to be a duel between American and Finnish runners, which was a little odd, since in 1935 Japanese runners had posted the three fastest times in marathon history. Japan's top man was Kitei Son, who, like many of the best racers wearing the Rising Sun on their tricots, was actually Korean—latter-day booty of Japan's 1910 annexation of the Korean Peninsula, which Japan still controlled. Son was a passionate Korean nationalist who ran for Japan only because he had no alternative. In Berlin he made a point of signing his Korean name—Sohn Kee-chung—and drawing a little map of Korea next to his signature. America's top threat was a twenty-two-year-old Narragansett Indian named Ellison "Tarzan" Brown—"Tarzan" because he enjoyed swinging from trees and yelling like the Johnny Weissmuller character. (Brown, by the way, was lucky to have made it to Berlin. In the 1936 Boston Marathon, a qualifying event for the U.S. Olympic team, he nearly destroyed himself in a duel over "Heart-break Hill" with the legendary John A. Kelley; Brown actually had to walk part of the race and almost staggered into the path of a car.) In addition to the Nurmi-trained Finns, other favorites included Carlos Zabala, an Argentinean who had won the Olympic marathon in 1932; and Ernest Harper, an aging Englishman who, in contrast to the stone-faced Asians and stoic Finns, ran with a look of epic agony on his well-lined face.

Unfortunately for the marathoners, the cool and cloudy weather that had prevailed so far through the track events turned warm and sunny on August 9, the day of the great race. As the runners left the stadium to the sound of blaring trumpets at 3:00 in the afternoon, many of them wore hats to shield themselves from the relentless sun. Zabala immediately took the lead in a very fast pace, challenging the other runners to stay with him. In light of the weather, the wiser ones let him go, sensing, correctly as it turned out, that he would pay for his wicked pace later on. One of those who held back—but not too far back—was Son. He was easily distinguishable by his bandy legs and weird-looking running shoes, which featured a split between the big toe and the rest of his foot, a design he had copied from the comfortable Japanese sandals he wore off the track. Son, who knew some English, ran and chatted for many kilometers with Harper, the old sage assuring him that Zabala would eventually blow up. Tarzan Brown surged to fourth place at twenty-five kilometers, but that was as far up the pecking order as he could go. The heat and fast pace duly overcame Zabala at twenty-eight kilometers; he slowed, then fell, and by the time he could get up Son and Harper were by him. Zabala dropped out of the race with leg cramps at thirty-two kilometers. Harper stayed with Son for a time, but after thirty-three kilometers the Korean had a lead of twenty-five seconds, which he kept widening for the rest of the race.

Son entered the stadium through the Marathon Gate all by himself, his appearance announced by another trumpet fanfare. He showed no sign of stress or strain as he crossed the finish line in 2:29:19, an Olympic record. Upon finishing he promptly removed his odd shoes and then ran barefoot another one hundred meters to the dressing rooms. Son was already out of sight when Harper crossed the line two minutes later, looking, in contrast to the winner, the way people are supposed to look after running forty-two kilometers under a hot sun. Third place went to Shoryu Nan, another Korean running for Japan.

"A Japanese wins the marathon! What a nation, what a race!" observed Goebbels in his diary. (Three months later Germany would join Japan in the so-called Anti-Comintern Pact, and then add Italy to form the Rome-Berlin-Tokyo Axis.) Son, for his part, modestly attributed his victory to Harper: "From the time we started," he said, "[Harper] kept telling me not to worry about Zabala, but to let him run himself out."

On the victory podium Son and Nan duly bowed their heads as the Japanese anthem was played. But Son courageously told reporters afterward that he had made this gesture not in reverence to Japan but in silent "shame and outrage" over Japan's occupation of Korea. As punishment for his outspokenness, Son was banned for life from competitive running by Japanese officials. In the same spirit of protest, a Seoul newspaper, *Dong-a Ilbo*, printed a retouched picture of Son on the podium showing him wearing a sweatshirt absent the Rising Sun emblem. The Japanese overlords in Korea immediately jailed the paper's editors and shut down publication for nine months.

After the Berlin games the name "Kitei Son" was chiseled into a stone pillar near the entrance to the Olympic Stadium along with the names of the other winners. Some thirty years later South Korean politicians asked the West German officials who then managed the stadium to change the name on the pillar to "Sohn Kee-chung" and the winner's national affiliation to the Republic of Korea. The West Germans turned the matter over to the IOC, which refused to countenance any changes.

But Sohn got the last laugh. His status as a national hero to the Koreans was such that, fifty-two years later, in the Seoul Olympics of 1988, he was given the signal honor of carrying the Olympic torch into the stadium. Weeping with joy, Sohn, aged seventy-three, looked almost as spry as he had in crossing the finishing line in Berlin.

Of Pools, Mats, Rings, and Rough Waters

▲

▲

WITH the conclusion of the track-and-field events, a bit of steam seemed to go out of the Berlin games. Some of the track athletes left the city as soon as their events were completed, and the fans who had come mainly to see Jesse Owens departed as well. But leaving these games early would have been a mistake, for many of the most impressive athletic efforts were still to come, including the majority of the Olympic and world-record-breaking performances set in Berlin. The 1936 games also produced the youngest Olympic medal winner and the youngest Olympic gold medal winner.

For those interested in the latest technical gadgetry to measure and record athletic achievement, there were, in addition to the photoelectric timing mechanism deployed in the Olympic Stadium, new electronic timing and photographic devices at the swimming stadium and the first-ever electronic scoring system for fencing. Up in Kiel the yachting competition was monitored by aerial photography from blimps. The technical innovations did not, however, prevent a flurry of complaints about judging and organization, whose quality, many believed, was not nearly as high as that prevailing for the track-and-field competition.

For the large German team, the events to come were especially important, for it was in competitions other than track and field in which Germany won most of its medals—enough of them, in fact, to come out on top in the national medal race for the first time in the history of the Summer Games. Thus while some foreign visitors, especially Americans, might have found the Berlin games less interesting once the track-and-field events were completed, the German fans became increasingly excited as more and more athletes wearing the swastika on their tunics mounted the victory podium.

Swimming and Diving

The venue for the swimming and diving competitions at the 1936 games was the twenty-thousand-seat Aquatic Sports Complex, which lay just to the north of the Olympic Stadium. Germany had never been much of a power in the water sports events, and despite a rigorous new training program the Reich remained weak in 1936. Lack of home-team strength, however, did not hurt attendance; the stadium was filled almost to capacity each day during the eight-day aquatic competition. Even Hitler showed up occasionally, although he had little interest in swimming.

Like a rehearsal for the upcoming Pacific war, the men's swimming competition turned out to be a battle between the United States and Japan, just as it had been in Los Angeles four years earlier. And just as in LA, the Japanese men's team accumulated more points than the Americans, prompting one American journalist to comment: "Four years ago at Los Angeles, it might have been an accident. Now we know that the world's greatest [men's] swimming team is the Japanese, if diving is excluded." Some American commentators attributed the Japanese success to oxygen priming—the inhaling of pure oxygen—but the American coach, Bob Kiphuth, knew the real reason had to do with good technique and hard work:

> To the uninitiated there are two outstanding characteristics to Japanese swimming—a remarkably high stroke by which I mean a considerable number of complete strokes per minute, and a remarkable ability to maintain this high stroke over a considerable distance. [But] that isn't all there is to this business. The Japanese boys aren't interested in the girls, they regard their swimming as a matter of national honor, and they work like the devil.

Standouts for Japan included Noburu Terada, who won the fifteen-hundred-meter freestyle, and Detsuo Hamuro, who took gold in the two-hundred-meter breaststroke. Japan also bested the United States in the eight-hundred-meter relay, perhaps the most accurate measure of overall team strength. Jack Medica of Seattle, a big lanky fellow with an enormous wingspan, who had won nine NCAA championships at the University of Washington, came in second to Terada in the fifteen hundred and hauled in a gold medal for the United States in the four-hundred-meter freestyle, his signature event. Eighteen-year-old Adolph Kiefer of Chicago, the world-record holder in the one-hundred-meter breaststroke, set Olympic records in each of his heats as well as in the final, to win another American gold. One prominent exception to the Japan-America standoff came in the one-hundred-meter freestyle, which saw Hungarian Ferenc Csik, a relative unknown, swim the race of his life for the gold. He profited from the preoccupation of the Americans and the Japanese with each other; they failed to notice Csik until his hand went up in victory. Csik was followed by two Japanese.

Oddly some of the American swimmers in the Berlin games wore the Rising Sun rather than the Stars and Stripes on their tank tops. This was not a case of confused loyalty but the result of financial hard times for the American swim program, whose members, like those in the other disciplines, had to cover a good part of their own costs. The suits in question were old ones the Americans had picked up in an earlier dual meet with Japan. Rather than outfit the entire team in new suits for Berlin, American swim officials recycled the Japanese models. Given the final swimming results in Berlin, the decision was perhaps a fitting one.

The star of the women's swimming competition—and indeed one of the stars of the 1936 games overall—was Holland's Rita Mastenbrock, who earned gold medals (and set Olympic records) in the one-hundred-meter and four-hundred-meter freestyle, took silver in the one-hundred-meter backstroke, and won a third gold medal in the four-hundred-meter relay. Mastenbrock's accomplishment was all the more impressive because, unknown to her or her coaches at the time, she had a chronic blood disease that drained her of oxygen.

At age seventeen Mastenbrock was among the younger competitors in Berlin, but she was a mature woman in comparison to little Inge Sørensen of Denmark, who took bronze in the two-hundred-meter breaststroke. Only twelve years and twenty-four days old on the day of competition, she became the youngest medal winner in modern Olympic history, a record she still holds despite a recent plethora of prepubescent girl gymnasts.

In men's springboard diving competition the central attraction was a tall, blond, perfectly proportioned Miamian named Marshall Wayne. Well before he began his diving career at the University of Miami, Wayne had learned acrobatics from members of the traveling circus with which his parents performed. Circuslike twists and flips became the hallmark of his diving style. In Berlin, Wayne and his fellow American diver Dick Degener psyched out their Japanese rivals by avoiding the pool entirely until the last day of workouts and then proceeding to execute a series of perfect practice dives. While Degener ended up narrowly beating Wayne in the springboard competition, Wayne took gold in the platform diving by a convincing margin over his Olympic Village roommate, Elbert Root. (Root was a Native American who, according to Wayne, threw up all over their room night after night after gorging himself on German sausage.) Apart from his roommate, Wayne's main irritation during the games involved the bathing trunks that the Germans required all the divers to wear in competition; they were much baggier than the close-fitting models he was used to. "Why [the suits]?" Wayne wondered in an interview fifty years later. "I don't know. German morality? Those guys? Moral? But there we were in these damn bathing suits."

In women's diving the crowd's attention was focused on America's beautiful Dorothy Poynton-Hill, who had almost as much star wattage as Eleanor Holm Jarrett. Unlike her straitlaced fellow competitors, Poynton-Hill comported herself like a movie star, plucking her eyebrows, wearing colorful waterproof lipstick, and strolling around the pool area in high-heeled shoes. She designed her own chic gold lamé swimsuits, which she modeled for the Olympic fans. Having won gold and silver medals in Los Angeles, Poynton-Hill added another gold medal in platform diving and a bronze in the springboard competition in Berlin. Immediately after the games she announced that she was turning pro. "You can't blame her for wanting to capitalize on her hard-earned fame," her father explained.

The women's diving competition, like the swimming, featured some very young athletes, among whom was the thirteen-year-old American prodigy Marjorie Gestring. If Inge Sørensen became the youngest medal winner in Olympic history, Gestring became the games' youngest gold medal winner by taking the springboard competition in 1936. Like many prodigies, Gestring had been pushed hard by her parents, who accompanied her to Berlin. According to her father, little Marjorie was so preoccupied with her diving that she had little interest in food or even sleeping. "She hasn't begun to think about boys yet," he added, in what may well have been an example of hopeless parental naïveté.

Gymnastics

While the German fans had few successes of their own to celebrate at the aquatic center, things were different at the Dietrich-Eckart Theater, site of the gymnastics competition. The Germans regarded gymnastics as *their* sport, having made *Turnen* into a kind of national religion in the nineteenth century. They had dominated the gymnastics events in the first modern Olympiad in 1896. Believing a similar dominant performance in 1936 was a matter of national honor, Germany had worked hard to put together an extremely strong team for the Berlin games. In this instance the preparation paid off handsomely. Twenty-four-year-old Alfred Schwarzmann won a gold medal in the long horse and two bronze medals in the horizontal bars and parallel bars; his point accumulation also gave him the overall individual championship. (Incidentally, because of Germany's absence from further Olympic competition until 1952, Schwarzmann was the only German participant in the 1936 games to participate in the Olympics again. In the Helsinki games in 1952, at age forty, he won a silver medal in the horizontal bars.) In 1936 Schwarzmann's German teammate Konrad Frey won gold medals both in the side horse and the parallel bars. In the team competition the victorious Germans' strongest rivals were the Swiss, who came in a close second. Swiss gymnasts took gold and silver medals in the free exercise; silver and bronze in the side horse; silver in the long horse and parallel bars. Eugen Mack of Switzerland was second to Schwarzmann in the all-around individual competition.

For the American gymnastics team, which had done well in Los Angeles, the Berlin games were a great disappointment; they ended up finishing tenth. The chairman of the American gymnastics committee attributed the team's weak showing to "the arbitrary action" of the Gymnastics Federation Technical Committee at Berlin, which, contrary to the usual procedure, did not have a public drawing for the starting positions and simply assigned the Americans to work first on the flying rings, a routine that because of its notorious difficulty and tendency to bind the muscles usually came last on the program. The United States also complained because other nations were allowed to name three judges but America got to choose only one, and this "in spite of the fact that America had demonstrated its gymnastic prominence and ability in handling the 1932 competition in Los Angeles to the complete satisfaction of the officers of the International Amateur Gymnastics Federation."

The 1936 games included the first-ever gymnastic competition for women, the events on hand being the side horse, balance beam, and parallel bars. However, since medals were awarded only to teams and not to individuals, there were no internationally famous stars like Olga Korbut or Mary Lou Retton in the Berlin games. The German team finished first, followed by Czechoslovakia and Hungary.

Fencing

In contrast to the women's gymnastics competition, women's fencing in Berlin attracted a tremendous amount of fan interest—and that largely because of one participant, Helene Mayer. The German press was under strict orders from the Propaganda Ministry not to say anything about Mayer's "non-Aryan" heritage," but it was widely known that Mayer was half Jewish and had been called back from America to compete for Germany. Some observers praised her for her "patriotic" willingness to represent her fatherland, while others condemned her for handing the Reich a fig leaf with which to cover its racism. One of her critics, Viktor Klemperer, had this to say in his now-famous diary about Mayer's silver medal performance for Germany in 1936: "I don't know which is more shameless, her participating as a German of the Third Reich, or the fact that her achievement is claimed by the Third Reich."

Reich officials had been hoping that their strategic concession in the Mayer case would be compensated by a gold medal rather than a mere silver in the women's foils, and they also cannot have been pleased that the gold medal winner turned out to be another "non-Aryan," Ilona Schacherer-Elek of Hungary. The Hungarian narrowly beat Mayer in their one head-to-head match and then went on to take the gold on points because Mayer fought to a draw in her contest with Austria's Ellen Müller-Preis, another Jewish athlete. (Müller-

Preis took the bronze medal, which meant every one of the medal winners in women's foils in the 1936 games was either Jewish or partly Jewish.)

At the awards ceremony Mayer did not hesitate to render a Nazi salute upon receiving her medal. Her continuing love for Germany and her deep frustration at being forced to live in exile were painfully evident in a bittersweet, confused, and painful letter she wrote from America to her German Olympic teammates in November 1936:

Dear Molly, Gisela, Tilly, Dolly, Doris, 'Mensch' Käthe, Elfriede, and all you others!

I think back sooo often on the days in Germany [during the games]. You cannot imagine how vividly this memory lives on in my mind. The whole German episode is well behind me and I'm now back in my old American university routine. Nobody gives a damn about the Olympics here. "That's past history," they say. Other events, like strikes, the presidential election, and football games command all the newspaper space. But that's always the way it is here in America.

Although I have a pile of work to do, I always find a quarter-hour free during the day when I can think back on the wonderful days in Germany and especially on you all. I won't embark here on some long speech of praise, but I truly mean it when I say that the days together with you in good comradeship count among the happiest in my life. . . . You were all so decent and good to me that I'll never forget it! I can only convey my heartfelt gratitude in awkward phrases, but I trust you understand me. . . .

Here in America the press has made the [German] Olympiad look extra-bad. Nothing but propaganda against Germany! So I guess it didn't help much that all of us, and by this I mean also the American Olympic competitors, worked against this propaganda.

Will we see each other again in the future? I don't know. I know only that I'd like to return to Germany, but that there's no place for me there now. . . . I belong to that part of humanity that has been hard hit by bitter fate. I love Germany every bit as much as you do and I feel just as German as you!

In true comradeship,
Your Helene

Mayer competed again for Germany in the World Fencing Championships in 1937 but did not return to live in Germany until 1953. She married a German citizen and died of cancer in 1961. Ten years later, in preparation for the 1972 Summer Games, the city of Munich named a street in her honor near the Olympic site. As for Schacherer-Elek and Müller-Preis, the former won another gold medal in the 1948 London games and a silver in 1952, while the latter took bronze in 1948.

While Central European Jews (or half Jews) dominated women's fencing in 1936, the men's division belonged largely to the Italians. Italian Giulio Gandini took the foil competition and teammate Franco Riccardi won the épée (rigid blade) competition, giving Italy the gold in team competition. A Hungarian, Endre Kobos, took gold in the third men's fencing event, the saber. (He had won this same event in 1932.)

In winning his medal in 1936, Kobos added to a long tradition of Hungarian Jewish excellence in fencing. Between 1908 and 1936, Hungarian Jews won an astounding total of eighteen medals in this sport. A primary reason for this success is worth noting: Austro-Hungarian Jews zealously took up fencing in the late nineteenth and early twentieth centuries in order to defend challenges to their "honor" from anti-Semites. As soon as the Jews began to show exceptional prowess in this sport, however, their antagonists often claimed they had no "honor" to defend, thereby sparing themselves the humiliation of getting properly cut up by a Jew.

In contrast to their relatively strong performance in Los Angeles, American fencers in Berlin fared poorly. An American fencing official attributed the weak U.S. showing to injuries, a dearth of international experience, and, above all, a lack of adequate financial and organizational support for the American team. Comparing American preparation for the games with that of the Italians, the American official reported: "In the months preceding the Games, while the American fencers were dividing their time between respective businesses and a mad scramble to obtain funds to finance their team, the Italians were confining their activities to fencing and general conditioning under some of the finest coaches in the world." This kind of complaint about disguised professionalism would be heard from the American side with increasing frequency in future Olympic competition, as Soviet and other Eastern European athletes began to muscle the Yanks aside in the international race for medals.

Boxing and Wrestling

Like fencing, the boxing competition in Berlin was truly cosmopolitan. More than two hundred athletes from thirty-four nations participated in the largest boxing tournament yet seen in the Olympics. The boxing matches, spread out over six days and nights, all took place in the cavernous Deutschland Halle, Europe's largest sports arena. For the occasion the hall was bedecked with swastika flags along with Olympic banners. During the early qualifying rounds matches went on simultaneously in two rings in order to more quickly cull the competition; sometimes the boxers in one ring mistook the bell sound in the neighboring ring for their own gong, resulting in much confusion.

For the large American team the dual-ring setup was not the only irritation. The Yank boxers resented having to weigh in every day, which according to their trainer kept them "half-starved and all dried out" for the duration of the tournament. The Americans, along with the British, also believed that the mainly Central European judges were biased in favor of fighters from that part of the world. In fact Central Europeans did end up winning most of the medals. For a time it looked as if Britain and America might even withdraw from the boxing competition in protest against the judging, but in the end they decided to remain in Berlin and accept their fate, which was to go away from these games without a single gold medal in boxing, an Olympic first.

While the British won no medals at all, American boxers managed one silver medal and one bronze. The silver went to Californian Jackie Wilson, one of six blacks on the American boxing squad. A veritable beanpole at 6 feet 2 inches and 117 pounds, Wilson was said by the American trainers to pack "the hardest punch of any bantam in the amateur field." The judging being what it was, however, Wilson would undoubtedly have had to knock out his Italian opponent, Ulderico Sergo, to win a gold medal. As it happened, Wilson looked dominant in every round but still lost on a split decision. (Wilson went on to have a successful pro career, ranked number 2 in the world at lightweight by *Ring* magazine in 1940, and number 2 at welterweight in 1941.) Flyweight Louis Lauria, another American black, received an award for being "the most scientific boxer" in the Berlin games but was judged the loser on points in his semifinal bout, thereby earning only a bronze. Apparently science wasn't enough.

In contrast to America and Britain, Germany, an upstart in the boxing world, put on a very strong performance with five medals, two of them gold.

One of the golds came in the premier event, the heavyweight division. The winner, Herbert Runge, won a hard-fought decision over Guillermo Lovell of Argentina.

After the games an American boxing official proposed only half in jest that one way to solve the problem of biased or incompetent judging at the Olympics would be to allow the host country "to supply all the officials" for the matches. "It could not be worse," he opined, "and [the host country judges] might be ashamed to take all the championships themselves, and award some of them on merit alone."

The wrestling competition, consisting of Greco-Roman and freestyle events, also took place in the Deutschland Halle, and like the boxing events employed two mats simultaneously for the qualifying rounds. Traditionally the Olympic wrestling matches attracted sparse crowds, but in Berlin wrestling drew almost as well as boxing. Hoping to spur on the local boys, the German fans gesticulated wildly and shouted advice such as "Put his ass on the mat, Jakob!" The Greco-Roman events, following the tradition of ancient wrestling, involved stand-up grappling in which the contestants were restricted to holds above the waist. In Berlin the most adept practitioners of this style tended to hail from Scandinavia and the Baltic countries. Wrestlers from Sweden, Estonia, Latvia, and Finland dominated the heavier weights, while a Turk won gold in the flyweight class and a Hungarian in the bantamweight. The freestyle competition also showcased northern Europeans in the heavier weights, but America, which had no entries in the Greco-Roman division, made its mark in the middle- and lower-weight classes of the freestyle events. American Frank Lewis won gold in the welterweight class, while Fred Flood got silver in the bantamweight and Franco Millard silver in the featherweight. All these men hailed from Oklahoma, America's premier incubator of world-class grapplers.

Perhaps the most intriguing contestant in the 1936 wrestling competition was the German middleweight Werner Seelenbinder. Coming from a working-class Berlin family, Seelenbinder had joined the Communist party at age twenty-four and participated in various worker-sports tournaments in the late 1920s. Forced to join a bourgeois sports club after the Nazis came to power, Seelenbinder won the national championship of his sports association in 1933. On the victors' podium he refused to give the Nazi salute, which prompted his immediate arrest. Fortunately for him, the Gestapo officer who interrogated him was a wrestling fan, and Seelenbinder was allowed to go free.

In 1935 Seelenbinder became the German national champion and also won all the Olympic qualifying bouts in his division, which put him on the German team for 1936. He and some of his Communist friends, now in the underground, decided that if Seelenbinder won a gold medal in the Berlin games he would speak out against the Nazi regime in the postgames interviews conducted with all Olympic champions. Alas, he never got the chance to carry out this courageous plan because he lost a first-round bout and ended up finishing fourth overall. A year later he took third in the European championships and retained his German title. Over the next four years he successfully defended his national title every year.

In February 1942, while he was a transport worker in an ammunition plant, Seelenbinder was arrested for sheltering a fugitive Communist operative. After being shuttled around between nine different concentration camps he was scheduled to be executed in September 1944. In a last-minute effort to avoid that fate, he lodged an appeal for clemency based on his contributions to German sport. He asked to be sent to the war front so he could serve the national cause as "a good German." His appeal was rejected, and he was hanged in the Brandenburg Penitentiary on October 24, 1944.

After the Nazi collapse a sports field in the working-class Neuköln section of western Berlin was named after Seelenbinder, but with the onset of the Cold War he was suddenly persona non grata in the West, and his name disappeared from the map. By contrast Communist East Germany named the first sports hall it constructed Seelenbinder Halle and held annual wrestling matches there in his honor.

Weight Lifting

The weight-lifting competition in Berlin saw the establishment of world or Olympic records in every weight division except one. A truly outstanding lifter, the Turkish middleweight Khadr El Touni, set a new world record in the press and equaled the existing world mark in the snatch. The total for his best three lifts in the press, snatch, and jerk surpassed the effort of the second-place finisher, Rudolf Ismayer of Germany, by an astounding thirty-five kilograms. Touni's teammate, Ahmed Mesbah, won the gold medal and set an Olympic record in the lightweight division with a total of 332.5 kilograms.

Josef Manger, a young German giant, won the gold and set yet another Olympic record in the heavyweight class.

Rudolf Ismayer, who as we have seen had the honor of reciting the Olympic oath at the beginning of the Berlin games, was one of those German Olympians who, at least at the time, believed fervently in the Nazi cause. He joined the party a year after the games and went on to become a Wehrmacht intelligence officer on the Eastern Front during the war. After the war, however, he had a major change of heart, becoming one of the founders of the left-wing German Peace Union. He had come to believe, he explained, that topflight athletes should use their prominence to promote world peace and brotherhood. Yet with respect to the 1936 games, he continued to insist fifty years later that Hitler had not intentionally violated the Olympic spirit and that the German games had genuinely fostered international understanding. Of course he was not alone in this. Like many of his former teammates, he simply could not accept the notion that the 1936 games, an enterprise for which he and his fellow competitors had sacrificed so much, had been "misused" by the Nazis or tainted in any way by their ideology.

One of the competitors in the weight-lifting competition who suffered under that Nazi ideology was Robert Fein, an Austrian Jew. Fein earned exactly the same number of points as Ahmed Mesbah in the lightweight division but was denied a share in the gold medal by the German judges on the grounds that he weighed more than Mesbah. Fein appealed this decision and was promised a gold medal by the IOC, but he never received it. Two years after the games, when Austria was taken over by the Nazis, Fein went into hiding to avoid being sent to a concentration camp.

Cycling

While the weight-lifting competition in Berlin had its share of rabidly partisan fans, the cycling events evoked national passions on a much grander scale. The shorter races attracted capacity crowds to the specially banked wooden track in the cycling stadium, and the one-hundred-kilometer road race brought tens of thousands of fans out to the twisting route that ran through the Grunewald Park west of Berlin. For decades big-time cycling had rivaled soccer as a primary index of national sporting prowess, especially in Western

Europe. In France, Germany, Italy, Switzerland, Spain, and Belgium the best riders were household names, and the stakes were so high in major races that egregious fouling was commonplace. In the Tour de France, for example, it sometimes happened that racers maneuvered their opponents off the road or even dropped tacks on the pavement to puncture the tires of pursuers. And of course the Tour became infamous for its doping scandals.

Sharp practices had become a tradition in Olympic cycling as well, and the Berlin games were no different. One of the most flagrant fouls to occur in any competition at the 1936 games occurred in the finals of the one-thousand-meter pairs race, which pitted two cyclists dueling each other around the sharply banked track. In the race for the gold a German competitor, Toni Merkens, brazenly blocked the Dutchman Arie Gerrit van Vliet, who was in the process of maneuvering around him for a sure victory. The Dutchman protested, but instead of disqualifying Merkens the German officials merely fined him one hundred reichsmarks and declared him the winner. It was decisions like this that prompted an American reporter to observe: "Outside of the main track and field events, the Olympic judges generally have proved astonishingly biased and incapable."

Organized ineptitude was certainly evident in the one-hundred-kilometer road race. For the first time in Olympic cycling competition, all the racers started together rather than beginning from a staggered start and running the course as an individual time trial. The potential for accidents was compounded by the narrowness of the road on which the racers jockeyed for position. Critics had warned that this setup could bring nasty spills, and sure enough, not far from the finish an inexperienced Peruvian rider tumbled and in the process brought down twenty of the world's greatest riders, including three of the faster Americans. The fans were as outraged as the riders, and a huge fight broke out in the stands. Commented a *New York Times* reporter: "The theory that international sport gatherings are conducive to international peace and understanding seemed at that moment like one more illusion." Deftly avoiding the pileup, Robert Charpentier of France sprinted to the finish just ahead of fellow Frenchman Guy Lapébie. This win brought him his third gold medal in the 1936 games. A Swiss rider took third. Overall in the team rankings France placed first, Switzerland second, and Belgium third. It was the first time since the institution of team rankings in 1920 that the Italians had not won the gold. American riders won no medals at all.

Rowing

In comparison with cycling, the rowing events in Berlin were a model of organizational competence, but there were complaints about the setup here too, especially from the Americans. The U.S. crews groused about inadequate practice time on the course, overly windy conditions, and inadequate quarters for the athletes (some of whom were put up in the Köpenick police station).

All the rowing, sculling, and canoeing events took place in Grünau, on the southeastern edge of Berlin. There the Berlin Regatta Club had its headquarters—a site that locals liked to call "Germany's Henley." The racing courses were laid out on the broad Müggelsee, which was expansive enough to accommodate six boats racing side by side. Along the course stood new grandstands that could seat twenty thousand spectators; the stands were filled to capacity for both days of the rowing competition, and thousands more sat on the grassy banks.

Britain and the United States were expected to make the strongest showings in rowing in 1936. Britain had invented the sport in the nineteenth century and continued to enjoy considerable success in international competition, although America had come on strong in the modern Olympics, especially in eight-oared skulls. U.S. boats had won this event six times since its Olympic debut in 1900. The Germans, for their part, had done relatively well in 1932, coming in second behind America in team points, but all told they had won only four gold medals over the forty years of modern Olympic history. Few foreign experts expected them to do well in 1936 despite the advantage of home waters and partisan crowds.

As it happened, however, German oarsmen shocked everyone by winning five gold medals in Berlin, one more than Britain's record bounty in 1908. German victories came in the single sculls, the pair-oared shells with coxswain, the pair-oared shells without coxswain, the four-oared shells without coxswain, and the four-oared shells with coxswain. Great Britain ended up taking only one gold medal, in the double sculls, while the United States, represented by the University of Washington, won the top prize in the eight-oared boats with coxswain, arguably the most prestigious of the rowing events.

The German victories were not only numerous but decisive; each of them left no doubt about who was the best. After the races the German coach attributed his team's success to meticulous preparation, extremely hard training, a "will to victory," the support of the home crowd, and "absolutely the presence of the Führer." Another factor, unmentioned by the coach, was a fleet of German-made boats significantly lighter than those of their competitors.

The lone British victory is noteworthy because Jack Beresford, who shared in that victory, was participating in his fifth Olympics and had medaled in all four previous tries, winning gold twice and silver twice. At age thirty-seven he was the second oldest rower in the competition. For much of their race, Beresford and his partner, Leslie Southwood, both of the Thames Rowing Club, looked as if they were going to lose to a German pair, but in the last three hundred meters they put on such a mighty sprint that they finished three lengths ahead of the Germans.

The American victory in the heavyweight eights also involved a tremendous sprint to the wire, but this win was a very close-run thing. The University of Washington crew, hailed as the "Husky Clipper" and unbeaten in American collegiate racing that year, did not jump off to a quick lead as was their wont; indeed, they were dead last for much of the race. At the head of the pack were Germany and Italy, whose boats were shielded from a strong headwind by a hill on the left side of the course. It so happened, moreover, that Husky stroke Don Hume was ill with walking pneumonia. At about three hundred meters into the race, with the U.S. boat still lagging in last place, Washington coxswain Bob Moch yelled at Hume to pick up the pace. Hume did not respond because he had passed out, dead to the world. But just as Moch, in desperation, decided to go to his number 7 man to take up the stroke, Hume suddenly came alive. With two hundred meters to the finish, and Hume back in the game, Moch raised the count to an unheard-of forty-four strokes a minute. The Huskies quickly shot past all the boats but the two leaders. In the final sprint the German crowd yelled "Deutschland, Deutschland" in unison with the withering stroke, drowning out Moch's plea to Hume: "Gimme 10 hard ones." Finally, with only a few meters to go, Washington passed Germany, then Italy. For many minutes after the race, Hume, drenched in sweat and vomit, was so disoriented that he did not even realize his crew had won the gold medal.

Team Sports

The United States had high expectations for its oarsmen in 1936 but not for its soccer team. Americans of course had long been notoriously indifferent to soccer. In previous Olympic competition U.S. teams had won only one silver and one bronze medal, both in the lightly contended home-turf St. Louis games of 1904, when America entered two different teams. Tellingly, there was no soccer competition in the Los Angeles Olympics in 1932. Many Americans, of course, would continue to disdain soccer as alien, wimpy, boring, elitist, and probably subversive.

As it turned out, the United States brought a surprisingly competent soccer team to Berlin in 1936, and the Americans played well enough, but what defined the football competition in this Olympics was not the play, good or bad, of any one team, but displays of fierce nationalistic passion among the fans. In one spectacular instance, the fan excitement exploded into open violence. There was also plenty of dirty play and poor sportsmanship among the players, many of whom were closet professionals.

The American team got a taste of this nastiness in its opening match with Italy. Unlike the United States, Italy took its soccer *very* seriously. As Winston Churchill once observed, "The Italians lose wars as if they were games of football; and lose games of football as if they were wars." Frustrated by their inability to score more than one goal against the underdog Americans in the first half of play, the Italians resorted to increasingly aggressive tactics in the second period, kicking, shoving, and punching their opponents. Two Americans had to be carried from the field, one after having been kicked in the stomach, the other with a torn ligament following a vicious shove out of bounds. Toward the end of the game the hapless German referee ordered Italian striker Achille Piccini to leave the pitch for punching an American player. But Piccini simply refused to vacate the field, and when the referee tried to enforce his order the other Italian players surrounded him, pinned his arms to his side, and clapped their hands over his mouth. Intimidated, the referee let play resume with Piccini still in the game. The Italians ended up winning, 1–0. The Americans protested, but their appeal was denied.

The American-Italian dustup was a minor fracas compared to what happened in a second-round match between Austria and Peru—a donnybrook that generated a full-blown international incident (not to mention a political windfall for the ruling Peruvian president). Austria, imposing what the United Press called "its manner of rough play," led Peru 2–0 at the half, but toward the end of the game Peru suddenly scored two quick goals, throwing the contest into overtime. In the first fifteen-minute overtime period neither team scored, forcing a second overtime and greatly heightening the emotional tension in the stadium. Near the end of the second overtime, with the score still tied, Peruvian spectators decided to take matters into their own hands. A few dozen Peruvian fans, some of them brandishing revolvers, stormed on to the field and attacked the Austrian players and referees. With the Austrian team more or less *hors de combat*, the Peruvian team promptly kicked two goals, thus winning 4–2.

Upon hearing this result over the international radio broadcast, the populace of Lima exploded in joy. The archbishop of Lima sent a telegram to the president of the Peruvian Olympic delegation at Berlin, saying, "I embrace you and bless you," and the president of the Peruvian Republic, Oscar Benavides, wired the following message of congratulation: "With all the Peruvian people I share intense patriotic emotion for you in your triumph and to the enthusiastic congratulations of our fellow citizens I add mine, being sure now that your gallant achievements will lead to greater national prestige."

While the Peruvians were celebrating, the Austrians were lodging an official protest with Olympic officials and with the International Federation of Amateur Football (FIFA). This time FIFA conceded the legitimacy of the protest and ordered a rematch. To ensure an absence of fan interference, the officials ordered that the rematch be played in an empty stadium.

The Austrians duly showed up for the scheduled rematch, but the Peruvians did not. Indeed, in high dudgeon over what President Benavides called "the crafty decision from Berlin," the entire Peruvian Olympic contingent at the games, on orders from the president, abandoned Germany and moved on to Paris (where presumably they could lick their wounds in comfort). On departing Berlin the head of the delegation stated: "We've no faith in European athletics. We have come here and found a bunch of merchants."

Meanwhile, back in Lima angry mobs tore down an Olympic flag from a travel agency and stormed the German consulate. Stevedores at the port of Callao refused to unload a German ship; the owner of the "German Tailor Shop" in Lima hastened to change his business's name. The newspaper *La Cronica* insisted that the "cunning and intrigue" by which Peru had been denied its legitimate victory revealed the Olympic project to be an example of latter-day colonialism and an affront to all of South America, which "through the medium of the Peruvian athletes" would certainly have won Olympic gold had not the FIFA officials found it necessary to "prop up" an old and decadent Europe.

Likewise claiming to speak for the entire South American continent, President Benavides announced that—in a gesture of solidarity with Peru—Argentina, Ecuador, Chile, Colombia, Uruguay, and Mexico all intended to vacate Berlin. Fearing that all the South Americans would in fact follow this call, Goebbels hastily made it known that the German government and the Berlin Olympic organizers had no control over FIFA, to which no Germans belonged. (In the end only Colombia joined Peru in leaving the games). Meanwhile, an "emergency fund" was established in Peru to help the Peruvian Olympic delegation survive the rigors of its sojourn in Paris. President Benavides himself contributed 35,000 francs to the fund.

If the Peruvian government seemed to be doing all it could to inflame national indignation over the soccer "scandal," this was not without good reason: Benavides faced parliamentary elections and needed to distract attention from his woeful record of incompetence and corruption. As the American chargé d'affaires in Lima noted: "President Benavides has found this to be a splendid opportunity to take action to endear him to the populace, particularly the laboring element which largely holds more radical views, and it is evident that the Peruvian Government has not neglected to take full advantage [of this incident] to reap political prestige from the affair." Once the president had secured the election, he recovered his true political bearings and blamed the entire affair on world communism.

As for the other party in this imbroglio, the Austrians, they were declared the winners over Peru by virtue of Peru's no-show; they then went on to defeat Poland and to face Italy in the match for the gold medal. The Italian-Austrian final also contained some very rough moments and went into overtime, Italy finally achieving victory with one goal. Mussolini, who continued to resent the Austrians for their long domination of northern Italy, was beside himself with joy; he personally congratulated every one of the Italian players on the team's return to Rome.

Germany had expected to be playing for the gold in soccer but had lost 2–0 in the second round against lowly Norway. "How could this happen?" moaned the national press. The explanation murmured by many Germans was that Hitler, all too confident of a German victory, had neglected to appear in the stadium for the Norway match.

Summing up all the passion and mayhem surrounding the soccer competition at the Berlin games, an American commentator opined: "Back on the [Olympic] program for the first time in eight years, [soccer] has demonstrated that it cannot be played safely internationally." In later years, of course, "football hooligans" around the world would do their best to prove this judgment correct.

IF soccer seemed alien to most Americans, basketball was anything but, and the United States had been lobbying for years to get it on the official Olympic program. In 1936 men's basketball finally appeared for the first time as an Olympic sport, though this was due less to American pressure than to the growing popularity of the game outside the United States. The tournament in Berlin drew twenty-three teams from four continents.

While American Olympic officials were pleased to see basketball on the program in 1936, they were considerably less pleased with the rules and regulations for play. During the elimination rounds in Berlin the newly constituted International Basketball Federation, under a Swiss president and a British secretary, debated an Uruguayan resolution that would have limited the players' height to five feet eight inches, then passed a rule that put the limit at about six feet one, which effectively banned three of the U.S. players. America protested vigorously, and the height restriction was rescinded at the last minute. America's efforts to institute U.S. collegiate conventions across the board, however, did not succeed, and the Olympic game, at least as it was played in Berlin, appeared about as familiar to the Yanks as cricket.

Rather than an indoor arena, with standard boundaries and a painted key, the basketball complex in Berlin was outdoors and consisted of four sunken clay tennis courts from which the nets had been hastily removed and makeshift lines chalked on the sandy surfaces. The official ball, a vaguely round German product called the "Berg," was so poorly balanced that it wobbled violently when thrown. These balls were also exceptionally light and therefore hard to shoot with any accuracy in the often windy conditions. But at least the players did not have to worry about crashing into the bleachers when going out of bounds: There were no grandstands because the German organizers foresaw little fan interest in this sport.

The U.S. squad consisted of fourteen players, half of whom came from the Olympic-trial-winning Universal Studios team. Among them was Sam Balter, one of six Jews representing America in all disciplines at the 1936 Summer Games. (After the games Balter hosted a radio program in Philadelphia in which he frequently criticized the AOC for whitewashing Hitler's racial policies. In response to the criticism, Frederick Rubien, the body's secretary, wrote to Avery Brundage: "I agree with you that it is highly desirable that we develop some plan to exclude individuals of Balter's type from future Olympic teams regardless of athletic ability.")

The American squad had no trouble getting into the gold-medal round against Canada, but the final game was a true test for the Yanks—a test less against the Canadians than against the conditions of play. Steady rains had left about six inches of standing water on the surface of the sunken court where the final game was scheduled to be played. The Americans pleaded with the German officials to move the game to an indoor arena but the officials refused, conceding only a shift to a neighboring tennis court that was slightly less drenched. As the U.S. captain, Francis Johnson, remembered the game:

> It was like a football game in the rain with people wrapped up in parkas and others with umbrellas, all outside watching a basketball game in the rain. Every time the ball would hit the ground, it would take up water just like a sponge. And being a clay court, when you went to stop you couldn't; you'd just slip and slide along. Our uniforms got discolored pretty good from those slides through the mud.

According to Sam Balter the officiating was equally bizarre, its complete lack of consistency proving "bewildering to the players."

The Americans led 15–4 at the half and went on to win 19–8. Mexico defeated Poland for the bronze. The winning Americans were awarded their oak-leaf crowns by none other than Dr. James Naismith, the aged inventor of basketball, who had traveled to Berlin courtesy of the U.S. Basketball Association.

Summing up this bizarre Olympic debut, sportswriter Arthur J. Daley considered it "far from sensational" in terms of organization but "worthwhile for the missionary effect" it would have on basketball around the world.

And of course, the rest of the world *did* become increasingly drawn to the American game—so much so that American colleges and the NBA would eventually start recruiting top foreign players, and the American Olympic teams of the 1970s and 1980s would find themselves not just seriously challenged but sometimes failing to win the gold, as happened in 1972 and in 1988. In 1992 the United States felt obliged to field a "dream team" of star professional players in order to reinstate the enormous talent gap that had existed in the first twenty years of Olympic basketball.

ALONG with soccer and basketball there were four other team sports at the Berlin Olympics: field hockey, field handball, polo, and water polo. Their results can be summarized briefly here. India, which had won field hockey in 1928 and 1932, dominated again in 1936, trouncing Germany 8–1. It was India's lone medal.

Field handball, played only in Central Europe, and combining the mayhem of rugby with the precision of soccer, was one of those sports that the host nation managed to add to the program as a probable medal source for the home team. Germany duly beat Austria for the gold, while Switzerland won the bronze. This event never again appeared on the Olympic program.

Polo, another sport that was dropped after 1936, attracted a mere five teams, and only one of them—Argentina—really counted. The Argentineans humiliated Britain 11–0 in the final. Mexico beat Hungary for the bronze. Germany and Hungary were considered so inferior they were not even allowed to play for the gold or silver medals.

Water polo, a sport so rough that the pool water sometimes became distinctly pinkish, offered a number of kicking, elbowing, and testicle-wrenching free-for-alls in 1936, including the final match between Hungary and Germany. Hungary, whose star, Oliver Halassy, had one leg amputated below the knee, and Germany, which had taken second place to Hungary in 1932, battled to a 2–2 tie, but Hungary's ratio of goals scored to goals given (10:2) over the entire tournament was rated higher than Germany's ratio (14:4), so Hungary got the gold. (A German mathematician disputed the arithmetic, but the result stood.)

Yachting, Shooting, Riding

The 1936 yachting competitions, held in the inner and outer harbors of the German naval base at Kiel, took on some of the warlike qualities of their surroundings. In no other sport category in the 1936 Summer Games, not even in soccer, were there more fouls, underhanded tactics, and contested results than in the "gentlemanly" yachting competition. The biggest rows came in the divisions involving boats of six and eight meters in length. In the six-meter race the judges on the spot set the order of finish Norway, Britain, and Switzerland, but the race had been so close that Britain appealed the decision to higher officials, who on the basis of aerial photography overturned the original ranking and gave Britain the gold and Norway the silver. Switzerland later lost its bronze to Sweden when it was discovered that one of the Swiss crew was not strictly an amateur—something that could have been said of dozens of others in the competition. In the eight-meter event the judges' ranking was again disputed. Italy was finally awarded the gold, but a sail-off between Norway and Germany was required two days later to establish the silver and bronze. Norway won. Incidentally, a member of the Norwegian crew, Jacob Thams, had also won the ski-jump competition at the Chamonix Olympics of 1924, making him the first Olympian to win a gold medal in both the Winter and Summer Games (and as yet one of only four athletes to achieve this feat in the history of the modern games).

UNLIKE yachting, the shooting competition at Berlin, which was held in a special pavilion at Wannsee (a large lake in western Berlin where, on January 20, 1942, Nazi officials would host a conference to work out the details for the extermination of Europe's Jews), generated only a few protests, but also, alas, relatively little interest. Many thought that shooting did not belong in the Olympics at all, but Coubertin's desire to attract military support to his project had secured a place for various shooting events from the very beginning of the modern games.

In 1936 there were three shooting events—rapid-fire pistols at moving targets at twenty-five meters; free (or target) pistols at fifty meters; and smallbore (.22 caliber) rifles at fifty meters. Germans placed first and second in the rapid-fire pistol; a Swede won the free pistol; and a Norwegian, Willy Røgeberg, won the small-bore rifle with a perfect score of 300 points, the first-ever perfect score in Olympic competition. Despite personal encouragement from Army Chief of Staff Werner von Fritsch, German marksmen could place no higher than sixth in this event.

As for the United States, its Pistol Shooting Committee objected to the use of .22 caliber guns, insisting they were too puny; the committee also complained that the Germans, in a breach of the rules, had been able to practice with these weapons before the competitions started. In the end the Americans decided not to compete in the miniature rifle event. Justifying this decision, the National Rifle Association insisted that these little toys were beneath the dignity of the manly marksmen from the United States.

THE equestrian events, like the marksmanship competition, were at the time of the Berlin Olympics still very much the province of the world's military establishments, which trained and supported most of the contenders. Indeed, at Berlin six of the equestrian events were open only to active military men. The American team for the military riding was composed exclusively of cavalry officers from Fort Riley, Kansas. The Germans, of course, all came from the Wehrmacht. With extensive financial and logistical support from that organization, German riders won every one of the individual competitions and team championships—an unprecedented and unequaled feat in Olympic equestrian history.

In the three-day individual competition the most demanding event was a twenty-one-mile cross-country obstacle race. Only twenty-seven of the fifty-six entries managed to finish this race, and three horses died trying. Never before in Olympic competition had an equestrian event taken such a toll.

In the opinion of an American sportswriter, Henry McLemore, this epic cross-country event amounted to "one of the dirtiest stories" of the 1936 games. (Whether the story was really dirty is impossible to say with certainty. In any case it shows once again that the "controversy" surrounding the Nazi games was hardly confined to politics.) In the account related by McLemore, who interviewed American competitors after the race, all the riders were given maps of the course showing the various obstacles. Obstacle number 4 consisted of a pool of water tucked behind a stone wall. The problem, the Americans told McLemore, was that they and the other foreign riders were advised by German officials that the pool in question was less than four feet deep, when in reality it was *ten feet deep*. The German riders alone seemed to have had advance knowledge of the obstacle's true treachery, for when it came time to negotiate this obstacle all three Wehrmacht officers jumped their horses to the extreme left of the wall, allowing them to land in about three feet of water on an artificial sandbar. They came through without mishap. By contrast twenty-eight of the foreign riders, including all the Americans, lost their mounts in the plunge. Of course the onerous process of regaining the saddle and getting out of the trap cost valuable time, not to mention the addition of about fifteen pounds of water weight.

For America's Capt. Raggs Raguse, the cross-country race ended with obstacle number 4. His horse, Trailolka, one of the best in the army's stables, broke his leg in the tumble, obliging Raguse to shoot his mount right then and there. "Tears trickled down the captain's water-drenched face," reported McLemore. "It was a pathetic sight."

The three-day equestrian team event produced another German hero of the Berlin games in the person of twenty-six-year-old Lt. Freiherr Konrad von Wangenheim. He broke his collarbone in a fall at an obstacle during the cross-country race but remounted and completed the course flawlessly. Riding with his arm in a sling in the last of the competitions, the Prix des Nations (a timed jumping event), he was again thrown, only to remount and finish perfectly. Due to his skill and courage, the Germans won the gold medal.

Like virtually all his teammates on the German equestrian squad, Wangenheim went on to serve in the war. Two of his fellow riders were killed in action, but Wangenheim himself survived the conflict only to perish in a Soviet prisoner-of-war camp in 1953. Another German gold-medal winner in the equestrian competition, Heinz Brandt, was among those officers fatally injured in the abortive attempt by Count Claus von Stauffenberg to blow up Hitler in his eastern headquarters on July 20, 1944.

The Pentathlon

The modern pentathlon, a five-day ordeal combining riding, shooting, fencing, swimming, and running, was the military version of the decathlon and in its way just as demanding. "There is probably no more terrible test of nerve and endurance than the pentathlon," wrote one observer. "It lasts five days and is enough to put the average man without military training in a madhouse or hospital." So far as is known, none of the 1936 competitors went to the madhouse, but several of them had to be hospitalized.

The scenario for the pentathlon seemed to have been taken from the pages of *The Three Musketeers*. A valiant soldier, ordered to deliver a message through enemy lines, gallops away on horseback, is forced to dismount and duel with swords, remounts but then has to shoot his way out of an ambush with a pistol, and finally, having lost his mount, has to swim a river and run through the woods to his goal. Sweden had dominated this event since its inception in the Stockholm games of 1912, the Olympics in which America's Lt. George S. Patton, Jr., might have won the gold medal had he not scored so poorly in the marksmanship section.

In 1936 a German, Lt. Gotthardt Handrick, broke the Swedes' streak and won the gold, followed closely by American Lt. Charles F. Leonard (who, unlike Patton, was especially strong in the shooting). Handrick's winning secret, he told an interviewer later, was not to focus on any one event but to be consistently good in all of them. In truth, however, he hated the running part, insisting he "would rather drive." Oddly enough, Handrick was a fighter pilot, not a member of the cavalry, the branch from which most of the contestants came. In July 1936 he had been seconded to the Condor Legion fighting in the Spanish civil war. He obtained special leave from his unit to compete in Berlin and returned to Spain as soon as the games were over. After his win Hitler personally promoted him one rank, as he did all the German military men who won medals in the 1936 games.

Handrick went on to become a member of the Luftwaffe's famed Richthofen squadron and to fight in the invasion of Poland and the Battle of Britain. Unlike so many of his buddies, he survived the war without a wound. In the postwar era he gave up flying to become a successful Mercedes salesman in Hamburg.

Demonstration Sports

The 1936 Summer Games offered two demonstration sports, gliding and baseball. These sports were on trial for possible acceptance in the official program at some future date. Only one of them, baseball, eventually became an official Olympic sport, though not until 1992.*

Gliding failed in part because it brought the 1936 games their only (human) fatality: that of Austrian pilot Ignaz Stiefson, whose craft plummeted to earth after a wing broke in flight. Gliding's prospects for the future were also damaged because the sport's chief backer was the German military, which had used gliding as a subterfuge to avoid the restrictions on air force development imposed by the Versailles treaty. Nazi Germany was to go on to use gliders very effectively in its invasion of the Low Countries in 1940.

Baseball produced no fatalities but it almost bored the bewildered Berlin

---

*Baseball had actually appeared in the Olympics once before, in the Stockholm games of 1912, when an American team beat host Sweden 13–3. In the 1952 Helsinki Games there appeared a modified version of the sport called "Finnish Baseball," whatever that was.

spectators to death. Due to extensive advertising and plain old curiosity, a capacity crowd of one hundred thousand showed up at the Olympic Stadium to watch two American teams—the "USA Olympians" and the "World's Amateurs"—play each other on August 12. This was the largest crowd ever to witness a baseball game in any country, including the United States.

American enthusiasts and a handful of baseball-savvy Germans had tried to prep the prospective audience in advance through a lecture series entitled "Baseball—Was ist Das?" The instruction included not entirely helpful translations such as *Einwerfer* (literally, "thrower-in") for pitcher and *Mittel-Aussen* ("middle-outside") for center fielder. A German expert from Goebbels's Propaganda Ministry set his countrymen straight on some of the arcane rules: "The thrower-in throws the ball at a certain height toward the catcher of his team against the hitters of the adverse team. The catcher must catch the ball if it is not captured by the wooden baton of the hitter."

As with the basketball competition, the physical setting was less than perfect: White tape on the infield grass marked the foul and base lines; a soccer net stood in as a backstop; and the stadium lights illuminated the field only to a height of fifty feet, making it impossible for players or spectators to track fly balls. The German announcer had not the slightest clue about what was going on. Nor, of course, did the spectators; they cheered wildly at pop-ups and fell silent at base hits. Well before the seven innings of play were completed, with the "World's Amateurs" on top of the "USA Olympians," the crowd had thinned out significantly. Nevertheless, determined to leave the impression that the German organizers had scored a home run even with this bizarre American import, Carl Diem assured both the teams after the game that their experiment had been a great success. "I have come officially to advise you that this has been the finest demonstration of any sport that any nation has ever put on at the Olympic Games," he declared.

Baseball was in fact voted on to the official program for the 1940 Tokyo games, but since there were no Tokyo games in 1940 the world missed the opportunity to see what the Japanese would have done with a sport that was becoming popular in their country even before the American occupation following World War II. (Baseball had been introduced to Japan from the United States in the early Meiji period.) Opposition from the Europeans in the IOC kept baseball out of the Olympics as a medal sport until the Barcelona games, when assistance from Japan and the Caribbean countries helped America finally get it placed on the official program.

Perhaps America should not have pushed so hard: Cuba won the first two Olympic gold medals in baseball. The Yanks won in Sydney in 2000, only to fail even to qualify for the baseball tournament in Athens in 2004, won again by Cuba. Fidel Castro, who according to legend had once dreamed of pitching in the American major leagues, made much of Cuba's supremacy playing in America's "national pastime." (Although baseball had become a true international sport, the IOC announced in 2005 that it would be dropped from the program for the 2012 London games.)

The "World Labor Athletic Carnival"

As the 1936 Summer Games were winding down in Berlin a competing "Olympiad" was taking place halfway around the world in New York City: the "World Labor Athletic Carnival." This affair was conceived as a "progressive" and "democratic" alternative to the Nazi-hosted games in Berlin.

The Labor Carnival was not meant to have been the main democratic alternative to the Nazi Games; that role was supposed to have been played by the "People's Olympics" scheduled to begin on July 19 in Barcelona. Thousands of leftist athletes and their supporters had indeed shown up for the People's games, only to find the city paralyzed by the violence attending the outbreak of the Spanish civil war. An American journalist traveling with some of the athletes described a scene of utter chaos:

As we reach Barcelona, the white flags are at all windows—towels, sheets, tablecloths hung over the windowsills for peace. Shooting is heard again and again—not cannons or machine guns (except once, but rifles). . . . Overturned cars, dead animals, coils and spires of smoke arising from burning churches. The coils of color climbing the architectural heart of the city, [Antoni] Gaudi's marvelous church [the unfinished Sagrada Familia], untouched by harm.

Under these conditions the People's games could obviously not go on, and the organizers called them off immediately. Most of the athletes soon found their way out of the city, but some elected to stay and fight Franco, or to go on to an athletic meet in Prague. Of the twelve sportsmen sent by America's

Committee on Fair Play in Sports to compete in the Barcelona alternative games, only seven came home. The rest stayed to fight in Spain. Among those athletes who returned home, three ended up participating in the New York City event.

Unlike the abortive Barcelona People's Olympics, the Labor Carnival was cast as a rather modest alternative to Berlin, consisting exclusively of track-and-field events and lasting only two days. The principal organizers were Charles Ornstein and Judge Jeremiah Mahoney, who as we recall had played major roles in the American effort to boycott the Berlin games. Both men saw the carnival as an opportunity "to avenge their humiliation at the hands of Brundage's clique and to vindicate their belief that American athletes should not lend tacit support to the Nazi government."

An important cosponsor was the Jewish Labor Committee (JLC), which had considerable clout in New York City. David Dubinsky, head of the International Ladies' Garment Union (ILGWU) and treasurer of the JLC, threw his powerful union's support fully behind the event. Also critical was the cooperation of the AAU, since the carnival could not have attracted any AAU-affiliated athletes without that organization's blessing. Daniel Ferris, secretary of the AAU, agreed to sanction the event only after gaining assurances from Ornstein "that there will be no attempt to interfere with . . . the Olympic Games themselves." Privately Ferris shared Avery Brundage's confidence that this "alternative" to Berlin would not amount to much: "I agree with you," he wrote Brundage in June, "that they will not be able to get any foreign athletes of any account. The good athletes will all be at the Olympic Games. I think it is just another track meet and up to date I have not found anything in connection with it to get excited about."

The venue for the Labor Carnival was the track stadium at Randall's Island, site of the 1936 Olympic track-and-field trials. Dubinsky, deploying his union clout, convinced New York Park Superintendent Robert Moses and Mayor Fiorello La Guardia to permit use of the Randall's Island facility. La Guardia promised his full support, though he was careful to frame the event as a benefit for his city's working-class population rather than as a leftist political protest. "I am not unmindful of the need for developing greater opportunities for physical culture and body building among the adults of our congested population," he told Dubinsky, "and any movement designed to implant in the hearts and minds of the workers a desire for more general participation in athletic endeavors is worthy of hearty cooperation and support. You will have that support from me in the splendid enterprise you now have underway."

New York governor Herbert Lehman, a track enthusiast since his days as manager of the Williams College track team, likewise offered his endorsement, even promising to attend the games in person if he could find the time. Notably absent among the sponsors was the American Communist Party, which was competing bitterly with the JLC and the ILGWU for influence among New York City's left-leaning workers. The animosity obtaining between these rival constellations in New York mirrored the split between old-line Socialists and Stalinist-Communists in Europe.

The carnival opened on August 15, the penultimate day of the Berlin games. The competition was divided between eight "closed" events reserved for male and female union members and twenty-three "open" events designed to attract top male (no female) athletes from America and around the world. This bifurcation reflected the organizers' twin desires to promote workers' sport in America and to offer a genuine alternative to the Berlin Olympics.

A few outstanding American athletes did show up for the carnival, some of them men who had failed to make the cut for Berlin. Among the "big names" were Eulace Peacock, the 1932 Olympic silver medalist in the one hundred meters who had outrun Jesse Owens shortly before the Olympic trials; Eddie Gordon, the gold medalist in the long jump in 1932; Charles Beetham, the AAU eight-hundred-meter champion; Ben Johnson, a former indoor sprint titleholder; Robert Rodenkirchen, schoolboy sprint sensation from Jersey City; and, perhaps most notably, George Varoff, the reigning world-record holder in the pole vault, whose surprisingly inadequate performance in the 1936 Olympic trials had caused him to miss the boat for Berlin. Most of the top athletes at the carnival participated not out of political motivation but out of a desire for redemption—to show they were just as good as the men who made it to Berlin. Varoff was a partial exception here. Known as "the Jumping Janitor," this custodian from San Francisco had decidedly left-wing views. The relatively small contingent of foreign athletes at Randall's Island also contained some political protesters. Among them was Canadian Henry Cieman, a Jewish racewalker of world-class stature who could have made the Canadian Olympic team had he not decided to boycott the Berlin games.

Despite the presence of these and a few other outstanding athletes, the Carnival turned out to be an athletic disappointment. Varoff provided the most noteworthy performance by vaulting fourteen feet four and a half inches, an inch and a half higher than Earle Meadows's gold-medal vault in Berlin. The janitor made a valiant try to better his own world-record mark of fourteen feet, six and a half inches but hit the bar three times.

Among the crowd of spectators cheering on Varoff and his colleagues was Governor Lehman, who kept his promise to attend the festival. He and the rest of the crowd sighed in disappointment when Eulace Peacock, whom fans had hoped might post a record time in the 100-yard dash, pulled up lame and limped to a lowly third place. The winner of that event, as well as of the 220-yard sprint, was an unheralded runner from Georgia named Perrin Walker. The American press made much of the fact that Walker was white, as were the other top finishers at the carnival. Caucasian runners had "monopolized the sprints for a change," observed the *New York American*, in an obvious reference to the contrasting scene in Berlin.

Ernest Federoff of the Millrose Athletic Association won the mile in 4:24:4, which the *New York Times* admitted "was nothing to become excited about." Charles Beetham, who had missed a trip to Berlin by falling down in the tryouts, won the 880-yard race in the comparatively slow time of 1:56:2. Eddie Gordon could place no more than second in the long jump, while Walter Marty, a former world-record holder from San Francisco's Olympic Club, cleared only six feet four inches in the high jump and finished third behind winner Al Treadgold, who managed six feet six (two inches less than Cornelius Johnson's gold-medal jump in Berlin). White guys may have dominated in New York, but for the most part they did so with relatively mediocre performances.

The carnival also flopped at the box office. Despite extensive publicity by the Jewish press and union papers, and block purchases of tickets by some unions, the turnout was disappointing—a mere eighteen thousand for the two days (instead of the anticipated thirty thousand). The less-than-hoped-for turnout could be attributed to a combination of factors: the unwillingness of radical leftists to attend an event organized by more moderate activists; too few big-name participants, especially from abroad; and New Yorkers' preference for basketball and baseball and boxing over track and field. Most of all, there simply was not much excitement about a competition that featured also-rans. The Labor Carnival may have been—as Governor Lehman put it—an "answer to the Nazi Olympics," but it was not a very convincing answer, or one that very many people paid much attention to.

Good-bye to Berlin

The Olympic athletes, officials, and spectators assembled in Berlin certainly had little interest in what was transpiring at the "alternative" games in New York. As the Summer Games wound down in the German capital, the central preoccupation of most of those present was the ongoing national medal count, which, it now became clear, would be won by Germany for the first time in modern Olympic history.

Of course the IOC, holding to the fiction that the games were strictly contests among individuals, discouraged the inclusion of national medal tallies in the official results, but unofficial national medal tabulations had been part of the modern Olympic story from the beginning, and the Germans could hardly have been expected to make an exception. Nor did they do so. While no national results were posted at the Reichssportsfeld, and the German press, with the exception of the *Völkischer Beobachter*, refrained, on orders of the Propaganda Ministry, from publishing national rankings until after the games, a giant scoreboard in front of the Ullstein press building in downtown Berlin showed how each nation was faring in the medals race throughout the games. Following the final competitions on August 16, the board had Germany at the top with 33 gold, 26 silver, and 30 bronze medals; the United States in second place with 24 gold, 20 silver, and 12 bronzes; and Italy a distant third with 8 gold, 9 silver, and 12 bronze medals.

With the completion of competition German leaders and the domestic press unleashed an orgy of national self-congratulation, along with varying explanations for the Reich's success. "Germany stands far and away on top with 33 gold medals," exulted Goebbels in his diary. "[We are] the premier sports nation in the world. That is wonderful!" *Der Angriff* gushed: "We can scarcely contain ourselves, for it is truly difficult to endure so much joy!" Comparing Germany's approach to the games with those of rival nations, the paper concluded that while the Reich did not dominate in any specific sport category the way the Finns did in middle-distance running, the Japanese in men's swimming, and the Americans, "with their dark-skinned warriors," in men's sprinting and jumping, Germany covered a wider range of sports and tried to make a mark even in events where they had never been strong before. The result was an exceptionally large haul of silver and bronze medals across a wide spectrum of competitions. (Oddly, the paper seemed to have forgotten about Germany's total domination of the military equestrian events.) But for *Der Angriff* (as for other German papers), the primary explanation for Germany's success had to do with the influence of one man: Adolf Hitler. The Führer, said the paper, had seen to it that the Reich's athletic institutions were regenerated along with the rest of German society, and his faithful presence at the games had constituted a tremendous stimulus to the German athletes. Germany's *Olympia-Zeitung* agreed. "Must we not conclude," declared this journal, "that the biggest victor of the Olympic Games was Adolf Hitler?"

Fully endorsing this assessment, Tschammer und Osten declared in a postgames speech, "We should lay on the altar of National Socialism the laurels we won for Germany. We should be thankful with all our hearts to the movement and above all to its Führer, who has not only revivified the German people but given great impetus to German sport."

American commentators agreed that Hitler's presence had been, as the *New York Times* put it, "a terrific mental impetus," for the German competitors, but U.S. writers were quick to add that the German athletes had been given fifteen months of state-subsidized training free of any other commitments—a practice one observer believed called into question their amateur status.

Of course, as everyone knew, Germany also had all the advantages that came with being the host nation. With minimal travel costs the Reich could enter full teams even in minor sports, as the United States had done to its great advantage in Los Angeles and earlier in St. Louis. Foreign observers also hastened to point out that the large German crowds helped inspire the Reich's athletes "to outdo themselves." Finally many outsiders noted that Germany's record bounty of medals also derived from the Reich's exceptionally strong women's contingents in most events. As one American observer archly commented: "This masculine Third Reich owes much of its success to its women athletes. The German women, taken as a whole team, were consistently better than their rivals everywhere except in the swimming pool."

While the achievement of the German women generated comment about the "masculine" look of some of the Reich's female competitors (anticipating that later jibe about the East German Olympic teams: "Where men are men, and so are the women"), a more pressing issue for most contemporary commentators involved the social implications of Germany's victory, especially when combined with the impressive performances by Italy and Japan and the relatively weak showings by some of the Western democracies, most notably Britain and France. Japan outstripped once-powerful Britain in total medals by winning eighteen to Britain's fourteen. Italy garnered twenty-two medals to France's nineteen. A lesson that many drew from these results was that, in comparison with the tough militarized dictatorships, the Western nations were "going soft." Hitler himself concluded on the basis of Britain's relatively poor showing in Berlin that "one can't expect much from such a nation in a crisis situation." Japan's military leaders saw their nation's strong performance in Berlin as a confirmation of Japanese "racial vitality" and as yet another indication that Japan was destined to replace America and Britain as the chief imperial power in East Asia. China, though it won no medals at all in 1936, drew its own positive "racial lesson" from the Berlin games. In reference to Jesse Owens's victories, one prominent Chinese journalist wrote that his performance "destroyed the poisonous myth of white supremacy," while another asked, "Now who says the colored races . . . are inferior to the white race?"

Even in the United States, which hardly did poorly in the Berlin games, the loss to Germany in the overall medal count occasioned more than just the predictable grumbling about alleged German cheating and deck stacking. It also brought on some introspection regarding the deeper meaning of the Yanks' less-than-stellar showing in premier events like swimming and long-distance running. As one concerned American put it, his nation's abject failure in the tortoise test of the marathon (as opposed to the hare hop of the sprints) suggested a profound spiritual weakness:

> Stamina is the life of a people, and our stamina has become weakened through too much soft living. After all, it is strong spiritual principles that strengthen the body as well as the soul, and of late years we Americans have become notoriously lax in religious and moral principles. We have plenty of churches, but there is no soul in them.

In Britain the weak Olympic showing in 1936 generated considerable hand-wringing about the sociopolitical inadequacies supposedly at the root of the nation's athletic decline. A clergyman writing to the editor of the *Daily Telegraph* lamented:

> A century ago Englishmen in general had two convictions: 1. That they could not be beaten; 2. That they would have to beat numerically superior foes. I believe that Nelson or Wellington never had, and never expected to have, as many men and guns as the enemy. Now, a maritime

people, we are beaten in rowing by the inland Swiss. In boxing (pre-eminently a British sport) we occupy a back seat. . . . What are the reasons for this decline in athletic prowess—in skill and will to win? We have much in our favour; we have a long tradition of supremacy; our people are the best fed in Europe; we have the highest standard of living and the greatest amount of leisure; our climate is perfectly adapted for outdoor exercise; we have not been distracted by revolution nor crippled by financial stringency.

So what was wrong? According to this clergyman, the problem was essentially too much "democracy"—a system that in his view encouraged mediocrity and sapped virility. "It is not pleasant to think of the Union Jack waving over a company of 'also rans,'" the cleric concluded. "And we need not wonder if this failure in manly sports on the world stage is interpreted by our rivals as another proof that England has 'gone soft.'"

This "going soft" business, not surprisingly, was seen to have ominous implications for the looming competition between the democracies and fascist powers on the political-economic front and perhaps eventually on the battlefront as well. No one had a clearer presentiment of this than Sir Robert Vansittart, the British diplomat whom the Germans thought they had charmed during his Olympics visit. On leaving Berlin, Vansittart sensed prophetically that the real contest of nations in the mid-twentieth century was just beginning. Referring to the Germans, he wrote: "These tense, intense people are going to make us look like a C 3 [third-class] nation if we elect to continue haphazard, and they will want to do something with this stored energy. . . . These people are the most formidable proposition that has ever been formulated; they are in strict training now, not for the Olympic Games, but for breaking some other and emphatically unsporting world records, and perhaps the world as well."

AS if to reinforce the anxiety of those foreign observers who, like Vansittart, saw something dangerous in the Germans' combination of organizational efficiency, growing military might, and evangelical Führer-worship, the closing ceremonies at the Berlin games looked much more like a Nazi Party rally than a tribute to peace and international goodwill. In contrast to the opening ceremonies, uniformed SA and SS units were visible everywhere around the stadium and along the route that Hitler took from the Wilhelmstrasse to the Reichssportfeld. And because the ceremony took place at night, the organizers could employ the same "cathedral of light" effects with upturned searchlights that Albert Speer had devised for the Nuremberg rallies. There were also plenty of open flames, evoking the Nazis' patented torchlight parades.

As protocol demanded, Baillet-Latour made a speech thanking the German organizers on behalf of the IOC for their "magnificent work" and calling on the youth of the world to assemble four years hence in Tokyo. "May [those games] display cheerfulness and concord so that the Olympic torch may be carried on with greater eagerness, courage, and honor for the good of humanity throughout the ages."

While a massed choir of a thousand voices sang hymns, artillery pieces boomed off in the distance, suggesting to one reporter the opening of a barrage. Following the lowering of the fifty-two Olympic flags by white-clad sailors, a red rocket went up over the stadium and the searchlights blinked off one by one, the encroaching darkness highlighting the Olympic flame that burned brightly for a few more minutes before slowly dying against an aural backdrop of funereal tolling from the giant Olympic bell. Through the loudspeakers came a ghostly message: "I call the youth of the world to Tokyo," while the chorus sang the farewell song, "The Games Are Ended."

The huge crowd, however, was not yet ready to leave, apparently expecting a final benediction from Hitler. As the Führer sat in the darkness, people in the stands began to yell "Sieg Heil!" and "Heil Hitler!" Then, as if from a hidden signal, the masses seemed to rise as one and, with right arms upraised, belted out the German national anthem and the "Horst Wessel Lied." The last words to echo across the giant Olympic Stadium on the closing night of the 1936 Olympic Games were those of the SA's fight song, and they emphatically had nothing to do with the Olympic ideals as enunciated by the soon-to-expire Baron Coubertin: *"Bald flattern Hitlerfahnen über allen Strassen, die Knechtschaft dauert nur noch kurze Zeit."* ("Soon Hitler flags will wave over all streets; our subjugation will last only a little longer.")

IX

Olympia

▲

▲

F the 1936 Berlin Olympics are still remembered as a triumphant success both in terms of organization and public relations, this probably has less to do with what the German media said about the games—or what the German media said the foreign media said about the games—than with the impact of a film that did not premier until about two years after the games were over: Leni Riefenstahl's *Olympia*. While the TV coverage of the games offered only a tiny taste of what was to come in this department, Riefenstahl's film laid out a cinematic smorgasbord of mythic proportions. It also gave the Germans another cause for gloating at the expense of the arrogant Americans: No film had been made of the 1932 Los Angeles games despite the proximity of the LA Memorial Coliseum to Hollywood.

The Making of Olympia

Leni Riefenstahl's road to her directorial role in *Olympia* was every bit as arduous as that of the athletes who competed before her cameras. Born on August 22, 1907, in Berlin, she had to fight to persuade her father, a plumber, to subsidize the ballet lessons that constituted the first steps toward her artistic career. By age seventeen she had already emerged as a star dancer on the Berlin stage, working in productions mounted by the great Jewish impresario Max Reinhardt. Her athletic dancing brought her to the attention of film director Arnold Fanck, who cast her as an adventurous climber in his "mountain movies," most notably *Der heilige Berg* (The Holy Mountain). In 1933 she also played a heroic pilot in *S.O.S. Eisberg* (S.O.S. Iceberg), a film about the *Titanic* disaster. In *Das blaue Licht* (The Blue Light), she both acted and made her debut as a director. This seminal film, which explored the "inner landscape" of its central character, a young female traveler and truth seeker, proved to be a milestone in Reifenstahl's career, for its "mystical" qualities greatly impressed Adolf Hitler, a man convinced that he was on a spiritual quest of his own.

When *S.O.S. Eisberg* opened at Berlin's Ufa-Palast am Zoo on August 30, 1933, Riefenstahl had to fly up for the premier from Nuremberg, where she was already embarked on her newest endeavor—directing a documentary record of the first annual Nazi Party Rally. Hitler himself, her important new fan, had instructed Propaganda Minister Goebbels to recruit her for this project at the last moment. Hastily put together, the film, entitled *Sieg des Glaubens* (Victory of the Faith) proved a flop and is now largely forgotten. Riefenstahl later claimed that Goebbels, ignoring Hitler's express orders to help her, put all sorts of obstacles in her path, though the real problem seems to have been the lack of preparation time, combined with insufficient funding and inadequate equipment.

The failure of *Sieg des Glaubens* did not deter Hitler from asking Riefenstahl to direct the filming of the next Nuremberg Party Rally in 1934. This time she would have a substantial budget and considerably more preparation time. The result was perhaps the most famous propaganda film of all time, *Triumph des Willens* (*Triumph of the Will*). To achieve the impressive atmospheric effects she wanted for the film, Reifenstahl employed innovative techniques like mobile cameras moving on rails above the action. "I discovered that I had a definite talent for documentaries," she wrote later. "I experienced the pleasure of a filmmaker who gives cinematic shape to actual events without falsifying them."

Triumph des Willens premiered in Berlin on March 28, 1935, with Hitler in the audience. Vastly pleased with the work, Hitler handed her a lilac bouquet. A few months later, in August 1935, he handed her a more significant reward: his request that she put together a documentary film on the upcoming Olympic Games in Berlin.

In her controversial memoirs, published in 1987, Riefenstahl did her best to obscure the true story behind her making of *Olympia*. She claimed that her Berlin opus was commissioned by the IOC (at the instigation of Carl Diem) and produced entirely by herself with financial backing from an independent distribution company, Tobis Films. The reality is quite different. Although she did indeed retain artistic control over the film, it was commissioned by the Propaganda Ministry and financed entirely by the Reich. Mindful, however, that it would certainly look better if the film *seemed* independent of the Nazi government, the authorities allowed Riefenstahl to establish a dummy corporation, Olympia-Film, G.m.b.H., which acted as a cover for the Propaganda Ministry (Promi), the actual owner of the film.

Riefenstahl also insisted in her memoirs that Goebbels opposed her making the film and, as with *Sieg des Glaubens*, obstructed her work at every opportunity. The reality is that Goebbels appreciated the propaganda potential in the film and tolerated Riefenstahl's involvement, although he would have preferred to have Hans Weidemann, the director of the Winter Games film *Jugend der Welt*, in charge of the movie. "Fräulein Riefenstahl reports on the preparation work for the Olympia film. She's a smart cookie," observed Goebbels in a diary entry dated August 17, 1935. The problem for Riefenstahl was that Goebbels ultimately took *too much* interest in the project, trying on several occasions to shape its design. She seems to have resisted this effort successfully—just as, at least so she claims, she successfully resisted the randy little womanizer's efforts to get her into his well-used bed.

Riefenstahl was determined not to make a traditional sports documentary or glorified newsreel. She wanted to capture the essence of the Olympic ideal as it had first presented itself in ancient Greece and then found its new home—so she too apparently believed—in Nazi Germany. Regarding what turned out to be the almost surreal, mist-enshrouded prologue to her film, she had an ecstatic vision:

> In my mind's eye I could see the ancient ruins of classical Olympic sites slowly emerging from patches of fog and the Greek temples and sculptures drifting by: Achilles and Paris, and then the discus thrower of Myron. I dreamed that the statue changed into a man of flesh and blood, gradually starting to swing the discus in slow motion. The sculptures turned into Greek temple dancers dissolving into flames, the Olympic fire igniting the torches to be carried from the Temple of Zeus to the modern Berlin of 1936—a bridge from antiquity to the present.

Because she could hardly include the entire Olympic festival of 1936 in her film, she elected from the outset to shape her work around key or representative moments, scenes, and performances. But since she also could not know in advance which scenes or events would be worthy of preserving in the final version, she decided she would have to film just about everything that transpired, relying on the editing process to come up with a movie that did not last as long as the games themselves. To her credit, the film she ended up with was only one hour and fifteen minutes longer than the winning time in the marathon.

Riefenstahl's strategy for *Olympia* entailed an enormous commitment in time, personnel, equipment, and money. The contract she signed with the Propaganda Ministry on December 1, 1935, reflected her grandiose ambitions. It called for a total budget of 1,500,000 reichsmarks, far larger than the outlay for *Triumph des Willens*. The funds were to be distributed in four allotments between April 15, 1936, and October 15, 1937. Riefenstahl herself was to be paid 250,000 reichsmarks. She would have artistic control over the film but was required to provide regular financial reports to the government. There was no mention in the contract of the IOC, which in theory controlled the rights to any commercial exploitation of the games. Nor did the GOC figure in the negotiations. The contractual and financial arrangements for *Olympia* showed once again how thoroughly the Nazi state had managed to hijack the ostensibly "independent" Olympic vehicle.

Taking advantage of her generous budget, Riefenstahl set up elaborate production facilities and hired a huge staff to assist her in planning and executing her project. Months before the games began she and four of her cameramen withdrew to the nearby spa town of Bad Harzburg to discuss strategy.

For her production headquarters she commandeered a spacious villa in Berlin-Spandau called Haus Ruwald. There she lived with her entire crew for the duration of the shooting process, in conditions that were anything but Spartan. Like a first-class hotel, Haus Ruwald had a full bar, maid service, library, and restaurant. Unlike most first-class hotels, Haus Ruwald's restaurant served opulent breakfasts at no cost to the residents. The villa's work spaces included state-of-the-art cutting and editing rooms, a theater for reviewing dailies, a large darkroom, and several offices that even Riefenstahl admitted were "sumptuously appointed."

For her cameramen and technical personnel, Riefenstahl turned largely to young sporting types from southern Germany, who, unlike many of Germany's top film people, expressed willingness to work for a woman; some of them, indeed, had worked for her before.

These men were also willing to experiment with new techniques. Chief cameraman Hans Ertl, one of the technical geniuses behind the Winter Games film *Jugend der Welt*, developed a special camera that could shoot underwater, a great advantage for the swimming and diving events. Walter Frentz, who had become an expert at shooting kayak racing, took charge of the boating and yachting photography. Guzzi Lantschner, a veteran of *Triumph des Willens* and a silver medalist in alpine skiing at Garmisch, shot most of the diving, gymnastics, and equestrian events.

The expert responsible for much of the spectacular close-up work in *Olympia*—shots of athletes' faces contorted in pain, muscles bulging with effort—was Hans Scheib, who deftly deployed a huge Leica 600 mm telephoto lens, the most powerful then in existence. With this cannon Scheib could capture a sweat-stained brow halfway across the stadium. Or, put more accurately, Scheib could get such shots when the conditions were right— meaning when there was enough natural light to guarantee a good exposure with the slow film stock then available. Alas, in the gloom and rain that prevailed during the early days of the games, good long-distance shots were virtually impossible, and much of the work that Scheib turned in during that period ended up being discarded.

The actual filming of *Olympia* began well before the games opened. In June 1936 Riefenstahl sent the brilliant but mentally troubled surrealist photographer, Willy Zielke, to Greece to assemble footage that might be appropriate for the prologue. Zielke, who was given leave from his sanatorium for this purpose, spent several weeks using smoke powder and gauze-covered lenses to generate hazy and dreamlike images of the Acropolis and the ruins at ancient Olympia. The photographer put together some additional footage for the prologue by filming among the lonely sand dunes along the Baltic Coast near Danzig. As we have seen, Riefenstahl also sent a team to film the torchlighting ceremony and first stages of the torch relay in Greece. Her tactic of filming staged recreations of parts of the relay anticipated a technique she would use occasionally for the competitions themselves.

As opening day drew near, Riefenstahl, determined to establish the best possible technical environment for filming the games, launched an assault on the Reichssportfeld and other Olympic venues that often put her at odds with the officials responsible for running the show. At first she demanded permission for her cameramen to roam around the stadium infield at will, but officials objected this would distract the athletes and possibly lead to accidents—say, a cameraman being skewered by a javelin or decapitated by a discus. Eventually she got authorization to construct two steel towers in the infield on which she mounted cameras; the towers were of course an eyesore and blocked the sightlines for some spectators. Even more problematic were the camera pits she ordered dug near the long jump, high jump, and sprint track to afford low-angle images of the action. The IOC was understandably concerned that an athlete might accidentally stray into one of these traps. Sure enough, Jesse Owens very nearly fell into one after completing his first one-hundred-meter heat. Furious, the IOC forced Riefenstahl to fill in all the camera pits save the ones near the jumping venues.

The filmmaker also installed an innovative rail system along which an unmanned camera could be propelled to photograph the sprinters as they raced down the track. The device was tested at the German National Track Championships in spring 1936 and found to work well. The IAAF, however, became concerned that the Olympic runners might be distracted by the speeding camera, and insisted on the eve of the games that the entire system be dismantled.

At the rowing course in Grünau, by contrast, Riefenstahl did manage to put into operation a one-hundred-meter-long platform along which a car pulled a camera for meter-by-meter coverage of the sprints to the finish line. Justifying this elaborate apparatus, Riefenstahl said she wanted shots "of struggle, final push, victory and exhaustion."

The filmmaker also wanted panoramic aerial shots of the rowing competition, and for this purpose she borrowed a military airship from the Luftwaffe. Yet once again officials foiled her plans, forbidding the use of the craft on safety grounds. As a last-minute alternative to the dirigible, Riefenstahl experimented with an unmanned balloon carrying a minicamera programmed to open its shutter at a specific height. The device worked well in tests, but the balloons she eventually launched during competition floated off course and produced no usable footage at all.

The numerous impediments Riefenstahl and her crew encountered in setting up for the games convinced them that the only way they were going to get some of the special shots they wanted was to gather footage of the Olympic training sessions, where fewer restrictions applied.

Most of the yachting footage in the final film came from shots Riefenstahl and cameraman Frentz took with boat-mounted cameras during German elimination races and training exercises at Kiel. Similarly, the coxswain-eye views of the rowing contests were taken by cameramen sitting in various sculls during training. Hans Ertl got some exciting shots while perched in a rubber raft during practice sessions in the swimming stadium. Additional dramatic swimming footage was obtained from minicameras affixed to toy boats that were pulled along in front of the swimmers' noses as they plowed through their training. Frentz was even able to persuade some of the marathoners to carry tiny cameras lodged in baskets suspended from their necks during training runs so as to yield action shots of running feet. In the race itself, of course, none of the runners carried cameras, but Riefenstahl did get good close-ups of Kitei Son and Ernest Harper via a camera towed along a rubberized track concealed in the bushes alongside the Avus Speedway portion of the marathon course.

Once the games began, Riefenstahl continued to struggle with officials over filming procedures and access to athletes. It did not help matters that the filmmaker, confident of backing from Hitler, strode around the Reichssportfeld as if she owned the place. She became livid every time the police, judges, or other officials got in her way. When a judge at the hammer throw stopped cameraman Lantschner from shooting the action, Riefenstahl rushed up to the poor official, grabbed him by the lapels, and screamed "You bastard!" She also knew how strategically to turn on the tears.

Observing Riefenstahl in action at the Reichssportfeld, Bella Fromm recorded a rather less-than-flattering portrait of the filmmaker as prima donna:

Leni Riefenstahl, official photographer, wearing gray flannel slacks and a kind of jockey cap, is obtrusively in evidence everywhere, pretending an untiring and exhaustive efficiency and importance. Meanwhile, her assistants quietly, expertly do the work, which Leni signs.

On and off, she sits down beside her Führer, a magazine-cover grin on her face and a halo of importance fixed firmly above her head. She has priority rights and cannot bear to have anyone else take a shot that she has overlooked. Page boys dash constantly from photographer to photographer, handing them the dreaded slip: "Leni Riefenstahl warns you to stay at your present position while taking pictures. Do not move around. In case of disobedience, press permission will be confiscated."

During the games Riefenstahl's team shot some 400,000 meters of film. In addition to the prologue work, the torch relay material, and the training shots, this imposing mass of celluloid contained at least some footage of every competitive event. Not all the "action" footage involved real-time coverage of the events purportedly on display, however. As we noted above, because darkness prevented good shots of the concluding phase of the pole vault, Riefenstahl, with the assistance of Glenn Morris, persuaded the finalists to jump again on the following day for her cameras. Morris also consented to rerun the five-thousand-meter race that had concluded his great decathlon victory, a sequence Riefenstahl had also failed to film. Some of the swimming, diving, and gymnastics footage was likewise obtained during arranged shoots after the games had concluded.

For all the difficulties Riefenstahl encountered in getting the games on film, her toughest task came with the editing process, which required that she get rid of about three-quarters of what her cameramen had shot. She planned the editing phase as carefully as she had the filming, drawing up a detailed index of all her material and setting a precise timetable for the work.

Before she could truly get going with the editing, however, she ran into a serious challenge from Goebbels, who now really did become her adversary. Goebbels did not approve of her plan to spend well over a year editing the film, which he believed could have a large-scale propagandistic effect only if it came out right after the games. According to her he also worried that the film would "show too much of the blacks." Furthermore he was angered by rumors that she had squandered government money during the filming. Finally his deep-seated misogyny kicked in, leading him to question whether a mere woman, even a "smart cookie" like Riefenstahl, was up to the task of molding her mountain of material into a hard-hitting piece of propaganda. He therefore proposed that Riefenstahl be replaced as the director of *Olympia* by Hans Weidemann, his lackey in the Propaganda Ministry. Riefenstahl immediately went to Goebbels to protest this intrusion. As he noted in his diary: "Riefenstahl has complaints about Weidemann. But she is badly hysterical. A further proof that a woman cannot master such assignments."

To intimidate and discredit Riefenstahl, Goebbels ordered a surprise audit of Olympia G.m.b.H.'s books in October 1936. The filmmaker was vulnerable here, for she and her crew had indeed spared no expenses and had not taken adequate care of the equipment entrusted to them. Predictably the government bean counter found all sorts of irregularities. For example, rather than procuring a safe for valuables, the firm's chief financial officer, Walter Groskopf, had carried thousands of reichsmarks around in his coat pockets, distributing them willy-nilly. Whether it had been necessary to spend so much time and money filming in the Baltic dunes the auditor could not judge, but he could not overlook the lavish spending of Riefenstahl's firm on food, drink, and tips in Berlin. Riefenstahl, moreover, had drawn on expense money from company coffers rather than taking funds out of her salary, as stipulated in her contract. The firm had purchased a car from Mercedes for 2,671 reichsmarks and then sold it to cameraman Lantschner for 1,000 reichsmarks. Much of the company's material inventory at Haus Ruwald, from dishes and clothing to cameras, had been sold off illegally or simply vanished after the conclusion of shooting. In short, as one witness testified to the auditor: "Money was not a concern. Every operator and technician procured whatever he wanted. Any private company employing such procedures would be quickly bankrupt."

For Goebbels the auditor's report showing that Riefenstahl had "supped like a pig" at the Reich trough provided more evidence that she should be fired forthwith. At the very least, he said, she should be put on a short financial leash.

But Riefenstahl was not the sort to be leashed. She responded to the criticism by demanding another five hundred thousand reichsmarks in postproduction subsidies to finish the project. She also formally proposed that *two* feature-length films be teased from the material at hand. Goebbels was flabbergasted by Riefenstahl's arrogance, although he claimed to have shown nothing but icy disdain on receiving the filmmaker's latest demands. As he wrote in his diary: "Fräulein Riefenstahl demonstrates her hysteria to me. It is impossible to work with this wild woman. Now she wants half a million more for her film and to make *two* out of it. Yet it stinks to high heaven in her shop. I am cool right down to my heart. She cries. This is the last weapon of women. But that does not work on me anymore. She should do her work and keep order."

Obviously at an impasse with Goebbels, but determined to retain control over *Olympia* and finish it as she saw fit, Riefenstahl now played her strongest card: her special relationship with Hitler. After much effort and considerable delay, she arranged a personal meeting with her benefactor, enlightening him as to her needs and her difficulties with Goebbels. She claims in her memoirs not to have mentioned "the sexual advances Goebbels had made to me," focusing exclusively on the "harassment" she and her crew had supposedly endured from the Propaganda Ministry. She said she could not continue to live and work in Germany under such circumstances.

Hitler, who theretofore had heard only Goebbels's side of the story, duly had words with his propaganda minister. It is not known exactly what was said at this meeting, but shortly thereafter Riefenstahl was informed by Hitler's adjutant that she would be granted an additional three hundred thousand reichsmarks for her work and need not worry about further difficulties from Herr Goebbels.

For the latter this outcome was deeply humiliating, but all he could do by way of revenge was to purge some of Riefenstahl's minor collaborators.

FREE from interference from Goebbels, Riefenstahl threw herself into editing *Olympia*, an extremely demanding undertaking she kept entirely under her own control in order to ensure a "consistent architecture" in the final product. Although she had an overarching design in mind, she put the individual pieces together according to their "rhythmic fit." This did not necessarily coincide with the actual sequence of events at the games. "It was like composing music, and just as intuitive," she later said of her method.

Like most documentaries Riefenstahl's film was to include a narrative voice-over, but in this case the filmmaker decided to have her main narrator, Paul Laven, a prominent radio announcer who had broadcast the games for German radio, actually appear in the film and re-create his role as broadcaster. In the movie Laven is of course narrating to the film audience, but it looks as if he is talking to an unseen radio audience. In this way Riefenstahl was able both to enliven the narrative and to put in a plug for German radio technology, which after all was one of the glories of the Berlin games.

During editing Riefenstahl was also obliged to dub new sound effects because during the actual shooting her recording engineers had been unable to pick up much beyond undifferentiated crowd noise. Hitler's fifteen-word sentence proclaiming the games open is the only moment in the film when synchronous sound is heard. To heighten the impression of verisimilitude in the soundtrack, Riefenstahl got American and Japanese students living in Berlin to record typical cheers from their respective homelands.

Music had played a crucial role in Riefenstahl's previous films, helping to shape their mood and message. In the opening scene of *Triumph des Willens*,

Hitler's airplane descends from the clouds to accompanying passages from Wagner's *Die Meistersinger*. Riefenstahl was determined to have an equally effective musical score for *Olympia*, so she turned once again to Herbert Windt, who had worked with her on *Triumph des Willens*.

Windt's specialty was "heroic" music for nationalistic radio programs and films. He was a member of the Nazi Party and one of Goebbels's favorite composers. In engaging him for *Olympia*, Riefenstahl was hoping to mend her fences with the Propaganda Ministry. What she wanted from her music man was a kind of parallel text: music that—in the fashion of Wagnerian leitmotifs—would help to tell the story. For example, regarding the prologue, she told Windt: "It would be beautiful, Herbert, if you could do it so that when new themes appear in the picture, the heads on the temples and so on, that you change the theme exactly synchronous with the picture." For the marathon Windt composed music that served as a counterpoint to the action, thereby getting at the inner essence of what was going on in the race. As he enthusiastically explained:

> Leni Riefenstahl had also produced shots that were shot from the heads of runners [the famous basket shots], so that the spectator, as it were, sees with the eyes of the runners. His view goes out over the ground, his legs fly unceasingly forward—under them the earth rushes behind. In these pictures, Leni Riefenstahl was able to create dramatically that condition that sets in after so many kilometers in every long distance run: exhaustion! His legs become heavier, his rhythm slower, his gait more sluggish, his image more oppressive. But the music does not accompany the sequence of events happening to his body. On the contrary, it, the music of the runner, his mood, his flight of ideas, his spirit, his will, his driving idea, elevates itself over the body which begins to tire, flies before him, and pulls the body further on. Here was a magnificent success in forming a dramatic counterpart of body and spirit as a thrilling experience.

A Monument of German Genius

Finally, in early March 1938, *Olympia* was "in the can." As promised, Riefenstahl had actually created two films: part 1, *Fest der Völker* (*The Festival of*

Peoples); and part 2, *Fest der Schönheit* (*The Festival of Beauty*). Like Wagner's demanding *Ring* tetralogy, the entire opus was designed to be seen in separate sittings. For international audiences, however, who might be expected to be less patient with a Wagnerian-length production, Riefenstahl created five foreign-language versions that were somewhat shorter than the German original. Advisedly the director eliminated some of the swastika imagery and shots of Hitler from these foreign versions. Shortly after the war Allied censors substantially cut the German original, and in 1958 Riefenstahl herself produced a foreshortened, sanitized version that was meant to further her own efforts at political decontamination.

Riefenstahl always insisted that *Olympia* was purely an art film with no political or ideological message. Many commentators at the time, and a few since, have also taken this view. How accurate is this perspective?

Assessments of *Olympia* are tricky because of the many different versions in which the film is now available. The truncated version of 1958 and the various foreign-language versions differ in subtle but significant ways from the original German edition. Few people these days see that original work, surviving copies of which were confiscated by the Americans after the war. The National Archives in Washington retains a copy, as does the Berlin branch of the German Federal Archives.

Even though the 1938 German edition was designed for local audiences, it does not, at least on the surface, come across as particularly partisan. Foreign victories are given due attention, as are foreign spectators (indeed, the film gives the erroneous impression that a huge part of the audience consisted of foreign fans). *Olympia* does not reveal that Germany won the unofficial national medals count and in fact records some embarrassing German defeats, most notably the lopsided loss to India in field hockey. This "neutral" approach, however, should not be read as a sign of Riefenstahl's independence from the official line. On the contrary, it mirrored Goebbels's mandate to the German press that it duly acknowledge foreign victories and desist from displays of national pride.

With particular respect to the performance of American black athletes, the film also seems at first glance to be more than fair. Jesse Owens is clearly the star. He is treated so favorably that Berliners made a little joke out of the matter: "Dem Führer zeigt die Leni dann / was deutsche Filmkunst alles kann / Da sah er dann im Negativ / wie positiv der Neger lief." ("Leni shows the

Führer too / all that German film can do / He saw in negative print / how positive the Negro could sprint.") On the other hand, while there is plenty of footage of Owens in action, there are no shots of the long lines of German kids patiently waiting to get the athlete's autograph. The film is rather less celebratory, moreover, when it comes to the performance of other American blacks. The only close-up shot of the men's four-hundred-meter race captures the British runner Godfrey Brown lunging for second place, not Archie Williams taking the gold. Footage of the eight-hundred-meter race focuses on the Italian team's cheering for their star runner, Mario Lanzi, not the spectacular come-from-behind triumph of John Woodruff. Neither Williams nor Woodruff is seen on the victor's podium. Riefenstahl, in other words, may not have downplayed "the blacks" as much as Goebbels would have liked, but she by no means gave the American blacks their full due.

In a variety of subtle ways, moreover, the film *does* reflect a bias in favor of German athletes. The best slow-motion shots are reserved for German performances. German victories are also emphasized by heightened musical pathos and close-ups of exulting national leaders. A huge amount of footage is devoted to the equestrian events, in which the Germans excelled. German athletes are sometimes featured even when they did not win medals. Thus Erich Borchmeyer is shown winning his heat in the one-hundred-meter dash though he finished out of the running in the final. Willy Schröder is shown as if he had been a finalist in the discus competition, though he had been eliminated in the early rounds. In the decathlon footage Erwin Huber is presented as a more serious challenger to the dominant Americans than he actually was. The German viewer could be forgiven for thinking that the Reich's track-and-field athletes had done better than they really had.

The film also favors athletes from states allied with or friendly toward Nazi Germany. The Japanese receive extensive coverage, as do the Italians. By contrast there is not a single shot of the medal winners from Czechoslovakia, whose country was then at loggerheads with Germany over the Sudetenland.

In the original German version Hitler is shown so frequently that he appears to have had an even larger role in the games than he actually had. In general the footage of the Führer in *Olympia* does not depict him as a glowering demigod, as is the case in *Triumph des Willens*, but as an everyday sports fan, a kind of Fritz-six-pack buoyed by home-team victories, saddened by their defeats. Most of the time he is seen laughing and smiling, just having a good time. (It would have been going too far in this direction, however, to show Hitler getting that famous kiss on the cheek from his grandmotherly American admirer at the swimming stadium. Hans Ertl's footage of this scene ended up on the cutting-room floor.) In her portrayal of Hitler as regular *Mensch*, Riefenstahl was perhaps putting on her own performance for her benefactor, handling him in the way a loyal court painter might approach the royal personage.

In the English-language edition of *Olympia* Hitler appears sporadically, and the only close-up shot of him during the opening-day ceremony occurs when he pronounces the sentence opening the games. Elsewhere in the film there are quick shots of him giving the Nazi salute to the Austrian team and laughing after a German victory. Similarly the swastika flag, which was all over the place at the games, and accordingly shown extensively in the original German version of the film, takes second place to the Olympic flag in the English-language cut and the other foreign editions of *Olympia*.

There are also significant differences in narrative tone between the German and foreign versions. While in the latter the narrative voice-over is studiedly neutral and banal, in the former the narrator often describes the games as racial and national battles. Thus in the one-hundred-meter dash we have black runners lining up against "the strongest representatives of the white race." The two-hundred-meter men's breaststroke at the swimming stadium is presented not as a competition among individuals but as a "blood battle" between Germany and Japan. Three Finish racers grouped together in the marathon are described as "three runners, one country, one will," an echo of the Nazi slogan, "One nation, one people, one leader." While the foreign-language versions carefully mention the athletes' names, the German version often identifies them only by nation. The *Olympia* that German audiences saw, in other words, reinforced the Nazi dogma that these games were above all a contest of nations and races, a sporting equivalent of the great battle for world supremacy among the peoples of the world.

Even the foreign-language versions of *Olympia*, however, are by no means free of National Socialist ideology. The film manages, sometimes subtly, sometimes fairly overtly, to convey some of the key principles and aesthetic ideals dear to the Nazis. *Olympia*'s prologue, dwelling as it does on classical Greek imagery, repostulates the alleged ties between ancient Greece and modern Germany. When Myron's statue of the naked discus thrower morphs into the perfect Aryan superman, we do not have to know that the model was Erwin Huber to get the point. Footage of the torch relay, by giving prominence to the starting point in ancient Olympia and the conclusion in Nazi Berlin, suggests an even greater spiritual connectedness between these two places than did the relay itself: One minute we are in the hallowed ruins at Olympia and practically in the next minute—interrupted only by the image of a black line snaking across a map of southeastern Europe—we are in the Berlin stadium, with Hitler presiding.

The prologue to part 2, *Fest der Schönheit*, takes us on a tour of the Olympic Village just as dawn is breaking. We see a beetle crawl through the underbrush; a heron flap its wings; a kangaroo, courtesy of the Australian team, hop across a field. A spiderweb is lit by the rising sun. It's morning in Nazi Germany. Here, amid the bucolic surroundings and the tasteful lodgings built by the Wehrmacht, athletes from all over the world are seen availing themselves of the local amenities: playing fields, ponds, lounge chairs, running paths through the woods, a Finnish sauna in which naked men, genitals a-dangling, happily lash each other with birch branches. The mood conveyed is one of playful exuberance, relaxation, and multinational togetherness on the eve of the serious business to come. The whole scene, as others have noted, is highly reminiscent of the footage of the Hitler Youth brigades frolicking before the Nuremberg Party Rally in Riefenstahl's *Triumph des Willens*. In *Olympia*, of course, most of the athletes are not Nazis, but we are meant to see the Olympic Village at Döberitz, like the Hitler Youth encampment at Nuremberg, as an expression of the profound communitarian ethos supposedly at the heart of the Nazi *Volksgemeinschaft*.

Finally, *Olympia*'s celebration of the "body beautiful" is not simply a reflection of Riefenstahl's personal aesthetic (much as she indeed loved a fine physique): It tied in closely with the National Socialist Germany's glorification of health, strength, and physical perfection. Of course other political philosophies, most notably communism, also idealized the strong and healthy body, but the Nazi aesthetic differed from the communist one in its preference for *naked* bodies in a natural setting—part of its Romantic "blood and soil" ethos. *Olympia* is particularly effective here, taking full advantage of the fact that in the Summer Games the athletes were scantily clad, and focusing enough on bare skin and thinly veiled musculature to create the illusion (almost) of ancient warriors doing heroic battle in the altogether.

"As Pretty as a Swastika"

Olympia premiered on April 20, 1938, Hitler's forty-ninth birthday, at the Ufa-Palast am Zoo in Berlin. The film was supposed to have opened a month or so earlier, but Hitler had something more important on his plate at that time—namely, the annexation of his native country, Austria. On March 13, 1936, German troops marched into Austria, meeting little resistance from either the Austrians or the international community, which by then had more or less written off Austria as an independent republic. By the time Hitler was ready to see *Olympia*, Austria was solidly in the German orbit, having on April 10 voted 99.75 percent in favor of the Anschluss in a Nazi-controlled plebiscite.

The *Olympia* premiere was a gala occasion. Speer designed a special facade for the theater, creating giant Olympic flags interspersed with swastika banners. Everybody who was anybody in the Reich's political, economic, and cultural establishments was there. In addition to the entire cabinet and members of the diplomatic corps, actors Gustav Gründgens and Emil Jannings showed up, as did Berlin Philharmonic conductor Wilhelm Furtwängler. Contrary to Riefenstahl's original intention, both parts of the film were shown together, with a short intermission. When the curtain finally came down after four and a half hours the entire audience stood and clapped for several minutes—perhaps as much out of relief as admiration. Hitler, the birthday boy, presented Riefenstahl with a bouquet of white lilacs and red roses. The Greek ambassador gave her an olive branch from a "sacred tree" at Olympia. Even Goebbels energetically shook her hand. "I was completely overcome by the power, profundity and beauty" of the film, he confessed in his diary.

The German press, not surprisingly, ladled on the praise. The Nazi film critic Frank Maraun hailed *Olympia* as the filmic embodiment of ideals derived from "the ideological realm of National Socialism." Goebbels, recognizing a winner, felt obliged to give Riefenstahl yet another one hundred thousand reichsmarks as a reward and to help her publicize the film. But *Olympia* hardly needed much promotion, at least not in Germany. Around the Reich it played to full houses night after night, becoming the biggest hit the Promi had produced to date. In May, Goebbels presented Riefenstahl with the National Film Prize, declaring that *Olympia* would "stand for German prowess in the eyes of the entire world and testify to the greatness of our people in these times."

To ensure that people everywhere had the opportunity to be impressed by this work of German genius, the Promi sent copies of the film to every country that had participated in the games, and even to some that had not. Iran had not sent a team to Berlin, but the Propaganda Ministry sent a copy to Tehran to give the Iranians a taste of what they had missed.

Believing that the propaganda value of *Olympia* would be enhanced if not only the film, but also the filmmaker, made the rounds abroad, the Promi sent Riefenstahl on a multination European publicity tour in the summer of 1938. At government expense Riefenstahl toured Zurich, Paris, Brussels, Copenhagen, Oslo, Helsinki, Stockholm, Rome, and Venice with her film.

The road show brought her additional praise and honors. In Paris she and her film were the sensations of the moment, partly, no doubt, because she had been clever enough to cut some of the Hitler and swastika scenes from the version she showed there. In Rome she was squired about by *Il Duce* himself, and at the Venice Film Festival she was awarded the prize for best film, the Coppa Mussolini.

Yet her tour was not without its mishaps and sour notes. At the premiere in Zurich someone detonated a stink bomb near Leni's seat. During showings in Antwerp leftists distributed anti-fascist leaflets and yelled "Bloodhound!" whenever Hitler appeared on the screen. Even in Venice, British and American members of the film festival jury condemned their group's award to Riefenstahl as an example of fascist cronyism (the Americans had voted for Walt Disney's *Snow White*). Meanwhile, back in Rome, Pope Pius XI put *Olympia* on the Catholic Film Index, condemning it as an exercise in paganism, "dangerous to morals."

The criticism Riefenstahl encountered in Europe anticipated the much more serious protests she met in the United States in the fall of 1938, when she sought to introduce her film to American audiences. Avery Brundage, an ardent admirer of Riefenstahl's, had feared early on that *Olympia* would never make it to America at all because of Jewish opposition. As he wrote to his Swedish friend Clarence von Rosen in May 1936: "I envy you your opportunity of seeing the Olympic Film which I understand is an artistic masterpiece. The Jews, who own all the picture theaters in America, will understandably prevent its being shown here." Goebbels, also doubtful about a warm welcome for *Olympia* in America, advised Riefenstahl not to take her movie to the United States. When he proved unable to dissuade the filmmaker from making the trip, Goebbels tried to reduce the potential political risk by inventing the cover story that she was traveling in a purely private capacity (in fact she used funds from the Reich Economic Ministry), and he instructed the German consulates in America not to make a fuss over her.

AUTUMN 1938 was not a good time for somebody like Riefenstahl to try to promote German genius in America. In September, a month before her planned departure, Europe seemed about to plunge into war over the Sudetenland issue. The crisis was defused at the last moment by the infamous Munich Agreement, but many in the United States (rightly) saw the deal as a shameful cave-in by the Western democracies to German saber-rattling. On November 3, 1938, the *New York Times*, in reporting that Riefenstahl was en route to America, made much of her friendship with Hitler, noting coyly that his car was often seen outside her Berlin apartment. (Riefenstahl claims in her memoirs that Hitler "desired me as a woman," but she always denied rumors that she became his lover, and in this case her story seems credible.) On November 4, as Riefenstahl's ship docked in New York City, the *Times* reported that two Jewish groups, the American Jewish Congress and the Jewish Labor Committee, were calling for a boycott of *Olympia*. In a telegram to leading film distributors and theater owners, the groups appealed for joint action against Riefenstahl's film, which they called "part of an attack on American institutions and American democracy." The organizations promised to picket any theater that booked "this fascist film."

Such advance protests notwithstanding, Riefenstahl at first enjoyed a friendly enough reception in New York. She was greeted at the dock by thousands of reporters clamoring to interview and photograph "Hitler's girlfriend." She took a suite at the Pierre Hotel and plunged into New York's nightlife. King Vidor, the noted director, traveled all the way from Hollywood to meet her.

But after a few days in New York she suddenly found herself caught up in the storm of agitation generated by the Kristallnacht pogrom of November 9–10, when, in supposed retaliation for the assassination of a German diplomat in Paris by a Polish Jew, Nazi thugs burned synagogues, smashed Jewish businesses, and physically accosted Jews in the streets of German cities. Thousands of Jews were rounded up and sent into "protective custody" in various concentration camps. The Reich government then imposed a large indemnity on German Jews to pay for the damage left behind by the pogrom. Asked for her response to this outrage, Riefenstahl replied that she did not believe any pogrom had actually occurred. The reports were simply "slanders," she said, typical of the baseless rumors circulating in the world about Nazi Germany. Statements like this naturally turned sentiment in America against her. In a comment conflating Riefenstahl's politics and putative beauty, the columnist Walter Winchell, a vocal opponent of Nazism, wrote she was "as pretty as a swastika."

Riefenstahl continued to play dumb about the pogrom even after being told the unvarnished truth by Germany's consul in New York, who advised her to return immediately to Germany. She refused, telling the consul she would hold tight in the States until "this damn Jewish thing is no longer in the headlines . . . and the American people have turned their attention to the next sensation."

New York, however, continued to be so inhospitable to Leni that she decamped for Chicago in mid-November. There she stayed with Avery Brundage, who organized a private screening of *Olympia* for thirty-five people at the Engineers Club. This was *Olympia*'s ignominious American "premiere."

While in Chicago, Riefenstahl received an invitation from Henry Ford to visit him in Detroit, which she promptly accepted. She hoped that Ford would use his money and influence to get *Olympia* distributed in the United States. The carmaker, however, was not really interested in the film. He simply wanted to inform Riefenstahl about his admiration for Hitler, instructing the filmmaker to "tell [the Führer] that I am looking forward to meeting him at the coming party rally in Nuremberg." (Ford ended up not going to the rally, and he never met Hitler.)

Still refusing to admit defeat, Riefenstahl went on to Hollywood in late November, naively imagining that among fellow film people she would find respect and support. Instead she found an announcement in *Variety* saying: "There is no place in Hollywood for Leni Riefenstahl." The left-wing Anti-Nazi League for Defense of American Democracy, which had an influential chapter in Hollywood, promised to picket any showing of *Olympia*. Gary Cooper, who had said he wanted to meet Riefenstahl, suddenly found himself otherwise engaged. Louis B. Mayer cancelled a meeting with her. The only studio boss who consented to see her was Walt Disney, who had a certain pro-German bent. Fearing retaliation against his own films if he openly supported Riefenstahl, however, Disney refused to get involved in *Olympia*'s distribution. He even refused to show her film in his own screening room.

In the end *Olympia* would have gotten no Hollywood screening at all had not Avery Brundage prevailed upon William May Garland to organize a private showing at the California Club in Los Angeles for 190 invited guests, among whom were swimmer Johnny Weissmuller and Olympic decathlon champion Glenn Morris, Riefenstahl's former flame. In the print used in the showing Riefenstahl had carefully cut out every appearance by Hitler. A *Los Angeles Times* critic who saw this cut hailed it for its "fair-mindedness" and lack of political content. But the positive reviews made no difference. No major studio or distributor would touch *Olympia*, and at last, in early June 1939, Riefenstahl gave up and returned to Germany. Before leaving America she issued a press release saying:

> Although America achieved great successes at the 1936 Olympiade [*sic*], my film with its triumphant athletes is not being shown here because the American film industry, including production and distribution, is controlled by people hostile to modern Germany. They have managed to ensure that Americans will not have the chance to see their own athletes putting the rest of the world in the shade, despite the fact that the Olympic Games were a purely sporting event and although the film has been shown everywhere else across the world.

Leaving aside its political and moral myopia, this statement was inaccurate regarding *Olympia*'s alleged presentation "everywhere else across the world." For reasons similar to those that blocked an American distribution, the film was not shown in Great Britain until after the war.

On returning to Germany, Riefenstahl was buoyed by yet another prize. In June 1939 the IOC voted to award her the Olympic Diploma, an initiative put forth by Avery Brundage. Brundage and the IOC were obviously not disturbed by the charges that Riefenstahl was a propagandist for a regime that was becoming increasingly belligerent, having just two months before—in violation of Hitler's promises at Munich—occupied the rest of Czechoslovakia. The IOC saw Riefenstahl's work as perfectly in tune with *"les idéals olympiques."*

WHATEVER Brundage and the IOC may have thought of Riefenstahl and *Olympia* in 1939, some commentators since have come to understand that

the film was in fact a work of propaganda, all the more brilliant for not seem-
ing to be propagandistic at all.

But even if the film constituted a form of advertisement for Hitler's Germany, it did not significantly change the way people around the world saw
the Third Reich. Like the games themselves, in its early showings the film
seems to have made a greater impact within Germany than abroad. It ran for
weeks on end in German theaters but soon disappeared from screens elsewhere on the Continent. Hitler-hostile foreign newspapers that found reasons
to praise the film did not, under its impact, revise their negative perception
of Nazi Germany. Of course the timing of *Olympia*'s foreign release undercut
whatever propaganda value the film might have had in those days. It was
increasingly difficult to sell the proposition of a peace-loving and tolerant
Germany given the regime's aggressive and brutal behavior from the
Anschluss through Kristallnacht and the occupation of Czechoslovakia. Thus,
at least with respect to *Olympia*'s foreign resonance, Goebbels may have been
right in thinking that the project's full impact depended on a quick release.
Although the film ultimately made money for the Reich—some 114,066
reichsmarks as of December 1942—on a strict cost-benefit analysis *Olympia*
cannot be said to have fully realized the hopes invested in it by the Propaganda Ministry.

AT the moment Leni Riefenstahl received the Olympic Diploma from the
IOC, the outbreak of war in Europe was only three months away. The battle
between nations and races celebrated in Riefenstahl's film segued into World
War II, the bloodiest military conflict in human history. At the conclusion of
the 1936 Summer Games the world had been invited to witness the games'
resumption four years hence in Tokyo. Of course there would be no Olympic
Games in Tokyo in 1940.

Epilogue

"The Games Must Go On"

▲

▲

TWO weeks after the closing ceremony at the Berlin games, Hitler instructed his chief aides that within four years' time Germany must be militarily and economically ready for war. As part of the Reich's military preparations, the Blaupunkt Company began producing field radios in the catacombs beneath the Olympic Stadium. Soon thereafter, the stadium itself underwent a symbolic transformation: the five Olympic Rings linking the two pillars in front of the building's main entrance came down, to be replaced by a giant swastika.

No longer in need of Theodor Lewald as a liaison to the international sporting community, Reichssportführer Hans von Tschammer und Osten forced the half-Jewish official to withdraw from the IOC in 1937. To replace Lewald on the committee, Tschammer proposed (and the IOC accepted) Gen. Walther von Reichenau, a man who could be trusted to put a greater emphasis on the ties between German sport and military preparedness. Justifying the Reichenau appointment, Ritter von Halt praised the general to Baillet-Latour as "an excellent athlete" and "one of the best protectors of sport." In Reichenau's own view the best "protection" German Olympic sport could enjoy was a close and enduring association with the Wehrmacht.

SS Chief Heinrich Himmler had a competing vision of Nazi Germany's Olympic program—one that reflected the SS's growing rivalry with the military. On November 8, 1936, he announced that henceforth the SS, the elite black-shirted security service that was rapidly becoming a state within the state, intended to provide the personnel for at least one-half of Germany's Olympic teams.

But Himmler was not the only Nazi leader to discover a belated interest in the Olympics and competitive sports. Caught up in a Reich-wide sports mania following Germany's impressive showing in the Berlin games, virtually every Nazi Party organization, from the Hitler Youth to the Labor Service, set up an athletic club of its own. Hitler himself promised that Germany's team for the Tokyo Games of 1940 would be the largest of all the foreign contingents and would go to Japan accompanied by several shiploads of German Olympic fans.

By way of publicly demonstrating Nazism's ongoing co-optation of the German Olympic program, the Nazi Party Rally of September 1936 featured a march-in-review of Germany's top Olympic performers. Organized by the Strength Through Joy organization, this "Parade of German Sport" served to remind the party faithful that Germany's great athletic triumph in the month past was yet another gift of the Führer. Meanwhile, over in "Gapa," the Nazi-dominated town council voted to give honorary citizenship to Reichssport-führer Tschammer und Osten and *Gauleiter* Adolf Wagner for their role in helping to bring off the Winter Games. German army ski troops began training for war on the slopes overlooking the twin villages.

FAR from being put off by the manner in which the Nazi regime was casting the recent games as a celebration of Hitler and National Socialist values, the IOC continued to portray Hitler's Germany as a great steward of Olympic ideals. IOC President Baillet-Latour agreed with Avery Brundage that the Berlin games were "the best ever." In 1937 the committee awarded the Olympic Cup to the Strength Through Joy organization for its services to Olympism during the 1936 Games.

As we have seen, in 1939 the IOC also saw fit to award Leni Riefenstahl the Olympic Diploma for her film, *Olympia*. She could not actually accept the award in person until 1948. In autumn 1939 she was serving as a war correspondent with General von Reichenau and the German tenth Army in its invasion of Poland. Put off by the atrocities she witnessed at the front (at least so she later claimed), she soon returned to Berlin, where she worked on her new film, *Tiefland*, for which she used Gypsy concentration camp inmates as extras. When German troops entered Paris in June 1940 Riefenstahl sent Hitler a telegram expressing her "indescribable joy."

While the IOC remained headquartered in Switzerland, modern Olympism's intellectual center of gravity shifted to Germany following the death of Coubertin in 1937. The Olympic "renovator's" body was laid to rest in Lausanne (minus his heart, which, per his request, was placed in an urn at ancient Olympia), but his personal papers ended up at a new International Olympic Institute in Berlin. This occurred because Hitler, seeing propaganda value in a continued exploitation of the Frenchman's legacy, dispatched an emissary to the old man just before his death and managed thereby to secure the rights to Coubertin's literary remains. With the deathbed blessing of Coubertin, and also with support from Baillet-Latour, Carl Diem assumed the directorship of the new Olympic Institute.

From 1937 until 1944 Diem's institute published *Die Olympische Rundschau*, which succeeded Coubertin's *Revue Olympique* as the IOC's official publication. Diem also took administrative charge of Germany's excavation work at ancient Olympia, a project personally ordered by the Führer in 1936. Having become in effect the Olympic world's new Baron de Coubertin, Diem took it upon himself to commission a monument to the great Frenchman in 1938. The statue went up in the German spa town of Baden-Baden.

JAPAN, the country scheduled to hold both the Winter and Summer Games of 1940 (in Sapporo and Tokyo, respectively) invaded China in March 1937. Like Germany's invasion of Belgium in 1914, Japan's attack on China immediately cast into doubt its suitability as a host for the games. Once again the IOC found itself faced by intense international pressure to shift the games to some other country. And once again, groups in the United States took the lead in a global effort to move the Olympics, or to boycott them if they were held in Japan after all. Writing to Avery Brundage, fellow AOC member A. C. Gilbert warned that "the opposition we had on the Jewish question [apropos the German Games of 1936] is nothing as compared to the reaction which would result in an open announcement that the American Olympic team is going to participate in a set of Games in Japan, if they are actually at war." But Brundage, persisting in his insistence that "politics" must not be allowed to disrupt the Olympics, argued that the games must be held in Japan as scheduled, and with full American participation. "Whether our Committee or athletes like or dislike Japan is beside the point," he said, adding, "We stuck to this [position] in 1936 when there was agitation to have America withdraw from the Berlin Olympics, and we shall not change now." To buttress his case, he published a screed entitled "The Olympic Show Must Go On."

Unknown to Brundage, the Japanese generals who had presided over their nation's invasion of China were, like some of the Nazi zealots in the early 1930s, distinctly unenthusiastic about the whole idea of international Olympic competition. They condemned the games as incompatible with the intensely nationalistic and militaristic code of Bushido, Japan's warrior code. Under pressure from the military, the Japanese cabinet renounced Japan's claims to the 1940 Games on July 12, 1938. The government further announced that Japan would put on its own national "Olympics" strictly for members of the Japanese nation, and that no Japanese athletes would be allowed to participate in an Olympic contest held outside Japan.

In a distant echo of Cincinnati's bid to step in for Berlin when the German capital was disqualified for the (later cancelled) 1916 Olympic Games, New York City offered to take over the 1940 Summer Games as an adjunct to its upcoming World's Fair, where Eleanor Holm Jarrett was scheduled to appear as an "Aquamaid." The IOC, having nothing but bad memories of its association with World's Fairs (and, for that matter, with Jarrett), voted instead to move the 1940 Summer Games to Helsinki, and the Winter Games to St. Moritz. The Olympic show, as Brundage had said, must go on.

It quickly became evident, however, that the winter festival, at least, would not be able to proceed in its newly designated replacement site. The Swiss insisted on having no alpine skiing at the 1940 games because the IOC would not drop its ban on the participation of professional skiing instructors. Unwilling to forgo alpine skiing, the IOC decided to shop for yet another replacement venue. Astoundingly, the site they finally came up with in June 1939 was Garmisch-Partenkirchen. The committee, in other words, was willing to honor Nazi Germany with another Olympic festival *even after* the Kristallnacht pogrom and the German occupation of Czechoslovakia.

Germany's Olympic officials, for their part, were quite pleased to be so honored. A new Organizing Committee for the Fifth Winter Games hastily set about upgrading the facilities at Garmish-Partenkirchen, which had been taken over by the municipal government directly following the 1936 games. Ritter von Halt, who along with Diem took charge of planning for the games, looked forward to playing host once again to his old friend Avery Brundage. In July 1939 Halt sent an official invitation to Brundage in the latter's capacity as head of the AOC, adding that he would be "extremely grateful for your personal assistance in order to obtain that our invitation be accepted at the earliest possible delay [*sic*]."

Alas, there was to be no Winter Olympiad in Garmisch in 1940, or, for that matter, a summer festival in Helsinki (the Finnish-Soviet war of 1940 guaranteed that). On September 1, 1939, Germany invaded Poland, precipitating the horrors that would become World War II. As was the case during the Great War of 1914–18, the bloody confrontation on the battlefield ultimately preempted the anticipated zestful competition on the sporting field.

Again as in 1914, however, the IOC sought for a time to proceed as usual with the preparations for 1940, hoping the war might come to a speedy end. Brundage, for one, held out the hope that "someone big enough and powerful enough" would come along to end a war he considered "utterly futile and unnecessary." (Brundage, along with Charles Lindbergh, later joined the America First Committee, which insisted that the United States must stay out of the fight against Nazi Germany.)

With respect to the projected Garmisch games of 1940, Ritter von Halt informed Baillet-Latour on September 9, 1939, that a rapid German success in Poland, leading to a "definitive adjustment" of Germany's eastern frontier and hence "true world peace," should by all rights allow the games to go on as scheduled. He admitted, however, that he would have to check with Hitler to ascertain whether Germany's preparations for the games could proceed under the existing conditions.

Hitler soon decided that Germany had more important matters to attend to than the Olympics. In late October he ordered a suspension of Germany's preparations for the Winter Games. This came as a great disappointment to Halt, though he had to agree with the Führer that the youth of Germany had more urgent business before them than taking part in the games. As he wrote Brundage in January 1940:

> I cannot believe that your fine idea of a truce in honor of the Olympic Games will be feasible. Life and death of peoples being at stake at present, sport has to resign in some way. There are still greater sacrifices to be brought by the youth than only the happiness in sporting activity. We have got anew the conviction that England and France are laboring again under the old delusion that they will be happier when Germany will be cut to pieces, and so we cannot but defend ourselves to the last. Both the countries have compelled us to do it thoroughly so that they

may learn to adapt themselves beside Germany. After this we trust that peace will prevail again all over the world.

In August 1940, following Germany's defeat of France and the opening of its air campaign against Britain, Halt expressed to Brundage his conviction that Germany's domination of Europe would be a great boon to Olympism. "We count with a rapid and complete victory although Germany is prepared to hold the struggle for any thinkable time. A new Europe will also give a better foundation for the Olympic movement."

Like Halt, Carl Diem sought during World War II—as he had in the 1914–18 conflict—to make sport a vital part of the German arsenal. Once it became clear that there would be no Winter Olympic Games in Garmisch in 1940, he put forth a plan for a "Greater German Olympia" designed to link the heritage of the ancient games with the nationalistic German gymnastics festivals and the German *Kampfspiele* of the 1920s. Planned to be held in four-year intervals, this "German Olympiad" would move from city to city across the Reich and be open only to athletes of "German blood." Diem's scheme never got beyond the planning stage, but it bore similarities to Hitler's own dream of a German-dominated Olympic festival, and we can safely assume that something like it would have come to pass had the Germans won the war.

Nazi plans for the future of the Olympic movement were also evident in a set of demands that Tschammer and Diem presented to IOC president Baillet-Latour in mid-1940, following the Wehrmacht's successful conquest of the Low Countries, including Baillet-Latour's Belgium. (Germany's invasion of Belgium, incidentally, was led by none other than the Reich's new man in the IOC, General von Reichenau.) The idea here was to ensure, as Tschammer put the matter to Hitler, that the IOC and all future Olympic Games would be "reoriented" in ways that reflected "the dominant position that German sport has attained across the board, particularly in the Olympic domain." When Diem met with Baillet-Latour in the summer of 1940 he informed him that London, which had been tapped by the IOC to host the games in 1944, must be made to step aside so that either Berlin or Rome could assume the host role. More important, with respect to the future composition and functioning of the IOC, the Germans insisted that the national governments be allowed to appoint, and to recall, their delegates without consultation with the international committee. Germany further insisted that

Berlin must control the IOC appointments from all the new states the Reich had managed to place under its "protection." Confident that the next IOC president would be a German, Diem stated that henceforth the IOC must be run according to the Nazi *Führerprinzip* (leadership principle).

Although these demands amounted to a total emasculation of the IOC, Baillet-Latour agreed to them, at least in principle. In practice, he managed to put off their possible implementation by putting the IOC "on vacation" for the duration of the war. The Germans had to be content with an assurance that once they had finished with their military business, they would thoroughly control the IOC and the Olympic movement.

Because Baillet-Latour had been so useful to them in connection with the 1936 games, and so compliant concerning their demanded future "reorientation" of the IOC, the Germans were genuinely saddened when the Belgian died suddenly of a stroke in January 1942. Hitler sent a delegation led by Halt and Diem to Baillet-Latour's funeral in German-occupied Brussels. Halt deposited a wreath from Hitler and Tschammer, while Diem left a similar memorial on behalf of the GOC. Halt made clear to Baillet-Latour's widow that she would be well taken care of by the German military governor of Belgium and by the Brussels branch of the Deutsche Bank (on whose board of directors Halt still sat).

As the war dragged on and expanded into a vast global conflict, the Nazi Reich abandoned an early wartime program involving "international" athletic contests among Germany's allies and a few neutral countries. Diem presided over "International Winter Sports Weeks" in Garmisch-Partenkirchen in 1940 and 1941, but after the invasion of the Soviet Union in June 1941 the Reich's alpine athletes focused on military skiing, not slalom and downhill.

Diem increasingly devoted his time to writing newspaper articles and giving inspirational speeches revolving around an old pet theme of his: the notion that sport in general, and Olympic sport in particular, constituted perfect preparation for the rigors of military conflict. Diem believed that the Germans had learned this lesson better than anyone else. Germany's victories in Poland, Norway, the Low Countries, and France, he claimed, had been nurtured on the playing fields of the Reich. The fact that the 1936 Olympic gymnastics champion, Alfred Schwarzmann, distinguished himself as a paratrooper in the early fighting illustrated, in Diem's view, the close relationship between sports and war: "Olympic victor and hero in battle at the same time.

. . . Sports-loving officers and sports-loving leaders! . . . Thus it came to the storming of Poland, Norway, Holland, Belgium and France—to the triumphant race to a better Europe!" In a speech he delivered in occupied Paris on "The Olympic Idea in the New Europe," Diem claimed that National Socialist ideology and German military strength were direct legacies of ancient Sparta (a view he shared with Hitler). In contrast to his earlier scheme for "racially pure" Germanic Olympics, in his Paris speech he hazarded the proposition that in future Olympic Games the white race should *not* exclude other races, though he justified this idea on purely racist grounds: "Only weaklings fear competition with other races. What the white race may lack in terms of innate physical endowments will be compensated for by higher intelligence and disciplined preparation. . . . He who wants to impress the world must be prepared to fight against the rest of the world."

Germany, of course, was now literally fighting against the rest of the world, or against most of it anyway, and in 1943–44 Diem traveled around Nazi-occupied Europe giving speeches to Wehrmacht soldiers on "Heroism in Sport" and the "Olympic Legacies" of iron discipline, strict obedience, national pride, and willingness for self-sacrifice. "Death is beautiful when a man experiences it as a hero," he told the soldiers.

The part in his speeches about self-sacrifice was becoming increasingly germane in late 1944 and early 1945, as the Wehrmacht began retreating back to German soil, leaving tens of thousands of fallen comrades behind and girding for the loss of legions more in the defense of the homeland.

In preparation for that final defense, the Nazi Reich, with its regular military forces stretched to the limit, established so-called Volkssturm battalions—ragtag units made up of the very young and the very old. One of these units was Volkssturm Battalion 3/107, which was stationed at the Reichssportfeld. It was headed by none other than Ritter von Halt, who had become Germany's new Sportführer in March 1943 following the death of Tschammer und Osten. Carl Diem served as one of Halt's adjutants. Another adjutant was Guido von Mengden, the former GOC press secretary. On November 12, 1944, Volkssturm Battalion 3/107 swore an oath to Hitler in the middle of the Olympic Stadium.

On March 18, 1945, Carl Diem delivered one of his patent inspirational speeches to a group of Hitler Youth attached to the Volkssturm unit at the Reichssportfeld. By this time the Americans had already crossed the Rhine, and Red Army soldiers stood on the Oder River some seventy kilometers east of Berlin. Diem's speech took place in the Kuppelsaal of the Sportforum, where in 1936 Olympic fencers had crossed swords. As he had in his pep talks to the Wehrmacht, Diem likened the Olympic spirit to the self-sacrificial fanaticism of the small band of Spartans at the Battle of Thermopylae (480 B.C.), who preferred death to surrender to the numerically superior Persian invaders. The difference between this Hitler Youth speech and his earlier talks to the Wehrmacht, of course, is that now Diem was addressing adolescent boys who faced an entirely hopeless situation. The scenario he conjured up for these teenagers was eerily reminiscent of the "hero's death" scene in his *Olympic Youth* drama of 1936. But again there was a big difference: this time the "martyrdom" would be for real.

On April 20, 1945, Hitler's fifty-sixth birthday, the Red Army attacked Berlin proper, and in a matter of days Soviet units reached the Reichssport-feld on the western edge of the city. The former Olympic complex had been transformed into a veritable fortress, replete with its own flak battery. A wall next to the Dietrich-Eckart-Theater served as an execution site for Wehrmacht soldiers and Volkssturm personnel who showed any signs of cowardice or defeatism. Between August 12 and April 14, 1945, SS execution squads shot more than two hundred "traitors" at this site, many of them young boys.

Red Army soldiers broke into the Olympic Stadium on April 25. This was not a key target for them, their main preoccupation being the core of the city, and above all Hitler's bunker under the Reich Chancellery. Three days later the Hitler Youth brigades in the area were ordered to take back the stadium at all costs. The boys did manage briefly to dislodge the Russians, but lost more than two thousand dead in the process. A few days later Berlin surrendered to the Soviets.

Diem, who had not witnessed the slaughter at the stadium because of a minor foot injury, walked the Olympic grounds directly after the German capitulation. Later, in his autobiography, he recalled what he had seen and felt on this grim occasion: "The field where the Olympic youth had once assembled, the buildings and monumental grounds that had once delighted the world, had become a deadly battlefield, revealing nothing but sickening remains and gruesome debris wherever one looked. . . . It struck me that not even the most fanciful poet could have imagined such a mad contradiction." This "mad contradiction" was in part of course a direct product of the mind-set that had always posited a glorious harmony between the Olympic spirit and heroic martyrdom.

THE leaders of Nazi Germany's Olympic movement fared somewhat differently in the immediate post–World War II era, but many of them went on to play important roles in West Germany's Olympic establishment in the 1950s and 1960s. This development was part of a broader pattern of continuity in leadership personnel between the Third Reich and the Federal Republic of Germany under Bonn's conservative first chancellor, Konrad Adenauer.

Theodor Lewald, who had spent the years since his forced retirement from the IOC in quiet retirement, was too old at the end of the war to return to active service in the German sports community. Sadly, he never came to grips with his own deeply problematical role in helping to organize the Nazi games of 1936. To the very end he continued to insist that these games had been entirely free of interference from the Hitler regime, for which imagined achievement he took personal credit. As he wrote Britain's Lord Aberdare on February 22, 1946: "You yourself have attested to the fact that under the surprisingly difficult conditions occasioned by Hitler's seizure of power I managed to carry out the 1936 games in a blameless fashion. The Olympic laws and regulations were followed to the letter. The IOC acknowledged this when it unanimously awarded the 1940 Winter Games to Garmisch-Partenkirchen. You can imagine how grateful I was for the recognition of the fact that I had been able to ward off all Hitler's attempts to change the character of the Games."

Lord Aberdare, Sigfrid Edstrøm, Avery Brundage, and other former Olympic colleagues helped keep their old friend Lewald materially afloat under the harsh conditions prevailing in Germany immediately after the war, sending him provisions and money. He died in April 1947, at age eighty-seven.

A year before he died Lewald wrote a letter in support of his colleague Carl Diem's campaign to clear his name with the Allied occupation authorities. Lewald declared that Diem, in private conversations with him, had "never made any bones about his rejection of National Socialism. His organizational talent and artistic sensibility had much to do with the success of the 1936 Olympic Games."

Diem did not rely solely on obfuscating affidavits from Lewald to airbrush his complicated relationship with the Nazi regime. In a questionnaire he was obliged to complete for the British military government, whose occupation zone in postwar Berlin included the Reichssportfeld, Diem claimed not only that he had never been a member of the Nazi Party (which was true), but also that he had never worked for any of the party's organizations. The second part of this statement was patently false, for his association with the Reichsausschuss für Leibesübungen qualified as work for a Nazi-run agency, and he had helped send Volkssturm youth to a needless death at the end of World War II.

If anyone in authority had objections to Diem's creative interpretation of his résumé, this did not prevent the now-sixty-four-year-old sports functionary from picking up his career almost seamlessly in the postwar era. In 1947 he was allowed to become the first rector of the Deutsche Sporthochschule in Cologne, which he helped to found. He served in this capacity until his death in 1962. Diem also became the head of a new International Olympic Academy in Olympia, Greece, which helped perpetuate Germany's long tradition of scholarship on the ancient games. Following Germany's formal division in 1949, Diem assisted in the establishment of a new National Olympic Committee for West Germany, on whose executive board he sat until 1952. In 1948 the IOC invited Diem to the London games as a special guest, the only German to be so honored (no German athletes competed in 1948). Four years later he led a German youth delegation to the games in Helsinki, the first postwar Summer Olympiad in which Germans participated. He was also a member of the German delegation at the 1956 games in Melbourne, Australia. In 1957 the IOC awarded him its highest honor, the Olympic Order. A year later, on Diem's seventy-fifth birthday, Willi Daume, the head of West Germany's National Olympic Committee (and a member of Germany's field handball team in the 1936 games) officially recognized the veteran functionary as "the most creative and all-encompassing personality in recent German sports history."

Like Lewald, Diem seems never to have had any second thoughts about the role he had played in the sports establishment of the Third Reich. On the contrary he felt pride for a job well done, and he continued to insist he was free of any moral taint. As he wrote in a letter in May 1946: "I remained true to myself, rejected any compromises with the Nazis, chose to forgo teaching and administrative opportunities [in the Third Reich] rather than to crawl on my knees before the regime."

When Diem died in 1962 he was heralded in West Germany as "Mr. Olympia." All across the country, sports facilities and schools adopted his name. The street in Cologne on which the Deutsche Sporthochschule stands was renamed "Carl-Diem-Weg." It remains so named today.

Karl Ritter von Halt also managed to expunge the brown stain on his vest and to reemerge in the postwar era as one of West Germany's most powerful sports officials, but his political resurrection took rather longer than Diem's. Believing himself politically and morally unmarked by his work in the Third Reich, Halt turned himself in to the Russian occupation authorities in Berlin in May 1945. This was a mistake: He spent the next four and one-half years in various Soviet internment camps, most notably in Buchenwald, the former Nazi concentration camp near Weimar that the Soviets utilized to lock away their own political enemies.

Learning of Halt's fate, Olympic colleagues like Brundage and Edström tried to free their old friend, but they had no leverage with the Russians, who had not even had a team in Berlin in '36. In early 1947 news reached the outside world that Halt had been one of the victims of a deadly epidemic at Buchenwald; his death was reported in German newspapers and over the radio. Diem duly informed Brundage of the demise of "our dear friend," who had been "united with us over decades in the fight for truth, beauty and honor." Fortunately for the sake of truth, if not necessarily beauty and honor, the reports of Halt's demise were soon revealed as erroneous; it seems that a certain "Herr von Anhalt" had died in Buchenwald, and the Soviets had gotten the names confused.

Upon his release from Buchenwald in 1950, Halt had to go through a denazification hearing, but with testimonials to his supposed "anti-Nazi" posture from Diem, Edström, and Brundage, he had no difficulty securing his official clearance certificate (a document the Germans mockingly called a *Persilschein*, after a popular brand of soap powder). Diem even claimed that Halt had worked hard to get Jews admitted to Germany's Olympic teams in 1936. Halt's rehabilitation came at a time when West German officials, who had recently taken over the denazification process from the Allies, were anxious to achieve "closure" relative to the Nazi past and to get on with the tasks of rebuilding the German economy and securing international recognition for the Federal Republic as the only legitimate German state.

For his part Halt now felt ready to "return to Olympia"—to resume his old career as a key player in the German and Olympic sports establishments. In fact, like his German IOC colleague the Duke of Mecklenburg, he had never lost his seat on the committee, and, after overcoming some objections from the Allied High Commission for Germany, which raised questions about his Nazi past, he was able in May 1951 to resume attending meetings of the committee. In 1958, on Avery Brundage's recommendation, he became a member of the IOC's Executive Commission, its governing body. Meanwhile, on the domestic sports front, Halt used his IOC clout to succeed Mecklenburg as president of West Germany's National Olympic Committee in January 1951. He ran the committee with an iron hand for a decade thereafter, presiding over West Germany's admission to the Olympic fold. When he died in 1964, the authorities in Garmisch-Partenkirchen named a new sports complex in his honor.

AS we have seen, after World War I the defeated and discredited Germans had been excluded from two Olympiads, those of 1920 and 1924, but in the wake of World War II and the collapse of the Third Reich they had only to sit out the 1948 Winter Games in St. Moritz and the Summer Games in London. They did not miss much in either case. The St. Moritz games were poorly attended and racked by disputes over professionalism among the ice hockey players. The London games, held against a backdrop of postwar Britain's grim austerity, featured a bare-bones Olympic Village thrown together by superannuated RAF pilots, and food portions for the participating athletes that barely matched the rations allotted to industrial workers. Due to inept handling, the Olympic flame briefly went out upon reaching England after its relay odyssey from Olympia.

Germany was a participant in the 1952 Oslo Winter Games and that year's Summer Games in Helsinki. The "Germany" in question, however, consisted solely of West Germany. East Germany, though it now had a national Olympic committee of its own, was excluded through the efforts of Halt and other West German officials. They received crucial backing in this endeavor from IOC president Edström, as well as from Brundage, who went on to succeed Edström as president of the committee in mid-1952.

West Germany's admission to the Oslo Winter Games in 1952 came over the strong opposition of many Norwegians, who harbored bitter memories of the German occupation of their land during World War II. As a condition of its participation in Oslo, Germany was not allowed to send to Norway any athletes or officials who had been part of the 1936 games. Thus Halt and Diem had to stay home. Helsinki imposed no similar restrictions on Germany, resulting not only in the attendance of Halt and Diem but also in the participation of the gymnast (and wartime paratrooper) Alfred Schwarzmann, the only German athlete from 1936 to compete in a subsequent Olympiad.

AT the time of Germany's return to Olympic competition, Berlin, Nazi Germany's erstwhile "Olympic City," was a shadow of its former self, littered with ruins, divided into four occupation zones, and, from the Western perspective, sadly isolated deep within the Soviet-dominated German Democratic Republic. Under these conditions Berlin's recent Olympic glory already seemed a distant memory.

One event that helped to reawaken that memory, and certainly to cheer up the Berliners, was the return of Jesse Owens to the Olympic Stadium on August 22, 1951. It was the first time he had been back to the scene of his greatest triumphs. Owens stopped in Berlin on a European tour with the Harlem Globetrotters. For his historic return to Berlin, Owens pulled out all the theatrical stops, arriving by helicopter in the middle of the stadium and then taking a "victory lap" around the track. A crowd of 75,000 cheered wildly. When he finished his lap, Owens gave a brief speech, calling on the Germans "to stand fast with us in the fight for freedom and democracy, under the protection of Almighty God." West Berlin's acting mayor, Walter Schreiber, stepped up to Jesse and said, "Hitler wouldn't shake your hand. I give you both hands." The crowd, which included thousands of people from Communist East Berlin, roared again. The Berliners' response to Owens, marked by a mixture of adoration and gratitude for his very presence in a time of trial, anticipated the outpouring of affection for President John F. Kennedy on the occasion of his "Ich bin ein Berliner" speech of June 1963. (Following Owens's death in 1980, West Berlin named a street leading to the stadium Jesse-Owens-Strasse.)

Owens's triumphal appearance at the stadium had an inspirational coda. According to a story he related three years later, he was heading to his dressing room after his speech when a young boy approached him for his autograph. The boy turned out to be the son of Lutz Long, the great German long jumper whom Owens had defeated in 1936, and come to regard as a friend. On signing the boy's autograph book, Owens learned for the first time that his German friend had been killed fighting in Sicily during the war. "We have to talk," said Owens to Long's son. "You and me have to talk and get to know each other." This encounter may or may not have played out exactly the way Owens recalled it, but in subsequent years Owens did maintain contact with Long's family, and in 1964, when he returned to Berlin again to film scenes for *The Jesse Owens Story*, he made sure that Long's son got a part in the movie.

JESSE OWENS experienced a host of frustrations and humiliations in the immediate aftermath of the 1936 Olympics. Because he chose to return to America rather than to continue competing in a series of postgames exhibition track meets around Europe put on by the AAU, that body summarily expelled him, ending his amateur career. Having decided in any case to turn professional, Owens soon discovered that the only way he could make any money was by participating in circuslike stunts such as racing against thoroughbred horses, cars, greyhounds, and even boxer Joe Louis (whom Owens was careful to let win). The money he made from these spectacles came back to haunt him because some of his black fans accused him of playing the "Negro-Clown," while the U.S. government slapped a lien on his 1936 earnings for failure to pay sufficient taxes. His effort to cash in on his Olympic gold was undoubtedly one of the factors in a decision by the AAU to give its Sullivan Memorial Award for the best amateur athlete of the year in 1936 to Glenn Morris rather than to Jesse.

JESSE OWENS'S sad fate after 1936 can be seen as part of a broader picture of ongoing racial prejudice in which even Owens's great victories in Berlin, and those of his fellow black Olympians, were reconciled with the prevailing racist views in America. The idea that blacks and other "primitive" peoples owed whatever athletic successes they might achieve was hardly unique to the Nazis. In the United States a basic shift in the thinking about connections between race and athletic prowess was under way. The prevailing view for much of the early twentieth century had held that white sporting successes derived from a combination of superior minds *and* superior bodies. The dominance in the early Olympic Games by whites of northern European extraction buttressed this perspective. In boxing, repeated victories over whites by black fighters like Australia's Peter Jackson and America's Jack Johnson generated some speculation about "inherent" Negro advantages in that brutal sport, but since blacks could compete only against other blacks in most athletic arenas the myth of white athletic supremacy went largely unchallenged.

This began to change in the early 1930s, due largely to the strong performances in the 1932 Olympic Games by the American blacks Eddie Tolan and Ralph Metcalfe (sprints) and Edward Gordon (long jump). Now some white (and even some black) commentators began to argue that blacks possessed certain anatomical advantages over whites that "explained" their recent successes in sprinting and jumping.

In America the main impact of the 1936 games in the area of racial think-ing was to harden such pseudoscientific nostrums and to give them wide cur-rency among sports commentators, officials, and coaches. Avery Brundage wrote that "one could see, particularly with Jesse Owens, how the Negroes could excel in track events. Their muscle structure lends itself to this sort of competition." Albert McGall, Yale's track coach, proposed that a projecting heelbone commonly found among blacks literally gave them leverage over white sprinters. Dean Cromwell, assistant coach of America's Olympic track team in 1936, observed in 1941: "The Negro excels in the events he does because he is closer to the primitive than the white man. It was not that long ago that his ability to spring and jump was a life-and-death matter to him." Even Owens's coach, Larry Snyder, proposed that the success of "his boy" and of other black sprinters derived from "the striation of the muscles . . . and the cell structure of the nervous system." It also helped, Snyder said, that Negro athletes like Owens were willing to take orders from their white coaches: "Most colored boys take to coaching very readily. They have perfect confi-dence in their coach . . . and are willing and glad to leave their training, their form, and their perfection of their technique up to him."

In a postgames essay entitled "The Real Winners in the 1936 Olympic Games," Charles D. Snyder, a professor of experimental physiology at Johns Hopkins University, insisted that the victories of the American blacks in Berlin did not necessarily undermine the doctrine of overall white supremacy on the athletic field. "Perhaps in the short races," he wrote, "some anatomi-cal advantages of bone or muscle structure gives the black man an advantage over the white. In any case, we must remember that the Negro boys were trained by white men in the white men's institutions." Moreover, the profes-sor went on, if one assessed national performances in 1936 on the basis of population size rather than on the sheer number of medals won, the small northern and central European countries with homogenous white popula-tions were still the clear winners. The best performers, he said, represented "the homelands of what remnants there are of the 'once great northern races,'" while the worst performers were "on the whole those [countries] whose populations represent the greatest racial mixtures."

While in America (as elsewhere) the 1936 Olympic Games helped to buttress an emerging stereotype of blacks as anatomically advantaged in cer-tain forms of athletic endeavor, they did little to break down old stereotypes of Negroes as inherently weak in character and intellect. Blacks might be talented at sprinting and jumping, the thinking went, but they would never be able to surpass whites in contests requiring stamina, discipline, team-work, and mental agility. Thus blacks would never excel, it was said, in sports like basketball and long-distance running. It would take many more black successes in the Olympics and other amateur contests, as well as the long-overdue integration of American professional sports, to undercut this dogma—but of course even then to undercut it only partially, and only, perhaps, in polite public discourse. As late as 1988 sports commentator Jimmy "the Greek" Snyder was famously dropped from the CBS show *The NFL Today* after declaring that blacks were better athletes than whites because they were "bred to be that way since the days of slavery." Following the firing thousands of viewers called the network to say that they agreed with Jimmy.

JESSE OWENS might have suffered humiliating treatment in the years fol-lowing the 1936 games, but at least he survived the horrors of World War II, which is more than one can say for many of his fellow Olympic competitors. Between 1939 and 1945 twenty-five members of the 1936 Polish Olympic team died fighting in the war, in the Polish resistance, or in concentration camps. Twenty-five German medal winners in the 1936 games died in World War II, thirteen of them on the Eastern Front.

Most of the German Olympians of 1936 who survived the war lived in quiet anonymity in subsequent years, holding menial jobs as construction workers, railwaymen, waiters, and bartenders. According to the equestrian champion Gotthardt Handrick, who (atypically) went on to prosper as the owner of West Germany's largest Mercedes dealership, many of the '36 Ger-man Olympians became alcoholics or drug abusers in later years. "By and large," Handrick says, "I'm afraid that for most German participants the Olympics were an experience which, if they didn't possess an excellent bun-dle of nerves, later on gave them a lot of difficulty to adjust to." Of course this assessment could apply to the postglory days of a great many Olympians, and indeed to the careers of high-performing athletes in general.

THE surviving German Olympic veterans of 1936 were fast approaching old age by the time their country—or more accurately, the western half of their former country—next got the opportunity to host an Olympic festival. In 1966 the IOC voted to award the 1972 Summer Games to Munich—partly, it seems, as consolation for its decision a year earlier to allow East Germany to field its own team in future Olympiads, which ran sharply counter to Bonn's claim to represent all of Germany.*

Thirty-six years may have separated Germany's two twentieth-century Summer Olympiads, but the 1972 Munich games were conducted very much in the shadow of the 1936 Berlin Olympics. The Munich organizers were determined that everything about their games should be different from those of 1936, reflecting their conviction that an "entirely new Germany" was hosting the festival.

For this reason the Munich organizers were not amused when Leni Riefenstahl, who had been banned from making films in postwar Germany because of her work for the Nazis during the Third Reich, showed up in Munich as a photojournalist for the British newspaper the *Sunday Times*. Nor were the German authorities pleased when theater owners in Munich took advantage of Riefenstahl's presence to show her film *Olympia* all over town during the '72 Games.‡

Riefenstahl notwithstanding, there was not much around Munich in 1972 that might have prompted Olympic visitors to draw parallels with the games of the Third Reich. In contrast to the neoclassical Olympic buildings of 1936, the Munich stadium, with its signature tentlike glass roof, represented a tour

---

*For the games of 1956 through 1964, Germany had had single Olympic teams combining athletes from both West and East Germany. The joint teams participated under a common flag— a black-gold-yellow tricolor inscribed with the five Olympic rings—and used the same hymn, the "Ode to Joy" section of Beethoven's *Ninth Symphony*. West and East Germany fielded separate teams from 1968 through 1988, returning to a single squad following German reunification in 1990. The bitter battle between the two Germanys over representation at the Olympics during the period of division constitutes a complicated and fascinating story of its own.

‡Other Olympic host cities, as well as the IOC, bore no similar grudge against the filmmaker. The Helsinki organizing committee offered her a contract to make a film about the 1952 games—she declined—while the IOC, and especially Brundage, remained on quite cordial terms with her throughout the fifties and sixties. In later years she reinvented herself as a photographer of African tribal peoples, particularly the Nuba and Masai. In her seventies she took up scuba diving and underwater photography. But throughout this period she was dogged by her earlier role as "Hitler's filmmaker" and by charges that she remained trapped in a Nazi-era mindset. In the penultimate year of her long life—she died in 2003 at age 101—she underwent a brief and inconclusive investigation in Germany involving accusations of race-hatred crimes.

de force of architectural modernism. The designers, the Stuttgart firm of Günther Behnisch and Partners, said their plan aimed to create "an atmosphere of openness, transparency, and clarity" rather than one of rigid monumentality. Werner March, the designer of Berlin's Olympic Stadium of 1936, had also submitted a design for the 1972 stadium, but even though his new conception was quite bold and modernistic, the Munich organizers were not about to reemploy the man who had worked for Adolf Hitler.

Although the new Munich stadium was undeniably large, and breathtakingly costly, in general the organizers strove to avoid "gigantism" and grandeur in favor of a low-key democratic transparency. Hoping to discourage nationalistic displays during the games, Willi Daume and company chose not to bedeck the town with national flags, preferring instead pastel-colored Olympic banners, which flew everywhere. To drive home the idea that the new Germany was not a police state, the Olympic security forces wore tasteful light-blue outfits and carried no weapons. As Daume put the matter: "We shied away from pathos and heroic exaggeration. Our colors were those of peace and relaxed cheerfulness. . . . The Munich Olympic Games were supposed to be embedded in the play of architecture, landscape and color. . . . In general, we tried to represent not the host country, but Olympic sports."

At first this strategy seemed to work. There were the usual complaints about price gouging, but otherwise visitors were impressed with the kinder and gentler Germany on display in the Bavarian capital. "The first thing you felt on arriving in Munich was this utter determination of the Germans, whether they be Olympic officials, policemen, journalists, or indeed the general population of Munich, to wipe away the past," wrote a reporter for the *Independent Television News* of Britain. "We were totally overwhelmed by the sense that this was the new Germany. It was a massive attempt, and it hit you right away that the Germans were determined to appear open and modern and shorn of their past." Vastly relieved that all was going so well, German radio boasted of a "wave of international praise" emanating from Munich: "Here is a new, a changed Germany, presenting itself to the world—a Germany of which nothing is reminiscent of the National Socialist dictatorship that politically misused the Olympics thirty-six years ago in Berlin. Munich need not fear comparisons."

Then came the horrific murder of eleven Israeli athletes and coaches on September 5, 1972, day eleven of the Munich Olympiad. The attack on the Israelis was carried out by Black September, an arm of the Palestinian Liberation Organization's Fatah group. Now the prevailing images emanating from Munich were those of masked terrorists holding Jewish Olympians hostage in the Olympic Village, followed some twenty hours later by grim-faced Bavarian officials announcing that an attempted (and, though they didn't admit it, horribly botched) rescue operation at Fürstenfeldbruck airfield had resulted in fifteen deaths—all nine Israeli hostages (two Israelis had been murdered earlier), five of the terrorists, and one German policeman. No one officially said it, but everyone thought the same thing: Once again, Jews have been murdered on German soil.

One of the bitterest ironies of the tragedy of September 5 is that it derived in part from the Munich organizers' well-meaning effort to distinguish their games from those of the Berlin games of 1936. Whereas the 1936 Olympic Village was situated on a heavily guarded army base a good distance from central Berlin, the Munich Village lay right next to the Olympic Stadium and well within the city limits. It was encircled by a six-foot-high security fence whose gates were locked at midnight but not guarded around the clock. By day entry to the village was almost as easy for autograph hunters as it was for athletes and officials. After midnight athletes who had gone out carousing in town could reenter the village by simply climbing over the fence.

This was the method employed by the terrorists. At 4:00 A.M. on September 5, they approached the fence and encountered no one except a group of drunken American athletes returning to their beds after a night on the town. The Americans and the terrorists, who were dressed like athletes, helped one another climb over the fence. When questioned after the tragedy about the lax security arrangements, Bavarian prime minister Alfons Goppel pointed out that, because of its past, Germany had to be very careful about any displays of uniformed authority: "*Man wollte eben nicht den Polizeistaat demonstrieren*" ("One simply didn't want to look like a police state").

On the day after the murders, at a memorial service for the dead Israeli athletes, Avery Brundage, still president of the IOC, announced that the Munich games would go on as scheduled after a single day of mourning. By way of justifying this decision, he (with breathtaking insensitivity) lumped the murder of the Israelis together with a threat by the black African states to boycott the Munich Olympics unless Rhodesia were excluded, a threat to which the IOC had succumbed. Having given in to the "naked political blackmail" of the Africans, Brundage said, the IOC could not buckle to Arab terrorism: "The Games Must Go On."

Brundage's statement shocked many observers, but it should not have. After all, it was what the man had been saying over the past forty years with respect to "threats" to the Olympic movement, most notably the boycott effort preceding the German games of 1936. His "the games must go on" refrain was yet another echo of the Nazi Olympics. Brundage stepped down as IOC president at the conclusion of the ill-starred Munich games. He died three years later while vacationing in Garmisch-Partenkirchen, a place he had come to love since his first visit there during the Winter Games of 1936.

In his last speech as IOC president, delivered at the committee's Munich session in 1972, Brundage had expressed pride in the games' global expansion during his twenty-year tenure in office, while lamenting their growing cost and commercialization. True to form, he inveighed against those who would lower Olympism's barriers to athletic professionalism or yield ground in the ongoing battle against "political interference" of any kind. He also took a parting shot at the Winter Games, which he said had become "seriously ill" in Innsbruck in 1964, "degenerated into a half-dozen world championships" in Grenoble in 1968, and cost the Japanese a whopping seven hundred million dollars in 1972. Concluding his Munich talk, Brundage said his fond wish was that the winter festival, now the target of "derision and ridicule in the world press," would "receive a decent burial at Denver in 1976." (Denver backed out of the '76 games, leaving Innsbruck to jump into the breach at the last minute. We can safely surmise that the Winter Olympics' further evolution through the scandal-wracked Salt Lake City Games of 2002 would not have caused Brundage to amend his hostility toward this IOC "mistake," though it is interesting to note that in all his denunciations of the winter festivals he always exempted the Garmisch games of 1936.)

EIGHT years after the Munich games, in another time of great political turmoil, the United States took a much different stance than it had in 1936 on the question of Olympic sanctity. As most adult Americans recall, America decided to boycott the Moscow games of 1980 as a protest against the Soviet Union's invasion of Afghanistan in 1979. Some sixty-one other nations, including West Germany, which was pressured hard by Washington to follow its example, also stayed away from Moscow. (On the other hand Britain, France, and Italy elected to send teams to the Soviet capital, much to Washington's dismay.)

As it happened, America's Olympic leaders at this juncture were actually no more enthusiastic about a boycott of Moscow in 1980 than Avery Brundage had been about possibly boycotting Berlin in 1936. The American officials, however, came under intense pressure from various quarters at home to reject Moscow's invitation, and the proboycott forces of 1980 invoked the experience of 1936 as part of their reasoning. "The Olympic Games gave the Nazis a period of respectability and glory which they otherwise could not have achieved," argued the Anti-Defamation League of the B'Nai B'rith. Like Nazi Germany, said the league, Soviet Russia was guilty of systematic "ethnic and religious discrimination. . . . Those wavering about a 1980 decision have learned nothing from the shameful 1936 Berlin Olympics experience." Similarly, James Burnham, writing in the *National Review*, argued that the impending Moscow games represented a propaganda opportunity for the Kremlin reminiscent of the Nazi games.

In the end, the decisive pressure on the American Olympic officials came from the Carter administration, which made a Soviet pullout in Afghanistan a precondition for American participation in the Moscow games. In January 1980 President Jimmy Carter personally wrote to USOC president Robert Kane, instructing him that if the Soviet Union did not vacate Afghanistan within one month, the American committee must try to get the IOC to move the games out of Moscow; failing that, the United States must work with other Western nations to stage a crushing boycott of the Soviet games. Such a "powerful signal of world outrage," Carter said, could "not be hidden from the Soviet people" and would "reverberate around the globe," perhaps deterring "future aggression." If America's Olympic establishment did not toe Washington's line, Carter threatened to withhold government financial support for the Olympic team and to bar U.S. athletes from traveling to Moscow.

Carter himself did not trot out the "analogy" of 1936 in justifying the boycott plan in 1980, but his secretary of state, Cyrus Vance, certainly did. He declared: "I look back to the 1936 Games, when I was in college, and I think in hindsight it was a mistake for us to have attended." Vice President Walter Mondale voiced similar sentiments. Speaking to the USOC on the eve of its vote on the Moscow games, Mondale insisted that the 1936 games offered a valuable lesson that must not be ignored. The American athletes of 1980 "may have been born a full generation after the Berlin Olympics," he said, "but as their advisers and trustees, you bear the responsibility of linking that history to their duty. For the story of Hitler's rise is more than a study in tyranny. It is also a chronicle of the free world's failure—of opportunities not seized, aggression not opposed, appeasement not condemned." (It was Mondale too who strenuously opposed curtailing U.S. grain shipments to Russia as punishment for the Afghan invasion. Such a tactic, he said, would only hurt American farmers.)

So what did the partial boycott of the Moscow games actually accomplish? The sixty-two nation no-show certainly did detract from the luster of the 1980 games, but it did not induce Moscow to change its policy in Afghanistan, nor is there any evidence that this move weakened the Kremlin internally. As for the Carter administration's references to the situation in 1936, this analogy seems rather off the mark. Whereas a large-scale boycott of the 1936 games could quite possibly have weakened Hitler at home—his three-year-old regime needed a splendid Olympic success to enhance its status in world opinion and with the German people at home—the 1980 boycott proved to be a poor substitute for harder sanctions that might in fact have gotten Moscow's attention. (That rejected embargo on U.S. grain exports comes to mind.) Ultimately the primary consequence of the boycott of the Moscow games was the eastern bloc's counterboycott of the Los Angeles games in 1984.

As in 1936 America's Olympic athletes had argued passionately against the boycott of the Moscow games, as had many former Olympians. Among the latter, interestingly enough, was Jesse Owens. Although extremely ill with the lung cancer that would end his life in March 1980 (he was a heavy smoker), Owens, after initially expressing his support for the boycott, came out against it on grounds that it would be cruel to the athletes. Sounding much like Avery Brundage, he wrote: "The road to the Olympics doesn't lead to Moscow. It leads to no city, no country. It goes far beyond Lake Placid or Moscow, ancient Greece or Nazi Germany. The road to the Olympics leads, in the end, to the best within us."

IF the ghosts of 1936 hovered in the background when Washington made its decision to boycott Moscow, those brown-sheeted ghouls were smack in the foreground when, in 1993, Berlin made a new bid for the Summer Games of 2000.

Berlin launched its 2000 Olympics drive in the wake of Germany's seemingly miraculous reunification in 1990 and the Bundestag's decision of 1991 to shift the capital from Bonn back to the old *Reichshauptstadt*. Berlin boosters cited the city's triumph over ideological division as a good reason to celebrate the millennial games in their town. In a decision reflecting amazing myopia, however, the Berlin Senate proposed the former Reichssportfeld and aging Olympic Stadium as the primary venue for the 2000 games. According to this plan, the Olympic dignitaries would salute the athletes from the very same podium used by Hitler sixty-four years before.

This idea did not go down well even among many Berliners, who argued that the Reichssportfeld was so closely associated with the 1936 games that trying to mount a new Olympiad there would represent an insult to the memory of all those who had suffered under the Nazis. The problem was compounded by the continuing presence of much of the heroic statuary installed for the 1936 games on the grounds outside the Olympic Stadium; like the arena itself, these statues were under a landmark protection law and therefore could not be removed. "There are bound to be embarrassing moments," wrote two members of the Olympic planning commission apropos the statues, "Photos of the remaining Nazi artifacts are sure to appear in the international press."

Opposition to a possible return to the haunted ground of 1936 was so heated that the assembly hall in which the debates over Berlin's Olympic bid took place had to be sealed off by the police. The atmosphere became even more explosive once the plan to reuse the Reichssportfeld garnered official approval. In the weeks and months thereafter, Berlin's ghosts of the past were joined by its demons of the chaotic present. A left-wing "NOlympia" movement, insisting that the games were nothing but a rich man's toy and subsidy to the ownership class, staged violent demonstrations and bombed buildings belonging to the Olympic campaign's sponsors. The bid became mired in scandal when the first head of the Berlin Olympic Committee was caught with his hand in the till, while his successor had to be fired when it was revealed that he had compiled dossiers on the private lives of the IOC members, replete with information on their drinking habits and sexual preferences. There would be no second Olympic act for Berlin in 2000.

If Germany *had* hosted the 2000 games on the grounds of Berlin's former Reichssportfeld, the organizers would have had to do more than exorcise a few ghosts to make the facilities there fit for a new Olympic festival. The entire complex, including the Olympic Stadium, was in need of extensive refurbishing following almost a half century of hard use and minimal upkeep by its various tenants.

The Red Army had camped on the site for a brief period after its conquest of Berlin, then turned the area over to the British, who made it their headquarters in the divided city for decades thereafter. They used the May Field for rugby matches and in May 1987 celebrated Queen Elizabeth II's birthday with a "Queen's Parade" on the grounds. They built barracks and civilian housing on a part of the complex near the old Sportforum.

The British began employing the partially damaged Olympic Stadium as early as September 1946 for athletic contests, at first solely among the Western Allied forces stationed in Berlin. Before reopening the facility they excised the names of Hitler, Tschammer, and Pfundtner from the bronze "Honor Tablet" near the main entrance.

Similarly, after changing the name of the Dietrich-Eckart-Freilichtbühne (Dietrich Eckart Theater) to Waldbühne (Forest Theater), the British staged professional boxing matches there. It was there, on October 31, 1948, that Max Schmeling ended his professional boxing career with a loss to Richard Vogt, who had won a silver medal in the light-heavyweight division in the Berlin Olympics.* Eventually the Waldbühne became a venue for major musical events, especially rock concerts. In 1965 the Rolling Stones played a show there that resulted in eighty-seven injuries and damages totaling three hundred thousand marks.

The Bell Tower at the May Field suffered a more ignominious fate, at least initially. Because it had been severely damaged in the war, the British decided in February 1947 to blow it up rather than to repair it. Before bringing down the tower, however, they removed the bell and buried it nearby to protect it from scrap-metal thieves. Ten years later, at the urging of Werner March, the British dug up the bell and placed it at one of the stadium entrances, where it enjoyed a rebirth as an official "Memorial for the Olympians of the World Who Lost Their Lives Through Tyranny." March also pleaded for a reconstruction of the Bell Tower itself, and in 1962, with money from West Ger-

---

*Like Leni Riefenstahl, Schmeling went on to enjoy an amazingly long life—he died in 2005 at age ninety-nine—but he proved more adept at shaking off his association with the Nazis in later years than did the filmmaker. Eventually becoming wealthy by dint of his ownership of several Coca-Cola distributorships in West Germany, he helped out Joe Louis financially and sent money to Louis's widow on the Brown Bomber's death in 1981. Schmeling's long post–Third Reich career, along with his self-serving memoirs, managed effectively to blur the fact that he had willingly served Nazi ends and was much closer to Hitler than he claimed.

many, a new tower went up exactly where the old one had stood. With the old bell serving its new memorial function (and badly cracked besides), however, a replacement *Glocke* had to be forged and installed in the newly rebuilt tower. Bearing images of the Brandenburg Gate and the German Federal Eagle, the new bell was about half the size of its predecessor.

Starting in 1949 the British began relinquishing control over some of the Reichssportfeld structures to the Germans. German football clubs made increasing use of the Olympic Stadium (no worries among them about "ghosts of the past"), while ordinary Berliners in their thousands flocked to the swimming stadium. On June 12, 1950, the Berlin Senate renamed the entire complex Olympia-Stadion. It was there that West German track athletes and swimmers competed in trials for the 1952 Helsinki games. In 1963–64, with the introduction of the Bundesliga (professional soccer league), the Olympic Stadium became the home field of the Berlin football club Hertha BSC, and it served as one of the sites for the 2006 World Cup, including the final.

In the mid-1990s, following the failure of Berlin's bid for the 2000 Olympic Games, the Olympic Stadium fell into even worse shape than it had been in for the past forty years, which was bad enough. Saplings grew out of the clock tower, and stalactites drooped from the ceiling joists where water had seeped through the mortar. Berlin politicians blamed the continuing deterioration on the federal government in Bonn, the official owner of the complex, which refused to spend much money on its upkeep. There were thoughts of tearing the whole thing down, but of course this would have been very difficult to do owing to the structure's status as a historic monument. "The Eiffel Tower doesn't look very pretty either," said one protective Berlin official, "but would you tear it down? Both [the tower and the stadium] are symbols. You have to retain them because of their historical dimension."

In 1998 the federal government and the *Land* (state) of Berlin joined in a major renovation of the stadium and its surrounding grounds. The reconstruction left the facade of the stadium more or less in its original state, but the interior was extensively remodeled, with colorful plastic seats, a partial roof, new lighting, and VIP seating in the area where the Honor-Loge used to be. Walking around inside the stadium today, one has to strain to imagine what the place must have looked like when Hitler sat in his box and Jesse Owens stood at the victor's podium.

THE Olympic Village experienced a quite different fate from that of the Reichssportfeld, largely because it stood in the Soviet occupation zone after the war. Having reverted to the Wehrmacht in the years immediately after the games, the complex remained under army control throughout the rest of the Third Reich, and it became the scene of fierce fighting in the last days of the war. After the conquest of Berlin the Red Army took over the complex and used it for military training and housing. The Russians salvaged the Hindenburg House, Dining Hall, Swimming Hall, and Gymnastics Hall, but tore down most of the athletes' huts with the exception of one small group. Unknown to them, the group of huts they decided to save was the very complex used by the American athletes in 1936. Jesse Owens, staunch anti-Communist and postwar Cold Warrior that he was, enjoyed a kind of sweet revenge.

Today the village grounds present a dismal picture of dilapidated buildings and rubble-strewn wasteland. The cinder track where Jesse Owens and Jack Lovelock trained is overgrown with weeds. The terraces where the athletes sunned themselves are long gone. So is the Finnish sauna. Signs on the surrounding security fence warn of unexploded ammunition. But there are a few vestiges of the past. On the front wall of the vestibule in the Hindenburg House one can barely make out the phrases: "*Ich baue fest auf Dich, deutsche Jugend!*" and "*Treue ist das Mark der Ehre.*" ("I build strongly on you, German youth!" "Loyalty is the mark of honor.") More prominent, however, is a remnant of the area's more recent tenants: a colossal portrait of Lenin in the central hall.

IN the summer of 2001, sixty-five years after the Berlin Olympics, the Nazi games were again in the news, though not because of anything that had recently happened in Germany. The reason for the recollections of Hitler's games was the IOC's award of the 2008 Summer Games to Beijing, which some critics claimed (in an echo also of the dispute over the 1980 Moscow games) amounted to a repeat of the "tragic error" of 1936. As François Londe, chairman of the French National Assembly's Foreign Affairs Committee, put the matter: "The decision of the IOC goes towards justifying a repressive political system that each day flouts freedom and violates human rights. Following the example of Nazi Germany in 1936 and the Soviet Union in 1980, Communist China will use [the games] as a powerful propaganda instrument destined to consolidate its hold on power."

Of course the comparison of Berlin 1936 and Beijing 2008 also elicited the counterargument that twenty-first-century China, for all its centralization of power in one party and abuses of human rights, hardly amounted to a replica of Hitler's Germany. Wrote *New York Times* sports columnist George Vecsey in 2001: "Some people compare Beijing's selection to the temporary prestige [gained by] Hitler's Berlin in 1936. There is no denying the similarities between the German concentration camps and the Chinese laogai, or labor camps. But this is a different time, and China is far different from the Germany of 1936. There is no charismatic leader, no rampant movement, no unity of purpose. If anything, the Chinese people clearly seem to want Western-style freedom and a Western-style economy. [The Chinese] people have reason to celebrate [the IOC decision]."

Whatever the differences (and similarities) between Communist China and Nazi Germany, the IOC, in justifying its Beijing decision, availed itself of a well-worn argument it had used in 1936, and again in 1980: namely, that putting on the Olympics would change the host country for the better. The buildup to the 2008 games, insisted the committee, would accelerate openness in China and facilitate improvements in its record on human rights. "We count on there being many changes in China in the next seven years," said one IOC official in 2001. The Olympics, in other words, would finally accomplish that long-held Western fantasy about this repressive and secretive Eastern colossus: turn it into a true "democracy," fully open to the world.

It is impossible to know whether the IOC actually believed that hosting the games—whether in China or anywhere else—invariably produced liberalizing consequences. Past examples were hardly very encouraging. Rather than promote greater tolerance of political diversity and dissent in authoritarian regimes, the prospect of inviting in the world had often prompted authorities in such countries to come down even harder on political opponents and potential troublemakers. This had been the case not only in Berlin in 1936, but also in Mexico City in 1968, where ten days before the games government snipers had fired into a crowd of protesters, killing at least thirty-eight and perhaps more than one hundred people. In 1987, a year before the Seoul games, police used tear gas and clubs against student demonstrators who dared compare the upcoming games to the Berlin Olympics, claiming that South Korean president Chun Doo Hwan, like Hitler before him, was intent upon using the Olympics to bolster his repressive regime. Residents in Seoul's poorer neighborhoods also protested an Olympic "beautification" program involving the elimination of tenement housing visible from the main roads and big hotels. Even democratic Greece sought in 2003 to allay foreign fears about security at the impending Athens games by rounding up fifteen members of a radical leftist group known as November 17 and putting them behind bars. Greek police and intelligence agencies also stepped up their activities in a predominantly Muslim area of Athens, prompting protests from local Muslims that all followers of Islam were being treated like potential terrorists. As for China, it continued to crack down on political and religious dissidents in the years leading up to the games, and it also pursued a different kind of sanitization by razing the vibrant (if unsanitary) *hutongs*—the old neighborhoods of twisting alleyways and ramshackle tenements in Beijing.

But whatever political consequences might come from hosting the games in China, the IOC, just as it had in 1936, also deployed the *opposite* argument to defend its choice of Beijing: The games, it insisted, were not about "politics" at all, but about bigger things, such as global togetherness and world peace, and therefore decisions about venue should not get caught up in petty political controversies of any sort. "I think the Olympics should supersede politics," said USOC president Sandra Baldwin. "It's the greatest peacetime event in the world."

One can almost hear Avery Brundage cheering from the grave.

Notes

▲

▲

Abbreviations Used in Notes

AAF	Amateur Athletic Federation (Los Angeles)
AAU	Amateur Athletic Union
AJCA	American Jewish Committee Archive (New York)
ABC	Avery Brundage Collection (Champaign-Urbana)
AOC	American Olympic Committee
BAB	Bundesarchiv Berlin
BAK	Bundesarchiv Koblenz
BHSA	Bayerisches Hauptstaatsarchiv (Munich)
BPP	Bayerische Politische Polizei
BSA	Bayerisches Staatsministerium des Äussern
BSI	Bayerisches Staatsministerium des Innern
BSUK	Bayerisches Staatsministerium für Unterricht und Kultus
CDA	Carl-Diem-Archiv (Cologne)
FAZ	*Frankfurter Allgemeine Zeitung*
FO	Foreign Office
GOC	German Organizing Committee
HI	Hoover Institution (Stanford)
IfZG	Institut für Zeitgeschichte (Munich)
IJHS	*International Journal for the History of Sport*
IOC	International Olympic Committee
IOCA	International Olympic Committee Archive (Lausanne)
JSH	*Journal of Sport History*

LC	Library of Congress (Washington, DC)
MAGP	Markt-Archiv Garmisch-Partenkirchen
NA	National Archives (Washington, DC)
NAACP	National Association of Colored People
NYT	*New York Times*
OKWS	Organisations-Komittee der IV. Olympischen Winter Spiele
ÖSA	Österreichisches Staatsarchiv (Vienna)
PAAA	Politisches Archiv des Auswärtigen Amts (Berlin)
PRO	Public Record Office (London)
RMI	Reichsministerium des Innern
RSA	Richard-Strauss-Archiv (Garmisch-Partenkirchen)
RPMI	Reichs- und Preussisches Ministerium des Innern
RSHA	Reichssicherheits Hauptamt
SAM	Staatsarchiv München
SZS	*Sozial- und Zeitgeschichte des Sports*
VB	*Völkischer Beobachter*
WP	*Washington Post*

NOTE: For purposes of consistency, I use throughout the notes the European day-month-year style of dating.

Introduction

3 "they ever were": GOC, ed., *The Olympic Games Berlin 1936. Official Report*, 2 vols. (Berlin, 1936), vol. 1, 518. (Hereafter cited as *Official Report*.)

3 "for an idea": "Before the Games," *NYT*, 29.6.03.

4 "entire German people": Quoted in Hajo Bernett, Marcus Funck, and Helga Woggon, "Der Olympische Fackellauf 1936 oder die Disharmonie der Völker," *SZS*, 10. Jg, Heft 2 (1996): 18.

4 "most glorious reawakening": "Wir holen das Olympische Feuer," *Die Olympia-Zeitung*, 29.6.03.

5 "symbol of purity": Carl Diem, ed., *Ewiges Olympia: Eine Quellensammlung antiker und moderner Texte* (Kastellaun, 1991), 17.

6 with the *Olympia* filming: Leni Riefenstahl, *A Memoir* (New York, 1992), 188–89.

6 "connected with the ancient Games": Richard Stanton, *The Forgotten Olympic Art Competitions* (Victoria, BC, 2000), 160.

6 "Heil Hitler!" as the torch went by: Victor Kuron, *The Messengers of Peace from Olympia to Berlin* (Berlin, 1936), 12.

8 "distorted by shouting": Ernst Rüdiger von Starhemberg, *Between Hitler and Mussolini* (London, 1942), 244.

8 "quite unexpected proportions": *Official Report*, vol. 1, 528.

8 "exceptionally regrettable": Hans Bohrmann, ed., *NS-Presseanweisungen der Vorkriegszeit: Edition und Dokumentation, Band 4/II: 1936* (Munich, 1993), 936.

8 "a singular provocation": Bernett, Funck, and Woggon, "Der Olympische Fackellauf," 16.

8 directly from Berlin: Marek Waic, "Die Beteiligung der Tschechoslowakai an den Olympischen Spielen im Jahre 1936 und die Sudeten-Deutschen in der tschecholslowakischen Representation," *SZS*, 10. Jg, Heft 2 (1996): 37–38.

9 "blue-eyed blonds were acceptable": "Ich trug das Olympische Feuer," *FAZ*, 1.8.86.

10 "and physical primacy": Willi Könitzer, *Olympia 1936* (Berlin, 1936), 32.

10 of Germanic origin: David Welch, *Propaganda and the German Cinema* (Oxford, 1983), 115.

10 cradle of Aryan culture: *Berliner Morgenpost*, 9.7.36.

10 of Gothic cathedrals: Robert Cecil, The *Myth of the Master Race: Alfred Rosenberg and Nazi Ideology* (London, 1972), 15.

10 half the known Olympic victors: Arnd Krüger and Dietrich Ramba, "Athens or Sparta? Classical Greek Ideals and the 1936 Olympic Games," in Roland Renson, ed., *The Olympic Games through the Ages: Greek Antiquity and Its Impact on Modern Sport* (Athens, 1991), 347–48.

11 "Greece was sealed": *Pädagogisches Zentralblatt*, Nr. 9/10, 1933, quoted in Ivone Kirkpatrick, *The Inner Circle* (London, 1939), 74.

11 "greatness of the Third Reich": Der Reichssportführer. Abschrift zu RK. 10921, 11.12.35, R 43II/729, BAB.

12 "spiritual mobilization": Richard Evans, *The Coming of the Third Reich* (New York, 2003), 396.

12 "most controversial Olympics": Allen Guttmann, *The Olympics. A History of the Modern Games* (Urbana, IL, 1992), 53–71.

13 archival record now available: The pioneering work in English on the 1936 Games is Richard D. Mandell, *The Nazi Olympics* (New York, 1971)—reprinted with a new preface in 1987. A lively account from the British perspective is Duff Hart-Davis, *Hitler's Games: The 1936 Olympics* (London, 1986). Neither of these authors made much use of unpublished sources. For book-length scholarly studies in German, see especially Arnd Krüger, *Die Olympischen Spiele 1936 und die Weltmeinung: Ihre aussenpolitische Bedeutung unter besonderer Berücksichtigung der USA* (Berlin 1972); and Thomas Alkemeyer, *Körper, Kult und Politik. Von der 'Muskelreligion' Pierre de Coubertins zur Inszenierung von Macht in den Olympischen Spielen von 1936* (Frankfurt, 1996). As my references will indicate, there is a wealth of specialized scholarly literarure on the games in German, English, and French.

14 "spoiled professionals of today": "Die Flamme war erloschen," *Garmisch-Partenkirchner Tageblatt*, 6.2.86; also "Da kann ich nur noch Nazi werden," *Der Spiegel*, 31/1986, 116–32.

14 games for political purposes: "Politisch missbraucht, das kann ich überhaupt nicht mehr hören," *FAZ*, 1.8.86. Among the surviving '36 veterans who disputed the notion that the Nazis had misued the games was Erich Borchmeyer, who had competed against Jesse Owens in the one-hundred-meter dash.

14 Hitler regime and the '36 games: W. P. Knecht, "Verwirrender Rückschau über fünf Jahrzehnte," *Olympisches Feuer* 36 (1986): 4. For a more moderate version of this perspective, see Christine Eisenberg, *"English Sports" und der Deutsche Bürger: Eine Gesellschaftsgeschichte 1800–1939* (Paderborn, 1996), 404–29.

I "Faster, Higher, Stronger"

17 conflict among nations: Andreas Höfer, *Der Olympische Friede. Anspruch und Wirklichkeit einer Idee* (Sankt Augustin, 1994).

17 War of 1870–71: John MacAloon, *This Great Symbol: Pierre de Coubertin and the Origins of the Modern Olympic Games* (Chicago, 1981), 5–6 ; Eugen Weber, "Pierre de Coubertin and the Introduction of Organized Sport in France," *Journal of Contemporary History* 5 (1970): 5.

18 cosmopolitan ideal: On Jahn and the *Turner* movement, see Christiane Eisenberg, "Charismatic National Leader: Turnvater Jahn," in Richard Holt, J. A. Mangan, and Pierre Lanfranchi, eds., *European Heroes: Myth, Identity, Sport* (London, 1996), 14–27.

18 "the ancient warriors": Quoted in Karl Lennartz, *Die Geschichte des Deutschen Reichsausschusses für Olympische Spiele. Heft 1: Die Beteiligung Deutschlands an den Olympischen Spielen 1896 in Athen* (Bonn, 1981), 54.

19 "of a German man": Quoted in ibid., 71.

19 in Asia Minor: Minas Dimitriou, "Athen 1896—die ersten Olympischen Spiele der Neuzeit im Schatten des Griechisch-Türkischen Krieges," *SZS*, 10. Jg, Heft 2 (July 1996): 7–13.

20 "on a junket": James B. Connolly, "Fifteen Hundred Years Later," *Collier's*, 1.8.36, 24.

20 him the edge: Burton Holmes, *The Olympic Games in Athens, 1896: The First Modern Olympics* (New York, 1984), 64–65.

20 "wild Indians": George Horton, "The Recent Olympic Games," *The Bostonian* 4, no. 4 (July 1896): 219.

20 "like overgrown children": Quoted in Guttmann, *The Olympics*, 18.

21 "the legendary inspiration": Quoted in Lennartz, *Geschichte des Reichsausschusses*, Heft 1, 119.

21 "vairy slow": Quoted in MacAloon, *This Great Symbol*, 217.

21 "bottle after bottle": Horton, "Recent Olympic Games," 223.

22 "the national hymn": Quoted in MacAloon, *This Great Symbol*, 232.

22 "it strengthens it": Quoted in Guttmann, *The Olympics*, 19.

22 "any other country": Horton, "Recent Olympic Games," 228.

22 "variety of aspect," Pierre de Coubertin, "The Meeting of the Olympic Games," *North American Review* 170 (1900): 802.

23 "*et très brilliant*": André Drevon, *Les Jeux Olympiques oubliés* (Paris, 1900), 87.

23 convenient shortcuts: David E. Martin and Roger W. H. Gynn, *The Olympic Marathon* (Champaign, IL, 2000), 28–37. See also Karl Lennartz, "Der Marathonlauf bei den Olympischen Spielen 1900 in Paris," *Deutsche Gesellschaft für Leichtathletik-Dokumentation Bulletin* 5, no. 17 (1987): 37–56.

24 *à bas la Prusse!*: Manfred Blödhorn and Walter Niegman, "Zur Ehre unseres Vaterlandes und zum Ruhme des Sports," in M. Blödhorn, ed., *Sport und Olympische Spiele* (Reinbek bei Hamburg, 1984), 31.

24 "without prestige": Pierre de Coubertin, *Une campagne de vingt-et-un ans* (Paris, 1908), 150.

25 "mediocrity of the town": Quoted in John Lucas, "Early Olympic Antagonists: Pierre de Coubertin versus John E. Sullivan," *Stadion* 3, 2 (1997): 267.

25 standing high jump: David Wallechinsky, *The Complete Book of the Summer Olympics: Athens 2004 Edition* (Toronto, 2004), 6.

26 Anglo-Saxon race: Robert Rydell, *All the World's a Fair* (Chicago, 1984), 157; Lew Carlson, "Giant Patagonians and Hairy Ainu: Anthropology Days at the 1904 St. Louis Olympics," *Journal of American Culture* 12 (1989): 19–26.

26 "doing with training"; "principles of amateurism": Quoted in S. W. Pope, *Patriotic Games: Sporting Traditions in the American Imagination 1876–1926* (New York, 1997), 43.

26 "amused spectators": Quoted in Bill Henry, *An Approved History of the Olympic Games* (New York, 1948), 57.

26 "to clothe her"; "that of the Thames": Quoted in Guttmann, *The Olympics*, 28, 29.

27 "earthly king"; OFF THE BRITISHERS: Quoted in Pope, *Patriotic Games*, 47.

29 "in taking part": Quoted in F. A. M. Webster, *The Evolution of the Olympic Games 1829 B.C.–1914 A.D.* (London, 1914), 214.

29 "and absolutely unfair": Quoted in Lord Killanin and John Rodda, eds., *The Olympic Games* (New York, 1976), 37.

29 "and German service": Lennartz, *Die Geschichte des Deutschen Reichsausschusses für Olympische Spiele: Heft 3: Die Beteiligung Deutschlands an den Olympischen Spielen 1906 in Athen und 1908 in London* (Bonn, 1985), 139–40.

30 "model of its type": Guttmann, *The Olympics*, 32.

30 cross-country race: Harold E. Wilson, Jr., "A Legend in His Own Mind: The Olympic Experience of General George S. Patton, Jr.," *Olympika* 4 (1997): 99–110.

30 "primitive blacks": Quoted in Guttmann, *The Olympics*, 32.

31 "flag up there": Quoted in Killanin and Rodda, *The Olympic Games*, 41.

31 "gentlemanly" competition: John Lucas, *The Modern Olympic Games* (Cranbury, NJ, 1980), 93.

31 "assimilation of many races": Quoted in Pope, *Patriotic Games*, 50.

32 play-for-pay: Jack Newcomb, *The Best of the Athletic Boys: The White Man's Impact on Jim Thorpe* (New York, 1975), 210.

32 "collected thereafter": Quoted in Wolfgang Schivelbusch, *The Culture of Defeat* (New York, 2003), 174.

33 "cultivating patriotic spirit": Quoted in Volker Kluge, *Olympiastadion Berlin: Steine beginnen zu reden* (Berlin, 1999), 36–37.

33 "by the sun"; "and militarily strong": Quoted in Achim Laude and Wolfgang Bausch, *Der Sport-Führer. Die Legende um Carl Diem* (Göttingen, 2000), 15, 25–26.

35 "all down the line"; "something about it": Quoted in Karl Lennartz, *Die VI. Olympischen Spiele Berlin 1916* (Cologne, 1978), 62, 132.

35 "and military might": Quoted in Laude and Bausch, *Der Sport-Führer*, 28.

36 his career prospects: Arnd Krüger, *Theodor Lewald: Sportführer im Dritten Reich* (Berlin, 1975), 18.

37 "dereliction of duty"; "on German soil": Lennartz, *Die VI. Olympischen Spiele*, 90, 95.

38 as did the British army: Martin Polley, "'No Business of Ours'? The Foreign Office and the Olympic Games 1896–1914," *IJHS* 13, no. 2 (Aug. 1996): 108–9.

38 "internationalist Olympic Games!": Quoted in Höfer, *Der Olympische Friede*, 141.

39 "in olden times": Quoted in Otto Mayer, *A travers les anneaux olympiques* (Geneva, 1960), 81.

39 "must be counted": Pierre de Coubertin, *Olympische Erinnerungen* (Berlin, 1936), 157.

40 "throughout the world": Quoted in Alfred E. Senn, *Power, Politics, and the Olympic Games* (Urbana, IL, 1999), 37.

41 "a winning side": Mark Dyreson, "Selling American Civilization: The Olympic Games of 1920 and American Culture," *Olympika* 8 (1999): 10–11.

41 "money at all": John Lucas, "American Preparations for the First Post–World War Olympic Games, 1919–1920," *JSH* 10, no. 2 (1983): 37.

41 "since the war": Dyreson, "Selling American Civilization," 40.

42 "German race unbeatable": Quoted in Arnd Krüger, "Deutschland und die Olympische Bewegung," in Horst Ueberhorst, ed., *Geschichte der Leibesübungen, Band 3/2* (Berlin, 1981), 1029.

43 "fully adequate replacement": Carl Diem, *Sport als Kampf* (Berlin, 1920), 38–39.

43 "a partial creation": Quoted in Laude and Bausch, *Der Sport-Führer*, 44.

43 "*völkisch* liberation ideal": Aufruf an sämtliche Gliederungen der NSDAP, *VB*, 16.6.23.

44 glory of France: Didier Braun, "Le sport français entre les deux guerres et les Jeux Olympiques en France en 1924," *Relations Internationals* 38 (Summer 1984): 193–211.

44 "most violent hatred" toward France: Andrew Barros, "Les dangers du sport et de l'éducation physique: Une evaluation des forces allemandes par le Deuxième Bureau français (1919–1928)," *Guerres mondiales et conflicts contemporaines* 210 (2003): 115.

44 games of 1924: Fabrice Auger, "Le Comité International Olympique face aux rivalités franco-allemandes (1918–1928)," *Relations Internationales* 112 (Winter 2002): 427–46.

44 separate Winter Games: Mayer, *A travers*, 113–14.

45 tough as nails: Lucas, *Modern Olympic Games*, 104.

46 "little sulking-corner": Quoted in Laude and Bausch, *Der Sport-Führer*, 46.

47 "were his road": Lucas, *Modern Olympic Games*, 115.

47 "war without weapons": John Lucas, "Architects of the Modernized American Olympic Committee, 1921–1928: Gustavus Town Kirby, Robert Means Thompson, and General Douglas MacArthur," *JSH* 22, no. 1 (Spring 1995): 43.

47 "to win decisively": Douglas MacArthur, *Reminiscences* (New York, 1964), 86.

47 "athletic escutcheon": Quoted in Lucas, "Architects," 44.

47 "a healthy people": Quoted in Laude and Bausch, *Der Sport-Führer*, 48.

II Enter the Nazis

49 "Freemasons and Jews": Quoted in Hart-Davis, *Hitler's Games*, 45.

50 in the ring: Neben Berlin und Nürnberg, auch Köln und Frankfurt als olympische Anwärter, R8077, 46/170/503, BAB. See also Hajo Bernett, "Die Bewerbung deutscher Städte um die Olympischen Spiele des Jahres 1936," *Stadion* 21/22 (1995–96): 210–27.

50 in the committee: Lewald assured Adenauer that Cologne's application would be given equal consideration. See Lewald to Adenauer, 7.2.30, Mappe 590, Nachlass Diem, CDA.

51 "*Auf Wiedersehen* 1936 in Berlin!": Bernett, "Die Bewerbung," 220.

51 games from Mussolini: Neben Berlin, R8077, 46/170/503, BAB.

51 Lausanne in May: Procès-verbal de la Séance du dimanche 26 Avril 1931, IOC Meetings File, IOCA.

52 Imperial German Army; positive effect: Bernett, "Die Bewerbung," 222.

52 to Lewald's efforts: Carl Diem, *Ein Leben für Sport* (Ratingen, 1974), 115.

53 "number of advantages": Garland to Coubertin, 24.3.21, Garland Correspondence, AAF.

53 shift to America: Coubertin to Garland, 6.2.22, ibid.

53 "for neo-Olympism": Robert K. Barney, "Resistance, Persistence, Providence: The 1932 Olympic Games in Perspective," *Research Quarterly for Exercise and Sport* 67, no. 2 (June 1996): 152.

53 "of this magnitude": Avery Brundage, "The Olympic Story," Manuscript, Boxes 330–331, ABC.

53 "on the map": John Lucas, "Prelude to the Games of the Tenth Olympiad in Los Angeles, 1932," *Southern California Quarterly* 64, no. 4 (Winter 1982): 313–18.

54 "Groceries Not Games": Barney, "Resistance," 154.

54 American menu: Mark Dyreson, "Marketing National Identity: The Olympic Games of 1932 and American Culture," *Olympika* 4 (1995): 23–25; Jeremy White, "'The Los Angeles Way of Doing Things': The Olympic Village and the Practice of Boosterism in 1932," *Olympika* 11 (2002): 79–116; *The Games of the Xth Olympiad. Official Report* (Los Angeles, 1932), 225–96.

55 "horse or cow": Andrew Morris, "'I Can Compete'! China in the Olympic Games, 1932 and 1936," *JSH* 26, no. 3 (Fall 1999): 548.

55 rest sailed home: Klaus Ulrich, "80 Jahre Olympische Spiele," in Hans-Jürgen Schulke, ed., *Die Zukunft der Olympischen Spiele* (Cologne, 1976), 29.

55 county and the city: City Attorney Report, 29.4.35, Olympic Funds Court Case, AAF.

56 "Games in Berlin": Quoted in Krüger, *Theodor Lewald*, 37; see also Lewald to Curtius, 15.5.31, R8077, 46/170/503, BAB.

56 dominate the LA games: "D. J. Ferris Predicts German Victory," *NYT*, 15.6.30.

58 "On to Berlin in 1936!": "*Auf nach Berlin!*" R8077, 46/170/503, BAB.

58 "white man ragged": Quoted in David B. Welky, "Viking Girls, Mermaids, and Little Brown Men: U. S. Journalism and the 1932 Olympics," *JSH* 24, no. 1 (Spring 1997): 37.

58 "protruding lips": Quoted in Hajo Bernett, "Deutsches Sport im Jahre 1933," *Stadion* 2 (1981): 267.

58 "We demand it": "Neger haben auf der Olympiade nichts zu suchen," *VB*, 19.8.32.

59 would join in 1933: On Halt, see Peter Heimerzheim, *Karl Ritter von Halt—Leben zwischen Sport und Politik* (Sankt Augustin, 1999).

59 "with great interest": Pressenotiz, 16.3.33, R43, 11/729 (film), BAB.

59 "danger is past": Adolf Hitler, *Mein Kampf* (Boston, 1943), 301.

59 "for a statesman": Quoted in Ulrich Popplow, "Adolf Hitler—der Nichtsportler und der Sport," in Heinz Nattkämper, ed., *Sportwissenschaft im Aufriss* (Saarbrücken, 1974), 41.

60 "gymnastics or games": Ernst Hanfstaengl, *Unheard Witness* (Philadelphia, 1957), 119–20.

60 and physical toughness: Hans-Joachim Teichler, *Internationale Sportpolitik im Dritten Reich* (Schorndorf, 1991), 21–31.

60 "sport and gymnastics": Hitler, *Mein Kampf*, 409.

60 "and the noblest soul": "and cowardly individuals": Ibid., 408.

61 "of the Nordic peoples": *VB*, 1.10.23.

61 "against the white race": Georg Haller, "Der Olympische Gedanke," *Nationalsozialistische Monatshefte* 3 (1933): 392.

61 "community morality in athletics": Bruno Malitz, *Die Leibesübungen in der nationalsozialistischen Idee* (Munich, 1933), 3.

62 "rest of the world"; "world of sport": Teichler, *Internationale Sportpolitik*, 45–47.

62 resignations of Lewald and Diem: "Die schuldigen Sportführer verteidigen sich," *Der Angriff*, 7.9.32; Teichler, *Internationale Sportpolitik*, 47.

62 coming to Germany for the games: Reichskanzlei to Küfner, 29.9.32, Question juive, IOCA.

63 "warmest congratulations": Lewald to Lammers, 6.3.33, R 43II/729, BAB.

63 "produced great results": Lewald to Lammers, 16.3.33, R8077, 46/173/612, BAB.

63 "terms of propaganda value": Lewald to Lammers, 16.3.33, R8077, 46/173/612, BAB.

64 "every manner possible"; "appropriate limits": "Hitler Promises Full Support," *NYT*, 17.3.33.

64 "a fighting race": Lewald to Hitler, 25.3.33, R 43II/729, BAB.

64 in the coming summer: Lewald to Lammers, 29.3.33, R 43II/729, BAB.

65 "grandparent is non-Aryan": Saul Friedländer, *Nazi Germany and the Jews. The Years of Persecution, 1933–1939* (New York, 1997), 27.

65 "drought and poison gas": *Der gelbe Fleck: Die Ausrottung von 500,000 Deutschen Juden* (Paris, 1936), 187–88.

65 "needs new leadership!": "Neue Männer an die Spitze," *VB*, 1.4.33.

65 "Diem equals Ullstein": "Es wird gesprungen: Lewald+Diem=Ullstein," *Der Angriff*, 3.4.33.

66 "all the attacks"; "a young boy": Lewald to Lammers, 3.4.33, R 43II/729, BAB.

66 "host of the 1936 Games": IOC to GOC, 3.8.33, ibid.

66 "essential matters of policy": Pfeiffer and Krüger, "Theodor Lewald: Eine Karriere," 254.

67 "and a nationalist": Diem to Breitmeyer, 5.4.33, Mappe 28, Nachlass Diem, CDA.

67 know something about athletics: Dieter Steinhöfer, *Hans von Tschammer und Osten* (Berlin, 1973), 15.

III Boycott Berlin!

70 "class, color, or creed": "Berlin Faces Loss of Olympic Games," *NYT*, 18.4.33.

70 were all that counted: Allen Guttmann, *The Games Must Go On. Avery Brundage and the Olympic Movement* (New York, 1984), 10–11.

71 "form of the Olympic Games": "Brundage's Views Stir Berlin Press," *NYT*, 20.4.33.

71 prevented at all costs: Karl Lennartz, "Difficult Times: Baillet-Latour and Germany, 1931–1942," *Olympika* 3 (1994), 101.

71 "plan and method": Baillet-Latour to Coubertin, 27.3.35, Baillet-Latour Correspondence, IOCA.

71 "participate in complete equality": Quoted in Hans-Joachim Teichler, "Zum Ausschluss der deutschen Juden von den Olympischen Spielen 1936," *Stadion* 15, 1 (1989), 47–48.

72 "cordially welcomed"; "circumstances and conditions": "Germans Reiterate Stand on Olympics," *NYT*, 23.4.33.

72 "any other country"; "toward the world": Kirby to Brundage, 19.5.33, Box 28, ABC.

72 at the 1900 Paris games: On Sherrill, see John Lucas, "An Analysis of an Over-Crowded Life: General Charles Hitchcock Sherrill's Tenure on the International Olympic Committee, 1922–1936," *Olympika* 11 (2002): 144.

72 "a world of pussyfooters": Quoted in *The Nation*, 11.12.35, 666.

73 "equal under the laws": "Olympic Policy Stated," *NYT*, 2.6.33

73 Nazi racial principles: Baillet-Latour to Halt, 26.5.33, Question juive, IOCA.

73 "membership in German teams": Teichler, "Zum Ausschluss," 50.

74 "no objection can be raised": "German Jews Face Exclusion from Olympics Despite Pact," *WP*, 6.8.33

74 "all but biting": Kirby to Brundage, 2.11.33, Box 28, ABC.

74 "next three years": Brundange to Kirby, 11.11.33, ibid.

75 "stirring the matter up": Brundage to Rubien, 5.11.33; Rubien to Brundage, 10.11.33, Box 35, ibid.

75 "not made as cleverly": Baillet-Latour to Brundage, n.d., Box 42, ibid.

75 "Olympic Games of 1936": "AAU Boycotts 1936 Olympics," *NYT*, 21.11.33.

76 "German sports teams": "Berlin Asked to Respect Pledge," *WP*, 23.11.33.

76 "feeling in the United States": "Sherrill Explains Views on Olympics," *NYT*, 1.12.33.

77 "kept within certain limits": Edström to Brundage, 4.12.33, Box 42, ABC.

77 America had shown in 1932: Luther to Hull, 30.1.34, Olympic Games, 862.4063, NA.

78 for Germany's Olympic teams: "Nazis 'Convicted' of World 'Crime' by 20,000 in Rally," *NYT*, 8.3.34.

78 "AOC in this controversy": Brundage to Kirby, 3.3.34, Box 28, ABC.

78 "up to their pledges": Hulbert to Brundage, 12.3.34, Box 27, ibid.

78 "AOC to do": Brundage to Kirby, 3.3.34, Box 28, ibid.

78 "compete in the Olympics": "Deutsch Asks for Olympic Inquiry," *NYT*, 10.3.34.

78 "as a member thereof": Kirby to Brundage, 21.4.34, Box 28, ABC.

79 "democracy of sport": "Brundage's Approval of Berlin's Conduct," *NYT*, 11.8.34.

79 "all the facts": Quoted in Krüger, *Die Olympischen Spiele 1936 und die Weltmeinung*, 52.

79 "liked very much": Brundage to Halt, 22.10.34, Box 57, ABC.

79 consistent with Olympic ideals: Krüger, *Die Olympischen Spiele 1936 und die Weltmeinung*, 52.

79 "will be fulfilled"; "other than sports": "U.S. Will Compete in 1936 Olympics," *NYT*, 27.11.34.

80 "disturb the situation": Brundage to Halt, 22.10.34, Box 57, ABC.

80 training for Olympic tryouts: "Sherrill Returns from Berlin Visit," *NYT*, 17.11.34.

81 halt the anti-Jewish actions: Volker Bloch, *Berlin 1936: Die Olympischen Spiele unter Berücksichtigung des jüdischen Sports* (Constance, 2002), 74.

81 "afraid of being arrested": Quoted in Friedländer, *Nazi Germany and the Jews*, 138.

82 "amicably resolved": "Olympic Committee Members Are Alarmed," *NYT*, 26.7.35.

82 "powerful Jewish financier": Quoted in Hajo Bernett, *Guido von Mengden. Generalstabschef des deutschen Sports* (Berlin, 1976), 47.

82 New York City's next mayor: Brundage to Baillet-Latour, 24.9.35, Box 42, ABC.

82 "make the trip to Berlin": *Commonweal*, 9.8.35, 353–55.

82 racial policies were intolerable: On Morrison, see Richard A. Swanson, "'Move the Olympics! Germany Must Be Told!' Charles Clayton Morrison and Liberal Protestant Christianity's Support of the 1936 Olympic Boycott Effort," *Olympika* 12 (2003): 39–49.

83 "sending a team [to Germany]": "Boycott the Olympics!" *The Nation*, 21.8.35, 201; Broun piece appeared in *New York World-Telegram*, 5.8.35.

83 and 57 percent against: H. Cantril, ed., *Public Opinion 1935–1946* (Princeton, 1951), 810–11.

83 "of Harvard University": German Consultate, Boston, to German Embassy, 7.9.35, 4555, PAAA.

83 "most unwarranted fashion": Brundage to Edstrøm, 29.8.35, Box 42, ABC.

83 "other German athletes": Edstrøm to Brundage, 12.9.35, ibid.

84 and Field Association: On Bergmann, see Bloch, *Berlin 1936*, 76-78; Bergmann "Je wütender ich war, desto besser sprang ich," *Die Zeit*, 19.7.96; "Der Fall Bergmann," *Die Zeit*, 24.7.61.

84 "the token Negro"; own political fortunes: Aufzeichnung über den Empfang am 24.8.34, 4508, PAAA. Lewald duly informed Baillet-Latour of Hitler's intransigence. See Lewald to Baillet-Latour, 7.9.35, Cojo-Comité d'Organisation des J.O. Correspondence 1935–37, IOCA. See also Arnd Krüger, "Once the Olympics Are Through, We'll Beat Up the Jew: German-Jewish Sport and Anti-Semitic Discourse," *JSH* 26, no. 2 (Summer 1999): 359.

85 for the international festival: Arnd Krüger, "'Dann veranstalten Wir eben rein deutsche Olympische Spiele': Die Olympischen Spiele 1936 als deutsches Nationalfest," in H. Breuer and R. Naul, eds., *Schwimmsport und Sportgeschichte: Zwischen Politik und Wissenschaft* (St. Augustin, 1994), 127–49.

85 "Mr. Roosevelt at Hyde Park": Sherrill to House, postcard, August 1935. E. M. House Papers, Stirling Library, Yale University; Cited in John Lucas, "An Analysis," 145.

85 "can't eat me": Quoted in Stephen R. Wenn, "A Tale of Two Diplomats: George S. Messersmith and Charles H. Sherrill on Proposed American Participation in the 1936 Berlin Olympics," *JSH* 16 (Spring 1989): 38–39. Sherrill also reported on this meeting to Baillet-Latour. See Sherrill to Baillet-Latour, 30.8.35, Question juive, IOCA.

85 "exactly on time": Quoted in Lucas, "An Analysis," 153.

85 "all German Olympic candidates": Tschammer to Sherrill, 21.9.35, 4519, PAAA.

86 "inadequate qualifying performance": Bloch, *Berlin 1936*, 77–78.

86 "only slightly abated": Quoted in ibid., 78.

86 as Jewish at all: German Consulate, San Francisco, to German Embassy, 18.11.35, 4520, PAAA.

87 "meeting you in Berlin": Quoted in Rürup, *1936: Die Olympischen Spiele und der Nationalsozialismus*, 57.

87 "Japanese in California": "Sherrill Rebuffs Olympic Ban Plea," *NYT*, 22.10.35.

88 compete in Germany: David K. Wiggins, "The 1936 Olympic Games in Berlin: The Response of America's Black Press," *Research Quarterly for Exercise and Sport* 54 (Sept. 1983). 278–92.

88 "Americans to compete at Berlin": Wilkins to Garland, 11.10.33, NAACP, C-384, LC.

88 "you have fought for": Quoted in Wiggins, "The 1936 Olympic Games in Berlin," 281.

89 "high plane of sportsmanship": Wilkins to Strauss, 15.11.35, NAACP, C-384, LC.

89 "treated like royalty": Quoted in Wiggins, "The 1936 Olympic Games in Berlin," 282.

89 "withdraw from the Olympics": Quoted in William J. Baker, *Jesse Owens. An American Life* (New York, 1986), 65.

90 felt on the matter: White to Owens, 20.11.35, NAACP, C-384, LC.

90 "right here at home?": Quoted in Baker, *Jesse Owens*, 66.

90 "regardless of race?": Text of article in NAACP, C-384, LC.

91 "only wise one": Baillet-Latour to Garland, Sherrill, and Jahncke, 5.10.35, JO Eté 1936, Correspondence, IOCA.

91 Nazis' state-sponsored persecution: On Jahncke's background and views on race, see John Lucas, "Ernest Lee Jahncke: The Expelling of an IOC Member," *Stadion* 17, no. 1 (1991): 53–65.

92 "instead of Hitler": Jahncke to Baillet-Latour, JO Eté 1936, Correspondence, IOCA.

92 "resignation can be expected": Baillet-Latour to Jahncke, 13.12.35, ibid.

92 "Olympic ideal of fair play": Mahoney to Lewald, 20.10.35, reproduced in 4509, PAAA.

93 "to be sufficient": Baillet-Latour to Brundage, 17.11.35, JO Eté, Correspondence, IOCA.

93 "recovered from the after-effects": American Olympic Committee, *Fair Play for American Athletes* (Chicago, 1935), 1-10. On this pamphlet and its distribution, see Arnd Krüger, "Fair Play for American Athletes: A Study in Anti-Semitism," *Canadian Journal of History of Sport and Physical Education* 9, no. 1 (May 1978): 43–57.

94 Germany regarding Jews and sports: George Eisen, "The Voices of Sanity: American Diplomatic Reports from the 1936 Berlin Olympiad," *JSH* 11, no. 3 (Winter 1984): 56–79.

95 "Olympic Games of 1936": Messersmith to State Department, 28.11.33, LM 193, Reel 25, NA.

95 no lasting significance: Geist to State Department, 15.12.33, Olympic Games, 862.4016, NA.

96 "from doing right": Messersmith to Hull, 15.11.35, ibid.

96 "opinion of National Socialist doctrine"; "is not exaggerated": Ibid.

97 "flagrant discrimination": Dodd report, 11.10.35, Olympic Games, 862.4063, NA.

98 a "grave mistake": Quoted in Stephen R. Wenn, "A Suitable Policy of Neutrality? FDR and the Question of American Participation in the 1936 Olympics," *IJHS* 8, no. 3 (Dec. 1991): 321.

98 "between our great countries": Quoted in ibid., 326. The German-American Olympic Fund Committee, headed by a German-born architect named Dietrich Wortmann, raised money for U.S. participation in the '36 games and conducted a vigorous public relations campaign in defense of Hitler's Germany. See Wendy Gray and Robert K. Barney, "Devotion to Whom? German-American Loyalty on the Issue of Participation in the 1936 Olympic Games," *JSH* 1, No. 2 (Summer 1990), 214-231. Brundage considered Wortmann "a loyal patriotic American citizen." Brundage to Early, 6.5.36, American Olympic Association, 811.43, NA.

99 "Jews, I think": Minutes of the 1935 AAU Convention, 155. Quoted in Stephen R. Wenn, "Death-Knell for the Amateur Athletic Union: Avery Brundage, Jeremiah Mahoney, and the 1935 AAU Convention," *IJHS* 13, no. 3 (Dec. 1996): 270.

99 "on the CIO": Edstrøm to Brundage, 22.12.35, Box 62, ABC.

99 "praise for your achievement": Baillet-Latour to Brundage, 12.12.34, Box 42, ibid.

99 "plus a high office": Sherrill to Baillet-Latour, 23.12.35, JO Été 1936, Correspondence, IOCA.

100 "ideals of the AAU": The 1935 AAU Convention, Report, Box 152, ABC.

100 "benefit of Nazi propaganda": Bush to Diem, 26.12.35, Box 155, ABC.

100 "useful in the future": Brundage to Lasker, 30.3.36, Box 234, ABC.

100 "misrepresent in your letter": Lasker to Brundage, 14.3.36, ibid.

101 "final arbiter of sportsmanship": Quoted in Hart-Davis, *Hitler's Games*, 82.

101 "[of such athletes] from competing": "British Consider Boycotting Games," *NYT*, 22.11.33.

101 "scarcely be exaggerated": Phipps to Sergent, 7.11.35, FO 371/18884, PRO.

101 incompatible with the Olympic spirit: Walter Citrine, "The Dictatorship of Sport over Nazi Germany," Trades Union Council pamphlet in AJCA, New York.

101 "he is of Jewish origin": Aberdare to Lewald, 1.1.34, Question juive, IOCA.

102 "way in England": Lewald to Aberdare, 10.1.34, JO Été 1936, Correspondence 1931–34, ibid.

102 "to watch the Games": Aberdare to Lewald, 5.2.34, ibid.

102 "Olympic Games of 1936": Aberdare to Lewald, 16.12.34, ibid.

103 "ambassadors of goodwill": Phipps report, 18.11.35, FO 371/18884, PRO.

103 beaten to death by Nazi fans: Wigand to Vansittart, 17.10.35, ibid.

103 cancel the match: National Association of Railwaymen to Foreign Secretary, 20.10.35, ibid.

103 "Home Office affair": Vansittart to Russell, 21.11.35, ibid.

103 "political trouble": Scott to Vansittart, 27.11.35, ibid.

103 "two Nordic countries"; "will be changed": Quoted in Hart-Davis, Hitler's Games, 89.

104 benefit to the German Jews: Treatment of Jews in Germany, 11.11.35, FO 371/18863, PRO.

104 "boycott has waned": Baillet-Latour to Le Fort, 21.10.35, R8076/G82, BAB.

104 overturning the Versailles treaty: The German Embassy in Paris certainly feared that France would boycott the Berlin games. See German Embassy, Paris, to Foreign Office, 14.3.36, 4556, PAAA.

105 remain "above politics": Bruce Kidd, "The Popular Front and the 1936 Olympics," Canadian Journal of History of Sport and Physical Education 11, no. 1 (1980): 1–18; William Murray, "France: Liberty, Fraternity, and the Pursuit of Equality," in Krüger and Murray, The Nazi Olympics, 87–112.

105 "pas un homme pour Berlin!": Quoted in Murray, "France," 92.

106 "despicable ideas to sport": Quoted in Jean-Marie Brohm, Jeux Olympiques à Berlin (Brussels, 1983), 86.

106 "Indians how to walk": "India's Reply to Hitler's Insult," Bombay Chronicle, 17.2.36.

106 quitting their national teams: Hajo Bernett, "The Role of Jewish Sportsmen during the Olympic Games in 1936," in Ulrich Simi, ed., Physical Education, 107–8.

107 their Boston rabbi: Susan D. Bachrach, The Nazi Olympics (Boston, 2000), 62–63.

107 "are held in Germany": "Neugrass Unwilling to Run," NYT, 12.12.35.

107 "[the Jews] if it could": Quoted in Bachrach, The Nazi Olympics, 70.

107 anti-Jewish persecution in Germany: "Revolt on Two Flanks," The Times (London), 9.7.36.

108 "against my conscience": Quoted in Rürup, 1936: Die Olympischen Spiele und der Nationalsozialismus, 63.

108 "disregard for the Olympic spirit": Quoted in Bachrach, The Nazi Olympics, 69.

108 into a new war: Detlev J. K. Peukert, Inside Nazi Germany. Conformity, Opposition, and Racism in Everyday Life (New Haven, 1987), 49–50.

IV The Winter Games

110 abuses of professionalism: Avery Brundage, "The Olympic Story," Manuscript, Box 330, ABC.

110 "reputation and greatness": Die Olympischen Spielen und Wir, LRA 61.944, SAM.

111 "Germany's Olympic bid": Lewald to Held, 4.2.31, MA 100242, BHSA.

111 footed most of the bill: BSUK to BSA, 16.2.31, MK 41598, BHSA.

112 no gouging in Garmisch: Scharnagl to Jahn, 4.7.31, ibid.

112 "Prussians" in the GOC: Industrie und Handelskammer, München, to BSA, 26.10.32, ibid.

113 and other revenues: Schäfer to Merz, 14.1.33, LRA 61.936, SAM; also Kollmann to BSUK, 5.5.33, BHSA.

113 through a bank loan: Jahn to BSI, 11.10.33, MK 41598, BHSA.

113 more funds were forthcoming: OKWS to BSI, 27.3.34, ibid.

113 "management of the Winter Games": BSUK to RPMI, 29.8.35, MK 41600, BHSA.

113 cost of 2.6 million reichsmarks: OKWS to RPMI, R8076, G110, BAB.

114 "ideas of the Olympic movement": "Coca-Cola at the Olympics," Woodruff Papers, Box 217, Folder 7, Emory University Archive.

114 athletes drinking his product: On Ovomaltine, see the correspondence in R8076, G50, BAB.

114 "carry the Olympic pin": OKWS to RPMI, 7.1.35, R8076, G110, BAB.

115 hearty thumbs-up: State of Preparations for the Fourth Winter Games, IOC Meeting, Athens, 5.5.34–23.5.35, Box 152, ABC.

115 shift the stadium location: Thoma to Halt, 14.9.34, Schriftverkehr 1931–1934, MAGP.

115 "the finest hotels"; "exceed normal levels": State of Preparations, Box 152, ABC.

116 stipulated by the agency: Olympia Verkehrsamt, Garmisch-Partenkirchen, to Halt, 9.5.35, LRA 61.942, SAM.

116 with severe penalties: Reichskommisar für Preisüberwachung to Bayer. Staatsregierung, 29.6.35, LRA 135.848, SAM.

116 "hospitable city in Germany": Landesverkehrsbund München to OKWS, 18.11.35, R8076, BAB.

117 "beggars and vagabonds": Rürup, *1936. Die Olympischen Spiele und der Nationalsozialismus*, 95.

117 "stabbed to death in the Alps": BPP to Bezirksvorstände und Staatskomissare in Oberbayern, 27.1.36, LRA 61.936, SAM; Bericht, Aussenstelle der BPP, 3.3.36, BHSA.

117 "Jew-free": Alois Schwarzmüller, "Juden sind hier nicht erwümscht! Zur Geschichte der jüdischen Bürger in Garmisch-Partenkirchen von 1933 bis 1945," Verein für Geschichte, Kunst- und Kulturgeschichte im Landkreis Garmisch-Partenkirchen, ed., *Mohr—Löwe— Raute: Beiträge zur Geschichte des Landkreises Garmisch-Partenkirchen*, vol. 3 (Munich, 1995), 186–93.

117 out of the Nazi Party; "endangered as well": Diem to Halt, 25.4.35, R8076, G158, BAB.

118 "on the Jewish question"; "relevant authorities": Halt to Lex, 14.5.35, R8076, G158, BAB.

120 "discipline in this matter": BPP to Bezirksamt, Garmisch-Partenkirchen, 9.9.35, LRA 61.941, SAM.

120 "who are masters'": Avery Brundage, "The Olympic Story," Box 330, ABC.

120 roadways in the "Gapa" area: Frick to BSI, 3.12.35, Reichsführer SS und Chef der deutschen Polizei, MA 400, IfZG.

120 "power of the Olympic movement": Brundage, "The Olympic Story," Box 330, ABC.

120 "fine gesture": Baillet-Latour to Sherrill, Garland, and Jahncke, 17.11.35, Box 63, ABC.

121 "blamed for that by Berlin!": Sherrill to Le Fort, 30.12.35, R8076, G122, BAB.

121 "looked upon as our friends": Le Fort to Sherrill, 13.1.36, ibid.

121 roads leading into the region: Reichsstaathalter Bayern to RPMI, 13.1.35, Reichsstaathalter von Epp 671, BHSA.

121 "notices will be replaced": British Consulate Munich to Phipps, 14.1.36, FO 371/19922, PRO.

121 and all Olympic sites: RPMI to BSI, 3.2.36, Reichsstaathalter von Epp 671, BHSA.

122 "remains irremovably fixed": Quoted in Peter Longerich, *Politik der Vernichtung: Eine Gesamtdarstellung der nationalsozialistischen Judenverfolgung* (Munich, 1998), 116.

122 "ordinary foreigners": Tätigkeiten von SS-Angehörigen gegen fremde Staatsangehörige und Juden, 28.1.36, Reichsführer SS und Chef der deutschen Polizei, MA 288, IfZG.

122 cosset the American scribes: Krause to Harster, 8.1.36, R8076, P34, BAB.

123 "Nazi officials there": William S. Shirer, *Berlin Diary* (New York, 1940), 44–45.

123 might have returned: Tschammer to Baillet-Latour, 2.2.36, R8076, G123, BAB.

124 close to the ski stadium: Himmler to BSI, 29.1.36, ED 60011, IfZG. See also Peter Hoffmann, *Hitler's Personal Security* (London, 1979), 91–92.

124 "been a fairy tale": Cigaretten-Bilderdienst, ed., *Die Olympischen Spiele 1936 in Berlin und Garmisch-Partenkirchen* (Hamburg, 1936), 4.

124 "an imperfect world": "Brilliant Setting," *NYT*, 9.2.36.

125 "Europe and America": Australian Sports Federation to GOC, 28.12.35, R8076, P31, BAB.

125 "American model": British Embassy Berlin to Eden, 13.2.36, FO 371/19940, PRO.

125 passing the reviewing stand: Lewald to Coubertin, 31.3.36, JO Eté, Cojo Comité, IOCA.

125 "come home to the Reich": Eröffnung der Winter-Olympiade, Österreichisches Generalkonsulat, München 7.2.36, Bundeskanzleramt, Neues Politisches Archiv, Karton 122, ÖSA.

126 "subject of comment later": "Hitler Opens the Winter Olympics," *NYT*, 7.2.36.

126 or embarrass the hosts: Hans Bohrmann, ed., *NS-Pressebestimmungen der Vorkriegszeit, Band 4/II:1936* (Munich, 1993), 46.

127 "especially during the Olympics": "Nazis Urge Swiss to Execute Killer," *NYT*, 7.2.36.

127 "demeaned the Olympic spirit": Quoted in Heimerzheim, *Karl Ritter von Halt*, 116–17.

128 "an unsportsmanlike racket": "Fight Is Renewed in Olympic Hockey," *NYT*, 10.2.36.

128 "one team from Canada": "Finnish Quartet," *NYT*, 11.2.36.

128 "the Latin temperament": "Cold Snap," *NYT*, 11.2.36.

128 best player for the *Herrenvolk*: See discussion of the Ball case in Osterreichisches Generalkonsulat, München, to Bundeskanzleramt, 27.2.36, Bundeskanzleramt, Neues Politisches Archiv, Karton 122, ÖSA; Bloch, *Berlin 1936*, 82.

129 reminded of World War I: "Tense Crowd," *NYT*, 13.2.36.

130 instructors were banned: Council of British Ski Clubs to Ostgaard, 18.4.35, R 8076, G111, BAB.

130 banning the alpine *instructors*: "Österreichs Teilabsage," *Die Stunde* (Vienna), 16.1.36.

131 on the Russian front: Rürup, *1936. Die Olympischen Spiele und der Nationalsozialismus,*, 99.

131 "become a public figure": "French Quartet," *NYT*, 11.2.36.

132 "Professional Amateur in Europe": Vinson to Brundage, 13.1.36, Box 152, ABC.

132 about Henie's professionalism: Brundage to Salchow, 19.3.36, ibid.

132 "came from *him*": Mandell, *Nazi Olympics*, 105.

133 never forgave her: Michael Boo, *The Story of Figure Skating* (New York, 1998), 32–33.

133 "half out of their seats": "Miss Herber," *NYT*, 14.2.36.

134 "is being considered": "Tense Crowd," *NYT*, 13.2.36.

135 attributed to "political grounds": Matti Goksøyr, "Norway: Neighborly Neutrality," in Krüger and Murray, *The Nazi Olympics*, 183.

136 "throughout the entire world": *Garmisch-Partenkirchner Tageblatt*, 20.1.36.

137 expenditures totaled 2,618,259 reichsmarks: Finanzbericht über die IV. Olympischen Winterspiele 1936, MK 41601, BHSA.

137 down on winter sports: Hinrichs to Propaganda Ministerium, 6.1.36, Olympiade 1936, PAAA.

138 leaders made an appearance: Ian Kershaw, *Making Friends with Hitler: Lord Londonderry, the Nazis, and the Road to War* (New York, 2004), 139.

138 "upsets the French": Harold Nicolson, *Letters and Diaries, 1930–1939* (New York, 1980), 245.

138 "leader of men": Quoted in Hart-Davis, *Hitler's Games*, 102.

139 dinner in *his* hotel: Killan to Le Fort, 8.1.36, Schriftverkehr, Winterspiele 1936, MAGP.

139 "abandon and general joyousness": "Cold Snap," *NYT*, 11.2.36.

139 "cultural-artistic" dimensions: Münchner Faschingsausschuss to Halt, 7.1.35, R8076, G158, BAB. See also OKWS, ed., *Die IV. Olympische Winterspiele 1936. Amtlicher Bericht* (Berlin, 1936), 234–45.

139 "attempted by the Nazi regime": "Reich Gives a Feast," *NYT*, 11.1.36.

140 "understanding among nations": Quoted in "Reich Gives a Feast," *NYT*, 11.1.36. For the German text, see OKWS, *Die IV. Olympische Winterspiele*, 239–41.

140 "just cannot believe it": Die IV. Olympische Winterspiele in Garmisch-Partenkirchen in politischer Beleuchtung, 18.2.36, Bundeskanzleramt, Neues Politisches Archiv, ÖSA.

140 "Cancan for Twelve": Mandell, *Nazi Olympics*, 104.

141 "heart for his German hosts": Brundage to Luther, 21.3.36, Box 152, ABC.

141 "was insignificant to us": *Garmisch-Partenkirchner Tageblatt*, 12.2.96.

141 "found the Germans friendly": "Athletes Desert Olympics," *WP*, 18.2.36.

141 "any heretofore held": Rubien to Le Fort, 4.5.36, R8076, G122, BAB.

142 "people and their Führer": *Petit Parisien* quoted in Heinrich Müller, "Die IV. Olympi-schen Winterspiele im Lichte ausländischen Presseberichte," *Die Neueren Sprachen: Zeitschrift für die neusprachliche Unterricht* 44 (1936): 369.

142 "thinks of anything else": Quoted in "Games in Garmisch," *Time*, 17.2.36, 37.

142 "country in Europe": "Crowded Program," *NYT*, 12.2.36.

142 "statesmen stood behind them": Die IV. Olympischen Winterspiele im Spiegel der Aus-landspresse, R8076, P61, BAB.

143 "and vice-versa": *Neuigkeits-Welt-Blatt* (Vienna), 9.2.36.

143 "all their predecessors": "Games in Garmisch," *Time*, 17.2.36, 40.

143 "their skiing outfits": Shirer, *Berlin Diary*, 46–47.

144 "men in uniform": "Military Display," *Chicago Daily News*, 17.2.36.

144 "have no understanding": Quoted in Krüger, *Die Olympischen Spiele 1936 und die Welt-meinung*, 174.

144 "way on the Winter Games": Halt to Reichsbahnzentralle, 26.3.36, R8077, 46/172/688, BAB.

144 countries around the world: Hilmar Hoffmann, *Mythos Olympia: Autonomie und Unter-werfung von Sport und Kultur* (Berlin, 1993), 90.

145 "important to me"; "kinds of technical aids": Leni Riefenstahl, *A Memoir* (New York, 1992), 180–81.

146 "dying to each detonation": "Olympic Explosives," *WP*, 17.2.36; "130,000 Stampede," *NYT*, 17.2.36.

V On to Berlin

149 "dares nothing wins nothing!": Elke Fröhlich, ed., *Die Tagebücher von Joseph Goebbels. Sämtliche Fragmente, Teil I, Aufzeichnungen 1924–1941*, 4 vols. (Munich, 1987), II: 577.

149 "legal nets and impenetrable pacts": Quoted in Krüger, *Die Olympischen Spiele 1936 und die Weltmeinung*, 179.

150 even more ominous intentions; in the face: William Murray, "France," in Krüger and Murray, eds., *The Nazi Olympics*, 94–95.

151 of national embarrassment: *Le Populaire*, 22.5.36.

151 "protect the Olympic ideal!": Quoted in Rürup, ed., *1936. Die Olympischen Spiele und der Nationalsozialismus*, 60.

151 whole boycott effort: Phipps to Foreign Office, 16.5.36, FO 371/19940, PRO.

152 athletes bound for Barcelona: Bruce Kidd, "The Popular Front and the 1936 Olympics," *Canadian Journal of History of Sport and Physical Education* 11, 1 (1980): 13–14.

153 "rest of the world": Vortrag, 14.12.33, R8076, G155, BAB.

153 "fills me with special joy": Abschrift, 14.12.33, MA 595, IfZG.

154 "modern glass box": Speer, *Inside the Third Reich* (New York, 1970), 80.

155 "eyes of the entire world": Quoted in Kluge, *Olympiastadion Berlin*, 73.

156 sounding off to his cronies: Henry Pickler, ed., *Hitlers Tischgespräche im Führerhaupt-quartier 1941-1942* (Stuttgart, 1963), 272–73.

156 "will and capacity to build": Quoted in Kluge, *Olympiastadion Berlin*, 76.

157 "simpler and more disciplined folds"; "only for me": Quoted in ibid., 132–33.

157 were delaying work: Frick directive, 18.7.35, Olympiade 1936, PAAA.

157 improving on it in every way: On the Olympic Village see Carl Diem, *Ein Leben für Sport*, 166–70; Hans Saalbach, *Das Olympische Dorf* (Leipzig, 1936).

159 extensively on the suicide: "Fuerstner Buried with Army Honors," *NYT*, 23.8.36.

160 "to their very best advantage": These preparations were the subject of a report from the American consul in Berlin. See Messersmith Dispatch, 25.7.36, Olympic Games, 862.4063, NA.

160 "of Adolf Hitler's Germany": *Der Mittag*, n.d., in Olympiade 1936, PAAA.

161 "visitors a good time": "Germany Puts on Her Best Face," *Manchester Guardian*, 22.7.36; see also Newton to Eden, 18.8.36, FO 371/19940, PRO.

161 Pierre Laval: Bülow-Schwarte to Deutsche Botschaft, Paris, 28.11.35, Olympiade 1936, PAAA.

162 "Games will be held": Olympic Games Press Release, Nr. 32, Box 152, ABC.

162 "wake-up call to the entire world": Quoted in Rürup, *1936: Die Olympischen Spiele und der Nationalsozialismus, 84.*

162 "among the German people": Pfundtner to Reichsstaathalter, 15.10.34, Reichsstaathalter von Epp, BHSA.

163 "and the Eleventh Olympic Games": Vortrag zu der Schrift über Goethe und der Olympische Gedanke," R8077, 46/109/449, BAB; see also "Goethe und der Olympische Gedanke," R8076, G33, BAB.

163 "documentation of the Eternal Germany": Goebbels speech in *Berliner Morgenpost*, 19.7.36.

163 "soul as a vital force": Quoted in Suzanne L. Marchand, *Down from Olympus: Archaeology and Philhellenism in Germany, 1750–1970* (Princeton, 1996), 351.

164 "task for the German people": Diem, *Ein Leben*, 175; GOC, *Official Report*, 365–69; "Olympia-Zug. 1000-km Werbefahrt durch Deutschland," Olympia-Werbung-Propaganda, CDA.

164 "Eleventh Olympic Games": GOC, *Guidebook to the Celebration of the XI. Olympiad Berlin 1936* (Berlin, 1936), 54.

165 "the upcoming competition": Abschrift, 14.12.33, Reichsministerium für die besetzten Ostgebiete, MA 595, IfZG.

165 candidates for Olympic training: "Wer macht's nach?" *VB*, 16.2.34.

166 version of solar energy: John M. Hoberman, *Mortal Engines. The Science of Performance and the Dehumanization of Sport* (New York, 1992), 131-45.

166 "bony and bare of womanhood": Quoted in *The Nation*, 18.7.36, 62.

166 female reproductive organs: Arnd Krüger, "Strength Through Joy: The Culture of Consent under Fascism, Nazism and Francoism," in J. Riordan and A. Krüger, eds., *The International Politics of Sport in the 20th Century* (London, 1999), 71.

167 "taken in the future": Quoted in Rürup, *1936: Die Olympischen Spiele und der Nationalsozialismus*, 75.

167 "necessary to be first!": Mussolini quoted in Die Vorbereitungen des Auslands für die Olympischen Spiele 1936, Vorbereitung, Vorbetrachtungen aus sportlicher Sicht, 017.425, CDA.

167 "*nel modo più degno*": Quoted in Harold Oelrich, "Hitler, Mussolini und der Sport," *Stadion* 24, no. 2 (1998): 296.

168 "through its superior performances": Die Vorbereitungen des Auslands, CDA.

168 team headed for Berlin: Ikuo Abe, Yasuharu Kiyohara, and Ken Nakajuna, "Fascism, Sport and Society in Japan," *IJHS* 9, no. 1 (Apr. 1992): 19–20.

168 "I can compete!"; than for the Netherlands: Andrew Morris, "'I Can Compete!' China in the Olympic Games, 1932 and 1936," *JSH* 26, no. 3 (Fall 1999): 545, 552.

168 weakness across the board: *Die Vorbereitungen des Auslands*, CDA; "La Préparation Olympique," *Le Populaire*, 25.5.36; "Les Français admettant que leur equipe olympique sera faible," *Le Messager*, 16.5.36.

169 "over the next four years": Quoted in Die Vorbereitungen des Auslands, CDA.

169 Malted Milk £52: British Olympic Association, *The Official Report of the XIth Olympiad Berlin 1936* (London, 1936), 47.

169 "and needs it soon": "Appeal for Funds," *NYT*, 14.4.36.

169 "New York City on July 15": Brundage to Edstrøm, Box 42, ABC.

170 "our two great countries": Wortmann solicitation letter, 28.4.36, Box 234, ABC.

170 "our people and fatherland": "Olympia-Werbung in Ausland," *Reichssportblatt*, 6.5.35.

170 "no other avenue of life": Bush to Rubien, 4.5.36, Box 35, ABC.

171 "precedent injurious to sport": "Offer Was Rejected," *NYT*, 17.6.36.

171 "true old Americanism": Randall's Island Tryouts, Box 152, ABC.

172 held later in Cambridge, Massachusetts: David Wiggins, "The 1936 Olympic Games in Berlin: The Response of America's Black Press," *Research Quarterly for Exercise and Sport* 54 (Sept. 1983): 283–84. See also Wiggins, *Glory Bound: Black Athletes in a White America* (Syracuse, 1997), 72–73.

172 "tested in Berlin this summer": "America Seen Facing Test in Berlin," *WP*, 21.2.36.

172 "American athletic supremacy"; "as *Kultur*": "Athletes of Europe See Chance," *NYT*, 24.2.36.

173 "We wuz robbed!": Max Schmeling, *An Autobiography* (Chicago, 1998), 82.

173 "one steal apiece": Quoted in David Margolick, *Beyond Glory. Joe Louis versus Max Schmeling, and a World on the Brink* (New York, 2005), 26.

173 sending him fan mail: On the Nazi leadership and Schmeling see, in addition to Margolick, ibid.; Hans Joachim Teichler, "Max Schmeling—der Jahrhundertsportler im Dritten Reich," *SportZeit* 1 (2001): 11–15; and Patrick Myler, *Ring of Hate* (Edinburgh, 2005).

174 "one for Adolf Hitler": Quoted in Jeffrey T. Sammons, *Beyond the Ring. The Role of Boxing in American Society* (Urbana, 1988), 106.

174 "I look like one": Quoted in Margolick, *Beyond Glory*, 40.

174 "on the right people"; "attend the Games": Schmeling, *Autobiography*, 109.

175 "Let's get Musso next": Sammons, *Beyond the Ring*, 102.

176 "(Kruel Kolored Klouter)"; "not much interest": McRae, *Heroes without a Country*, 62.

177 "moral support for him": Quoted in ibid., 120.

177 "I zee zomezings": Margolick, *Beyond Glory*, 121.

177 didn't look scared: *Joe Louis, My Life Story* (New York, 1947), 68.

177 "so many left hands"; "*einen Schönen geholt*": Max Schmeling, "This Way I Beat Joe Louis," *Saturday Evening Post*, 5.9.36, 10, 11.

178 "until the finish"; "delirious with joy": "Schmeling Stops Louis in Twelfth," *NYT*, 20.6.36.

178 "let my friends down": Louis, *My Life Story*, 75.

178 by white doctors: "Bomber's Kin," *Chicago Defender*, 11.7.36.

178 "an Alabama cabin"; "bum in the country": Quoted in McRae, *Heroes Without a Country*, 129.

178 "defeated Nigger-boy": Quoted in Bernett, Funck, and Woggon, "Der Olympische Fackellauf 1936 oder die Disharmonie der Völker," *SZS*, 10. Jg, Heft 2 (1996): 18.

179 "was a German!": Fröhlich, *Die Tagebücher von Joseph Goebbels*, vol. 2, 630. Goebbels was so pleased with Schmeling's victory that he waived the taxes on the boxer's earnings.

179 "several times over": Schmeling, *Autobiography*, 130.

180 he reinstate her: "Eleanor Holm Whalen," *NYT*, 2.2.04; "I Like Champagne," *Time*, 3.8.36, 21.

180 "in maintaining discipline": "Star's Attack Bitter," *NYT*, 26.7.36.

181 "cover up any racial angle": "Homesick Boxers," *NYT*, 30.7.36; "Ousted Boxer," *New York Amsterdam News*, 8.8.36.

181 "officials of the Nazi Party": *Sydney Morning Herald*, 23.6.36.

181 "wearing Western suits!": Quoted in Morris, "'I Can Compete,'" 555.

182 "whip him next time": Quoted in McRae, *Heroes Without a Country*, 144.

183 "the whole works": Quoted in William O. Johnson, Jr., *All That Glitters Is Not Gold: The Olympic Games* (New York, 1972), 29.

183 "an undignified manner": Krüger, *Die Olympischen Spiele 1936 und die Weltmeinung*, 194.

184 "than the New Yorkers": Quoted in [Janet Flanner], "Berlin Letter," *The New Yorker*, 1.8.36, 40.

185 after the Nazi defeat: Michael H. Kater, *Different Drummers: Jazz in the Culture of Nazi Germany* (New York, 1992), 36–38.

185 placed on every bottle: Mark Pendergrast, *For God, Country and Coca-Cola* (New York, 1993), 218–26; Helmut Fritz, *Das Evangelium der Erfrischung: Coca-Colas Weltmission* (Hamburg, 1985), 72–80.

186 "South American herbs": "What Is Coke?" broadside, Robert Woodruff Papers, Box 10, Folder 5, Emory University Archive.

186 "Berlin Means Boys": Christopher Isherwood, *Christopher and His Kind* (New York, 1976), 2.

186 "under police control": Quoted in Michael Peppiatt, *Francis Bacon. Anatomy of an Enigma* (New York, 1996), 29.

187 up from 938 in 1934: Eric Johnson, *Nazi Terror. The Gestapo, Jews, and Ordinary Germans* (New York, 1999), 288.

188 "Germany's prosperous facades": [Flanner], "Berlin Letter," 40.

188 Carl von Ossietzky: Lewald had promised Coubertin that "the Nobel Prize will certainly be handed over to you" after the conclusion of the Berlin games. See Lewald to Coubertin, 12.2.36, JO Eté 1936, Cojo Comité, IOCA. On the failed Nobel Peace Prize campaign, see Hans Joachim Teichler, "Coubertin und das Dritte Reich," *Sportwissenschaft* 12, no. 1 (1982): 28–29.

188 "traitor to its interests": Quoted in Lucas, "Ernest Lee Jahncke: The Expelling of an IOC Member," 68.

189 "100% female": "Olympic Games," *Time*, 10.8.36, 41

VI "Holy Flame, Burn"

191 "Berlin's schoolchildren": GOC, ed., *Official Report*, I: 537.

192 "senate of physical culture": Ibid., 126. On the Olympic chains, see Karl Lennartz, "More on the Olympic Chains: Setting the Record Even Straighter," *Olympika* 6 (1997): 65–71.

192 "never go out": Quoted in Hart-Davis, *Hitler's Games*, 152.

192 "of human understanding"; "Eleventh Olympiad, Berlin, 1936": GOC, *Official Report*, I: 541–43.

193 "or Messiahs use": Thomas Wolfe, *You Can't Go Home Again* (New York, 1940), 628.

195 "Germany's western neighbor": Albert Speer, *Inside the Third Reich*, 73.

195 "dip our flag": Rubien to Hull, 5.11.36, American Olympic Committee, 811.43, NA.

196 "by Nordic immigrants"; "of the modern era": "100,000 Hail Hitler," *NYT*, 2.8.36.

196 compose the music: Lewald to Strauss, 1.4.35, RSA. See also Albrecht Dündling, "Zwischen Autonomie und Fremdbestimmung. Die Olympische Hymne von Robert Lubahn und Richard Strauss," *Richard-Strauss-Blätter*, Heft 38 (December 1997): 71.

197 "first master of sport": Hajo Bernett, "Die Olympische Hymne in 1936. Ein Preisausschreiben und seine Folgen," in Gerhard Hecker, ed., *Der Mensch im Sport. Festschrift zum 70. Geburtstag von Professor Liselott Diem* (Schondorf, 1976), 51.

197 "be the highest": Dündling, "Zwischen Autonomie und Fremdbestimmung," 72–76; Bernett, "Die Olympische Hymne," 49–50.

197 "Olympic Hymn for all time": Lewald to Strauss, 24.9.34, RSA.

197 "for the proletarians": Quoted in Dündling, "Zwischen Autonomie und Fremdbestimmung," 77.

198 candidate for this job: Lewald to Lammers, 21.4.36, R 43II/730, BAB.

199 "bridged the millennia": Quoted in Hart-Davis, *Hitler's Games*, 159.

199 "to that of Richard Strauss": The Berlin Olympics Fine Arts, Box 152, ABC.

200 "brilliant new nocturnal beauty": [Flanner], "Berlin Letter," *The New Yorker*, 15.8.36, 35.

200 "brim of a felt hat": *Time*, 10.8.36.

201 "hill of peace": "100,000 Hail Hitler," *NYT*, 2.8.36.

201 "the German cause": Fröhlich, *Die Tagebücher von Joseph Goebbels*, vol. 2, 635.

202 "not be welcome in Germany": Quoted in Rürup, *1936: Die Olympischen Spiele und der Nationalsozialismus*, 123.

202 "suppression of civil liberties": "C. S. Cadman Quits," *NYT*, 2.2.36.

202 "clique of stateless émigrés: Hans Bohrmann, ed., *NS-Pressebestimmungen der Vorkriegszeit*, Bd. 4/II: 1936, 838.

202 "head of a friendly nation": Quoted in Rürup, *1936: Die Olympischen Spiele und der Nationalsozialismus*, 61.

203 "appropriateness for the Eckart Theater": GOC, *Official Report*, vol. 1, 506.

204 "excelled at water sports": The Berlin Olympics Fine Arts, Box 152, ABC.

205 "than the League of Nations": "English the International Tongue," *NYT*, 7.8.36.

205 "if possible, the unattainable": Quoted in Hart-Davis, *Hitler's Games*, 186.

206 "brave, sturdy and fit": Quoted in Karl E. Meyer and Shareen Blair Brysac, *Tournament of Shadows: The Great Game and the Race for Empire in Central Asia* (Washington, DC, 1999), 520.

206 "function in Germany": Hill to Sportärtzte-Kongress, 26.11.35, Olympiade, 4512, PAAA.

207 "other cultural offerings": Fiehler to Baillet-Latour, 28.11.35, Correspondence, 1934-36, IOCA.

207 "the great [Wagner] legacy": Quoted in Brigitte Hamann, *Winifred Wagner oder Hitlers Bayreuth* (Munich, 2002), 318.

208 "over the world": Truman Smith, Air Intelligence Activities, Truman Smith Papers, Box 1, HI.

209 "pushed for an interview": Shirer, *Berlin Diary*, 64.

209 "It is invincible'": Bella Fromm, *Blood and Banquets: A Berlin Social Diary* (New York, 1990), 224.

209 "may they fly swifter"; "popular of Nordics"; "bare to bombardments": "Hitler, Lindbergh, Göring," *Time*, 3.8.36, 16.

210 "in America and England": Lindbergh to Smith, 3.7.36, Truman Smith Papers, Box 1, HI.

211 "without some fanaticism"; "perfectly thrilling"; "a broad view": Quoted in Scott Berg, *Lindbergh* (New York, 1998), 381, 362. [Emphasis in original]

211 "was so happy"; "music in the air"; "ever been built": Wolfe, *You Can't Go Home Again*, 621, 622, 625.

212 "necessary to invent one": Quoted in David Herbert Donald, *Look Homeward: A Life of Thomas Wolfe* (New York, 1988), 385.

212 "come to be": Wolfe, *You Can't Go Home Again*, 625–26.

212 "so I yelled": Donald, *Look Homeward*, 386.

213 "alliance with Great Britain": Oswald Hauser, *England und das Dritte Reich: Zweiter Band 1936 bis 1938* (Göttingen, 1982), 42.

213 "had been asked": Joachim von Ribbentrop, *Ribbentrop Diaries* (London, 1954), 63.

213 "reinforced their thesis"; "without a sour look": Quoted in Hart-Davis, *Hitler's Games*, 180.

214 "over to us"; "opened his eyes"; "impression on him": Fröhlich, *Die Tagebücher von Joseph Goebbels*, vol. 2, 656, 568.

214 "by the regime"; "pervaded the Games": Quoted in Hajo Bernett, "National Socialist Physical Education as Reflected in British Appeasement Policy," *IJHS* 5, no. 2 (Sept. 1988): 169.

215 "with a crater"; "as cutting"; "opening it"; "command of English": Quoted in Hart-Davis, *Hitler's Games*, 181–82.

215 "unquestionably a great leader"; "with us again": Quoted in Richard Griffiths, *Fellow Travelers of the Right. British Enthusiasts for Nazi Germany 1933–39* (London, 1980), 223–24.

216 "for a rest!"; "a good lilt"; "new regime": Henry Channon, *"Chips": The Diaries of Sir Henry Channon* (London, 1953), 106–7.

217 "stroke my hair": Mary S. Lovell, *The Sisters: The Saga of the Mitford Girls* (New York, 2002), 206.

217 "a poor Indian": Hart-Davis, *Hitler's Games*, 184.

218 "assurance and self-content": André François-Poncet, *The Fateful Years*, 206.

218 "White House in Washington"; "could have added": Dodd, *Ambassador Dodd's Diary*, 340–43.

219 "he was breathless": François-Poncet, *Fateful Years*, 206.

219 "in despair with jealousy"; "noise was deafening": Channon, *"Chips,"* 111–12.

219 "of government money": Dodd, *Ambassador Dodd's Diary*, 343.

220 "oasis of freedom": Diem, *Ein Leben*, 95.

221 "their work ethic": Quoted in Hans-Norbert Bukert, Klaus Matussek, and Wolfgang Wippermann, *"Machtergreifung." Berlin 1933* (Berlin, 1982), 67.

221 "grave moral danger": Wolfgang Wippermann and Ute Brucker-Boroujerdi, "Nationalsozialistische Zwangslager in Berlin III. Das 'Zigeunerlager' Marzahn," in Wolfgang Ribbe, ed., *Berlin Forschungen*, II (Berlin, 1987), 191.

221 "on high alert": Preussische Geheime Polizei, Tätigkeit der Politischen Polizei, 18.7.36, R58, 2320, BAB.

222 "to disseminate propaganda"; "preaches racial hatred": RSHA, Olympische Spiele, R58, 2320, BAB.

223 "king of England": RSHA, Olympische Spiele, R58, 2320, BAB.

224 "Jewish-looking" customers had to be served: RSHA, R58, 2322, BAB.

225 "I would have saved!": Quoted in Hart-Davis, *Hitler's Games*, 245.

225 their lack of vigilance: See report on this incident by Ambassador Dobbs, 2.9.36, Olympic Games, 862.4063, NA.

225 "enemies of the people": Quoted in Rürup, ed., *1936. Die Olympischen Spiele und der Nationalsozialismus*, 131.

226 "of the German Jews": Quoted in Jörg Titel, "Die Vorbereitung der Olympischen Spiele in Berlin 1936," *Berlin in Geschichte und Gegenwart: Jahrbuch des Landesarchivs Berlin* (1993), 154.

226 "things out on the Jews": Klemperer, *I Will Bear Witness: A Diary of the Nazi Years 1933–1941* (New York, 1998), 181.

226 *"Juden zu Brei"*: Titel, "Die Vorbereitung der Olympischen Spiele in Berlin 1936," 154; also Arnd Krüger, "'Once the Olympics Are Through, We'll Beat Up the Jew': German Jewish Sport 1898–1938 and the Anti-Semitic Discourse," *JSH* 26, no. 2 (Summer 1999): 353–75.

VII "Darktown Parade"

227 "entirely political enterprise": Klemperer, *I Will Bear Witness*, 182.

228 "cancel its message": Hart-Davis, *Hitler's Games*, 171; see also "Die Zielphotographie bei der Olympiade," *Pester Lloyd*, 8.8.36

228 cork on his face: "Negro Athletes," *New York Amsterdam News*, 18.7.36.

228 "darktown parade": Quoted in McRae, *Heroes Without a Country*, 154. On the American Negro victories in 1936, see also Charles H. Williams, "Negro Athletes in the Eleventh Olympiad," *The Southern Workman* 56 (1937): 45–56; David Clay Large, "Afro-Amerikaner und die Olympischen Spiele 1936," in Ruprechts-Karls Universität, Heidelberg, ed., *Olympia—Sieg und Niederlage* (Heidelberg, 2005), 107–23.

230 women in just six: Michaela Czech, *Frauen und Sport im nationalsozialistischen Deutschland* (Berlin, 1999), 95.

231 as a "Siegfried" type: "Die Stimme aus dem Innenraum," *Stuttgarter N.S.-Kurrier*, 8.9.36.

231 the Führer's box: Henry J. Kellermann, "From Imperial to National Socialist Germany. Recollections of a German-Jewish Youth Leader," *Leo Baeck Institute Yearbook* (1999) xxxix, 327.

231 "and threatening rain": Richard Mandell, *Nazi Olympics*, 228.

233 "hands with a Negro?": Baldur von Schirach, *Ich glaubte an Hitler* (Hamburg, 1967), 217–18.

233 "me a telegram": Olympic File, NAACP, Box 384, LC.

233 "waved back at him": Quoted in Donald E. Fuoss, "An Analysis of Incidents in the Olympic Games from 1924 to 1948 with Reference to the Contribution of the Games to International Good Will and Understanding" Ed.D. thesis, Columbia University Teacher's College, 1951, 186.

233 "and other American blacks": Larry Snyder, "My Boy Jesse," *Saturday Evening Post*, 7.11.36, 97.

233 "the hour in Germany": Quoted in Fuoss, "An Analysis," 186.

233 "man of dignity"; "socialist": Quoted in Baker, *Jesse Owens*, 137.

234 "are traditionally taboo": Quoted in Wiggins, "The 1936 Olympic Games in Berlin: The Response of America's Black Press," 286.

234 "supreme colored athletes": "Jewish War Veterans Condemn Snub of Jesse Owens," Olympics Press File, NAACP, Box 384, LC.

234 "in every respect": Carlson and Fogarty, *Tales of Gold*, 181.

235 "more aggressive than Churchill": "Da kann man nur noch Nazi werden," *Der Spiegel*, 81/1986, 126–27.

236 "'should be running for Germany'": Carlson and Fogarty, *Tales of Gold*, 132.

237 "male sexual characteristics": Quoted in Hajo Bernett, "'Frauengeschichten' von den Olympischen Spiele in Berlin 1936," *Olympisches Feuer* 4 (1996): 36.

237 "honor and glory of Germany": Ibid. See also "Are Girl Athletes Really Girls?" *Life*, 7.10.66, 66.

237 never find a husband: Gigliola Gori, "A Glittering Icon of Fascist Femininity: Trebisonda 'Ondina' Valla, *IJHS* 18 (Mar. 2001): 177–78.

239 "animal in the wild": Quoted in Rürup, *1936: Die Olympischen Spiele und der Nationalsozialismus*, 145.

240 "was for shit": Carlson and Fogarty, *Tales of Gold*, 149.

240 "cords of wood"; "Mr. Consistency": Ibid., 155, 151.

240 "enough in one Olympics"; "last few days": "Owens Out of Relay," *NYT*, 5.8.36.

241 "and were coached": Quoted in Peter Levine, "'My Father and I, We Didn't Get Our Medals': Marty Glickman's American Jewish Odyssey," *American Jewish History* 78 (Mar. 1989): 408.

241 "a sensational time"; "around that corner": "Nazi, Dutch Threats Are Reason," *NYT*, 8.8.36.

241 a fourth gold; "world-class sprinters": Levine, "'My Father and I'," 410, 415.

241 "in my life": "50 Years Later," *NYT*, 10.8.86.

242 "pupils to run": Quoted in Levine, "'My Father and I'," 412–13.

243 coaches were "absurd": Ibid., 416.

243 "evidence was there"; "what [Hybl] said": "Glickman Shut Out," *NYT*, 30.3.98.

244 "not be trampled upon": Hans Bohrmann, ed., *NS-Presseanweisungen der Vorkreigszeit*, Bd.4/II: (1936), 831.

244 "of the ancients": Quoted in "Da kann man nur noch Nazi werden," *Der Spiegel*, 31/86, 117.

244 "racially conditioned athletic advantages": Speer, *Inside the Third Reich*, 70–73.

244 "shame for the white race": Fröhlich, *Die Tagebücher von Joseph Goebbels*, vol. 2: 655.

244 avoid future embarrassments: Rede an die Männer der 8. [SS] Klasse, 3.7.38, MA 312, IfZG.

245 "the track events": Martha Dodd, *Through Embassy Eyes* (New York, 1939), 212.

245 "government can play": Quoted in Mark Danner, "The Secret Way to War," *New York Review of Books*, 9.6.05, 73.

246 "sank to zero": Paul Wolff, *Was ich bei den Olympischen Spielen sah* (Berlin, 1936), 18.

246 in his case: Lothar Rübelt, *Sport: Die wichtigste Nebensache der Welt: Dokumente eines Pioneers der Sportphotographie 1919–1939* (Vienna, 1980), 22.

246 "is under suspicion": "Writer Charges Police Shadow Games Scribes," *Los Angeles Times*, 7.8.36.

247 plenty of negative reporting: The original Promi collection of reports appeared fifty years later in book form: Jürgen Bellers, ed., *Die Olympiade 1936 im Spiegel der ausländischen Presse* (Berlin, 1986).

247 "Hold 'em Yale!": Quoted in Krüger, *Die Olympischen Spiele 1936 und die Weltmeinung*, 208.

247 "as a sporting event"; world wasn't watching: Bellers, *Die Olympiade 1936*, 28, 31.

248 "profoundly distorted": Les Jeux Défigurés," *L'Auto*, 17.8.36.

248 "know how to use it": Quoted in Julian Hale, *Radio Power* (London, 1975), 1.

249 up to that point: Arnd Krüger, "Germany: The Propaganda Machine," in Krüger and Murray, *The Nazi Olympics*, 34.

249 to the Olympic venues: "Die Fernmeldungenanlagen auf dem Reichssportfeld," *Deutsche Allgemeine Zeitung*, 9.7.36.

250 every German living room: Heiko Zeutschner, *Die Braune Matscheibe* (Hamburg, 1995), 59–84.

252 "blurs in a milky mass". "Olympics in Television," *NYT*, 6.8.36.

253 "officials of the Olympic Committee," Carlson and Fogarty, *Tales of Gold*, 174.

254 "was utterly amazing": "400-Meter Title," *NYT*, 8.8.36.

254 "near him again"; "such passion": Riefenstahl, *A Memoir*, 196, 199.

256 grown into a tree: Neal Bascomb, *The Perfect Mile* (New York, 2004), 13.

256 "passing people without effort": Quoted in Hart-Davis, *Hitler's Games*, 201.

258 rest of the race: Martin Gynn, *The Olympic Marathon*, 170–72; "Japanese Smash Olympic Mark," *NYT*, 10.8.36.

259 "what a race!": Fröhlich, *Die Tagebücher von Joseph Goebbels*, vol. 2, 658.

259 "run himself out"; for nine months: Gynn, *Olympic Marathon*, 172–76.

259 countenance any changes: Karl Lennartz, "Kitei Son and Spiridon Louis: Political Dimensions of the 1936 Marathon," *Journal of Olympic History* 12 (Jan. 2004): 26.

VIII Of Pools, Mats, Rings, and Rough Waters

261 "diving is excluded": "U.S. Swim Teams," *NYT*, 16.8.36.

261 "like the devil": Quoted in James Olson, "Japan at the Olympic Games, 1909–1936," M.A. thesis, California State Polytechnic University, Pomona, 1991, 153.

263 "damn bathing suits": Carlson and Fogarty, *Tales of Gold*, 162.

263 "hard-earned fame": "Dorothy Poynton-Hill," *L.A. Times*, 14.8.36.

264 "about boys yet": "Olympic Diving Queen," ibid., 13.8.36.

265 "International Amateur Gymnastics Federation": Rubien, *Report*, 224.

265 "claimed by the Third Reich": Klemperer, *I Will Bear Witness*, 182.

266 "just as German as you!": Quoted in Rürup, *1936: Die Olympischen Spiele und der Nationalsozialismus*, 182.

267 "finest coaches in the world": Rubien, *Report*, 204.

268 "all dried out"; "in the amateur field"; "most scientific boxer": Ibid., 174–76.

269 "on merit alone": ibid., 176.

269 "the mat, Jakob!": "Geh aufs ganze, Jakob!," *Rheinische Landeszeitung*, 10.8.36.

270 national title every year: Klaus Ullrich, "Werner Seelenbinder—a Hero," *Fifth Symposium on the History of Sport and Physical Education* (Toronto, 1982), 363–68.

270 "a good German": Rürup, *1936. Die Olympischen Spiele und der Nationalsozialismus*, 214.

271 fostered international understanding: "Da kann man nur noch Nazi werden," *Der Spiegel*, 31/86, 130.

271 to a concentration camp: Rürup, *1936. Die Olympischen Spiele und der Nationalsozialismus*, 213.

272 "biased and incapable"; "one more illusion": "Kisses and Tears," *NYT*, 12.8.36.

273 "presence of the Führer": "30,000 erlebten den Triumph unserer Ruderer," *Berliner Journal Nachtausgabe*, 16.8.36.

274 had won the gold medal: "Huskey Crew—U.W. Rowers Recall Gold Medal Day in '36," *Seattle Times*, 4.5.96; "Reliving an Olympic Victory," ibid., 25.10.2000.

275 "as if they were wars": Quoted in Tobias Jones, *The Dark Heart of Italy* (New York, 2004), 75.

275 "manner of rough play"; "greater national prestige": Quoted in U.S. Consular Report, Lima, Peruvian-Austrian Football Game, 862.4063 Olympic Games, NA.

276 "crafty decision from Berlin"; "a bunch of merchants": *Time*, 24.8.36, 57.

276 old and decadent Europe; "prestige from the affair": U.S. Consular Report, Lima, 862.4063, NA.

277 on world communism: "Peruvian Eleven," *NYT*, 14.8.36.

277 "How could this happen?": "Furor over Reich Defeat," *NYT*, 9.8.36.

277 "played safely internationally": "Top Honors," *NYT*, 17.8.36.

279 "regardless of athletic ability": Rubien to Brundage, 19.8.36, Box 234, ABC.

279 "through the mud": Carlson and Fogarty, *Tales of Gold*, 191.

279 "bewildering to the players": Quoted in Adolph H. Grundman, "A.A.U.–N.C.A.A. Politics: Forrest C. 'Phog' Allen and America's First Olympic Basketball Team," *Olympika* 5 (1996): 121.

279 "the missionary effect": Arthur J. Daley, "Olympic Basketball at Berlin," *Spalding's Official Basketball Guide, 1936–37* (New York, 1937), 46–47.

280 the result stood: "Haben unsere Wasserballer das Olympiaturnier doch gewonnen?" *Stuttgarter Neues Tageblatt*, 29.9.36.

281 marksmen from the United States: Rubien, *Report*, 236–38.

283 "was a pathetic sight": "Dirtiest Stories," *WP*, 29.9.36.

283 "madhouse or hospital": "Pentathlon Won by German Star," *NYT*, 7.8.36.

284 "would rather drive": "Der Fünfkämpfer muss sich selbst besiegen," *Berliner Lokal-Anzeiger*, 8.8.36.

285 "wooden baton of the hitter": Quoted in *Time*, 24.8.36, 57.

285 "put on at the Olympic Games": Quoted in Mark Maestrone, "A 1936 Olympic Baseball Extravaganza," *Journal of Sports Philately* 36, no. 3 (Jan./Feb. 1998): 15.

286 "untouched by harm": Muriel Rukeyser, "We Came for the Games," *Esquire* 82 (1974): 368.

287 "support to the Nazi government": Edward S. Shapiro, "The World Labor Carnival of 1936: An American Anti-Nazi Protest," *American Jewish History* 74 (1985): 260.

287 "Olympic Games themselves": "Labor Track Meet," *NYT*, 28.5.36.

287 "get excited about": Ferris to Brundage, 5.6.36, Box 23, ABC.

288 "now have underway": Quoted in Shapiro, "The World Labor Carnival," 264–65.

289 "sprints for a change": Quoted in ibid., 270.

289 "become excited about": "Walker Captures Honors," *NYT*, 16.8.36.

289 "answer to the Nazi Olympics": Quoted in Shapiro, "World Labor Carnival," 271.

290 "That is wonderful": Fröhlich, *Die Tagebücher von Joseph Goebbels*, vol. 2, 663.

290 "endure so much joy": *Der Angriff* quoted in "Reich's Olympians," *NYT*, 17.8.36.

291 "Olympic Games was Adolf Hitler?": *Die Olympia-Zeitung*, no. 30, 19.8.36

291 "impetus to German sport": "Bekenntnis zu Führer und Reich," *Der Leichtathlet 1938*, Heft 14, 2.

291 question their amateur status: "Reich's Olympians," *NYT*, 17.8.36.

291 "except in the swimming pool": "4,500,000 Admissions," *NYT*, 17.8.36.

292 "in a crisis situation": Quoted in Hans-Adolf Jacobsen, *Nationalsozialistische Aussenpolitik 1933–1938* (Frankfurt, 1968), 352.

292 "to the white race?": Quoted in Andrew Morris, "'I Can Compete!': China in the Olympic Games, 1932 and 1936," *JSH* 26, no. 3 (Fall 1999): 556.

292 "soul in them": Letter to editor, *WP*, 25.8.36.

293 "by financial stringency"; "'gone soft'"; "world as well": Hart-Davis, *Hitler's Games*, 231, 227.

294 Wilhelmstrasse to the Reichssportfeld: Schlusstag-Minutenprogram, R 43II/730, BAB.

294 "throughout the ages": "Games in Berlin Close Amid Pomp," *NYT*, 17.8.36.

IX Olympia

296 spiritual quest of his own: On Riefenstahl's early life and career, see especially Rainer Rother, *Leni Riefenstahl: The Seduction of Genius* (London, 2002), 11–41; Lutz Kinkel, *Die Scheinwerferin: Leni Riefenstahl und das 'Dritte Reich'* (Hamburg, 2002), 10–44.

296 and inadequate equipment: Rother, *Riefenstahl*, 45–58.

296 "without falsifying them": Leni Riefenstahl, *A Memoir* (New York, 1992), 160.

297 distribution company, Tobis Films: Ibid., 172–73.

297 "smart cookie": Fröhlich, *Die Tagebücher von Joseph Goebbels*, vol. 2, 503.

297 "antiquity to the present": Riefenstahl, *A Memoir*, 171.

298 and October 15, 1937: Propaganda Ministerium Bericht, 16.10.36, R 055/503, PAAA.

298 were "sumptuously appointed": Taylor Dowling, *Olympia* (London, 1992), 36–38.

300 "victory and exhaustion": "Leni Riefenstahls Vorarbeiten in Grünau," *Das 12-Uhr Blatt*, 13.6.36.

301 training exercises at Kiel: "Leni Riefenstahl bei der Olympia-Auswahl der Sieger in Kiel," *Lichtbild Bühne*, 9.6.36.

301 "You bastard!": Riefenstahl, *A Memoir*, 194.

301 "will be confiscated": Bella Fromm, *Blood and Banquets*, 225–26.

302 "too much of the blacks": Riefenstahl, *A Memoir*, 201.

302 "master such assignments": Fröhlich, *Die Tagebücher von Joseph Goebbels*, vol. 2, 680.

303 "would be quickly bankrupt": Bericht über die Zeit von 3. bis 8. Oktober 1936 statgefundene Kassen und Regierungsüberprüfung bei der Olympia-Film G.m.b.H., R 055/505, BAB.

303 "supped like a pig": Fröhlich, *Die Tagebücher von Joseph Goebbels*, vol. 2, 707.

303 "and keep order": Ibid., 717.

303 "the sexual advances Goebbels had made to me": Riefenstahl, *A Memoir*, 202.

304 "and just as intuitive": Ibid., 205.

305 "synchromous with the picture"; "as a thrilling experience": Quoted in Cooper C. Graham, *Leni Riefenstahl and Olympia* (Metuchen, NJ, 1986), 174–76

306 "positiv der Neger lief": Quoted in Kinkel, *Die Scheinwerferin*, 152.

309 heart of the Nazi *Volksgemeinschaft*: Graham McFee and Alan Tomlinson, "Riefenstahl's Olympia: Ideology and Aesthetics in the Shaping of the Aryan Body," *IJHS* 16, no. 2 (June 1999): 91; Kinkel, *Die Scheinwerferin*, 153; Martin Loiperdinger, "Die XI. Olympischen Spiele in Berlin als internationaler Reichsparteitag," in Thomas Alkemeyer, ed., *Olympia-Berlin: Gewalt und Mythos in den Olympischen Spielen von Berlin 1936* (Berlin, 1986), 167–76.

309 strength, and physical perfection: Thomas Alkemeyer, "Images and Politics of the Body in the National Socialist Era," *Sport Science Review* 4, 1 (1995), 60–61. On Riefenstahl's obsession with the "body beautiful" and her Nazi sympathies, see Susan Sontag's famous essay, "Fascinating Fascism," *New York Review of Books*, 6.2.75, 23–30.

310 "power, profundity and beauty": Quoted in Kinkel, *Die Scheinwerferin*, 154.

310 "ideological realm of National Socialism": Quoted in Hajo Bernett, *Untersuchungen zur Zeitgeschichte des Sports* (Schondorf, 1973), 126.

310 "people in these times": Quoted in Kinkel, *Die Scheinwerferin*, 154.

311 they had missed: Deutsche Botschaft, Tehran, to Auswärtiges Amt, 1.11.36, PAAA.

311 bomb near Leni's seat: Voigt to Deutsche Gesandtschaft, Bern, 18.5.38, PAAA.

311 "Bloodhound!": Deutsches Konsulat Belgien to Auswärtiges Amt, 12.12.38, PAAA.

311 "dangerous to morals": "Riefenstahl Film," *Preussische Zeitung*, 9.1.39.

311 "prevent its being shown here": Brundage to Rosen, 16.5.38, Box 62, ABC.

312 make a fuss over her: Cooper Graham, "'Olympia' in America: Leni Riefenstahl, Hollywood, and the Kristallnacht," *Historical Journal of Film, Radio and Television* 13, no. 4 (1993): 435.

312 "this fascist film": "Protest Olympia Movie," *NYT*, 4.11.38; Kinkel, *Die Scheinwerferin*, 160.

313 "as pretty as a swastika": "Walter Winchell on Broadway," *Daily Mirror*, 9.11.38.

313 "the next sensation": Quoted in Kinkel, *Die Scheinwerferin*, 163.

313 American "premiere": Riefenstahl, *A Memoir*, 238; Graham, "'Olympia' in America," 439.

313 "rally in Nuremberg": Leni Riefenstahl, *The Sieve of Time* (London, 1992), 238.

314 "fair-mindedness" and lack of political content: "XIth Olympiad," *L.A. Times*, 17.12.38.

314 "across the world": Quoted in Rother, *Leni Riefenstahl*, 93–94.

314 "*les idéals olympiques*," Guttmann, *The Games Must Go On*, 91.

Epilogue "The Games Must Go On"

316 a giant swastika: Hajo Bernett, "Symbolik und Zeremoniel," 368–69.

316 "protectors of sport": Halt to Baillet-Latour, 23.12.37, Halt Correspondence, IOCA.

316 Germany's Olympic teams: Joseph Ackermann, *Heinrich Himmler als Ideologe* (Göttingen, 1970), 242–43.

317 German Olympic fans: "Germany Prepares for the 1940 Olympics," *NYT*, 23.8.36.

317 gift of the Führer: Hajo Bernett, "Vor 60 Jahren: Olympia-Parade auf dem Nürnberger Reichsparteitag," *Olympisches Feuer* 4 (1996): 43–47.

317 the Winter Games: Beschlüsse Markt Garmisch-Partenkirchen, 8.1.35 bis 5.12.44, MAGP.

317 "indescribable joy": Text of telegram in Kinkel, *Die Scheinwerferin*, 223.

318 in Japan after all: Hajo Bernett, "Das Scheitern der Olympischen Spiele von 1940," *Stadion* 4 (1980): 251–70.

318 "actually at war": Gilbert to Brundage, 7.2.38, Box 26, ABC.

318 "shall not change now": "Olympics Must Be Held in Japan," *NYT*, 13.1.38.

320 "earliest possible delay": Halt to Brundage, 1.7.36, Box 57, ABC.

320 "futile and unnecessary": Brundage to Babcock, 4.11.36, Box 14, ABC.

320 the existing conditions: Halt to Baillet-Latour, 9.9.39, Halt Correspondence, IOCA.

321 "over the world": Halt to Brundage, 10.1.40, Box 57, ABC.

321 "for the Olympic movement": Halt to Brundage, 28.8.40, ibid.

321 of "German blood": Laude and Bausch, *Der Sport-Führer*, 146.

321 "in the Olympic domain": Quoted in ibid., 161.

322 Halt still sat: Von Halt to Edstrøm, 31.1.42, Halt Correspondence, IOCA.

323 "a better Europe!": Quoted in Rürup, *1936. Die Olympischen Spiele*, 204.

323 "of the world": Quoted in Laude and Bausch, *Der Sport-Führer*, 174–75.

323 "as a hero": Quoted in ibid., 184.

324 would be for real: Hajo Bernett, "Bevor die Waffen schwiegen: Das Berliner 'Reichssport-feld' als Kriegsschauplatz," *Stadion* 18, no. 2 (1992): 261–63.

324 "a mad contradiction": Quoted in Laude and Bausch, *Der Sport-Führer*, 187.

325 "character of the Games": Lewald to Aberdare, 22.2.46, Nachlass Diem, 647b, CDA.

325 "of the 1936 Olympic Games": Diem to Brundage, 21.11.46, Nachlass Diem, 647b, CDA.

326 "recent German sports history": Quoted in Laude and Bausch, *Der Sport-Führer*, 199.

326 "before the regime": Quoted in ibid., 196.

326 "Carl-Diem-Weg": "Finaler Opfergang," *Der Spiegel*, 2/02, 44–45.

327 "beauty and honor": Diem to Brundage, undated, Correspondence, Roll 20, Nachlass Diem, CDA.

327 the names confused: Heimerzheim, *Ritter von Halt*, 182–83.

328 ice hockey players: Brundage to Diem, 1.6.48, Correspondence, Roll 20, Nachlass Diem, CDA.

328 West German officials: On the East German exclusion, see Wolfgang Buss, "Die Ab- und Ausgrenzungspolitik der westdeutschen Sportführung gegenüber der DDR in den frühen 50er Jahren," *SportZeit* 1 (2001), 35–56.

329 "give you both hands": "75,000 in Berlin Hail Jesse Owens," *NYT*, 23.8.51.

329 "know each other": Quoted in Baker, *Jesse Owens*, 174.

332 "difficulty to adjust to": Quoted in Johnson, *All That Glitters*, 194–95.

333 represent all of Germany: Noel Cary, "Playing Politics: The Cold War, the Berlin Wall, and the Origins of the Munich Olympics," unpublished conference paper, 2002. See also "Die Olympischen Spiele 1972 in München," *FAZ*, 27.4.66.

333 "entirely new Germany": Arnd Krüger, "Berlins Schatten über München," *Leistungssport* 4 (1972): 251–56. For a lively day-to-day account of the Munich Games, see Richard D. Mandell, *The Olympics of 1972. A Munich Diary* (Chapel Hill, 1991).

333 race-hatred crimes: "Leni Riefenstahl, 101," *NYT*, 10.9.03.

334 "openness, transparency, and clarity": Quoted in Gavriel D. Rosenfeld, *Munich and Memory. Architecture, Monuments, and the Legacy of the Third Reich* (Berkeley, 2000), 155.

334 "but Olympic sports": Quoted in Rürup, *1936. Die Olympischen Spiele*, 225.

334 "shorn of their past": Quoted in Simon Reeve, *One Day in September* (New York, 2000), x.

334 "not fear comparisons": Quoted in Noel Cary, "Murder and Memory at the Munich Olympics," unpublished conference paper, 2001.

335 "look like a police state": Quoted in Cary, "Murder and Memory."

335 "Games Must Go On": Guttmann, *The Games Must Go On*, 252–55.

336 "Denver in 1976": Brundage speech, IOC Munich Session 1972, Friedrich Ruegsegger Papers, Box 1, Folder 38, University of Illinois Archives.

337 "Berlin Olympics experience": "Myths and Realties of the 1936 Nazi Olympics," Anti-Defamation League pamphlet, AJCA.

337 "future aggression": Quoted in Gaddis Smith, *Morality, Reason and Power: American Diplomacy in the Carter Years* (New York, 1986), 227.

337 "to have attended": Quoted in ibid., 226.

338 "appeasement not condemned": Quoted in ibid., 227–28.

338 "best within us": Quoted in Baker, *Jesse Owens*, 225.

339 "the international press": Quoted in "Herrenmenschen in Cellophan," *Der Spiegel*, 14/93, 68.

339 and sexual preferences: "Picture Is Dimming for Games in Berlin," *NYT*, 14.7.92.

341 "their historical dimension": Quoted in "Hitler's Glory Slowly Decays," *Sunday Star-Times* (Wellington, New Zealand), 21.7.96.

342 American athletes in 1936: "Auf den Spuren von Jesse Owens," *Der Tagesspiegel*, 11.9.04.

342 "its hold on power": CNN.Com/World, 14.7.01.

343 "[the IOC decision]": "Being the Host Keeps the Pressure on China," *NYT*, 14.7.01.

343 "next seven years": Quoted in "Ein Meer der Freude," *Der Spiegel*, 29/01, 175.

343 open to the world: Susan Brownell, "China and Olympism," in John Bale and Mette Krogh Christensen, eds., *Post Olympism? Questioning Sport in the Twenty-first Century*, 60.

343 more than one hundred people: "Files Point to Official Use of Snipers," *NYT*, 2.10.03.

343 bolster his repressive regime: Alfred E. Senn, *Power, Politics and the Olympic Games*, 223–25.

344 big hotels: Helen Jefferson Lenskyj, "Making the World Safe for Global Capital: The Sydney 2000 Olympics and Beyond," in Bale and Christensen, *Post Olympism?*, 138.

344 putting them behind bars: "Experts Say Greek Verdicts Don't Dispel Olympic Threat," *NYT*, 10.17.03.

344 like potential terrorists: "Stepped-up Police Activity Irks an Arab Area in Greece," *NYT*, 26.4.04.

344 ramshackle tenements: "Better Race to Beijing before Olympics," *San Francisco Chronicle*, 29.9.05.

344 "in the world": "Delegates Hope Choice Spurs Openness," *NYT*, 14.7.01.

Index

Aberdare, Lord, 101–2, 325
Abrahams, Harold M., 45, 107
Abramson, J. P., 247
Adenauer, Konrad, 50, 325
advertising rights, 114, 171
Afghanistan, 194
  Soviet invasion of, 336–38
Albert I, King of Belgium, 41
Albritton, David, 89, 230–31
Alexandra, Queen of England, 27, 28
Alfonso XIII, King of Spain, 51
Amateur Athletic Union (AAU), 29, 32, 41,
    56, 74–76, 81–82, 97, 229, 287, 330
  anti-German sentiment within, 74–75
  boycott resolution of, 75–76, 77, 80,
    98–100, 175
  Jewish members of, 80
  Sullivan Memorial Award of, 90, 330
  track-and-field certifications of, 74, 78, 83,
    93, 101
American Jewish Congress (AJC), 72–73, 75,
    78, 81, 107, 312
American Jewish Labor Committee (AJLC),
    81, 312
American Olympic Committee (AOC), 31,
    40–41, 47, 134, 141, 144, 174, 180,
    181, 195, 222, 236, 243
  Balter's criticism of, 278–79
  fund-raising by, 98, 100, 169–71
  U.S. boycott movement and, 70, 71, 73,
    74–75, 76–77, 78–80, 82–83, 91,
    93–95, 96, 97, 100, 175
  see also Brundage, Avery

Amsterdam Summer Games (1928), 46–48,
    49, 53, 57, 62, 86, 114, 195, 248
Anglo-German Fellowship, 103–4, 213
Anglo-German Naval Agreement (1935), 102
Angriff, Der, 62, 65, 177, 184, 239, 290–91
Anthropology Days contests, 25–26
"Anti-Capitalist Olympiad," 55
anti-Jewish persecution, 14, 43, 44, 58, 64–68,
    69–109, 147, 154–55, 173, 175, 184,
    209, 224, 281
  Berlin violence in, 81–82
  of businesses, 64, 69–70, 114, 123, 160, 220
  cataloging technologies for, 211
  cultural, 201–2
  of doctors, 220
  of Dutch Jews, 238
  in Kristallnacht pogrom, 127, 312–13, 315,
    319
  in Munich violence, 81
  at 1936 Garmisch games, 114, 117–23,
    127, 128, 142
  in Nuremberg laws, 84, 85, 86, 91, 107
  "Olympic pause" and, 220
  post-Olympic, 226
  Strauss's disregard for, 197–98
  in *Stürmer,* 117, 120, 121, 142, 184
  U.S. consular reports of, 94–97
  see also boycott movement, international;
    Jewish athletes, German
anti-Semitism, 79, 107, 151, 242–43
  see also anti-Jewish persecution; racism
Antwerp Olympic Games (1920), 39–42, 45,
    52, 190

Antwerp Olympic Games (*continued*)
  black athletes in, 58
  inadequate facilities of, 40, 41
  innovations of, 42
  nonparticipants in, 39–40, 42–43, 104
  travel to, 41
Anzaña, Manuel, 152
Aquatic Sports Complex, 261–64
Argentina, 258, 269, 280
arts competitions, ancillary, 30, 201–3
Aryans, 10, 58, 83, 86, 128, 154, 157, 173,
        174, 176, 182, 220, 236, 244, 309
  Jewish marriages prohibited with, 84
  non-Aryans vs., 64–65, 128, 183, 265–66
  Nordic types as, 231, 235, 239
  Tibet as cradle of, 205, 206
Athens, 10–11, 46
  Acropolis in, 10, 11, 299
  torch relay in, 6
Athens "Olympiad" (1906), 34
Athens Olympic Games (1896), 6, 18–22,
        108, 252, 264
  marathon of, 21–22, 194
  political issues in, 19–20
Athens Summer Games (2004), 3*n*, 286, 344
Auden, W. H., 186
Australia, 21, 30
  boycott movement in, 106
Australia, Olympic team of, 24, 29, 223
  arrival of, 181
  kangaroo mascot of, 158, 181, 309
  in 1936 Garmisch games, 124–25
Australian Olympic Federation, 125
Austria, 39–40, 43, 140, 142–43, 203
  anti-Semitism in, 107
  German annexation of, 271, 310
  national anthem of, 135
  Nazi Party of, 7–8
Austria, Olympic team of, 265–66, 271,
        275–77, 280
  in 1896 Athens games, 19
  in 1936 Garmisch games, 125–26, 129–30,
        133, 135
  personal boycotters of, 107–8
  in procession of athletes, 125–26, 194
"Axel Paulson" jump, 132

Baarová, Lida, 219
Baer, Max, 173–74, 176
Baier, Ernst, 133
Baillet-Latour, Count Henri de, 40, 41, 49, 52,
        58–59, 188, 207, 294, 316, 317, 318,
        320
  on British boycott movement, 104

death of, 322
Hitler's snubbing behavior protested by,
        231, 233
Jahncke's rebuke of, 91–92
Nazi co-option sanctioned by, 321–22
1936 Garmisch games and, 120–21, 123,
        127
  in opening day ceremonies, 191, 192, 194,
        195
  U.S. boycott movement and, 71–72, 73, 75,
        90–93, 99
Baldwin, Sandra, 344
Baldwin, Stanley, 161
Ball, James, 47
Ball, Rudi, 87, 128–29
Ballangrud, Ivar, 131
ballooning, 23
Balter, Sam, 278–79
Bannister, Roger, 256
Barbuti, Raymond, 47
Barcelona, 51
  "People's Olympics" in, 152, 286–87
  as potential 1936 venue, 51, 52
Barcelona Summer Games (1992), 285
baseball, 284–86
  "Baseball—Was ist Das?" lecture series, 285
basketball, 278
Bavaria, 111–12, 113, 116, 121, 335
Bavarian Political Police (BPP), 117, 119, 123,
        124, 137
Bayreuth Wagner Festival, 193, 207–8
Beccali, Luigi, 255–56
Beer Hall Putsch, 60, 190
Beetham, Charles, 288, 289
Beijing Summer Games (2008), 184*n*, 342–44
Belgium, 40, 318
  German occupation of, 321, 322
  Olympic team of, 272
Bell Tower, 156, 164–65, 194
  postwar reconstruction of, 340–41
Benavides, Oscar, 276–77
Beneš, Edvard, 8
Beresford, Jack, 274
Bergmann, Gretel, 83–84, 85–86, 236–37
Berlin, 50–51, 156, 162, 164–65, 179,
        183–89, 211–12, 216
  amenities provided by, 184
  anti-Jewish displays removed from, 184
  anti-Jewish violence in, 81–82
  avant-garde art exhibits in, 185
  black athletes as well-treated in, 234
  as capital of German Empire, 33
  Coca-Cola in, 185–86
  cultural events in, 203–6

expanded North-South Railway in, 155, 159–60
IOC meetings in, 29–30, 188–89
jazz in, 185
Olympic Institute in, 318
Olympic Press Headquarters in, 122, 246
Owens's return visits to, 329
People's Court in, 223
prostitutes in, 183, 186
public radio loudspeakers in, 250
scaled-down militarism in, 187
sex scene in, 186–87
Soviet occupation of, 324, 327
2000 venue bid of, 338–39, 341
Unter den Linden, 160, 177, 187, 191
Berlin Olympic Games (1916), 18, 30, 32–39, 44
cancellation of, 38–39, 48, 50, 319
as "Fifth Olympiad," 39
funding of, 35–36, 37, 155
Olympic trials for, 37–38
proposed venue change of, 38–39
stadium built for, 32–33, 38, 50–51
training for, 35
Berlin Summer Games (1936):
as above politics, 8, 16
"alternative games" vs., 55, 152, 202, 286–89
competitions of, 205, 216, 217, 227–59, 260–94; see also specific events
cost of, 155–56, 223
expected revenue of, 50, 63
fatalities of, 282–83, 284
female athletes' housing at, 159
fiftieth anniversary commemoration of, 14, 86, 235
funding of, 63, 64, 113
Hitler salute vs. Olympic salute in, 194–95
Hitler's endorsement of, 58–59, 63–64
ideological elements of, 5, 14, 232, 271
IOC venue award of, 12, 44–45, 48, 49–57, 111
militaristic closing ceremony of, 293–94
national medal tabulations of, 290–93, 306
oak tree symbolism in, 232, 256
Olympic oath swearing at, 199
opening day ceremonies of, 11, 191–201, 210, 223, 224, 247, 304, 308
postgames interviews of, 270
procession of athletes in, 194–95
propaganda value of, 15, 35, 59, 63, 85, 96–97, 100, 101, 108–9, 136, 140, 156, 160, 213, 222, 247–48, 271, 337
protest demonstrations at, 222–23

security system of, 124, 193, 220–26, 245–46
VIP visitors to, 208–20
Berlin Summer Games (1936), preparations for, 4–5, 33, 35, 59, 62–64, 66, 147–89
athletic, 165–72
Los Angeles innovations emulated in, 56–57, 157, 182
municipal, 183–88
publicity and propaganda campaign in, 64, 161–65
regime's behind-the-scenes control of, 66, 67, 73
Rhineland remilitarization and, 147–52, 162
Schmeling and, 172–79
see also building program
biathlon, 134
Bingham, William J., 83
Birchall, Frederick T., 125, 142, 247
black athletes, 15, 25, 31, 58–59, 62–63, 89, 170, 171–72, 175, 179, 181, 228–29, 230–31, 238–45, 268
as "black auxiliaries," 239, 240, 244
British, 58
Canadian, 256
female, 228
Hitler's snubbing of, 12, 230, 231, 232–34, 247
in 1904 St. Louis games, 25
in 1924 Paris games, 45
in 1932 Los Angeles games, 58, 229, 330
in Olympia, 302, 306–7, 308
in U.S. boycott movement, 87–90
as well-treated in Berlin, 234
see also Owens, Jesse; racism, anti-black
Blake, Arthur, 21
Blask, Erwin, 234
blaue Licht, Das, 144, 296
Bleibtrey, Ethelda, 42
Blomberg, Werner von, 124, 194
Blum, Léon, 150–52
bobsledding, 105, 107
Garmisch course for, 112–13, 114–15, 127, 139, 145
in 1932 Lake Placid games, 56
in 1936 Garmisch games, 127, 134, 145
Bogner, Willy, 126
Bohemia, 43
Borchmeyer, Erich, 229, 232, 307
Bormann, Martin, 121–22
Böss, Gustav, 50
Boston, Ralph, 239

Boston Athletic Association (BAA), 19–20
Bote, Wilhelm, 223
boxing, 30, 65, 107, 168, 181, 268–69, 330
    Hitler's interest in, 60, 179
    professional heavyweight, 167, 172–79, 340
boycott movement, international, 12, 13,
        69–109, 117, 118–19, 123, 147
    alternative venues and, 69–70, 71, 73, 77,
        92–93, 119
    cultural boycotts in, 201–2, 203, 206
    in France, 69, 104–6, 107, 150–52
    German promises vs., 71, 72, 73–74, 75,
        77, 78, 81, 82–83, 92, 97, 101–2, 111,
        174
    in Great Britain, 69, 76, 101–4, 107, 213
    personal boycotts in, 105, 106–8, 136, 288
    potential result of, 108–9
    see also United States, boycott movement in
Brandt, Heinz, 283
Bräutigan, Hans, 223
Brazil, Olympic team of, 55, 223
Breitmeyer, Arno, 79
Breker, Arno, 156–57, 203
British Football Association, 102–4
British Olympic Association (BOA), 76, 101–4
British Olympic Council (BOC), 27, 38, 169
Broun, Heywood, 82–83
Brown, Arthur, 240
Brown, Ellison "Tarzan," 258–59
Brown, Godfrey, 256, 307
Brown, Ivan, 134
Brundage, Avery, 53, 87, 134, 139, 188,
        278–79, 287, 317, 318–21, 325, 333n,
        344
    AAU victory of, 98–100, 175
    America First Committee joined by, 320
    anti-boycott stance of, 70–71, 72, 74–75,
        76–77, 78–79, 82–83, 93–94, 318–19,
        336, 337
    background of, 70
    on blacks' anatomical advantages, 331
    Canadian protest supported by, 128
    death of, 336
    female gender verification proposed by, 189
    fund-raising efforts of, 100, 169, 171
    German construction contract awarded to,
        99
    in Glickman/Stoller affair, 242, 243
    Halt's rehabilitation aided by, 327–28
    on Hitler's banning of anti-Jewish displays,
        120
    Jarrett dismissed by, 180–81, 255
    and massacred Israeli athletes, 335–36
    in 1912 Stockholm games, 31, 70

at 1936 Garmisch games, 134, 139,
        140–41, 336
    1940 Tokyo venue supported by, 318–19
    Olympia admired by, 311, 313, 314
    personal "fact-finding" mission of, 77,
        78–80, 95
    Schmeling's meeting with, 174–75
    Sonja Henie's amateurism doubted by, 132
    Winter Games denounced by, 110, 336
Buchner, Ernst, 139
building program, 85, 113, 147, 152–61, 162,
        165
    beautification/sanitization projects in,
        160–61, 162, 220–21
    municipal infrastructure improved in, 155,
        159–60
    Olympic Village in, 157–59
    Reichssportfeld in, 152–57
Bulgaria, 7, 39–40, 195
Burke, Henry Penn, 170
Burnham, James, 337
Busch, Adolphus, 25
Busch, Christian, 165
Bush, Clarence, 93, 100, 170

Cadman, Charles Wakefield, 202
Cahners, Norman, 107
Canada, 44, 236, 256
    boycott movement in, 106, 288
Canada, Olympic team of, 29, 47, 256, 279,
        288
    in 1936 Garmisch games, 127–28, 129, 145
    personal boycotters of, 107, 288
Canadian Amateur Hockey Association, 128
Carnera, Primo, 167, 175–76
Carpenter, J. C., 28
Carpenter, Kenneth, 252–53
Carter, Jimmy, 337
Castro, Fidel, 286
Catalonia, Republic of, 51
"cathedral of light" effect, 146, 294
Celler, Emanuel, 79
Chamberlain, Neville, 215
Chamonix Winter Games (1924), 44–45, 281
Chandler, Harry, 53
Channon, Henry "Chips," 215–17, 218, 219
Chariots of Fire, 45
Charpentier, Robert, 272
Chicago, 24, 70, 79, 162, 170, 178, 229, 240,
        313
Chile, 51
China, People's Republic of, 184n, 342–44
China, Republic of, 54–55, 292
    Boxer Rebellion in, 24

Japanese invasion of, 318–19
Olympic team of, 55, 168, 181, 182
Chun Doo Hwan, 343
Church, Joe, 18
Churchill, Winston, 138, 217, 235, 275
Cieman, Henry, 288
Citrine, Walter, 101
Clark, Robert, 254
Coca-Cola, 114, 185–86, 340n
Colgate, Gilbert, 134
Colledge, Cecilia, 132
Cologne, 49–50, 326
Committee Against the Hitlerian Games, 105
Communist Party, 60, 71, 93–94, 221, 269,
    270, 309
  French, 104, 150–51
  German, 213–14, 222–23
  U.S., 55, 288
concentration camps, 97, 108, 131, 160–61,
    220–21, 223, 270, 271, 312, 317, 327,
    343
Condor Legion, 158, 207, 284
Connolly, John, 20
Cook, Theodore, 38
Coolidge, Calvin, 47, 91
Cooper, Gary, 313
Coubertin, Baron Pierre de, 17, 28–30, 38, 43,
    71, 190, 199, 281, 294
  ancillary arts competitions advocated by, 30,
    201
  on Anthropology Day contests, 26
  Berlin venue favored by, 51
  on counting Olympic games, 39
  death of, 318
  female athletes opposed by, 30
  five-ringed Olympic symbol designed by, 6,
    42
  literature competition won by, 30
  Los Angeles venue decision supported by,
    52–53
  marathon as viewed by, 21
  1900 Paris games and, 22, 24
  1904 St. Louis games and, 24–25, 26
  1912 Stockholm games and, 30
  1916 venue change rejected by, 39
  1920 Antwerp Games and, 41
  as Nobel Peace Prize candidate, 188
  Olympic Games restarted by, 3, 17–19
  Olympic ideals propounded by, 17–18, 27,
    28–29, 30, 92
  "Olympic truce" promoted by, 17, 39
  recorded voice of, 195–96
  "sporting war" as concept of, 17, 32
  Winter Games as viewed by, 44

Crabbe, Buster, 255
Cranz, Christl, 131, 145
Cromwell, Dean, 240, 242, 243, 331
Csák, Ibolya, 236
Csik, Ferenc, 262
Cuba, 286
cultural events, 201–8
  arts competitions in, 201–3
  Dutch alternative art exhibition in, 202
  exhibitions in, 162–63, 204–5
  lectures in, 205–6
  music in, 202, 203, 204, 207–8
  popular entertainments in, 204
  scientific congress in, 206
  theatre in, 203
Cunningham, Glenn, 255–56
Curley, James, 82
Curtius, Ernst, 9, 50
cycling, 168, 271–72
Czechoslovakia, 8, 167, 223
  German occupation of, 314, 315, 319
  Olympic team of, 31, 107, 129, 182, 265,
    307

Daley, Arthur J., 279
Dallkolat, 166
Daume, Willi, 326
Davison, Harry, 210–11
decathlon, 11, 31, 59, 254–55, 283, 302, 307,
    314
Degener, Dick, 263
"Degenerate Art" exhibit, 185
Delphi, Greece, 6
demonstration sports, 284–86
Dempsey, Jack, 176, 278
Denmark, 262
Depression, Great, 52, 53–54, 56, 108, 211
Deutsch, Bernard, 73, 74, 78, 80
Deutsch, Judith, 107–8
Deutsche Hochschule für Leibesübungen,
    66–67, 84
Deutscher Reichsausschuss für die Olympische
    Spiele (DRAFOS), 33, 34, 35, 37, 42,
    46
Deutscher Reichsausschuss für Leibesübungen
    (DRL), 9, 42, 65, 66, 67, 326
Deutsches Stadion, 32–33, 38, 50–51
Deutschland Halle, 268–70
de Vries, Carla, 225
Dhunen, Felix, 203
Didrickson, Mildred "Babe," 229
Diem, Carl, 18, 33–35, 47, 56–57, 108, 112,
    166, 194, 201, 220, 296, 319
  background of, 33–34

Diem, Carl (*continued*)
  baseball teams praised by, 285
  Berlin's venue bid supported by, 51, 52
  death of, 326
  denazification of, 325–26
  as DRAFOS general secretary, 34, 35
  Garmisch anti-Semitism deplored by,
    117–18
  "German Olympiad" proposed by, 321
  on German team's 1928 victories, 47–48
  IOC criticized by, 42–43
  IOC gold chains contributed by, 192
  Jewish associations of, 66–67
  military potential emphasized by, 34
  national games approved by, 42, 43
  national pride encouraged by, 46
  Nazi press attacks against, 66, 67
  1916 venue change rejected by, 38
  1932 Los Angeles games supported by, 56,
    62
  on oak-leaf crowns, 232
  Olympic flame as viewed by, 5
  as Olympic Institute director, 318
  Olympic torch relay planned by, 5, 6–7, 34
  pageant written by, 199–201, 324
  propaganda of, 35
  in publicity campaign, 161, 162–63, 164
  sports and war linked by, 10, 191, 321,
    322–23
  U.S. games arrangements studied by, 35,
    56–57
  wartime inspirational speeches of, 322–24
Diem, Gudrun, 194
Dietrich, Sepp, 124
Dietrich-Eckart Theater, 153, 156, 203,
    264–65, 324
  postwar usage of, 340
discus throw, 11, 20, 23, 252–53, 307
  women's, 234–35
Discus Thrower (Myron), 11, 157, 297, 308–9
Disney, Walt, 311, 313
diving, 30, 263–64
Döberitz, *see* Olympic Village in Döberitz
Dodd, Martha, 244–45
Dodd, William E., 97, 143, 212, 218, 219
Döhlemann, Friedrich, 119
Dollfuss, Engelbert, 8
Dörffeldt, Ilse, 236
Dorian tribe, 10
double-shot running-deer event, 42
Douglas MacArthur Award, 243
Draper, Arthur S., 41
Draper, Foy, 240–42
Dreyfus case, 22

Dr. Wander Pharmaceuticals, 114
Dubinsky, David, 287–88
Dunn, Gordon, 253

East Germany, 328
Edström, J. Sigfrid, 76–77, 83, 99, 169, 325,
    328
Edwards, Phil, 256
Edward VII, King of England, 27
Edward VIII, King of England, 137, 223
Egk, Werner, 199, 200, 203
Egypt, 130–31, 194
eight-hundred-meter race, 21, 234, 240, 307
eighty-meter hurdles race, women's, 237–38
"Emperor Hymn," 135
Enabling Act (1933), 64, 108
Epp, Franz Ritter von, 121, 207
equestrian events, 37, 46, 207, 282–83, 290,
    299, 307, 332
Ertl, Hans, 145, 299, 301, 308
Estonia, 269
Ewing, Alfredo, 52

Fairbanks, Douglas, Jr., 54
Fair Play for American Athletes (Brundage),
    93–94
Fanck, Arnold, 144, 295
Farmer, Zack, 53
Farrère, Claude, 150
Fauré, Felix, 24
Federoff, Ernest, 289
Fein, Robert, 271
female athletes, 30, 83–84, 85–87, 262,
    265–66
  Berlin housing of, 159
  black, 228
  gender verification of, 189, 236, 237
  German, 131, 133, 166, 229–30, 234–37,
    291
  Italian, 237–38
  Nazi opinion of, 166
  in 1932 Los Angeles games, 54, 159, 180,
    229, 237
  in 1936 Berlin track and field events, 166,
    228, 229–30, 234–38
  U.S., 41, 42, 125, 170, 180–81, 228,
    235–36, 263–64
fencing, 23, 37, 107, 180, 260
  by Hungarian Jews, 267
  women's, 86–87, 265–67
Ferris, Daniel J., 41, 56, 287
Fiehler, Karl, 207
field handball, 280, 326
field hockey, 180, 280, 306

fifteen-hundred-meter race, 254, 255–56
fifty-kilometer walk, 227, 256–57
figure skating, 56, 115, 127, 132–34, 135
    pairs, 133–34
Finland, Olympic team of, 27, 45–47, 182, 269
    in 1912 Stockholm games, 31
    in 1920 Antwerp games, 42, 45
    in 1924 Paris games, 45
    in 1928 Amsterdam games, 46–47
    in 1932 Los Angeles games, 56
    in 1936 Berlin track and field events, 230,
        231, 252, 255, 257, 258
    in 1936 Garmisch games, 131
Finnish-Soviet War, 320
firefighting, 23
Flack, Edwin, 21
Flanner, Janet, 187–88, 200
Flatow, Gustav Felix and Alfred, 108
Fleischer, Tilly, 229–30, 249
Flood, Fred, 269
Ford, Henry, 313
Fosdick, Harry Emerson, 82
4 x 100–meter relay race, 240–43
four-hundred-meter hurdle race, 231, 253
four-hundred-meter race, 25, 239–40, 307
    in 1896 Athens games, 20
    in 1904 St. Louis games, 25
    in 1908 London games, 28
    in 1924 Paris games, 45
    in 1928 Amsterdam games, 47
    in 1932 Los Angeles games, 58
four-hundred-meter relay race, women's, 236
four-minute mile, 256
Fox, Donna, 134
France, 17, 22–24, 25, 39, 43–45, 102, 138,
        148–52, 161, 214, 248, 336
    anti-German sentiment in, 38
    boycott movement in, 69, 104–6, 107,
        150–52
    Communist Party of, 104, 150–51
    1894 Sorbonne conference in, 18–19
    1916 Berlin venue opposed by, 38–39
    1923 Ruhr Valley occupation of, 43
    German occupation of, 317, 323
    Popular Front government of, 150–51, 213
    Rhineland remilitarization and, 148–50
France, Olympic team of, 106, 168, 182, 222,
        272, 291–92
    funding of, 105–6, 150–52, 168
    in 1932 Los Angeles games, 56
    in 1936 Garmisch games, 106, 125, 128,
        134, 148–49, 150
    personal boycotters of, 105, 107
    in procession of athletes, 194–95

Franco, Francisco, 197, 207, 213, 286
Franco-British Exhibition, 26–27
François-Poncet, André, 214, 218, 219
Franco-Prussian War, 17
Frankfurter, David, 126–27
Franz Ferdinand, Archduke, 38
Freisler, Roland, 223n
French Gymnastics Union, 18–19
Frentz, Walter, 299, 301
Frey, Konrad, 264
Frick, Margarete, 184
Frick, Wilhelm, 63, 65, 119, 120, 124, 152,
        153, 156, 157, 187, 194
Friesenhaus dormitory, 159
Fritsch, Hans, 195
Fritsch, Werner von, 281
Fromm, Bella, 209, 301
Fürstner, Wolfgang, 159
Furtwängler, Wilhelm, 207, 310

Gallico, Paul, 141, 173
    on militaristic closing ceremony, 146
Gamelin, Maurice, 150
Gandini, Giulio, 267
Garland, William May, 52–53, 72, 90–91,
        188, 314
Garmisch-Partenkirchen, 322, 336
    inter-village competition in, 115
    as 1940 Winter Games venue, 319, 320,
        321, 325
Garmisch-Partenkirchen Winter Games
        (1936), 13, 14, 59, 81, 104, 105, 106,
        110–46, 147–49, 150, 164, 172, 199,
        206, 227, 248, 317, 336
    advertising rights of, 114
    alpine skiing in, 129–31, 135, 139, 299
    amateurism and, 129–30, 132–33
    anti-German sentiment and, 116, 117
    anti-Jewish persecution at, 114, 117–23,
        127, 128, 142
    athletes' evaluation of, 141
    athletic housing of, 115
    attendance figures for, 136
    bobsled course of, 112–13, 114–15, 127,
        134, 145
    bobsledding in, 127, 134, 145
    Coca-Cola as "official sponsor" of, 114
    competitions of, 127–35
    contention in, 127–30, 143
    criminal elements barred from, 116–17
    entertainment facilities of, 138–39
    false public image created for, 121–23, 124,
        126–27, 137, 138, 140, 141–42,
        143–44

Garmisch-Partenkirchen Winter Games (continued)
figure skating in, 115, 127, 132–34, 135
foreign visitors to, 115–18, 121, 122–23, 136–41, 142, 144
funding of, 111–12, 113–14
as "Gapa" games, 112, 116
"Hitler salute" vs. Olympic salute at, 125–26
Hitler's attendance at, 123–24, 125–26, 130, 133, 138, 143–44, 146, 147
ice hockey in, 87, 115, 127–29, 141, 145
ice skating in, 112–13, 131, 141
IOC venue award of, 74, 111–12
Jewish visitors to, 117–19
in Jugend der Welt film, 142, 144–45, 297, 299
letdown parties at, 139
local visitors to, 136
militaristic closing ceremony of, 115, 146
military patrol skiing in, 134–35
new construction for, 112–13, 114–16
Nordic skiing in, 130, 131
official pin of, 114
Olympic flame of, 126
Olympic oath at, 126
opening ceremony of, 115, 124–26, 127, 145
opening day of, 113, 123–26, 138, 147–48
pairs figure skating in, 133–34
pickpocket incidents at, 117
preparations for, 112–24
price gouging at, 112, 116
procession of athletes in, 124–26, 145, 194
restrained German press reportage during, 126–27, 128
revenues of, 111, 113, 136–37
security system of, 117, 123–24
skating stadium of, 112–13, 115
ski instructors vs. ski trainers in, 129–30
ski jumping in, 123, 127, 131, 141
ski-jump stadium of, 14, 112–13, 115, 124
snow at, 123, 127
social scene of, 136–41
team boycotts of, 130, 134–35
Gebhardt, Willibald, 19, 22
Geist, Raymond, 94–95, 97
General Mills, 171
George II, King of Greece, 6
George V, King of England, 125
German Boxing Federation, 101
German Democratic Republic, 50, 329
German Gymnastics Festival (1923), 43

German Organizing Committee (GOC), 4, 5, 7, 30, 46, 63, 65, 82, 92, 105, 195, 196–97, 198–99, 246, 298
advertising deals made by, 114
building program and, 152, 158
cultural events sponsored by, 162–63, 201–6
nations formally invited by, 77, 79–80
1936 Garmisch games and, 110, 111, 112, 113, 114, 116, 125, 127, 139
Olympic bell donated to, 164–65
preparatory activities of, 161, 162, 164, 174, 184, 185, 187
radio broadcast facility created by, 249
see also Diem, Carl; Lewald, Theodor
German Swimming Association, 65
German Track and Field Association, 84
German Winter Sports Championships (1935), 113
Germany, Federal Republic of, 50, 325, 327
Germany, Imperial, 32–39, 52, 191
Berlin as capital of, 33
1912 bid withdrawn by, 29–30
Interior Ministry of, 36–37
international sporting contests opposed in, 17–18, 19, 20, 25, 38
Olympic team of, 18–19, 20–21, 24, 25, 29, 31, 34, 36, 108
Germany, Nazi:
Air Ministry of, 208–10
ancient Greeks' affinity with, 5, 9–11, 37, 196, 206, 308–9
annual rituals of, 190
bringing ethnic Germans back to, 206
British alliance sought by, 212–15
Catholic youth groups disbanded by, 82, 105
Communist Party in, 213–14, 222–23
concentration camps of, 97, 108, 131, 160–61, 220–21, 223, 270, 271, 312, 317, 327, 343
Depression in, 108, 211
Foreign Ministry of, 122, 125
Interior Ministry of, 63–64, 66, 68, 73, 118, 119, 121, 153, 155
IOC's tacit endorsement of, 111
national anthem of, 135, 194, 195, 294
1933 Enabling Act of, 64, 108
positive side of, 14
Propaganda Ministry of, 5, 8, 64, 68, 122–23, 144, 145, 161, 179, 197, 202, 244, 245, 246–47, 249, 251, 265, 290, 296–97, 298, 302–4, 305, 310, 315; see also Goebbels, Joseph

racism of, *see* anti-Jewish persecution; racism
Reich Commission for Price Control of, 116
"spiritual mobilization" of, 12
Vatican Concordat with, 82
Germany, Nazi, Olympic team of, 71, 165–72,
    182, 216, 260–61, 264–67, 268–70,
    271, 273–74, 277, 280, 281, 282–83,
    284
  female athletes of, 131, 133, 166, 229–30,
    234–37, 291
  medal count of, 60, 260, 290–93, 306
  Nazi members of, 227, 230, 235, 271
  in 1936 Garmisch games, 87, 125, 128–29,
    130, 131, 133, 135
  oath sworn by, 166–67
  performance enhancement of, 165–66
  postwar experiences of, 332
  in procession of athletes, 195
  SS and, 316
  as "state amateurs," 165, 291
  track and field, 229–31, 232, 234–35,
    238–39, 241, 242, 252–53
  World War II fatalities of, 283, 332
Germany, Weimar Republic of, 12, 42, 50, 52,
    157, 173, 204, 250
  Finns as athletic model for, 45–46
  military restrictions on, 40, 44
  national games preferred by, 42–43
  Olympic exclusion of, 18, 39–40, 42–43,
    328, 104, 328
  Olympic team of, 46–48, 55–56, 58, 62,
    86, 87, 111, 199
  sex scene in, 186
  sport and war linked by, 44
"Germany-Olympia" exhibition, 162–63, 204
Gestapo, 141, 182, 186–87, 198, 221–22,
    223, 224, 269
Gestring, Marjorie, 263–64
Gilbert, A. C., 318
Gilsa, Werner von und zu, 159
Glickman, Marty, 240–43
gliding, 284
Goddet, Jacques, 248
Goebbels, Joseph, 8, 10, 63, 65, 68, 129, 152,
    177, 180, 192, 201, 207, 213, 217,
    259, 277
  anti-black racism of, 244
  Jugend de Welt subsidized by, 144, 145
  media controlled by, 126–27, 128, 244,
    245–46, 248–50, 265, 290, 306
  official reception attended by, 140
  Olympic party hosted by, 219
  physical defect of, 59–60
  publicity campaign run by, 64, 161, 163

Rhineland remilitarization supported by,
    149
  Riefenstahl and, 296, 297, 302–4, 305, 306,
    307, 310, 311–12, 315
  Schmeling and, 177, 179
  Shirer chastised by, 122–23
  Strauss and, 197–98
  television promoted by, 250
  Vansittart and, 214, 215
Goethe, Johann Wolfgang von, 9, 106, 163,
    203, 205
Goldner, Lucie, 107–8
Goppel, Alfons, 335
Gordon, Eddie, 288, 289, 330
Göring, Emmy Sonnemann, 216, 219
Göring, Hermann, 129, 180, 192, 197, 213,
    214
  Coca-Cola promoted by, 186
  Lindbergh and, 208–10
  Londonderry's admiration of, 137–38
  Olympic parties hosted by, 215, 218–19,
    236
  physical appearance of, 59–60
  Vansittart and, 214, 215
Graham, Martha, 201–2
Great Britain, 33, 119, 121, 130, 143, 161,
    206, 247, 314, 336, 340
  anti-German sentiment in, 38, 103
  appeasement policy of, 215
  Blitz in, 138
  boycott movement in, 69, 76, 101–4, 107,
    213
  Foreign Office of, 38, 103, 104, 213
  Nazi sympathizers in, 137–38
  1916 Berlin venue opposed by, 38
  1935 British-German football match in,
    102–4
  Rhineland remilitarization and, 148, 150
  VIP visitors from, 137–38, 212–18
Great Britain, Olympic team of:
  black athletes of, 58
  in 1896 Athens games, 19
  Jewish athletes of, 45, 107
  in 1924 Paris games, 45
Great Britain, Olympic team of (1936), 222,
    225, 268, 273, 274, 280–81
  arrival of, 181–82
  funding of, 168–69
  medal count of, 291–93
  in 1936 Berlin track and field events, 236,
    240, 256–57, 258–59
  in 1936 Garmisch games, 125, 127–28,
    129, 132, 143, 145
  Olympic Village houses of, 181–82

Great Britain, Olympic team of (1936)
  (*continued*)
  in procession of athletes, 125, 195
Greece, 124, 194, 224, 299, 310, 344
  see also Olympia, Greece
Greeks, ancient, 39, 163, 297, 308–9
  athletic aesthetics of, 11, 60, 244
  athletic architecture of, 153–54
  athletic statuary of, 157
  democracy as downfall of, 10–11
  German affinity with, 5, 9–11, 37, 196,
    206, 308–9
  open-air theaters of, 153
  wrestling style of, 269
  see also Olympic Games, ancient Greek
Greek Torch Relay Committee, 7
Green, Milton, 107
Grenoble Winter Games (1968), 336
Groskopf, Walter, 303
Grosz, George, 173
Grünau, *see* rowing
Gründgens, Gustav, 203, 310
Gustav V, King of Sweden, 31
Gustloff, Wilhelm, 126–27
Guttmann, Allen, 70
gymnastics, 20–21, 24, 25, 29, 43, 108,
    264–65, 299, 302, 321
  women's, 262, 265
Gypsies, 221, 317

Haakon VII, King of Norway, 132
Halassy, Oliver, 280
Halswelle, Wyndam, 28
Halt, Karl Ritter von, 58–59, 62, 73, 79, 80,
    81, 83, 127, 144, 231, 316, 319–21
  at Baillet-Latour's funeral, 322
  concentration camp internment of, 327
  death of, 328
  denazification of, 327–28
  Garmisch anti-Semitism protested by,
    118–19
  in postwar era, 326–28
  as Reichssportführer, 323
Hamas, Steve, 174
Hamburg, 206, 221
hammer throw, 20, 234, 252, 301
Hamuro, Detsuo, 261
Handrick, Gotthardt, 284, 332
Hanfstaengl, Ernst "Putzi," 60
Hardin, Glenn, 253
Harper, Ernest, 258–59, 301
Harrer, Heinrich, 130
Harvard University, 19–20, 83, 107, 166
Hayes, John Joseph, 28

Hearst, Mrs. William Randolph, 211
Hedin, Sven, 205–6
Heiden, Eric, 131
heilige Berg, Der, 144, 295
Hein, Karl, 234
Heine, Heinrich, 9, 205
Held, Heinrich, 111
Helldorf, Wolf Heinrich von, 225
Helsinki Summer Games (1940), 319, 320
Helsinki Summer Games (1952), 264, 284*n*,
    326, 333*n*
  German participation in, 328
Henie, Sonja, 132–33, 138
Henry, Bill, 144, 249
Herber, Maxi, 133
Hercules, 10
Hess, Rudolf, 121, 188, 194, 204, 206
high jump, 25, 230–31, 289
  women's, 83–84, 85–86, 236–37
Hill, A. V., 206
Himmler, Heinrich, 123–24, 186–87, 316
  anti-black racism of, 244
  Hedin's theories shared by, 205, 206
  physical defect of, 59–60
Hindenburg, Paul von, 47, 50, 59, 63, 199
Hindenburg zeppelin, 179, 193–94
Hitler, Adolf, 4, 5, 8, 13, 15, 59–65, 68, 108,
    111, 136, 179, 180, 190, 199, 213,
    271, 278–79, 292, 316, 320
  on ancient Greek racial affinity, 10
  anti-black racism of, 228, 233, 244
  archaeological excavations approved by, 11,
    192, 318
  architectural display envisaged by, 25, 113,
    152–57
  assembled athletes reviewed by, 194, 225
  athletic warriors summoned by, 165
  attempted assassination of, 283
  at Bayreuth Wagner Festival, 207–8
  Berlin games approved by, 58–59, 63–64
  on black athletes' anatomical advantages,
    244
  black athletes snubbed by, 12, 230, 231,
    232–34, 247
  boxing as interest of, 60, 179
  boycott movement and, 72, 73, 78
  Breker's art favored by, 157, 203
  Brundage and, 140
  chancellorship assumed by, 49, 59, 62, 104
  Coubertin's literary remains obtained by,
    318
  flag of, 194
  Ford's admiration of, 313
  Franco's rebellion supported by, 207

Garmisch anti-Jewish displays prohibited by, 119, 120–21
German Jewish athletes prohibited by, 84–85
German medal count credited to, 291
GOC honorary chairmanship refused by, 63
grandmotherly visitor's kissing of, 225, 308
Gustloff funeral attended by, 127
Hedin and, 205
in Landsberg Prison, 60
Lindbergh's impressions of, 210–11
Londonderrys entertained by, 137–38
Mein Kampf of, 59, 60, 205
military medal winners promoted by, 284
in 1923 Munich protest, 43
at 1936 Garmisch games, 123–24, 125–26, 130, 133, 138, 143–44, 146, 147
new construction approved by, 113
official reception shirked by, 140
in *Olympia,* 304, 306, 307–8, 309, 311, 314
at Olympia Stadium, 212, 215, 216, 225, 227, 230, 231, 232, 234, 235–36, 252, 294
Olympic games denounced by, 49
in opening day ceremonies, 192–93, 194, 196, 198–99, 225, 304, 308
Owens's praise of, 233
personal bodyguard of, 124, 138, 187, 224
physical fitness demanded by, 60–61
physical ideal as unattained by, 59–60
on radio propaganda, 248
rearmament program of, 108
Rhineland remilitarized by, 146, 147–52, 162
Riefenstahl admired by, 144, 296, 301, 303–4, 310, 312, 317
Schmeling admired by, 173–74, 179, 340*n*
security arrangements for, 123–24, 193, 224–25, 235
Sonja Henie and, 132
sports eschewed by, 59–60
Stephens's private meeting with, 235–36
Strauss and, 197
strident partisanship of, 232, 247
television approved by, 250
Unity Mitford's attraction to, 217–18
Vansittart's impressions of, 214–15
Wolfe's yelling disliked by, 212, 225
"Hitler as Art Patron" cartoon, 202
"Hitler salute," 125–26, 194–95, 223, 230, 235, 266, 269
"Hitler weather," 123
Hitler Youth, 9, 191, 192, 196, 237, 309, 323–24
Hockert, Gunnar, 255

Hoffman, Fritz, 24
Homer, 10
Hoover, Herbert, 91
Horse Rider (Wackerle), 157
Horss, Maria, 3*n*
"Horst Wessel Lied," 4, 8, 195, 216, 223, 294
House, Edward M., 85
Hubbard, William DeHart, 45
Huber, Erwin, 11, 307, 309
Hull, Cordell, 77, 195
U.S. boycott movement and, 95–97
Hume, Don, 274
Hungary, 7, 39–40
Hungary, Olympic team of, 107
in 1896 Athens games, 19
in 1932 Los Angeles games, 56
in 1936 Berlin games, 236, 262, 265, 267, 269, 280
in 1936 Garmisch games, 128, 129
Husing, Ted, 249
Hybl, William J., 243

ice hockey, 87, 115, 127–29, 141, 145, 328
in 1932 Lake Placid games, 56
ice skating, 23, 112–13, 141
figure, 56, 115, 127, 132–34, 135
speed, 125, 131
India, 106, 130
Olympic team of, 24, 181, 182, 280, 306
Innsbruck Winter Games (1964), 336
International Amateur Athletic Federation (IAAF), 78–79, 83
International Jump Hill Commission, 115
International Olympic Committee (IOC), 3, 5, 12, 20, 24, 31, 32, 35, 38, 66, 236, 286, 290, 294, 316–22, 328, 333
advertising rights sale approved by, 114
Beijing venue award of, 342–44
Berlin venue award of, 12, 44–45, 48, 49–57, 111
Lausanne headquarters of, 39, 51, 52
Los Angeles venue award of, 49, 52–53
meetings of, 25, 26, 29–30, 32, 43–44, 49, 50–51, 53, 70, 72–74, 75, 76, 77, 101, 111, 188–89
Nazi co-option of, 316–18, 321–22
1904 St. Louis games and, 24–25, 26
1916 venue change resisted by, 38–39
1920 Antwerp games and, 40, 42–43
1924 Paris venue award of, 43, 52, 53
at 1936 Berlin games, 191–93, 194
1936 Garmisch games and, 74, 111–12, 115, 116, 119–21, 125, 127, 128, 129–30, 139–40

International Olympic Committee (IOC)
    (*continued*)
    1940 venue controversy in, 318–21
    official publication of, 318
    Olympia film and, 296, 298, 300, 314, 315,
        317
    Olympic Cup award of, 317
    Olympic Diploma award of, 314, 315, 317
    Olympic hymn and, 196, 197, 198
    Olympic Order award of, 326
    racial issues and, 58–59, 62
    U.S. boycott movement and, 69, 70, 71–73,
        75, 76, 77, 83, 84–85, 88, 90–93, 99,
        188–89
    Winter Games established by, 44–45
International Skating Union, 132
Iran, 311
Ireland, 19, 27
Isherwood, Christopher, 186
Ismayer, Rudolf, 199, 270, 271
Israeli athletes, massacre of, 334–36
Italy, 26, 44, 51, 77, 106, 148, 152–53, 175,
    203, 259, 336
Italy, Olympic team of, 222, 267, 268, 275,
    277, 281
    female athletes of, 237–38
    medal count of, 290, 291, 292
    in 1932 Los Angeles games, 56, 63, 167
    in 1936 Berlin track and field events, 242,
        255–56, 307
    in 1936 Garmisch games, 125, 128, 134,
        135
    in procession of athletes, 125, 195
    training of, 167

Jackson, Peter, 330
Jacobs, Joe, 173, 174, 175
Jacobs, Mike, 175, 176
Jahn, Ludwig "Turnvater," 18
Jahncke, Ernest Lee, 72, 90–92
    IOC expulsion of, 188
    U.S. boycott movement supported by,
        91–92, 188
Jalkonen, Kalle, 131
Jannings, Emil, 310
Japan, 24, 106
    as alternative 1936 venue, 77
    Asian expansionism of, 54–55, 167–68, 292
    as Axis power, 259
    baseball in, 285
    IOC membership of, 51–52
    Korea annexed by, 257, 259
    1940 Tokyo games renounced by, 319
Japan, Olympic team of, 181, 182, 261–62

government subsidies of, 168
medal count of, 291–92
in 1932 Los Angeles games, 54–55, 56, 166,
    261
in 1936 Berlin track and field events, 252,
    253, 255, 257–59, 307, 308
training of, 167–68
Jarrett, Eleanor Holm, 180–81, 255, 263, 319
javelin throw, 23, 252
    women's, 229–30
jazz, 185
Jenner, Bruce, 255
Jesse Owens Story, The, 329
"Jeux Défigurés, Les" (Goddet), 248
Jewish athletes, 58–59, 118
    Austrian, 265–66, 271
    British, 45, 107
    Czech, 107
    French, 105, 107
    Polish, 107
    U.S., 78, 107, 175, 240–43, 278–79
Jewish athletes, German, 75–77, 83–87,
    101–2, 128–29, 142, 327
    in concentration camps, 97, 108
    Hitler's prohibition of, 84–85
    purging of, 65–68, 72, 73–74, 78, 83–84,
        85–86, 91, 95–96, 97, 236–37
    token, Sherrill's proposal of, 84–87
Jewish Labor Committee (JLC), 287–88
Jewish Welfare Board, 80
Jews, 14, 43, 49, 58, 80, 173, 180–81, 234,
    288
    Diem's links to, 66–67
    Dutch, 238
    French, 105, 151
    Gustloff murder and, 126–27
    horses compared to, 59
    Hungarian, 267
    Israeli, Munich massacre of, 334–36
    in Lewald's ancestry, 36, 65, 66
    as Olympic visitors, 117–19
    in U.S. boxing, 173–74
    in U.S. boycott movement, 69–70, 71,
        72–73, 74–75, 77, 78, 80, 81, 100,
        107, 169–70
    see also anti-Jewish persecution; racism
Johnson, Ben, 288
Johnson, Cornelius, 89, 230–31, 289
Johnson, Francis, 279
Johnson, Jack, 174, 176, 330
Johnson, Jon, 255
Johnson, Rafer, 255
Johst, Hanns, 202–3
Jonath, Arthur, 58

Jugend der Welt, 142, 144–45, 297, 299
Juliana, Crown Princess of Netherlands, 137
Junghans, Carl, 145

Kalevala, 47
Kane, Robert, 337
Kapp Putsch, 157
Kaun, Elfriede, 236
kayak racing, 299
Kelley, John A., 258
Kennedy, John F., 329
Kiefer, Adolph, 262
Kiel, *see* yachting
King, Howell, 181
Kiphuth, Bob, 261
Kirby, Gustavus, 41, 72, 99, 170
  at New York anti-Nazi rally, 78
  in shipboard festivities, 180
  U.S. boycott movement supported by, 74,
    75, 76, 78, 188–89
Klemperer, Viktor, 226, 227, 265
Knecht, Willi, 14
Kobos, Endre, 267
Koenitzer, Willi, 10
Kohlemainen, Hannes, 31
Kolbe, Georg, 156–57
Korea, 257–59
Kotkas, Kalevi, 231
Kraenzlein, Alvin, 35
Krauss, Käthe, 235
Kristallnacht pogrom, 127, 312–13, 315, 319
Krupp, 7, 37
Krupp von Bohlen und Halbach, Gustav, 37,
  155

La Guardia, Fiorello H., 78, 82, 84, 287–88
Lake Placid Winter Games (1932), 49, 56, 87,
  132
  attendance figures for, 136
  pairs figure skating event at, 133–34
Lammers, Hans, 65–66, 81
Landon, Alf, 233
Langemarck Hall, 156, 194
Langer, Ruth, 107–8
Lantschner, Ludwig "Guzzi," 130, 299, 301,
  303
Lanzi, Mario, 307
Lapébie, Guy, 272
Larsson, Eric-August, 131
Lasker, Albert, 100
Latvia, 128, 269
Lauria, Louis, 268
Laval, Pierre, 161
Laven, Paul, 304

Law for the Restoration of the Professional
  Civil Service, 64–65
Le Fort, Baron Peter, 104, 114, 115, 121, 139
Lehman, Herbert H., 288, 289
Lehtinen, Lauri, 255
Leonard, Charles F., 284
Leopold II, King of Belgium, 30
Lermusiaux, Albin, 21
letdown parties, 139
Levy, I. P., 105
Lewald, Theodor, 33, 35–37, 46, 164, 166,
  188, 194, 196, 197, 198, 201
  background of, 35–36
  Bavarian funding sought by, 111–12
  Berlin's venue bid submitted by, 49–52
  boycott movement and, 71, 73, 76, 77, 80,
    81, 91, 92–93, 96, 97, 101–2, 174
  building program and, 152, 153
  death of, 325
  forced retirement of, 316, 325
  GOC established by, 63
  Hitler's support sought by, 63–64
  in IOC, 43–44, 49–50
  Jewish ancestry of, 36, 65, 66
  Los Angeles games supported by, 56, 57, 62
  Mahoney's rebuke of, 92
  Nazi press attacks against, 65–66
  regime's pressure on, 94–95, 96
  in Reich Interior Ministry, 36–37
Lewis, Frank, 269
Lex, Hans Ritter von, 118–19
Liddell, E. H., 45
Lindbergh, Anne Morrow, 209, 210, 211
Lindbergh, Charles E., 208–11, 320
Liu Changchun, 55
Lloyd George, David, 215
Londe, François, 342
London, 25, 26, 33, 162, 186
  as 1944 Olympic venue, 321
  Ribbentrop as ambassador to, 213, 214,
    215, 216, 218
Londonderry, Lord and Lady, 137–38
London Olympic Games (1908), 26–29, 195,
  273
  political issues in, 27–29, 31
  White City Stadium of, 27, 28, 29
London Summer Games (1948), 198, 267,
  326, 328
Long, Lutz, 238–39, 329
long jump, 45, 238–39, 288, 289
Longuet, Jules, 105–6
Los Angeles Memorial Coliseum, 53, 54, 57,
  153, 295
Los Angeles Organizing Committee, 53–55

Los Angeles Summer Games (1932), 49,
        52–58, 63, 77, 93, 168, 200, 248, 275,
        291
    advantages offered by, 53
    "Anti-Capitalist Olympiad" alternative to,
        55
    black athletes in, 58, 229, 330
    competitions of, 55, 56, 166, 180, 199,
        238, 253, 258, 261, 264, 265, 273,
        288, 330
    documentary film lacked by, 295
    East Coasters' view of, 53
    female athletes in, 54, 159, 180, 229, 237
    funding of, 53–54
    German officials' emulation of, 56–57, 157,
        182
    German team in, 55–56, 58, 62, 86, 111,
        199
    innovations of, 54, 57
    IOC's venue decision on, 49, 52–53, 55
    nations participating in, 54–56
    Olympic flame of, 57
    Olympic hymn of, 196, 198
    "Olympic Village" of, 54, 56, 157
    protest movement against, 54
    revenues of, 53, 55
    spectators of, 55
    travel to, 53, 54, 55
Los Angeles Summer Games (1984), 338
Louis, Joe, 172, 175–79, 182, 330, 340n
Louis, Spiridon, 21–22, 194, 198–99
Louisiana Purchase Centennial Exposition,
        24–26, 36
Lovell, Guillermo, 269
Lovelock, Jack, 256
Lubahn, Robert, 197
Luckenwalde, 9
Luftspring, Yisrael "Sammy," 107
LuValle, James, 239–40
Luxembourg, 206

MacArthur, Charles, 180
MacArthur, Douglas, 47, 195
Maccabi Union, 107
McGall, Albert, 331
Machon, Max, 177
Mack, Eugen, 264
McLemore, Henry, 282–83
Mahlo, Friedrich, 162
Mahoney, Jeremiah T., 80, 287
    Brundage's defeat of, 98–99
    Lewald rebuked by, 92
    U.S. boycott supported by, 81–82, 83,
        92–93

Malitz, Bruno, 61, 65, 166
Mandell, Richard, 231
Manger, Josef, 271
Mann, Heinrich, 151, 173
Mann, Thomas, 151, 184–85, 205
marathon, 13, 131, 258, 298
    in 1896 Athens games, 21–22, 194
    in 1900 Paris games, 23
    in 1908 London games, 27, 28
    in 1936 Berlin track and field events, 227,
        253, 257–59, 292
    in Olympia, 301, 305, 308
    standard distance of, 28
Marathon, Battle of, 21
Maraun, Frank, 310
March, Werner, 152–54, 155 157, 203, 324,
        340
Martin, Paul, 182–83
Marty, Walter, 289
Mastenbrock, Rita, 262
Mathias, Bob, 255
Mauermayer, Gisela, 234–35
Maurras, Charles, 20, 22
Max Schmelings Sieg—Ein Deutscher Sieg, 179,
        204
Mayer, Helene, 86–87, 265–67
Mayer, Louis B., 313
May Field parade ground, 153, 154, 156,
        164–65, 194, 340
Meadows, Earl, 253–54, 289
media coverage, 13, 63, 110, 159, 200–201,
        228–29, 242–43, 245–52
    of black athletes, 233–34, 239, 244
    Goebbels's control of, 126–27, 128,
        245–46, 248–50, 265, 290, 306
    of 1936 Garmisch games, 110, 118, 119,
        121, 122–23, 124, 126, 127, 128, 133,
        134, 140, 141–46, 248
    by photojournalists, 245–46
    by print journalists, 245–48, 249
    radio broadcasting in, 248–50, 251, 276,
        304
    recent, 249
    television in, 13, 250–52, 295
    of U.S. boycott movement, 75, 82–83, 85,
        88, 90, 101
Medica, Jack, 262
Melbourne Summer Games (1956), 198, 326
Meller, Willy, 156–57
Mengden, Guido von, 82, 323
Merkens, Toni, 272
Mesbah, Ahmed, 270, 271
Messersmith, George, 94–97
Metcalfe, Ralph, 58, 89, 229, 232, 241–42, 330

Mexico, Olympic team of, 279, 280
Mexico City Summer Games (1968), 343
Miklas, Wilhelm, 8
military patrol skiing, 134–35, 317, 322
Millard, Franco, 269
Miller, Douglas, 143
Miller, Franz, 232, 235
Miller, K. A., 70
Mitford, Diana and Unity, 217–18
Moch, Bob, 274
Mollenhauer, Paula, 235
Mondale, Walter, 337–38
Morris, Glenn, 254–55, 302, 314, 330
Morrison, Charles Clayton, 82
Moscow Summer Games (1980), 336–38, 342
Mosley, Sir Oswald, 217
Mount Temple, Lord, 103–4
Müller-Preis, Ellen, 265–66, 267
Munich, 110, 111, 112, 113, 114, 115, 120,
    121, 160, 217, 218
  aircraft collision over, 126
  anti-Jewish violence in, 81
  cultural and social functions hosted by, 81,
    139–40, 206–7
  Fasching (Carnival) Season of, 116, 139
  horseracing in, 207
  1923 Nazi protest demonstration in, 43
  visitor accommodations in, 116, 136
Munich agreement (1938), 8, 215, 312, 314
Munich Summer Games (1972), 267, 333–36
  Israeli athletes massacred at, 334–36
  Olympic Village of, 335
  public image created for, 333–34, 335
  threatened African boycott of, 335
Murakoso, Kohei, 255
Mussolini, Benito, 51, 56, 63, 71, 152–53,
    167, 187, 222
  Ethiopia invaded by, 148, 175
  female athletes approved by, 237, 238
  Riefenstahl and, 311
  soccer win enjoyed by, 277
Myron, 11, 157, 297, 308–9

Naismith, James, 279
Nan, Shoryu, 259
national anthems, 57, 135, 194, 195, 255,
    259, 294
National Association for the Advancement of
    Colored People (NAACP), 88–90
National Rifle Association, 281
Nazi Party:
  anti-black racism of, 58, 62, 87, 88, 185,
    228, 233, 239, 244–45
  Austrian, 7–8

book burnings of, 184
collectivism of, 61
cultic practices of, 170
"Degenerate Art" exhibit of, 185
election of, 12, 57, 63, 108, 117
English sympathizers of, 137–38
in "Gapa" region, 117, 317
homosexuality criminalized by, 186–87,
    221, 223–24, 239
international sporting contests disdained by,
    57–58, 165
jazz attacked by, 185
military sport approved by, 61
neo-Dorian architectural style of, 10
1920 platform of, 60
1923 Munich protest demonstration of, 43
Olympic movement disdained by, 12,
    61–62
Olympic program co-opted by, 316–18,
    312–22
Olympic team members of, 227, 230, 235,
    271
physical ideal of, 11, 59–60, 308–9
politics in sports approved by, 61, 102
Schmeling and, 173–79
sport and war linked by, 158, 308
sportsmanship of, 57–65
support of German youth sought by, 96–97
women's role as viewed by, 166
Netherlands, 137, 168, 202
  German occupation of, 238
  Olympic team of, 222, 232, 238, 241, 242,
    262
Neue Wache monument, 191
Neugrass, Herman, 107
Neurath, Konstantin von, 80
New York, N.Y., 33, 75, 76, 82, 83, 84, 107,
    161–62, 171, 172, 173, 174–79
  anti-Nazi demonstrators in, 81
  mass anti-Nazi rally in, 77–78
  1940 venue bid of, 319
  Riefenstahl in, 312–13
  "World Labor Athletic Carnival" in,
    286–89
New York Times, 75, 78, 124, 127, 142, 172,
    177–78, 200–201, 231, 242–43, 247,
    254, 257, 291, 312
New Zealand, 255–56
Nibelungenlied saga, 10
Nicolson, Harold, 138
Niebuhr, Reinhold, 82
Niedecken-Gebhard, Hanns, 199
Nishida, Shuhei, 253
Non-Sectarian Anti-Nazi League, 79

Norway:
  "alternative winter Olympics" in, 135
  German occupation of, 131, 133, 328
  Sonja Henie and, 132–33
Norway, Olympic team of, 277, 280–81
  military patrol skiing event boycotted by,
    134–35
  in 1936 Garmisch games, 130, 131,
    132–33, 135
Nuremberg, 49–50, 154, 160, 181, 184
Nuremberg laws, 84, 85, 86, 91, 107
Nuremberg Party Rallies, 84, 85, 100, 144,
    146, 154, 160, 190, 294, 296, 309,
    313
Nurmi, Paavo, 42, 45, 46–47, 241, 255

oak tree, symbolism of, 232, 256, 279
Oberammergau passion plays, 117
Odam, Dorothy, 236
"Ode to Joy" (Schiller), 199, 333n
"Ode to Sport" (Coubertin), 30
Oe, Suoe, 253
Olympia, Greece, 3–6, 17, 198, 299, 309, 310
  archaeological excavations at, 11, 37, 50,
    192, 318
  Coubertin's heart buried at, 318
  flame-lighting ceremony at, 3–4, 11
  International Olympic Academy in, 326
Olympia (documentary film), 11–12, 15, 145,
    295–315, 317, 333
  ancient Greek imagery in, 11, 297, 308–9
  black athletes in, 302, 306–7, 308
  budget of, 298, 302–4, 310
  close-up work in, 299, 301, 307
  decathlon footage in, 254–55, 302, 307
  editing of, 298, 302, 304–5
  equestrian events in, 307
  European objections to, 311, 314
  foreign-language versions of, 306, 308–9,
    311, 314
  Hitler in, 304, 306, 307–8, 309, 311, 314
  ideological bias in, 306, 308–9, 310
  making of, 295–305
  marathon footage in, 301, 305, 308
  musical score of, 304–5, 307
  narrator of, 304, 308
  Nazi physical aesthetic in, 11, 308–9
  Olympic torch relay in, 5–6, 299, 302, 309
  Olympic Village in, 309
  Owens in, 244, 306–7
  pole vault footage in, 255, 302
  political bias in, 306–8
  premiere of, 310
  prologue of, 111, 297, 299, 302, 305, 308

  Propaganda Ministry's backing of, 296–97,
    298, 302–4, 305, 310, 315
  propaganda value of, 302, 311, 314–15
  rowing footage in, 299, 300, 301
  sound effects of, 304
  staged recreations in, 254–55, 299, 302
  swimming footage in, 299, 301, 302, 308
  training shots in, 300–301, 302
  as two feature-length films, 303, 305–6,
    309, 310
  U.S. opposition to, 311–14
  yachting footage in, 299, 300–301
  see also Riefenstahl, Leni
Olympia (Koenitzer), 10
"Olympia" soft drink, 186
Olympic bell, 164–65, 194, 294
  postwar fate of, 340–41
Olympic flag, five-ringed, 42, 123, 196, 199,
    310
Olympic flame, 3–9, 57, 196, 198, 297, 328
  lighting ceremony of, 3–4, 11
  of 1936 Garmisch games, 126
  symbolism of, 5
Olympic Games:
  as above politics, 70, 105, 318, 336, 338,
    344
  alleged democratizing effect of, 343–44
  amateurism of, 26, 31–32, 129–30, 132–33,
    165, 167, 257, 281, 291
  ancillary arts competitions in, 30, 201
  counting of, 39
  disguised professionalism in, 267, 275, 328
  five-ring symbol of, 6, 42, 139, 196, 316,
    333n
  "gentlemanly" competition ethos of, 31, 32
  governmental promotions regulated by,
    161
  home-team favoritism in, 26, 27–29
  host's building of stadium for, 27, 30
  ideals and principles of, 9, 12, 17–18, 27,
    28–29, 31, 40, 42–43, 44, 61–62, 70,
    91–92, 120, 192, 247, 294, 297, 314,
    317
  invented traditions of, 4, 13, 27, 42, 56–57
  nationalism in, 17, 20, 22, 26, 31, 39–40,
    334
  postwar, 165
  protest counterattractions to, 55, 104, 135,
    152, 202, 286–89
  resumption of, 3, 17–18
  ritual opening invocation of, 126, 196
  as sporting war, 44, 47, 308
  victory crowns of, 232
  victory podium of, 57, 232, 259, 269, 307

Olympic Games, ancient Greek, 3, 4, 6, 17,
    26, 37, 42, 57, 58, 124, 190, 192, 194,
    297, 321
  characteristics of, 9
  city-state subsidies of, 165
  discus throw in, 11, 20
  false starters flogged in, 235
  five-ring symbol ascribed to, 6
  Hercules as mythic founder of, 10
  landed estates awarded to victors of, 234
  marathon lacked by, 21, 257
  "Messengers of Elis" in, 161
  performance-enhancing substances in,
    165–66
  Sparta in, 10
  winter sports lacked by, 44, 110
Olympic history exhibitions, 162–63, 204
Olympic hymn, 196, 197, 198, 333n
Olympic Hymn (Pindar), 3
Olympic Hymn (Strauss), 188, 196–98
  composition of, 196–97
  revised libretto of, 197
Olympic oath, 42, 107–8, 126, 199
Olympic salute, 125–26, 194–95, 200
"Olympic Show Must Go On, The"
    (Brundage), 319, 336
Olympic Stadium, 13, 14, 183, 193, 194, 204,
    249, 259, 261, 316, 329
  construction of, 153, 154, 155–56
  cost of, 155–56, 179
  historic monument status of, 339, 341
  Hitler at, 60, 212, 215, 216, 225, 227, 230,
    231, 232, 234, 235–36, 252, 294
  "Honor Tablet" at entrance of, 239, 340
  photoelectric timing system of, 227–28,
    237, 260
  postwar deterioration of, 339, 341
  reconstruction of, 341
  torchbearer's arrival at, 4, 9, 191, 192, 196,
    198
  Volkssturm Battalion in, 323–24
  see also track and field events (1936)
"Olympics Under Dictatorship, The" art exhi-
    bition, 202
Olympic Symphony Orchestra, 193, 195, 198,
    203
Olympic torch relay, 3–9, 13, 34, 147,
    191–92, 259, 297, 299
  flame-lighting ceremony of, 3–4, 11
  radio coverage of, 248
  route of, 5–8
  torchbearers of, 4, 5–6, 9, 191, 192, 196,
    198
  torch design in, 6–7

Olympic Train, 163–64
Olympic truce, 17, 39, 320–21
Olympic Village, 328
  Los Angeles, 54, 56, 157
  Munich, 335
Olympic Village in Döberitz, 13–14, 115, 145,
    157–59, 164, 181–83, 193, 207, 209,
    211, 246, 249
  amenities of, 158, 182
  house nomenclature of, 158, 181–82
  isolation of, 182
  in Olympia, 309
  police presence at, 222
  postal interceptions at, 222
  postwar deterioration of, 342
  sexual contacts in, 182–83
  Wehrmacht administration of, 158–59, 309,
    342
Olympic Youth pageant, 199–201, 203, 324
Ondra, Anny, 173
one-hundred-meter race, 21, 228–29, 231–32,
    244, 300, 307, 308
  in 1896 Athens games, 24
  in 1924 Paris games, 45, 107
  in 1932 Los Angeles games, 58, 288
  women's, 235–36
110-meter hurdles race, 253
Ornstein, Charles, 80, 99, 287
Osendarp, Martin, 232, 238, 242
Oslo Winter Games (1952), 328
Ossietzky, Carl von, 188
Ovomaltine, 114
Owens, Jesse, 14, 15, 89, 212, 217, 244, 249,
    252, 260, 288, 292, 329–30, 342
  death of, 338
  FDR condemned by, 233
  film produced by, 239
  in 4 x 100-meter relay, 240–43
  four gold medals won by, 12, 232, 238,
    239, 240, 242
  Hitler praised by, 233
  in long jump, 238–39
  Long's friendship with, 238–39, 329
  Moscow games boycott opposed by, 338
  in Olympia, 244, 306–7
  in Olympic trials, 172
  in one-hundred-meter dash, 228–29, 232,
    235, 244, 300
  personal story of, 228–29
  postgames experiences of, 330, 332
  protest declaration recommended to, 222
  records set by, 229, 238, 239, 242
  return visits of, 329
  Schmeling's visit to, 182

Owens, Jesse (*continued*)
  "snubbing" of, 12, 230, 231, 232–34
  in two-hundred-meter race, 238
  in U.S. boycott movement, 88, 89–90
  and young autograph seekers, 307, 329
oxygen priming, 166, 261

Palestinian Liberation Organization, 334–35
Panathenian Stadium, 6
Paris, 33, 43–44, 317
Paris International Exposition (1900), 22–24,
  36
Paris Olympic Games (1900), 22–24, 35, 72,
  190, 273
  eccentric facilities of, 23
  German team in, 24, 36
  political issues in, 23–24
Paris Summer Games (1924), 43–46, 52, 53
  competitions of, 45, 58, 107, 241, 254
  German exclusion from, 39–40, 43–44,
    104, 328
Parker, Jack, 254
Patton, George S., Jr., 30, 283
Paulson, Axel, 132*n*
Pausin, Erik and Ilse, 133
Peacock, Eulace, 89, 288, 289
Pegler, Westbrook, 143–44
Peloponnesian War, 10
pentathlon, 30, 31, 37–38, 283–84
Peru, 272, 275–77
Pfnür, Franz, 130, 131
Pfundtner, Hans, 73, 77, 118, 155, 156–57,
  162
Philippides, legend of, 21
Phipps, Eric, 214
phosphate additives, 166
Picart, Alfred, 22
Piccini, Achille, 275
Pietri, Dorando, 28
pigeons, release of, 196
pigeon shooting, 23
Pindar, 3
Pius XI, Pope, 237, 238, 311
Poage, George, 25
Podbielski, Viktor von, 33
Poland, 158, 235, 236
  German invasion of, 317, 320
  Olympic team of, 107, 277, 279, 332
pole vault, 252, 253–54, 255, 288–89, 302
police procedures, 117, 119, 123–24, 137,
    141, 182, 186–87, 193, 198, 220–26,
    245
polo, 280
Potsdam Garrison Church, 199

Poynton-Hill, Dorothy, 263
Prenn, Daniel, 65, 101–2
Primo de Rivera, Miguel, 31
Princess Matoika, 41
Princeton University, 19–20, 252
Princip, Gavrilo, 38
Prometheus, mythic cult of, 5
Prussian Meteorological Institute, 51

Raabe, Peter, 202
racism, 15, 58–59, 61, 62–63, 182–83,
    278–79, 323
  ancient Greeks and, 9–11
  of Anthropology Day contests, 25–26
  eugenics in, 205
  Gypsies and, 221
  Moroccan troops and, 43
  at 1912 Stockholm games, 2, 31–32
  Spartan, 10
  white athletic supremacy in, 330–32
  see also anti-Jewish persecution; Aryans
racism, anti-black, 88, 89, 90, 91, 171–72,
    178, 212, 292
  anatomical advantages and, 244, 330–32
  Nazi, 58, 62, 87, 88, 185, 228, 233, 239,
    244–45
radio broadcasting, 5, 248–50, 251, 276, 304
Raguse, Raggs, 282–83
Rampling, Godfrey, 256
Rathke, Kurt, 249
Ratjen, Dora, 236
  actual male gender of, 237
Rattenhuber, Hans, 124, 224
Recresal, 166
Reichenau, Walther von, 316, 317, 321
Reich Railway Central Office for Tourism,
    161–62, 170
Reichsbund für Leibesübungen, 82
Reichssportfeld, 13, 14, 159, 162, 164, 187,
    193, 216, 246, 249
  artistic decoration of, 156–57
  classical architectural style of, 10, 153–54
  construction of, 152–57
  corporate contributions to, 155
  cost of, 153, 155–56, 179
  heroic statuary of, 14, 157, 339
  laborers hired for, 154–55
  limestone in, 154
  nomenclature of, 156
  as Olympia-Stadion, 341
  postwar deterioration of, 339–41
  in proposed 2000 games venue, 338–39
  Riefenstahl and, 299–300, 301
  surviving sites of, 13–14

in World War II, 323–24, 340
Reichstag, 36–37, 57, 64, 149
Reimer, Jules, 105
Reinhardt, Max, 295
Resat, Erces, 130–31
Resting Athlete (Kolbe), 157
Rheims, Jean, 105
Ribbentrop, Joachim von, 137, 244–45
    as London ambassador, 213, 214, 215, 216,
        218
    Olympic party hosted by, 218
Riccardi, Franco, 267
Rice, Grantland, 247
Riefenstahl, Leni, 5–6, 11–12, 15, 100, 130,
        244, 295–315
    appearance of, 144, 313
    contractual arrangements of, 298, 303
    denazification efforts of, 306
    extravagance of, 298, 302–3
    film career of, 295–96
    Garmisch games film assignment rejected
        by, 144–45
    in Hollywood, 313–14
    innovative filming procedures of, 296,
        299–302
    Kristallnacht pogrom denied by, 313
    later years of, 333n
    memoirs of, 145, 254–55, 296–97, 303–4,
        312
    Morris's affair with, 254–55
    in New York, 312–13
    Nuremberg Party Rallies filmed by, 296
    postwar banning of, 333
    as prima donna, 301, 303
    prizes awarded to, 310, 311, 314, 317
    production headquarters of, 298, 303
    production staff of, 298–99, 301
    publicity tour of, 311–14
    skiing in bathing suit enjoyed by, 145
    see also Olympia (documentary film)
Riley, Charles, 229
Ritola, Ville, 45
Roberts, Bill, 256
Robertson, Lawson, 240–43
Robinson, Mack, 238
Rodenkirchen, Robert, 288
Rogeberg, Willy, 281
Rogers, Will, 54
    on black athletes' success, 58
Rome, 5, 26, 43, 51, 53, 153, 321
Rome Summer Games (1960), 239
Roosevelt, Franklin Delano, 85, 169
    Owens's condemnation of, 233
    U.S. boycott movement and, 94, 97–98

Roosevelt, Theodore, 29
Roosevelt administration, 94–98
Root, Elbert, 263
Rose, Billy, 180–81
Rosen, Clarence von, 311
Rosenberg, Alfred, 10, 61
Rosenman, Samuel I., 98
Rothschild, Philippe de, 105
rowing, 13, 50, 159, 170, 273–74
    in 1900 Paris games, 23
    in 1924 Paris games, 45
    in 1932 Lake Placid games, 56
    in *Olympia,* 299, 300, 301
Rübelt, Lothar, 245, 246
Rubien, Frederick, 74, 75, 141, 195, 278–79
Rugby Union football, 45, 102–4
Runge, Herbert, 269
Ruperti, Oskar, 43–44
Russia, 24, 27, 31, 40, 188
Ruud, Birger, 131, 141

SA (*Sturmabteilung*), 4, 60–61, 64, 67, 81,
        165, 166, 191, 226, 230, 293–94
Sachsenhausen concentration camp, 220–21
Salchow, Ulrich, 132
Salminen, Ilmari, 255
Salt Lake City Winter Games (2002), 336
Sandler, Joseph, 25
Schacherer-Elek, Ilone, 265–66, 267
Schäfer, Ernst, 206
Schäfer, Karl, 135
Scharnagl, Karl, 112
Scheib, Hans, 299
Schilgen, Fritz, 198
Schiller, Friedrich, 9, 106, 199, 200, 203, 205
Schirach, Baldur von, 192, 233
Schmeling, Max, 172–79, 340
Schmidt, Theodor, 7
Schmitz, Ernst, 161–62, 170
Schreiber, Walter, 329
Schröder, Willy, 252, 307
Schwab, Arthur, 257
Schwarzmann, Alfred, 264, 322, 328
schweigsame Frau, Die (Strauss), 197–98
Seelenbinder, Werner, 269–70
Seldte, Franz, 186
Seoul Summer Games (1988), 259, 343–44
Sergo, Ulderico, 268
Seven Years in Tibet, 130
Sharkey, Jack, 167, 172–73, 175
Sherrill, Charles, 72, 76, 80, 90–91, 95, 98,
        99, 188
    anti-Jewish displays protested by, 121
    background of, 72

Sherrill, Charles (*continued*)
   Hitler's meeting with, 84–85
   token Jewish athlete proposed by, 84–87
Shirer, William L., 122–23, 209
   false public image exposed by, 143–44
shooting, 37, 42, 281
shot put, 20, 230, 252
Sieg des Glaubens, 296, 297
Simmons, Floyd, 255
sixteen-hundred-meter relay race, 256
skiing, 13
   alpine, 129–31, 135, 139, 299, 319
   military patrol, 134–35, 317, 322
   Nordic, 130, 131
   by Riefenstahl, 145
ski jumping, 112–13, 115, 123, 127, 131,
   141, 281
Slater, William, 249
Sloane, William Milligan, 20
Smith, Al, 78, 82
Smith, Truman, 208, 209, 210
Snyder, Charles D., 331
Snyder, Jimmy "the Greek," 332
Snyder, Larry, 90, 233, 331
soccer, 167, 168, 249, 274–78
Son, Kitei (Sohn Kee-chung), 257–59, 301
Sørensen, Inge, 262, 263
S.O.S. Eisberg, 296
South Africa, 29
Southwood, Leslie, 274
Soviet Union, 40, 50, 127*n*, 151, 181, 224,
   267, 283, 320, 322
   Afghanistan invaded by, 336–38
   Berlin occupied by, 324, 327
   German invasion of, 206, 322
Spain, 49, 51, 106, 122, 152, 207, 213
Spanish-American War, 24, 26
Spanish civil war, 147, 152, 158, 207, 213,
   284, 286–87
Sparta, 10, 46, 323, 324
Speer, Albert, 146, 154, 195, 244, 294, 310
Spock, Benjamin, 45
"Sport in Hellenic Times" exhibition, 11, 163,
   204
SS (*Schutzstaffel*), 68, 79, 122, 124, 130,
   160–61, 165, 206, 224, 230, 237, 238,
   246, 293–94
Starhemberg, Ernst Rüdiger von, 8
Stauffenberg, Claus von, 283
Stephens, Helen, 235–36
Stiefson, Ignaz, 284
Stierstorpff, Count Adalbert von, 38
St. Louis Olympic Games (1904), 24–26, 53,
   275, 291

Anthropology Day contest in, 25–26
German team in, 25, 36
St. Moritz Winter Games (1928), 46, 47, 111,
   112, 132
St. Moritz Winter Games (1940), 319
St. Moritz Winter Games (1948), 328
Stöck, Gerhard, 230
Stockholm Olympic Games (1912), 30–32,
   34, 35, 70, 283, 284*n*
Stoller, Sam, 240–43
Straus, Roger, 209
Strauss, Richard, 188, 196–98, 199
Streicher, Julius, 184
Strength Through Joy program, 136, 183–84,
   204, 206, 317
Stresemann, Gustav, 50
Stribling, William Young, 173
Stürmer, Der, 117, 120, 121, 142, 184
Sullivan, John, 29, 32
Swahn, Oscar, 42
Sweden, 76–77, 83, 99
Sweden, Olympic team of, 224, 234 255, 269,
   281
   in 1932 Los Angeles games, 56
   in 1936 Garmisch games, 131
swimming, 52, 166, 261–62
   in 1900 Paris games, 23
   in 1904 St. Louis games, 25
   in 1928 Amsterdam games, 46
   in *Olympia*, 299, 301, 302, 308
   women's 41, 42, 30, 107–8, 180–81, 262
Switzerland, 44, 126, 319
   boycott movement in, 106
Switzerland, Olympic team of, 181–82, 257,
   264, 272, 280–81
   in 1936 Garmisch games, 128, 129–30, 134
Sydney Summer Games (2000), 286

"Table Talks" (Hitler), 156
Tarzan's Revenge, 255
television, 13, 204, 250–52, 295
ten-thousand-meter race, 31, 230, 255
Terada, Noboru, 261, 262
Thams, Jacob, 281
Thermopylae, Battle of, 10, 324
Thorak, Josef, 156–57
Thorpe, Jim, 31–32
Thurber, Delos, 230–31
Tibet, 130, 205, 206
Tiefland, 317
Tiller Girls, 204
Tisdall, R.M.N., 58
Tokyo Summer Games (1940), 51–52, 188,
   285, 294, 315, 317

Tolan, Eddie, 58, 238, 330
Torrance, Jack, 230
Toscanini, Arturo, 203
Touni, Khadr El, 270
Towns, Forrest "Spec," 253
track and field events, 20, 21, 24, 28, 31, 84,
    89
    AAU's certifications of, 74, 78, 83, 93, 101
    in 1900 Paris games, 23, 25, 72
    in 1904 St. Louis games, 25
    in 1924 Paris games, 45, 107
    in 1928 Amsterdam games, 46–47
    in 1932 Los Angeles games, 58, 288
track and field events (1936), 227–59
    decathlon, 254–55, 307
    discus throw, 252–53, 307
    eight-hundred-meter race, 234, 240, 307
    female athletes in, 166, 228, 229–30,
        234–38
    fifteen-hundred-meter race, 254, 255–56
    fifty-kilometer walk, 227, 256–57
    4 x 100–meter relay, 240–43
    four-hundred-meter hurdle race, 231, 253
    four-hundred-meter race, 239–40, 307
    hammer throw, 234, 252
    javelin throw, 229–30, 252
    long jump, 238–39
    men's high jump, 230–31
    men's sixteen-hundred-meter relay, 256
    number of participants in, 228
    one-hundred-meter dash, 228–29, 231–32,
        235, 307, 308
    110–meter hurdles, 253
    marathon, 227, 252, 257–59, 292
    pole vault, 252, 253–54, 255, 288–89, 302
    records set in, 229, 234, 235, 238, 239,
        242, 253, 254, 255, 256, 258
    shot put, 230, 252
    spectators of, 228
    ten-thousand-meter race, 230, 255
    two-hundred-meter race, 238
    women's discus throw, 234–35
    women's eighty-meter hurdles race, 237–38
    women's four-hundred-meter relay, 236
    women's high jump, 236–37
    women's javelin throw, 229–30
    women's one-hundred meter dash, 235–36
Treadgold, Al, 289
"Tree Trunk Exercise," 204
Triumph des Willens, 100, 144, 296, 298, 299,
    304–5, 307, 309
Tschammer und Osten, Hans von, 11, 79,
    123, 124, 139, 152, 155, 174, 192,
    291, 317, 321

British-German football match approved by,
    102–4
    death of, 323
    Garmisch anti-Jewish displays ignored by,
        118
    in publicity campaign, 161
    as Reichssportführer, 67–68, 73–74,
        166–67, 188, 207, 316
    token Jewish athlete approved by, 85, 87
tug-of-war, 23
    in 1908 London games, 28
Turkey, 19, 39–40
    Olympic team of, 195, 269, 270
Turnerschaft, 18, 19, 29, 35, 38, 46, 57, 58,
    61, 264
Twain, Mark, 33
two-hundred-meter race, 58, 238
Tydings, Millard, 78

Ufa-Palast am Zoo, 146, 296, 310
ultraviolet radiation baths, 166
Umberto, Crown Prince of Italy, 194
Union Racing Club, 32
United States:
    anti-black racism in, 88, 89, 90, 91,
        171–72, 178, 212
    anti-German sentiment in, 12
    athletic training in, 20, 35
    Communist Party of, 55, 288
    Diem's study trips to, 35, 56–57
    GOC's formal invitation to, 77, 79–80
    isolationist sentiment in, 40, 320
    manifest destiny of, 26
    1929 stock market crash of, 52
    Olympia opposed in, 311–14
United States, boycott movement in, 69–100,
    120–21, 174–75, 188–89, 247, 287,
    318–19, 336–38
    anti-Nazi demonstrations in, 77–78, 81, 86
    black athletes in, 87–90
    Catholic support of, 82, 83
    defeat of, 98–100
    Jewish groups in, 69–70, 71, 72–73, 74–75,
        77, 78, 80, 81, 100, 107, 169–70
    left-wing support of, 82–83
    Nuremberg laws and, 84, 85, 86, 91, 107
    press coverage of, 75, 82–83, 85, 88, 90,
        101
    Protestant support of, 82
    public opinion on, 83
    Roosevelt administration and, 94–98
    Sherrill's token Jewish athlete and, 84–87
United States, Olympic team of:
    in 1896 Athens games, 19–20, 252

United States, Olympic team of (*continued*)
  in 1900 Paris games, 23, 24, 72
  in 1904 St. Louis games, 25
  in 1908 London games, 27–29
  in 1912 Stockholm games, 31–32, 70
  in 1920 Antwerp games, 40–41, 42
  in 1924 Paris games, 45
  in 1928 Amsterdam games, 46–47
  1980 Moscow games boycotted by, 336–38
  processional flag not lowered by, 27, 125, 195
  vociferous fans of, 20, 45
United States, Olympic team of (1936),
     169–72, 182, 212, 261–62, 263–65,
     267, 268, 269, 273, 274–75, 278, 281,
     282–83, 284–85, 286
  dismissed members of, 180–81
  female athletes of, 41, 42, 125, 170, 180–81
     228, 235–36, 263–64
  funding of, 169–71, 262, 267
  in Garmisch games, 121, 125, 133–34, 135,
     141, 172
  Jewish athletes of, 78, 107, 175, 240–43,
     278–79
  medal count of, 290, 292
  Olympic trials of, 171–72, 240, 288
  in procession of athletes, 125, 195
  shipboard festivities of, 179–81
  track and field, 228–29, 230–31, 235,
     238–45, 252–56, 257–58
  see also black athletes
United States Figure Skating Association
     (USFSA), 132
United States Olympic Committee (USOC),
     243, 337, 344
Untermeyer, Samuel, 79
Uruguay, 278
Urusov, Prince Lev, 40
Uzcudun, Paulino, 174, 177

Valla, Trebisonda "Ondina," 237–38
Vance, Cyrus, 337
Vansittart, Sir Robert, 213–15, 293
van Vliet, Arie Gerrit, 272
Varoff, George, 288–89
Vatican, 82
Vecsey, George, 343
Venice Film Festival, 311
Versailles, Treaty of, 40, 44, 57–58, 104, 147,
     148, 158, 284
Via Triumphalis, 160, 193, 198, 224
Vidor, King, 312
Vogt, Richard, 340
Völkischer Beobachter, 58, 61, 62, 65, 66, 165,
     176–77, 290

Volkssturm Battalions, 323–24

Wackerle, Joseph, 156–57
Wagner, Adolf, 119, 124, 136, 317
Wagner, Richard, 193, 194, 207–8, 305,
     306
Wagner, Winifred, 207
Wajsowna, Jadwiga, 235
Walasiewiczówna, Staneslawa (Stella Walsh),
     235
  actual male gender of, 236
Walker, Perrin, 289
Walsh, Davis, 178
Walterspiel, Alfred, 139
Wangenheim, Baroness Johanna von, 159
Wangenheim, Konrad von, 283
Warngard, Oskar, 234
Washington, George, 93
water polo, 280
Watson, Thomas J., 211
Wayne, Marshall, 263
Wehrmacht, 5, 68, 146, 191, 194, 204, 238,
     271, 282–83, 316
  Döberitz Olympic Village administered by,
     158–59, 309, 342
Weidemann, Hans, 144, 145, 297, 302
Weigand, Theodor, 163
weight lifting, 56, 270–71
Weissmuller, Johnny, 255, 258
West Germany, 325, 326–28, 332–33, 336
White, Walter, 89–90
Whitlock, Harold, 256–57
Wigman, Mary, 200
Wiklund, Elis, 131
Wilhelm Gustloff, 127
Wilhelm II, Kaiser of Germany, 19, 29, 32–33,
     179
  medal endowed by, 37
Wilkins, Roy, 88–89
Williams, Archie, 239–40, 253, 307
Williams, Joe, 180
Wilson, Jackie, 268
Winchell, Walter, 313
Winckelmann, Johann Joachim, 9, 50
Windt, Herbert, 305
Wing, Howard, 168
Wolfe, Thomas, 193, 211–12, 225
Wolff, Albert, 107
Wolff, Frederick, 256
Wölke, Hans, 230
Woodruff, John, 234, 240, 307
Woodruff, Robert, 185, 186
World Alpine Ski Championships, 130, 135
World Fencing Championships, 267

World Four-Man Bob Championships (1934),
        114–15
"World Labor Athletic Carnival," 286–89
World War I, 9, 18, 31, 33, 38–40, 85, 93,
        129, 148, 191
    Central Powers of, 39–40, 44
    Germany's use of poison gas in, 39
    Versailles Treaty of, 40, 44, 57–58, 104,
        147, 148, 158, 284
World War II, 49, 50, 68, 99, 108, 127*n*, 130,
        131, 133, 136, 138, 141, 156, 165,
        181, 206, 218, 223*n*, 239, 255, 259,
        271, 283, 284, 293, 306, 312, 315,
        316–24, 332, 340
Wortmann, Dietrich, 169–70

wrestling, 21, 46, 56, 269–70
Wykoff, Frank, 241–42

yachting, 159, 260, 280–81
    in *Olympia,* 299, 300–301
Yale University, 45, 166
You Can't Go Home Again (Wolfe), 193, 211
Yugoslavia, 7

Zabala, Carlos, 258–59
Zehnkämpfer (Breker), 157
zeppelins, 33, 162, 179, 193–94
Ziegler, Adolf, 202
Zielke, Willy, 299
Zweig, Stefan, 197–98